THAMES VALLEY
THE FINAL DECADE
1961 - 1971

Written and published by Paul Lacey

Best Wishes
Paul

Bristol FLF6G-type Car 851 (WJB 235) was new in November 1961 and seated 70 passengers. It is seen on the forecourt of the Maidenhead garage in Bridge Street. Note the cream surrounds on the glazing and destination apertures, the latter still bearing a full display. The Maidenhead garage was one of the earliest to be established in the days of the pioneering British Automobile Traction Branch in the Thames valley. The site originally had a large old house The Cedars, the central portion of which was demolished and replaced with the first phase of the garage, with the side wings adapted for Company use. Indeed, the building seen to the left formed the Thames Valley offices from 1920 to 1922, when the Head Office returned once more to Reading. That location saw much activity in the handling of ex-War Department lorries, bought on behalf of both the local company and also associated operators much further afield, with the once rear garden turned into a parking yard. Over the years the Company acquired many of the surrounding cottages, some used for providing cheap lodgings for crews, though ultimately most were demolished to extend the garage, rearwards and further eastwards in a number of phases, which made it almost self-sufficient for maintenance and even re-painting. Other demolitions allowed the frontage to be extended for vehicle parking, both towards Bridge Street and also on the western border. Unfortunately, with the closeness of the Slough Trading Estate, along with the developing Heathrow Airport, Maidenhead garage was beset by constant staff shortages throughout the 1960's.

THAMES VALLEY - THE FINAL DECADE, 1961 - 1971

© Copyright Paul Lacey 2012
First published 2012

*No part of this work may be reproduced
without the prior permission of
the author and publisher
other than for the
purposes of
review*

Written, designed, typeset and published by
Paul Lacey, 17 Sparrow Close
Woosehill, Wokingham
Berkshire, RG41 3HT

ISBN 978-0-9567832-1-9

Printed by the MPG Group Bodmin and King's Lynn

This contrast of South Midland coaches at Victoria Coach Station also illustrates the development of the Bristol coach over a decade. On the right is LS6B-type 91 (TWL 56) which had been delivered in 1953 and carried ECW coachwork. Note also the Non Stop Express board in the nearside window, indicating that this journey ran without stopping between Headington on the outskirts of Oxford and Shepherds Bush in west London. On the left is the prototype high-floor RE-type, Car 867 (521 ABL), which was also South Midland's first 36-footer when delivered in 1963, carrying a 47-seater body also by ECW. The Lodekka-style grille actually worked quite well, though it left no room for the fleetname device carried by the previous MW-types and also retrospectively fitted to older vehicles. Note also the intake vents above the windscreens, which supplied air to the forced air ventilation, as the coach lacked opening side windows, though roof vents could also be opened in fine weather if required. The REX was modified quite a bit over the first few years, though the only change affecting its appearance was the removal of the fog lights from under the front bumper, as they were very prone to damage from low kerbs etc.

The parking yard off Stations Square was generally known as the Southern Yard, having originally been the goods yard of the Southern Railway. Thames Valley's presence there expanded over the years, though in this view taken in the Summer of 1967 some ground has been lost to car parking on the right following the demolition of the old Southern Station. Seen here are also a typical selection of buses awaiting their next duties, though the fact that there are two with blinds for Route 6A to Odiham rather belies the level of service to that location, this being because the Reading single-deck duties saw buses switching between a number of routes during the day. On the left is Car S310 (HMO 836) a Bristol LS6B converted from a coach for bus work in 1964. To its right is Bristol MW6G Car 852 (VJB 943), one of a pair with dual-purpose bodies and livery to match. On the right is Bristol KSW6B Car 749 (JRX 824), the last of that type bought new, and now rebuilt with a T-type destination aperture, with FLF6G Car D17 (DRX 121C), along with a pair of Bristol LS-types in the background.

CONTENTS

Subject	Page	Subject	Page
Chapter 1961	5	**Chapter 1971**	187
Chapter 1962	27	*Appendix 1* Fleet List	207
Chapter 1963	41		
Chapter 1964	57	*Appendix 2* Service Vehicles	219
Chapter 1965	73	*Appendix 3* Garages and outstations	220
Chapter 1966	89		
Chapter 1967 (Part 1)	103	*Appendix 4* Working Arrangements 1.11.61	221
Colour Section	113	*Appendix 5* Official Fleet Allocations 1.7.63	222
Chapter 1967 (Part 2)	129		
Chapter 1968	131	*Appendix 6* Official Fleet Allocations 1.6.68	223
Chapter 1969	149	**Index and Acquired Operators**	224
Chapter 1970	165	**Route Map at 1966**	118

Standard Body Codes - Throughout this work the standard codes are used to describe the configuration of bodywork, e.g. B32F is a single-deck bus seating 32 with a front entrance. See Appendix 1 Fleet List on page 207 for full listing of codes.

OTHER TRANSPORT TITLES FROM PAUL LACEY

The Independent Bus & Coach Operators of the Newbury Area, 1919 –1932 A History of Newbury & District Motor Services Ltd., 1932 – 1952 A History of the Penn Bus Co. Ltd., 1920 –1935 Thames Valley – The British Years, 1915 –1920	Sorry, these titles are now out of print

A History of the Thames Valley Traction Co. Ltd., 1920 –1930 £15.00

The detailed history of this vibrant period, including the 207 other operators sharing the roads with TV, published in 1995, 144 pages A4, perfect bound, 144 half-tones, route map, full fleet list, line drawings.

A History of the Thames Valley Traction Co. Ltd., 1931 – 1945 £25.00

Continuing the story of development through the expansion of the 1930's, railway shareholdings, and then through the difficult years of the wartime era, published in 2003, 208 pages A4 with laminated covers, 300 half-tone illustrations, maps and plans, full fleet lists and specialised appendices.

A History of the Thames Valley Traction Co. Ltd., 1946 - 1960 £25.00

This third volume covers the period of post-war reconstruction and through the busy 1950's, including the significant additions of Newbury & District and South Midland. Published in 2009, 224 pages A4 with laminated covers, 544 half-tone illustrations, route maps, full fleet list, allocations and service vehicles.

Thackray's Way – A Family in Road Transport £10.00

An in-depth study of this enterprising family, written with assistance from their descendants, published in 2001, 136 pages A5, perfect bound, 62 half-tones, plans of premises, route maps, full fleet list. Contains much of relevance to the Thames Valley story.

50 Years of South Midland, 1921 – 1970 £11.00

A comprehensive study of Oxford's premier coach operator and express service pioneer, <u>written by David Flitton</u>. Published in 2004, 192 A5 pages and laminated covers, 142 half-tone illustrations, full fleet list, details of premises and period adverts.

The Newbury & District Motor Services Story £25.00

A very detailed study of the origins and development of Newbury & District, along with the numerous other operators with which it shared the roads over a vast hinterland surrounding the west Berkshire market town of Newbury. Published in 2011, 224 pages A4 with laminated covers, 310 half-tones, fleet lists for N&D and absorbed operators, many detailed biographies, route maps and details of premises.

All titles in print are available direct from the author, or through good book suppliers
Prices shown above are inclusive of postage when ordered direct
For further details, offers and news see the website at www.paullaceytransportbooks.co.uk
Celebrating 50 years of Thames Valley research

ACKNOWLEDGEMENTS

This work is dedicated to all those who were involved in the daily operation of *Thames Valley*, many of whom I have had the interesting task of interviewing during 50 years of research. I also wish to say a big *Thank You* to everyone who has helped me in any way, <u>no matter how small</u>, to piece together this interesting history. So many people have been consulted over all those years, it is difficult to try to list them all, so my apologies for any unintentional omissions. However, special thanks must go to those who have offered their constant support for this massive four-volume history, Bob Crawley, Michael Plunkett, Peter Pribik, Dave Wilder and Peter Wilks. From the Company ranks I must thank Ernie Church, Nobby Clarke, Bill Cripps, Les Dearlove, Michael Dearlove, Charlie Hampton, Reg Hibbert, Vashti Hill, David Howard, Jim Lewington, Jack Lambden, Nigel Purssell, Jim Vockings, Arthur Waldron, Mike Waring, Alf Waterman, Ian White, Frank Williams and Bert Woods.

Other enthusiasts have also shared their knowledge, including Maurice Doggett, Brian Hawes, Peter Jaques, Thomas Knowles, Ed Maun, Allan Macfarlane, Bob Mack, Phil Moth, Frank Ranscombe, Mike Stephens, Steve Wimbush, as well as my old school friends and fellow bus spotters Phil Birtchnell, Andy Goddard, David Nicholls and Stephen Oliver. Judy Cox (nee Kercher) and Cyril Harding also provided photos of their relatives on the buses. In respect of photographs I have been fortunate in having many contributors, who have either supplied their own photos or brought to light archival material. However, the work of several local photographers is especially welcome for the diversity they have added, so particular thanks go to Graham Low, Martin Shaw and Philip Wallis. My thanks also go to the photographers, whose names are often unrecorded, who had the fore-thought to record the daily activities of the erstwhile '*Thames Valley Traction Company Limited*' and its fleet for posterity.

1961

Thames Valley bus services covered a roughly diamond-shaped area, bounded to the east by Slough, to the north by Aylesbury and Oxford, westwards to Swindon, and to the south at Aldershot, Camberley, Guildford, Odiham and Basingstoke. In addition there were also the pair of Reading to London express routes, plus the services and extended tours operated under the *South Midland* name and based on Oxford.

An official route map can be found on page 118.

The operational area of Thames Valley had evolved over four decades, through expansion and numerous take-overs. The Hampshire town of Odiham was first reached in May 1932, with the purchase of Lintott's Direct Bus Service, and even had a dormy shed from 1932 to 1937. Bristol LS6B Car 716 (HMO 862) is seen at the stop in St. Mary's Butts, Reading.

The fleet at the start of 1961 had reached a fair degree of standardisation, with various models of Bristol chassis carrying bodies by Eastern Coach Works. The exceptions to this were the solitary AEC 'Regal' MkIV coach with *South Midland* and the Guy 'Arab' MkIII with Duple bodies inherited from *Newbury & District*, all legacies of the era of *Red & White* control.

The oldest native vehicle was 1946 Bristol K6A Car 439 (CRX 548), though some of the secondhand purchases of 1959/60 actually had older chassis, albeit with newer bodies. The fleet comprised 376 vehicles:

Double-deckers (total 221)

<u>Bristol K5G (total 13, with ECW or Brush bodies)</u>
Cars 438, 460-465 and 472-477 (475 Brush body)
<u>Bristol K6A (total 20, with ECW bodies)</u>
Cars 439-452, 456-459, 466 and 467
<u>Bristol K6B (total 41, with ECW bodies)</u>
436, 437, 453-455, 468-471, 492-519 and 524-533
<u>Bristol KS6B (total 15, with ECW bodies)</u>
586-594 and 595-600 (coach seats and doors)
<u>Bristol KSW6B (total 76, with ECW bodies)</u>
601-603, 634-636, 637-639 (coach seats and doors), 640-670, 694-705, 726-737, 738-743 (coach seats and doors) and 744-749
<u>Bristol LD5G (total 13, with ECW bodies)</u>
765-769, 780-785, 789 and 791
<u>Bristol LD6B (total 7, with ECW bodies)</u>
755-757, 810, 811, 815 and 816
<u>Bristol LD6G (total 18, with ECW bodies)</u>
750-754, 760, 763 and 764 (coach seats and doors) 758, 759, 761, 762, 786-788, 790, 792 and 793
<u>Bristol LDL6G (total 1, with ECW body)</u>
779
<u>Bristol FLF6B (total 1, with ECW body)</u>
834 (coach seats and doors)
<u>Bristol FLF6G (total 9, with ECW bodies)</u>
835-838, (coach seats and doors) and 839-843
<u>Guy 'Arab' MkIII 6LW (total 7 with Duple bodies)</u>
170 and 171 (lowbridge bodies and doors) and H10, H13-H16 (highbridge bodies)

Certainly the most exotic buses in the fleet were the former Newbury & District Guy 'Arab' MkIII 6LW's, and H13-6 (HOT 391-4) had seen a short spell in the Venture fleet before reaching Newbury in 1951. The Duple-built highbridge bodies were well constructed, and H15 stands at Oxford's Gloucester Green Bus Station ready for the almost 30-mile run up and over the Berkshire Downs on Route 112 back to Newbury.

Single-deckers (total 97)

<u>Bristol LL5G (total 10, with ECW bodies)</u>
794-799 and 817-820
<u>Bristol LL6B (total 15, with ECW bodies)</u>
559-560 and 564-576
<u>Bristol LWL6B (total 30, with ECW bodies)</u>
577-585 and 613-633
<u>Bristol LS5G (total 6, with ECW bodies)</u>
686, 687 and 706-709

Bristol LS6B (total 16, with ECW bodies)
710-725
Bristol LS6G (total 9, with ECW bodies)
677-685
Bristol SC4LK (total 5, with ECW bodies)
774-778
Bristol MW6G (total 6, with ECW bodies)
852 and 853 (coach seats) and 854-857

Coaches (total 58, Thames Valley/South Midland)

AEC 'Regal' MkIV (total 1, with ECW body)
85
Bristol L6B (total 2, bodies by ECW or Windover)
73 (ECW body) and 555 (Windover body)
Bristol LL6B (total 13, with 8ft ECW bodies)
75-78 and 821-829
Bristol LWL6B (total 6, with ECW bodies)
607-612
Bristol LS6B (total 12, with ECW bodies)
90-95 and 688-693
Bristol LS6G (total 12, with ECW bodies)
79-84 and 671-676
Bristol MW6G (total 12, with ECW bodies)
800-807 and 830-833

A full fleet list for the period 1961 to 1971 appears in Appendix 1 on pages 207 to 218.

The conductor sets blinds for the working of Route 20, which covered 35-miles from Aylesbury to Windsor via Princes Risborough, High Wycombe, Bourne End and Maidenhead. In the period under review the size and scope of destination screens would be much reduced, resulting in most of these 3-piece displays showing 'Thames Valley' in the intermediate box, which later gave way to over-painting in red, whilst a fair number of buses were rebuilt with a T layout.

Apart from the vehicles based at the main garages in Bracknell, Desborough Road, Maidenhead, Newbury, Oxford, Reading and Wycombe Marsh, a number were kept at various dormy sheds and outstations, and the situation at the start of 1961 was as follows:

Baughurst (Wilts & Dorset dormy shed) – 1 double-decker for Route 9 (Reading – Mortimer – Tadley – Baughurst);

A pair of these sliding-doorway coach-seated Bristol FLF's were kept overnight at Victoria to cover the early-morning departures towards Reading, being crewed by London-based staff. These were rotated at the Reading end on a regular basis.

Fingest dormy shed – 2 single-deckers for Routes 36 (High Wycombe – Lane End – Cadmore End) and 37 (High Wycombe – Lane End – Fingest – Henley);
Hungerford outstation – 2 contract coaches taken home by part-time drivers for Chilton Foliat – Harwell (AERE) and Great Bedwyn – Harwell (AERE);
Kingsclere outstation – 1 double-decker for Route 122 (Newbury – Kingsclere – Basingstoke);
Lambourn outstation – 1 double-decker for Route 106 (Newbury – Lambourn – Swindon) and 2 contract coaches with part-time drivers for Lambourn – Didcot (ROF) and Ramsbury – Harwell (AERE), one of which also covered the Wednesdays-only Route 106a (Lambourn – Shefford – Hungerford);
London outstations – 2 double-deckers for Route B (Reading – Maidenhead – London Victoria) garaged at Samuelson's, plus 2 South Midland coaches for the routes to Oxford via Henley and High Wycombe and garaged by London Transport;
Princes Risborough dormy shed 2 double-deckers for Routes 20/20a (Aylesbury – Princes Risborough – High Wycombe – Maidenhead – Windsor);
Stokenchurch dormy shed – 2 double-deckers for High Wycombe services to Watlington (Route 39), Radnage (Route 40) and Ibstone (Route 41);
Worcester outstation – 1 South Midland coach for the express service Worcester – Oxford – London, plus a second one in Summer for the Southsea service.

A full review of all garages, dormy sheds and other outstations appears in Appendix 3 on page 220.

Thames Valley was operating 95 numbered public bus routes, along with the 2 London expresses. Under the *South Midland* name there were the express services to London from Worcester and Oxford, running by way of Henley or High Wycombe, plus the seasonal routes to Southsea, Worthing, Brighton, Eastbourne and Margate. *Thames Valley* also had seasonal operations from either Booker or High Wycombe to Southsea, Bournemouth and Hastings. The full listing of routes, as published in the timetable book for January 1961, is reproduced below in 2 parts:

LIST OF SERVICES

No.	Route
1	MAIDENHEAD, Twyford, READING, Theale, NEWBURY
1a	READING, London Road, WOODLEY
1b	READING, Winnersh, Hurst, Twyford, SHURLOCK ROW
2	READING, Wokingham, Bracknell, Ascot, WINDSOR
2a	ASCOT, Cheapside, Sunninghill, SUNNINGDALE
2b	ASCOT, Brockenhurst Road, Sunninghill, SUNNINGDALE
2c	ASCOT, Ascot Station, SUNNINGDALE
3	READING, Wokingham, Crowthorne, CAMBERLEY
3a	READING, Wokingham, Barkham, FINCHAMPSTEAD
4	READING, Farley Hill, Eversley, Yateley, CAMBERLEY
4a	READING, Arborfield, Barkham, WOKINGHAM
5	READING, Streatley, Wallingford, OXFORD
5a	READING, Blewbury, Harwell, Chilton, WANTAGE
5b	READING, Pangbourne, Yattendon, NEWBURY
6	READING, Riseley, Sherfield, BASINGSTOKE
6a	READING, Riseley, Rotherwick, Hook, ODIHAM
6b	READING, Grazeley, Stratfieldsaye, BRAMLEY
7	READING, Sonning Common, Peppard, Stoke Row, NETTLEBED
8	READING, Binfield Heath, HENLEY
9	READING, Burghfield, Mortimer, Tadley, BAUGHURST
9a	READING, Grazeley, Padworth, TADLEY
11	READING, Bradfield, BUCKLEBURY COMMON
12	READING, Riseley, Hartley Row, ALDERSHOT
15	MAIDENHEAD, CURLS LANE ESTATE
16	MAIDENHEAD, Warren Row, HENLEY
17	MAIDENHEAD, Hurley, HENLEY
18	MAIDENHEAD, MARLOW, MARLOW COMMON or DANESFIELD
18a	MAIDENHEAD—PINKNEYS GREEN
18b	MARLOW, Little Marlow, BOURNE END
19	MAIDENHEAD, Craufurd Arch, COURTHOUSE ROAD
20/20a	AYLESBURY, HIGH WYCOMBE, MAIDENHEAD, WINDSOR
21	MAIDENHEAD, Woodlands Park, Waltham St. Lawrence, WOKINGHAM
	FOR SERVICES BETWEEN MAIDENHEAD and SLOUGH AND INTERMEDIATELY SEE UNDER ROUTE NOS. 60/68.
23	MAIDENHEAD, Furze Platt, COOKHAM DEAN (Church)
24	MAIDENHEAD, Cookham Station, COOKHAM DEAN (Chequers)
25	HIGH WYCOMBE, Loudwater, FLACKWELL HEATH
26	LOCAL SERVICE—Wycombe Marsh or New Bowerdean Road—SANDS
27	HIGH WYCOMBE, The Kingshills, GREAT MISSENDEN
28	HIGH WYCOMBE, Marlow, Henley, Wargrave, READING
31	HIGH WYCOMBE, Naphill, Walter's Ash, LACEY GREEN
32	HIGH WYCOMBE, West Wycombe, Bledlow Ridge, CHINNOR
33	LOCAL SERVICE—Desborough Castle—HIGH WYCOMBE
34	HIGH WYCOMBE, North Dean, SPEEN
35	HIGH WYCOMBE—DOWNLEY
36	HIGH WYCOMBE, Sands, Lane End, CADMORE END
37	HIGH WYCOMBE, Piddington, Lane End, Fingest, HENLEY
38	HIGH WYCOMBE, Sands, BOOKER
39	HIGH WYCOMBE, Stokenchurch, Lewknor, WATLINGTON
40	HIGH WYCOMBE, Piddington, RADNAGE
41	HIGH WYCOMBE, Stokenchurch, IBSTONE
42	LOUDWATER, High Wycombe, West Wycombe, BOOKER HILL ESTATE
50	READING, Streatley, Dorchester, ABINGDON
51	WINDSOR LOCAL SERVICES
52	BRACKNELL LOCAL SERVICE
53	WINDSOR, Bracknell, Easthampstead, CROWTHORNE

The services from Reading to Abingdon and Oxford were joint operations with City of Oxford MS, and No.740 (WJO 740) a Willowbrook B43F-bodied AEC 'Reliance' of 1955 is seen on the Oxford service.

The 28.5-mile Route 75 (Reading – Wokingham – Bracknell – Bagshot – Guildford) was jointly operated by Thames Valley and Aldershot & District, though it had not started until April 1954. A&D's No.376 (XHO 376) was caught by Graham Low as it passed through Wokingham town centre past old buildings long gone.

LIST OF SERVICES (continued)

No.	Route
60	MAIDENHEAD, Main Road, SLOUGH
61	SLOUGH, Bath Road, CIPPENHAM
62	SLOUGH, Chalvey, CIPPENHAM
63	MAIDENHEAD, Dropmore, Burnham, SLOUGH
64	SLOUGH, Farnham Road, BRITWELL
65	MAIDENHEAD, Burnham, SLOUGH
66	MAIDENHEAD, Hitcham Park, Burnham, SLOUGH
67	SLOUGH, PRIORY ESTATE
68	MAIDENHEAD, Burnham, Everitts Corner SLOUGH
69	LENT RISE, Priory Estate, Everitts Corner, WEST GATE
	Services showing "a" operate via SLOUGH TRADING ESTATE
75	READING, Bracknell, Bagshot, GUILDFORD
80	HIGH WYCOMBE, Lacey Green, Princes Risborough, AYLESBURY
81	HIGH WYCOMBE, Desborough Avenue, BOOKER
101	NEWBURY, East Ilsley, HARWELL
101a	NEWBURY, Chieveley, PEASEMORE
102	WEST ILSLEY, East Ilsley, READING
103	NEWBURY, Greenham, ECCHINSWELL
104	NEWBURY, Headley, Ashford Hill, KINGSCLERE
105	NEWBURY, Shefford, Fawley, WANTAGE
106	NEWBURY, Lambourn Upper Lambourn, SWINDON
106a	LAMBOURN, Shefford, HUNGERFORD
108	NEWBURY, Wickham, HUNGERFORD NEWTOWN
108	NEWBURY, Wickham, Lambourn Woodlands, LAMBOURN
109	NEWBURY, Thatcham, COLD ASH
110	NEWBURY, Thatcham, TADLEY
111	NEWBURY, Thatcham, BUCKLEBURY
112	NEWBURY, Abingdon, OXFORD
113	NEWBURY, Inkpen, HUNGERFORD
114	NEWBURY, Ball Hill, EAST WOODHAY
114a	NEWBURY, Ball Hill, WEST WOODHAY
115	NEWBURY, Woolton Hill, HIGHCLERE
116	NEWBURY, Bath Road, HUNGERFORD
120	NEWBURY, Hermitage, FRILSHAM
120a	NEWBURY, Hermitage, Ashampstead, ALDWORTH
121	SHAW, Newbury (Broadway), Newtown Common, PENWOOD
122	NEWBURY—Kingsclere—BASINGSTOKE
126	NEWBURY—CROOKHAM COMMON
127	SHAW, WASH COMMON
128	SHAW ESTATE, Newbury, VALLEY ROAD ESTATE
128a	NEWBURY (Broadway), BARTLEMY CLOSE
129	NEWBURY—DIDCOT

SUMMARY TIMETABLES

READING—WOKINGHAM
READING—ARBORFIELD
READING—STREATLEY
READING—Spencers Wood, WELLINGTON MONUMENT
READING—THEALE

EXPRESS SERVICES

A	READING, Wokingham, Ascot, LONDON
B	READING, Maidenhead, Slough, LONDON
—	HIGH WYCOMBE, Maidenhead, SOUTHSEA
—	OXFORD, Henley, Maidenhead, LONDON
—	OXFORD, High Wycombe, LONDON
—	WORCESTER, Oxford, Maidenhead, LONDON
—	WORCESTER, Oxford, Newbury, SOUTHSEA
—	WORCESTER, Oxford, Maidenhead, BRIGHTON
—	OXFORD, Maidenhead, MARGATE
—	OXFORD, Maidenhead, EASTBOURNE

7

Route 12 from Reading – Aldershot was also jointly operated with Aldershot & District, and their East Lancs-bodied Dennis 'Lance' K4 No.207 (LOU 35) of 1954 is seen at Stations Square, Reading.

There were also joint-working arrangements with the *London Transport Executive* on Local Services in High Wycombe and Slough, though in both towns the routes were not actually identical. The cross-town 26 and 26a service of *Thames Valley* in High Wycombe ran as Mill End Road – Desborough Road – Newland Street – Duke Street, then onto New Bowerdean Road (26a) or through to Cricket Ground – Wycombe Marsh – Micklefield Estate (26), with a few early-morning projections eastwards to Sands. However, the *London Transport* Route 326 covered a route largely similar to the 26a, but traversed the town via Easton Road, with town centre journeys starting from Rutland Street, just west of its garage in Queen Alexandra Road.

The Bristol K6B's allocated to Desborough Road were ideal for the sometimes narrow streets and for quick loading at stops on the busy cross-town local services 26/26a. 1950 Car 533 (FMO 8) emerges from Totteridge Road for Mill End Road, these buses working high mileages on all-day turns through until withdrawal in 1965-7.

At Slough the *'Valley* operated its Route 64 as Slough (Station) – Salt Hill – Farnham Road – Britwell, and on the timetable was also shown the weekday *London Transport* Route 400, though that only covered roads from Slough (The Crown) as far as Wentworth Avenue, whereas the 64 penetrated further into the Britwell estate to Calbroke Road. On Sundays Route 64 operated in similar fashion, but *London Transport* covered the road with its 441a.

As already noted, the services out to Oxford and Abingdon were jointly operated with *City of Oxford*, though the latter used its own route numbers of 34 and 40 respectively. On the other joint operation between those partners, the Newbury – Oxford Route 112 of the *'Valley* was still the 12 with *City of Oxford*, having originally shared that number when operation began with *Newbury & District*.

Wilts & Dorset No.542 (JMR 638) was typical of the bus kept outstationed at Newbury in the 1960's. This 1953 Bristol LS6G with dual-purpose ECW DP41F body was originally intended for express duties, hence the coach seating and the additional bright-work on the waistrail, quite different from TV's own examples.

Route 122 (Newbury – Kingsclere – Basingstoke) was jointly operated with *Wilts & Dorset*, though one *TV* bus was outstationed at Kingsclere to provide the early service into Newbury on this 17-mile long route. There was no joint-working on the Newbury – Andover or Salisbury Route 80 of *Wilts & Dorset*, though some years before the matter had been raised by the *W&D* management. Nor had the 6 (Reading – Basingstoke) ever been discussed for joint operation despite being 17.5 miles long and without dormy shed assistance. However, *TV* did continue the facility of garaging a bus for *W&D* at Newbury to cover the 135 service (Newbury – Sydmonton or Whitchurch), which had its origins with *Venture* of Basingstoke and even made some connections with the *King Alfred* service at Whitchurch for travel onto Winchester.

However, *United Counties* (as successor to *Eastern National*) had, despite being involved in the original purchase with *Thames Valley* of the competition on the Aylesbury – High Wycombe road in the 1930's, shown no inclination towards any joint operation.

Whereas the previous decade had seen significant increases in the operational area, such acquisitions in the 1960's were rather modest by comparison. Indeed, due to pressures of rising costs and the increase in car ownership, this period would see a number of services abandoned. As some of these owed their origins to the Country Carriers, this led to villages being without a bus service for the first time in 40-50 years, reversing many of the social changes brought with those early operations. Better prospects for services lay in the expansion of Bracknell New Town, along with discussions over joint operation with Reading Corporation, though the latter would drag on until 1964.

It should also be noted that *Thames Valley* schedules staff were wise to the value of the various composite timetables that appeared in the booklets, as a number of places benefited from the passing of various services. Thus residents of the relatively rural village of Pangbourne could make use of buses on Routes 5 (from Oxford), 5a (from Wantage), 5b (from Newbury), 50 (from Abingdon) and Route 102 (from West or East Ilsley), along with the *City of Oxford* workings on Routes 34 (from Oxford) and 40 (from Abingdon), all of which gave an average wait between buses towards Reading of 16 minutes (sometimes as little as just 2 minutes), even taking into account the whole day from 7.09am through to 11.44pm!

32 Grosvenor Road in Caversham for his occupation. The former Chief Engineer Ian Campbell had moved to *United Automobile Services* at Darlington, so his former residence at Pangbourne was disposed of shortly afterwards.

The other pair of coach-seated saloons were Bristol MW6G's of 1960, and Car 853 (VJB 944) was seen in Wokingham working Route 75 by Garaham Low, whilst below is the interior view looking forward. Note the hopper windows, deep luggage racks and the warning signs advising 'lower your head when leaving your seat' on the seat-backs!

Most of the Reading one-man-operated routes were inter-worked duties, but those for the London Victoria A and the 75 to Guildford were on a separate rota. In the same way, it was the quartet of coach-seated saloons from the Reading allocation that were the usual performers on those routes. 1955 Bristol LS6B Car 723 (HMO 869) is seen at Victoria.

In the meantime the new Chief Engineer, Phillip Robinson, took up his duties from 1st January, and he came from *Cumberland Motor Services*. As was the custom at the time for senior officials moving between associated operators, a lease was taken on a house at

Other appointments from January were Arthur Waldron as Traffic Superintendent at Reading (after the unexpected death of Jack Dear in the previous December), Arthur having looked after the Newbury area, whilst C.S. Anderson became his Assistant. Inspector Reg Pembroke of Reading was made up to Chief Inspector, whilst Les Mercer became Depot Inspector at Newbury, Frank Williams became DI at Bracknell and E.H. Mitchell took the same role at Oxford. Two further appointments took effect from 25th February, when G.A.E. Archer and W.V. Summers were made up to Inspector at Reading.

Despite some recent losses amongst their number, long-serving employees going back to the 1920's were still in evidence, and early during 1961 it became necessary to consider the ill-health of Driver Ernie Pembroke (brother of Reg), something that the Company was noted for. Ernie was found alternative employment in the Traffic Office, where he became responsible for the (at times) time-consuming issuing of Scholar's Season Tickets. Also, in respect of personnel, it should be noted that Frank Robinson ('Mr. Rob') of the Traffic Office, was also in charge of the Reception Desk in the Head Office at 83 Lower Thorn Street, so sometimes it was necessary to cover absence of the switchboard operator Rosemary Jenkins, this often falling to Peter Wilks. More of life in the Traffic Office already appears in the preceding volume, but we shall also hear more of him in due course.

Bristol FLF6G Car 842 (WJB 226) is seen passing The Ship into Peach Street, Wokingham, having worked there from Maidenhead on Route 21.

New buses for January were further Bristol FLF6G's with ECW H38/32F bodies, as Cars 841-3 (WJB 225-7). 841/3 were sent to Wycombe Marsh for duties on the 22.8-mile Route 28 (High Wycombe – Marlow – Henley – Wargrave – Reading), whilst 842 went to Maidenhead for the 15.5-mile long Route 21 (M'h – Woodlands Park – White Waltham – Waltham St. Lawrence – Shurlock Row – Binfield – Wokingham).

The only bus sold during January was 1951 Bristol LL6B-type Car 572 (FMO 954), with ECW B39R body, whilst in the early months of the year 1952 Bristol LS6G coaches 79-84 (SFC 565-70) were re-seated from 37 to 39 for mainly contract duties.

On 6th January there was a collision between a train and car at the level crossing at Strand Castle on the line between Maidenhead and Cookham, so a single-decker provided a temporary service for several hours. Co-operation of another kind was evident a few days later, when one of a series of regular meetings took place between *Thames Valley* and local coach operators. These were to agree on fares for excursions, and such meetings were held with *Jeffways & Pilot Coaches* of High Wycombe, *Smith's Luxury Coaches*, of Reading, *Alpha Coaches* of Maidenhead, *Reliance Motor Services* of Brightwalton, along with *Dring's Coaches* and *City of Oxford* in connection with those operated by *South Midland* Such meetings eliminated very time-consuming battles via the Traffic Courts in respect of renewals of licenses, but on the other hand could also be undeniably construed as price-fixing!

Over at Oxford, staff representatives had requested a concession to use the London express routes via High Wycombe or Henley, and from January this was granted to allow travel at 25% of fares, which was in line with the concession also available for staff on the Reading – London Routes A and B.

Apart from the carriage of passengers, parcels still provided some additional income and, from the previous January, facilities offered by neighbouring concerns had been linked. This meant that parcels could be consigned from any bus station office in one participating company to another in a wide area which embraced *Thames Valley, Hants & Dorset, Wilts & Dorset,* and parts of *Bristol Omnibus, Southern* and *Western National*. No figures are recorded of how much such a facility was actually used.

Bristol FLF6G Car 843 (WJB 227) was initially sent to Wycombe Marsh, though it would not be long before it was transferred to Bracknell in boost the double-deck contingent there.

Early February saw the end of a significant service, when Ted White finally hung up his familiar hat at the Newbury Enquiry Office. His father had founded *W.J. White & Son* at Hermitage from a carrier's business to coach and bus operation, joining forces with *Newbury & District* in March 1934. Part of the deal was that Ted should be employed and he became the bookings manager for coach work, his many local connections adding considerably to the success of *N&D* and, in due course *Thames Valley* in that area. Ted had been aided for many years by Frances Ravening (nee Walters), a former conductress at *TV's* Newbury Shed and who had married Walter Ravening in due course. The latter had started out as a young man with *Denham Bros.*, such were the strands connecting many local busmen still in evidence in the 1960's.

Delivered slightly earlier was Bristol FLF6G Car 840 (WJB 224), which was also sent to Wycombe Marsh. Normally this would have been found on the trunk services, but as the 'Marsh covered the routes in the Stokenchurch area on Sunday, it is seen laying over at Ibstone when working Route 41.

The extended tours operated by *South Midland* were quite an upmarket affair, not universally affordable, and it is also noted that a number of clients came from the USA or Canada. Preparing each season's brochure took many months of work, most of which was done by 'Mr. Rob', which in those days entailed numerous visits to the printers with proofs. From 24th March 1961 an agency was also granted to *Smith's Luxury Coaches* at Mill Lane in Reading.

Despite many newer buses, the Bristol K-types were still the backbone of many services. Car 499 (EJB 221) was on Route 62 at Cippenham (The Green).

As already noted, the expanding population at Bracknell called for changes to bus services, and it soon became apparent that Route A was not meeting the needs of the Newtowners or their relatives visiting from London. Mainly due to the high provision of public transport 'up the smoke' few Londoners owned cars, so they naturally looked to the rail and bus links when visiting those who had moved into the country. Some used the trains, with many opting for the familiar *Green Line* service, though that only reached Ascot (Horse & Groom). Although some tolerated the need to complete the journey by bus or by being met, it was not ideal, and there was the inevitable call for the route to be extended onto Bracknell.

Thames Valley, on the other hand, had been slow to respond to the increased demand, resulting in relief buses having to duplicate busy journeys, whilst the single-deckers allocated to those duties could not cope with typical weekend loadings. Clearly this needed some re-thinking by the *TV* management, which we will hear more of soon.

Amongst the other K-types still active were the former United Counties K5G's fitted with 8ft-wide 1952 ECW bodies, and Car 464 (FPU 511) had just run in from Lambourn on Route 106 on a wet morning.

On the subject of Bracknell it is worth noting, that the original New Town was based on the estates built in Priestwood 1 (between the Wokingham and Binfield Roads), Priestwood 2 (between the Binfield Road and Bull Lane/Sandy Lane), the Bullbrook developments and new housing in Easthampstead (between Rectory Lane and South Hill Road/Bagshot Road). In that guise, no homes were particularly far from the town centre, whilst each neighbourhood had shops for daily needs, along with convenient primary schools. In the first instance, therefore, improving or modifying existing services was considered, together and travel for workers to reach the new industrial estates.

Whereas the Bristol LS-types at Bracknell were one-man-operated, a number of those at High Wycombe were still crew-operated. Route 25 (High Wycombe – Wycombe Marsh – Loudwater – Flackwell Heath) was a service not authorised for double-deck operation, mainly due to concerns over the steep Treadaway Hill. Car 679 (HBL 81) dated from 1953 and still had seats for 45, the conductor placing any pushchairs etc. in the rear boot if so required.

Easter saw the annual 'Ban the Bomb' march organised by the Campaign for Nuclear Disarmament, which now started from the AWRE Aldermaston base and went up to London. In 1961 it started on Good Friday 30th March. This provided both opportunities and inconveniences for the Company, as extra people used the buses, but there was also traffic congestion and some temporary road closures. However, it was an invariably peaceful progress, so the Police had only to deal with the associated traffic issues. That year *TV* carried an additional 530 passengers in 7 loads from Reading between 8am and 12noon, whilst others arrived from the west via service buses form Newbury on Route 1, Inspectors reporting 175 extra journeys.

When the March reached Reading that evening the Police closed St. Mary's Butts between 6.30 and 8pm, whilst similar temporary closures followed the progress of the march through Cemetery Junction and onwards to Maidenhead and Slough over the next two days.

Philip Wallis observed the transport associated with this event, noting the extra shuttle buses, which often resulted in types not usually seen along the Bath Road. Numerous other vehicles brought participants from further afield, with various independents there, along with the Company fleets as diverse as *Western National* and *Scottish Motor Traction*! There was also a sizeable contingent of *Eastern National* 'Lodekkas' on hire through *Tillings Transport* from London, as *London Transport* had declined to hire any buses out. These were drawn up around the triangle of roads near The Falcon at Aldermaston, close to the entrance to the controversial bomb-making establishment.

Whilst reviewing this event, it is worth noting that such a colourful selection of vehicles could be seen on any working day. Again, Philip recalls that a bus station area had been set aside about a quarter of a mile from The Falcon on the Baughurst Road, where the double-deckers of *Thames Valley, Wilts & Dorset, Reliance* of Brightwalton, *Lovegrove's* of Tadley and *Smith's* of Reading, along with the coaches of *Kent's* of Baughurst, *Ford's* of Silchester and *Porter's* from Dummer were seen. In the morning these arrived between 7.30 and 8am, but the afternoon exit was just after 5pm and was known locally as 'the camp rush'.

H10 (FMO 517) was caught by the camera of Philip Wallis at Heath End Crossroads on a contract run from AWRE Aldermaston in 1964, with a Smith's of Reading Leyland double-decker following on.

Worker's transport was also an important feature of the service routes too, and the Company had a long history of meeting such needs, particularly in the High Wycombe, Woodley, Slough and Newbury areas. More recently the post-war factories at the former RAF White Waltham airfield had resulted in numerous short-workings on Route 21 from Maidenhead, whilst at Bracknell the developments at the Eastern Industrial Estate (off the London Road) and the Western Industrial Estate (off Wokingham Road) had seen short-workings on Route 2 to bring workers in from the Ascot and Binfield directions. Such was the importance of these new large employers that representations from the union shop stewards at Sperry Gyroscopes on the Downshire Way led to some suitable short-workings for those needing to get into town and back at lunchtimes, whilst the Company also undertook to address the now inadequate capacity provided by the Bristol LS saloons on Local Service Route 52 from the South Hill Road area. Elsewhere, changes of working patterns notified to the Company often resulted in modified timings to suit.

Further conversions of Bristol LS-type saloons took place to 41-seaters equipped for one-man-operation, during this year, with Car 683 (HBL 85) dealt with in May, followed by Cars 717-9 (HMO 863-5) in September, and from November by Car 709 (HMO 855) which joined the Bracknell allocation.

Agreement was reached to continue the long standing arrangements whereby passengers could make use of combined travel by bus and the scheduled public boat trips along the River Thames operated by *Salter Bros.*, with various embarkation points between Oxford and Kingston, operational between Whitsun and the first week of September. Annual events such as the Taplow Horse Show were also afforded enhanced bus services, and in 1961 this occurred on 15th April, with a regular shuttle service from Maidenhead.

In the meantime the Company had attended the Irish Tourist Board conference in Dublin on 25th March, leading to agreement with Irish air operator *Aer Lingus* to convey passengers for the Irish Tours of *South Midland*. In order to drum up more clients for the programme of extended tours, it was arranged for new Bedford SB8 coach 861 (WRX 776) to be put on a series of static displays, starting out at Swindon on 11th April, in an echo of the once popular *TV* practice of displaying the season's latest edition to the coach fleet.

Bedford SB8 coach 861 (WRX 776) carried a 37-seater 'Super Vega' body by Duple, which was built to 7ft 6ins width for tours along narrower roads. It is seen here In October 1961 helping out on express services after a season on touring.

The other new coaches for the 1961 intake were a trio of Bristol MW6G's with ECW C34F bodies, as Cars 858-60 (WRX 773-5), which along with 861 were for *South Midland* touring work. 858/9/61 were all licensed in May, followed by 860 in June. For that season it was decided that drivers on tours would be issued with a two-piece suit in clerical grey. However, the new coaches still fell one short of the touring requirement, in that a second 7ft 6ins vehicle was used for the Wye Valley tour, so 1950 Bristol LL6B coach 73 (EBD 236) was given a reprieve for the season.

Coach 73 (EBD 236) had a fully-fronted ECW body with seating for 31, though of the 'interim' style with exposed radiator and originally delivered to United Counties. It is seen at Victoria Coach Station ready for the Wye Valley tour.

Bristol MW6G coach 860 embarks on the Cornish Riviera tour from Gloucester Green at Oxford, with the South Midland café behind.

The full 1961 programme of extended tours by *South Midland* was as follows:

Scotland	10 days
Ireland (Western & Northern Counties)	9 days
Ireland (Southern Counties)	9 days
Welsh Coast	8 days
Central Wales	8 days
North Wales	8 days
English Lakes	8 days
Cornish Riviera	8 days
North Devon	8 days
South Devon	8 days
Wye Valley	8 days

All of the above could be joined at Victoria Coach Station, High Wycombe, Maidenhead, Henley and Oxford, and bookings could be made through a wide network of agents. Each year the Company hosted a conference for the latter, as it was good business.

Apart from annual Agent's Conference, the Company also had a stand at various national and local events, promoting both the bus services and extended tours, the Thames valley still being a leisure area for many.

As already noted Route 75 (Reading – Wokingham – Bracknell – Bagshot – Guildford) was a long run, and it took 1 hr 35mins each way. The first run of the day for *TV* crews left Reading at 7.12 on weekdays, in order to give the driver a break and clear the stand at Farnham Road Bus Station, arrangements were made to proceed to the Woodbridge Road *Aldershot & District* garage for that layover.

Whereas once it had been the practice for conductors to hand in their ticket machines and racks each end of day, in an era where racks were replenished against waybills, that was no longer so relevant, and from 29th April Bracknell joined the garages where individual machines were issued.

Bristol MW6G coach 858 (WRX 773) 'somewhere in Scotland', caught by the camera on a wild stretch of road in August 1961 by well-known bus photographer Bob Mack of Leeds.

Another aspect of the *South Midland* portfolio not noticed by the public was the express services for RAF personnel going on leave from Abingdon or Benson airfields, these being operated on the basis of set fares, but with a guarantee of a minimum income for the Company by the Air Ministry.

On the services front a new Route 1c commenced on 6th May in response to new housing developments in the Woodley area. This was a one-man-operation and ran from Mondays to Saturdays only, as Reading (Stations) – London Road – The Drive – Whitegates Lane – Church Road – Wokingham Road – Loddon Bridge Road – Woodley (Roundabout).

Above: Bristol LL5G Car 820 (FMO 24) was a regular performer on Route 1c. *Below:* K6B-type Car 497 (EJB 219) is seen on a Route 70 to Lent Rise.

Reorganisation of services in the Slough area from 3rd June saw Routes 68 (Maidenhead – Lent Rise – Burnham – Slough) and 69 (Lent Rise – Slough Trading Estate) being withdrawn, some workings covered by amendments to Route 65 (Maidenhead – Taplow – Lent Rise – Burnham – Slough), whilst a new Route 70 between Maidenhead and Slough by way of Taplow - Lent Rise - Burnham – Britwell (Calbroke Road) started, though mostly operating between Slough and Lent Rise throughout the day.

Service improvements for residents in new housing at Purley was forthcoming in response to a request from the Parish Council, with buses on some journeys of Routes 5a (Reading – Wantage) and 102 (Reading – East or West Ilsley) diverted via St. Marys Avenue from 9th June. However, there were additional reasons for this compliance, as *Pangbourne Coaches* applied for an express service between Purley and Reading to meet the aspiration of local residents, and *TV's* action ensured that this was not granted a Road Service License. This actually led to *Pangbourne Coaches* airing its dissatisfaction with what it saw as Traffic Commissioner bias towards *Thames Valley,* though in reality the TC's merely favoured modifications to an existing facility in preference to additional operations.

Early in June the London-based Inspector, Mr. Rooke, resigned, whilst at Maidenhead G.C. Walker was made up to Inspector. During that same month Peter Wilks returned to the Company, having successfully completed his Institute of Transport studies at North West London Polytechnic. It is worth noting that such studies were actively encouraged by bus companies, whilst other training came from placements between associated operators, trainees spending some time in a number of different departments, all seen as for the overall good of the industry.

The Royal Counties Show was a hugely popular annual event, and in 1961 it was held in Windsor Great Park for four days from 21st June. On this occasion *TV* and *London Transport* shared a special service between Windsor town centre and the site, it being a border town for the two operators. Each ran three double-deckers, charging an adult fare of 8d, with half fares for children, and pooled the revenue.

June was a traditionally busy month for Thames Valley, with the annual Royal Ascot Week, and 1946 Bristol K6A Car 449 (DBL 157) is seen at the Grange Car Park, where a temporary bus station was once again set up to cater for the many relief buses helping out Route 2 towards Windsor or Reading.

The centre for South Midland operations was Botley Road garage, the original front portion having come from United Counties with the X8 service to London via High Wycombe. Accommodation was much enlarged by Thames Valley, allowing the old Iffley Road site to be disposed of in June 1961.

However, over at Maidenhead, the staffing situation had become so bad that it was necessary for Reading garage to take over its duties on Route 1 between the two towns, with four double-deckers being transferred from 26th June. Also in an effort to address the shortage of drivers, a driving school was set up at Maidenhead from 19th July.

Both *Thames Valley* and *South Midland* kept coaches for excursions and private hire, though the activities from *TV* garages had not been expanded under Tom Pruett, who had of course come from the only Tilling company not to operate coaches, with *Brighton, Hove & District* leaving that role to *Southdown* and its large coaching fleet. It had also been deemed a waste of staff time to endeavour to lodge new applications for licenses, given that every other coach firm, along with the (now State-owned) railways put forward their objections! Staff shortages had also rendered such duties harder to cover.

Even so, from 1961 there was still a regular excursions programme from each of the main garages, running from Whitsun through to mid/late September.

One of the newest attractions at that time was the new terminal at London's Heathrow Airport, which in those days of lesser security was the destination not only of air passengers, but also conducted coach parties. The new Europa and Oceanic Terminals had replaced the original tented village of ex-Army origins on the northern edge of the site, these being better known today as Terminals 2 and 3. There was also a restaurant and roof garden open to the public at the Queen's Building administration block.

Bristol LS6B coach 691 (HMO 837) is seen from the roof of the Queen's Building on one of the afternoon tours to the airport, the guide standing in the footwell and introducing the tour. This cost 6 shillings from Reading and proved very popular.

From Oxford *South Midland* operated a programme of day and half-day excursions ranging from seeing the Colleges & Blenheim Palace to coastal resorts, places of interest and a Wye Valley tour.

From Reading there were almost daily trips to London Airport, plus other more local places such as Woburn Abbey, Blenheim Palace, Windsor & Runnymeade, and Beaconsfield (for the Model Village) and Whipsnade Zoo, some circular tours to Savernake & Vale of the White Horse, the Surrey Hills and a South Coast all-day tour, together with coastal excursions to Bognor Regis, Hayling Island and Southsea. Rather more special was the coach trip to Hythe-on-Solent, followed by a 2-hour steamer cruise on Southampton Water, the brainchild of the late Reading Traffic Superintendent Jack Dear and Commander Percy of the Hythe Ferry Company. The latter would set you back 15 shillings 6 pence, whilst Southsea was 11 shillings, Whipsnade Zoo 9 shillings and Blenheim Palace 6 shillings. On almost all Reading excursions passengers could also board at The Colonnade, which echoed the early post-war years when the coaches were actually based at that location.

Also from Reading, as well as other locations, there were special excursions to annual events, including the major features of the racing calendar in the south, with the Derby at Epsom, Royal Ascot and Goodwood and included the motor-racing held at the latter.

From Newbury the basic pattern of excursions was similar to those above, though there was also a weekly Wednesdays and Fridays evening trip leaving at 5.30pm for performances at the Oxford Theatre, the coach booking included reserved seating at the venue, running throughout the year. Passengers from Thatcham could also be picked up on the excursions.

Newburians could also make use of the ever-popular daily Summer express service operated by *South Midland* from both Worcester and Oxford, which headed south through Winchester to Portsmouth and Southsea. Offering single, day and period return fares, this was a popular choice for both day trips and those wishing to stay for a week in those areas, or crossing to the Isle of Wight. This operated daily from 1st June to 1st October and passengers could also be picked up south of Oxford from Drayton, Abingdon, Steventon, Rowstock Corner, Harwell, Chilton, East Ilsley, Beedon, Chieveley and Wickham, whilst beyond Newbury it also served Whitchurch, and other points beyond Winchester, thereby drawing from a wide area. There were two departures a day, the first from Oxford at 8.30am, calling at Newbury at 9.37 to reach Southsea at midday, which ran daily as noted above. A second coach left Worcester at 9am, reaching Oxford at 12.30, Newbury at 1.37pm and Southsea at 4pm, though it only operated on Saturdays during June, then daily from 1st July to 30th September. Those wanting a day out from Newbury would book the Oxford-based coach down and the Worcester-based one back, as the latter left Southsea at 6pm.

Bristol MW6G coach 802 (ORX 633) is seen leaving The Wharf at Newbury on the 1.37pm departure to Southsea on an evidently very warm day.

From Oxford there were other seasonal express options for reaching coastal destinations, as *South Midland* had developed joint services to Worthing and Brighton or Eastbourne (with *Southdown*) and to Margate (with *East Kent*), but these operated only on specific dates and via Henley – Maidenhead – London (Victoria), so were really links of convenience.

From High Wycombe there were some also dedicated seasonal operations, with coaches from Booker to Bournemouth and Eastbourne, which called into High Wycombe and had been inherited from *Crook of Booker*. Also with similar 1930's origins was the seasonal express service to Southsea, which also picked up at Wycombe Marsh, Loudwater, Wooburn Green, Bourne End, Cookham village, Maidenhead, Braywick and Holyport, operating on specific Saturdays and Sundays between June and September.

Excursions from High Wycombe were similar to those offered at Reading, as were those from Maidenhead. It seems likely that the Reading-based London Airport tour also picked up at Maidenhead, as in due course staff shortages effectively killed off coach work from that location, leaving the town with only that and the Southsea express emanating from High Wycombe now provided by *Thames Valley*.

However, despite the Company's now rather reduced role in that field, the loss was certainly made up by other local firms, with *Smith's Luxury Coaches* serving not only Reading, but also many points southwards and eastwards en route to coastal destinations, then Bracknell and Wokingham covered by *Gough's Coaches* and *Brimblecombe Bros.*, the Maidenhead and Cookham areas by *Alpha Coaches*, High Wycombe by *Jeffways & Pilot Coaches*, whilst *Reliance Motor Services* had for many years built up its empire in west Berkshire and beyond.

Numerically the largest type present in the fleet was the 76 Bristol KSW6B-types delivered between 1950 and 1955, as Thames Valley were late converts to the 'Lodekka'. Therefore, they were still very widespread and a number of routes were still in their hands. Car 668 (HBL 70) is seen laid over in the Southern Yard at Reading between turns on busy Route 4 (Reading – Shinfield – Arborfield – Yateley – Camberley).

The early 1960's saw an increase in the pace of what would now be termed traffic management, consisting of by-passes and one-way traffic schemes, all of which inevitably affected bus operations. Although the intention was to avoid traffic hold-ups, therefore in theory making bus services more reliable, the often tedious diversions used more fuel, took additional time and were soon as full as traffic as ever! This was also a headache for schedulers and passengers alike, as stopping places going back to pioneering days had to be re-sited, often divorcing the inward and outward stops to some distance apart.

On 26th June the Maidenhead By-pass opened, whilst at Burnham there was a one-way traffic scheme introduced through the village from 6th July. The latter saw Route 63 (Maidenhead – Taplow – Cliveden (The Feathers) – Dropmore – Burnham – Slough Trading Estate – Salt Hill – Slough) now take in some rather narrow stretches, so it was restricted to 7ft 6ins buses.

Belying its true age, Bristol K5G Car 476 (GNO 688) had been laid down in 1938, but by the time it was sold to Thames Valley it had received a PV2 radiator and was fitted with an ECW 55-seater body of 1948 vintage removed from another United Counties bus.

Another enforced change of working arrangements came in effect from 27th June, due to the closure of Windsor Road between Holyport turning and Fifield turning, anticipated to last for some 6 months. A shuttle bus was provided for passengers on Routes 20/20a (Aylesbury – Princes Risborough - High Wycombe – Maidenhead – Windsor), to transfer passengers between Fifield (Memorial Hall) and Dedworth (Nags Head). For this duty Car 476 (GNO 688) was loaned from Maidenhead to Bracknell.

Route 3 was still single-decked, and Car 717 (HMO 863) has just passed under the low railway bridge on the Finchampstead Road onto Camberley past the Two Poplars. We shall hear more of this bridge later!

17

Route 3 (Reading – Wokingham – Crowthorne – Camberley) also had some short-workings taking in the backroads between Wokingham and Crowthorne, along with some Crowthorne – Little Sandhurst runs, all of which needed reconsideration as part of the plan to double-deck the main route. At the same time there were requests from residents of new housing in the Lily Hill and Deepfield Road areas of Bracknell for better bus services. As a result of these factors, some journeys on Route 53 (Windsor – Winkfield – Chavey Down – Bracknell – Easthampstead – Crowthorne) were diverted via Lily Hill Road and Deepfield Road, then extended onwards from Crowthorne (Iron Duke) to Little Sandhurst (The Stores), these journeys being designated 53a and operational from 1st July.

There had also been calls for better links to the large ICI Plant Research Establishment at Jealotts Hill, a site variously served by the Company, independents, contract coaches and even ICI itself over the over 30 years it had been open. However, with an increase population in Bracknell, more workers were now from that town than before, so a new Route 55 (Bracknell – Park Road – Newell Green – Warfield - Jealotts Hill – Hawthorn Hill) was instigated from 1st July, with some journeys travelling more directly between the town centre and Warfield via Maidenhead Road to the Plough & Harrow crossroads and known as 55a.

Although the passenger fleet was highly visible, the same could not be said of the Service Vehicles, and the staff cars were totally anonymous. However, all were an essential part of daily operations, and during 1961 a number of changes took place. Out went 1950 Morris 'Oxford' cars (FRX 9 and FRX 647), replaced in February by Austin A40 (WMO 52) and Morris 'Oxford' (WMO 279) cars for the Traffic Supervisors at High Wycombe and Reading. In June Oxford's 1951 Vauxhall 'Wyvern' (RWL 72) went, followed by Reading pool car Vauxhall 'Velox' (GJB 786) in July, these being replaced by Vauxhall 'Victor' cars (YBL 283/4).

Relatively few photos of the Staff Cars have come to light, but new Austin A40 (WMO 52) is included in this shot of Car 796 (DMO 666), a Bristol LL5G with 1958 body seen at Maidenhead Bus Station.

Above: Car 448 (DBL 156) is seen after rebuild and with Route 60 via the Main Road (i.e. the Bath Road A4) displayed at Maidenhead Bus Station. Below: Car 452 (DBL 160) is seen at Reading after its rebuild.

As previously noted, there remained a trend towards further double-decking of services, in a continued effort to reduce the once widespread need for relief workings or to meet housing developments locally. A start was made in rebuilding the best of the 1946 Bristol K6A's, with Car 447 (DBL 155) being the first out-shopped from The Colonnade in May. This work generally took a couple of months, but on this occasion there were no outward signs of any changes, as was the case with Car 440 (CRX 549) which was completed in October. However, also emerging later that month were Cars 448/52 (DBL 156/60), both of which had lost the upper-deck beading that had contained a cream band. These were followed by Car 441 (CRX 550) in November, but oddly this retained the upper-deck beading. Also, all of those buses still had the original 2-piece destination apertures taking the 49-inch wide blinds, and these refurbished buses were to outlast their untreated contemporaries by 2 to 3 years and were seen out on a daily basis.

Graham Low was in Weldale Street just as Car 845 (WJB 229) arrived from Lowestoft, showing it had been collected by a Thames Valley driver on Trade Plate 190 RD. Curiously, the author, Graham Low and Philip Wallis were all taking photos at this time, yet none of us met until many years later!

In the meantime, in July a further 5 Bristol FLF6G's with ECW H38/32F bodies arrived as Cars 844-8 (WJB 228-32), and these were allocated to Reading (844-6), Bracknell (847, the first 70-seater there) and Wycombe Marsh (848). These differed from previous examples by having illuminated advert panels fitted to the offside 'tween-decks area, and these were on the same circuit as the interior lighting. As new they did look effective, though if any of the fluorescent tubes failed, then the appearance could look rather poor.

Car 845 (WJB 229) is seen after entering service on Route 9 to Mortimer (Station) and with an illuminated advert for Wellsteads of Reading.

No vehicles were withdrawn as a result of the above new deliveries, as it gave respite for the rebuilding of the K6A's mentioned earlier, which in turn would see further withdrawals from the single-deck fleet.

A further incentive to reduce the need for relief workings came with an increase in the cost of diesel fuel by 3d per gallon, which equated to an additional cost of £15,000 to the annual fuel bill. However, one improvement for PSV operators was an increase in the legal speed limit being raised from 30 to 40mph.

Even rural routes like the 5b (Reading – Pangbourne – Yattendon – Newbury) had required regular reliefs until double-deckers had been introduced, especially between Reading and Pangbourne. Bristol K6B Car 526 (FBL 28) is seen in Reading garage ready for service. Note the typical row of K-types at the rear towards the Weldale Road entrance.

Further housing in the Woodley area resulted in Route 1a journeys to Colemans Moor Road operating from Woodley Roundabout via Colemans Moor Lane to that point, returning directly to the Roundabout, effective from 5th August. Woodley & Sandford PC had also requested that a bus reached Reading by 9am, so slight adjustments were made from 9th September.

A number of services had been under review at this time, some because of the need to increase capacity, whilst others were being unrenumerative. Route 17 (Maidenhead – Burchetts Green – Hurley – Henley) fell into the latter category, so its timetable was reduced from 26th August, though the peak journeys were retained in recognition that a good number of school children used the buses in Maidenhead or Henley.

Revisions were also intended for the Marlow local journeys from that date, with the 18b (Bourne End – Marlow) now to operate through from Maidenhead and onto Chisbridge Cross, thereby replacing the Route 18 'shorts' Marlow – Marlow Bottom. However, the Union felt it had not been sufficiently consulted, whilst the proposals were due to became effective during one of the recurrent overtime bans in forced by the Union. In due course the changes were introduced on 16th September, the Chisbridge Cross stop serving the HM Borstal at Finnamore Wood.

The annual Newbury Agricultural Show was held at Elcot Park, on the Bath Road halfway between Hungerford and Newbury on 16th September, and the *'Valley's* buses carried 4,300 passengers there, which was 700 more than the previous year. Buses left both Newbury and Hungerford throughout the morning and afternoon peaks at the behest of Inspectors, whilst any passengers travelling in between could use the service buses on Route 116 along the main road.

One of Newbury's 1952 Bristol LS6G coaches, 673 or 676 (HBL 75 or 78) got a rare chance to reach pastures new with an extended hire by the Women's Auxillary of the Licensed Victuallers from Bracknell, Reading and Newbury. The party left for the Irish Republic on Monday 18th September, with a guided tour of the Guinness Brewery and Dublin, followed by day trips out to the mountains, before returning home on Friday 22nd.

Many of the Newbury area routes were very rural in nature, and ideally suited to 7ft 6ins wide Bristol LL's converted for one-man-operation. Car 565 (FMO 947) had a tow-bar fitted at the rear in lieu of a breakdown wagon, and is seen at East Woodhay.

On the latter day the Traffic Manager went up to High Wycombe for a meeting regarding plans for a new bus station in the town, with *London Transport* also there at the Town Hall. However, he did not use his allocated car, Vauxhall 'Velox' (LBL 331) on that occasion, as someone had managed to crush it whilst reversing a bus in Reading garage the evening before!

From 30th September Maidenhead's driver situation had improved, so the Route 20/20a shuttle bus went over to its care, with K5G Car 476 (GNO 688) going back to there from Bracknell from 11th October.

The Company had over many years acquired various cottage properties around the Maidenhead and Reading garages, many having been demolished to allow yard or garage extensions. However, in September a clear out occurred with the sale of Nos.60-66 Bridge Street in Maidenhead and Nos. 74/80/2/4 Chatham Street in Reading, whilst the garden area behind the rented out shop at 2 Market Place in Marlow was also sold off.

One of the old Petrol Tanker drivers was still driving buses at Reading, but from early October Driver Wyeth was put on light duties, looking after the dispatch of newspaper bundles from Stations Square, many such dispatches reaching local shops by bus.

As already noted, *South Midland* handled a number of daily contracts to Harwell (Atomic Energy Research Establishment), and on the morning of 6th October 1952 Bristol LS6G coach 84 (SFC 570) was involved in a very bad smash at Ashridge Hill near East Ilsley some 3 miles from its destination. The coach was descending the hill when it mounted the nearside grass verge, taking out a telegraph pole, the impact of which spun the coach out across the road. It was then struck by two lorries, one a car transporter, which sliced the rear end completely off. Two passengers died and another five were injured, the victims coming from the Hungerford and Shaw areas. In due course it had to be considered as a write-off, being dismantled for parts until the remains were sold in May 1962.

The sorry state of the rear end of Car 84 (SFC 570) following the early-morning collision. The rear boot area and 7 seats had all been demolished.

Meanwhile, over to the north-east of *Thames Valley's* territory, further housing developments at Flackwell Heath led to consideration of double-deck operation. The route traversed the notorious steep Treadaway Hill, with the added complication that the railway line had a gate-operated crossing across it. A site meeting was held on 12th October with the East Midlands Traffic Commissioner to determine if double-deckers could be substituted in place of the restriction then in place. After a trial run it was agreed that they could be used on Route 25, but with a limit to 60-seaters at most, plus an instruction for drivers to stop dead and engage low gear before descending the hill.

Also considered that same week was the possible use of double-deckers on Route 5 (Reading – Oxford), as that would necessitate passing under the arched bridge at Pangbourne, itself set at an angle to the road. The County Surveyor met with the Traffic Manager, which presumably led to the signs warning that large vehicles might be using the middle of the road, as only the centre of the arch was high enough, but as it was that route remained a single-deck operation.

As noted earlier, the Little Sandhurst journeys had already been taken off Route 3's timetables, as part of preparations to double-deck that route throughout. Also for that aim, it was necessary to transfer the runs from Wokingham – Crowthorne via Gardeners Green – Crooked Billet – Crowthorne (Station). These were rolled into new Route 54 starting at Bracknell (Regal Cinema) – Binfield (Shoulder of Mutton) – Wokingham (Town Hall), then as before to terminate at Crowthorne (Iron Duke), a total of 10.5 miles, and operation commenced from 28th October.

Route 54 passed along some very winding lanes with little advance view of oncoming traffic. Bristol LS5G Car 709 (HMO 855) ended up in a ditch after its driver suddenly had to avoid a collision, though damage was only minimal.

At the same time Route 53/53a was extended onto Camberley to provide more capacity past new housing developments in Sandhurst and College Town. The 53a designation stayed with the journeys via Little Sandhurst, which left the main route by turning into Longdown Road, then via High Street – Church Road – Lower Church Road (A321) and under the very low railway bridge by Sandhurst station to rejoin the main route at the New Inn and Sandhurst High Street. Towards the eastern end of the route, all journeys now ran by way of Lily Hill Road – Bullbrook Shops – Deepfield Road, the full Windsor – Camberley journey taking 1hr 12mins and covering 20.6 miles (or 21.5 for 53a). A later journey from Camberley at 10.40pm was put on, also in order to work the last incoming bus on the 3 back to Bracknell Garage.

The staff situation at Maidenhead had improved to the extent that the Route 1 workings could be handed back from 28th October, so Bristol K6A Car 441 (CRX 550), K5G Car 477 (GNO 698) and KS6B Cars 598/9 (FMO 980/1) were returned to that allocation.

Other route alterations from that date saw Route 1c (Reading – Loddon Bridge – Woodley) extended onto Tippings Lane. Route 6a (Reading – Odiham) was altered to run via Whitley Roundabout – Christchurch Road – Shinfield Road – School Green – Hyde End Road – Spencers Wood, instead of running straight along the Basingstoke Road, which took in new housing in those areas, along with school children in an effort to make the service more profitable.

However, some services were reduced from the same day, with Route 9a (Reading – Grazeley – Tadley) at a reduced frequency, and also Route 16 (Maidenhead – Warren Row – Crazies Hill – Henley), though the latter reductions caused an outcry due to the number of school children who were adversely affected.

In response to calls for more capacity on Route A (Reading – Wokingham – Bracknell – Ascot – Staines – London Victoria), it was double-decked from 28th October, so a pair of coach-seated Bristol 'Lodekkas' were drafted over from Newbury, these being Cars 750/1 (MBL 831/2), which when new in 1956 had worked Route B (Reading – Maidenhead – Slough – London Victoria). In order to compensate Newbury for their loss, a pair of the slightly earlier generation of buses from the latter route, coach-seated Bristol KSW6B-type Cars 742/3 (JRX 817/8) were sent there to work on longer routes.

The pair of coach-seated Bristol LS-types Cars 723/5 (HMO 869/71) were displaced from the A onto other Reading-based services, whilst the dual-purpose MW-types tended to cover Route 75 (Reading – Guildford), a duty previously shared by all four. Car 852 (VJB 943) of the latter is seen at Reading when on Route A.

It was also possible for Route 3 to go over to double-deckers from 28th October, using a mix of 55 and 70-seaters, with FLF6G Car 843 (WJB 227) being transferred from Wycombe Marsh to Bracknell.

Following conversion of Route 3 Bristol FLF6G Car 847 (WJB 231) turns into Wellington Road from Wokingham railway level crossing, caught by local enthusiast Graham Low. Note the illuminated off-side advert panel, which interrupted the upper-deck beading. To the right are the works of the Electro-heat Company, whilst over in the background stands the old coal office and the storage shed of Hurst-based corn merchants Geo. Ford & Son.

Although the 70-seaters tended to be Cars 843/7 (WJB 227/31), the other duties were taken by 55-seaters, so those provided by Reading garage varied considerably. 1950 Bristol K6B Car 529 (FBL 31) is seen passing Rackstraw Farm, heading towards Sandhurst High Street and with the Owlsmoor turn behind where the van is. The stop was the Bull & Butcher, but the pub has gone and the farmhouse is now a restaurant, and is all surrounded by new housing estates.

Another scene much changed through time shows Bristol LS6B Car 716 (HMO 862) in one of Graham Low's photos. This was Station Road, Bracknell before all the existing buildings were swept away, a road of nice houses, plus a few shops and businesses. To the right is a tractor parked outside W.J. Coles, local Agricultural Engineers, and where the author's father worked for a time. The 53 was by then going through to Camberley.

In order to work Route 3 with double-deckers, buses now needed to take a diversion south of Wokingham town centre by travelling down Denmark Street, then turning right into Wellington Road, over the railway level crossing at the Station into Barkham Road, then left into the now improved Molly Millars Lane, with its developing industrial estate, before regaining the Finchampstead Road south of the low railway bridge of the Reading – Tonbridge line.

However, as the route had been worked with single-deckers since 1925, old habits die hard, with severe consequences in this case! So, it was not many weeks later that the first *Thames Valley* double-decker came to grief when its driver went straight on along the Finchampstead Road and struck the bridge with predictable results! The bus was former *Bristol O.C.* K6B Car 436 (KHU 624), which was certainly the best condition of all the buses from that source. In view of the latter, it was decided to hastily add it to the similar buses then being rebuilt.

Car 436 (KHU 624) emerged from the Colonnade in December, minus the upper deck beading, and also sporting a full 3-piece destination aperture, fitted in place of its single BOC-style box. This was the only one from that source treated to this, the others either having T-style boxes or shorter lives retaining their original single boxes. Due to this accident this bus was to survive through to July 1966.

Needless to say, further Staff Bulletins were issued on the subject of the low bridge on Route 3, whilst signs were erected at the junction of Finchampstead Road and Wellington Road and at the junction with Molly Millars Lane, instructing all *TV* drivers to turn off. Despite these precautions there would be two more such collisions in the following year!

Whereas the earlier months had been remarkably quiet in terms of disposals, October saw a seasonal clearout of old coaches. Former *United Counties* Bristol LL6B coaches with 8ft-wide ECW 'Queen Mary' FC37F bodies of 1951, Cars 821/6/8/9 (FRP 835/41/3/5), were all disposed of, these having latterly covered contract workings now assigned to older saloons.

Bristol LL6B coach 821 (FRP 835) at Victoria Coach Station when working the London – High Wycombe – Oxford route, also acquired from United Counties, though not actually at the same time.

The other coaches sold were both Bristol L6B's, but quite unalike in appearance. One was Car 73 (EBD 236), with fully-fronted, but exposed radiator 7ft 6ins ECW FC31F body new in 1950, and inherited with the Oxford – High Wycombe – London service from *United Counties* two years later. Latterly it had seen use on the Wye Valley tour, but a new Bedford was on order to replace it from 1962. A photo of this coach appears on page 13.

The other L6B had a half-cab Windover body and was new in 1950 to the *Thames Valley* fleet, being one of a number transferred in 1960 to help out at Oxford with *South Midland* fleetnames. Car 555 (FMO 937) was the last of that type in either fleet, working through on express services to the end.

Car 555 (FMO 937) was photographed by Martin Shaw at Oxford on 18th March 1961, looking a little worn around the edges, and minus the Bristol oval from the radiator top.

Also disposed of were Bristol LL6B saloons with ECW B39R bodies, Cars 570/3/5/6 (FMO 952/5/7/8), which had been in store at Stokenchurch, but could now be released following the rebuilding of the Bristol K-type double-deckers for further service.

The ECW bodies on the FLF6G deliveries from Car 848 onwards had cream rubber window surrounds instead of the black previously used. Car 850 (WJB 234) is shown at Maidenhead soon after entering service and on Route 21 to Woodlands Park.

The final incoming vehicles of the year were another trio of Bristol FLF6G's with ECW H38/32F bodies, as Cars 849-51 (WJB 233-5), all of which featured the offside illuminated advert panels. Car 849 went into service at Reading, the others going to Maidenhead in December. The only other fleet changes that month involved the transfer of 1952 Bristol LS6G coach 673 (HBL 75) and 1953 Bristol LS6B coach 688 (HMO 834) over to *South Midland,* both with ECW bodies.

Bristol FLF6G Car 849 (WJB 233) is seen just about to enter service at Reading on the long Route 28 up to High Wycombe. The cream rubber surrounds were also used on the destination apertures, whilst note the Dulux advert – painted on of course!

Rising costs were causing concerns for the Company at this time, and the first ever recorded instances of redundancies took place during October/November, when it was decided to dispense with a junior typist and a clerk at Maidenhead, along with two female clerks at the Reading Enquiry Office. At Maidenhead bus duty plates were introduced from 10th November, in an effort to provide efficient use of buses allocated there. However, the Duty Inspectors at the Bus Station soon found this system had its drawbacks, so they took to allocating the plates as the day went by, which also meant that any missing plates required the bus to be marked with crayon or chalk numbers instead. Also at Maidenhead the conductors were issued with individual ticket machines from 13th November.

At Bracknell a further Inspector was appointment with the promotion of Driver H.S. Stone from 28th October, in anticipation of the retirement of Arthur ('Nobby') Clarke at the end of the year.

On Sunday 12th November the sudden death of William ('Stan') Tucker, the Bracknell Garage Foreman, occurred at the age of 61. He had been born at Basingstoke in 1899 and was apprenticed at the Thornycroft vehicle works, where he would have been very familiar with the J-type chassis of wartime fame. *Thames Valley* had built up of such a fleet of that type by the opening of the new Ascot garage in 1924, that Stan was very suitable for the appointment of Garage Foreman there. He was indeed an excellent engineer and pivotal to the success of operations there in many ways, that location often being chosen for experiments with engines or the running of demonstrators. Indeed, former Chief Engineer Basil Sutton once said 'he had no worries with the Ascot allocation under Mr. Tucker', a fine compliment when one considers that the buses in his charge worked the highest weekly mileages of any in the fleet.

Stan had transferred to Bracknell when the new garage replaced Ascot and Crowthorne dormy shed in June 1960, moving there from his South Ascot home. Outside of work he was a keen participant in the busy social life of Ascot Garage and a Freemason of some distinction, whilst his work colleagues formed a guard of honour at his funeral. As a result of this unexpected vacancy, it was decided that Reading Garage Foreman E.J. Dickenson would now assume responsibility for over-seeing maintenance at Bracknell as well.

Bristol LS6B Car 724 (HMO 870) was for many years at Bracknell, but was still at Newbury in 1961.

THAMES VALLEY
THE FINAL DECADE
1961 – 1971

Written and published by Paul Lacey

THE FINAL VOLUME IS NOW AVAILABLE, SO ORDER YOUR COPY AT THIS OFFER PRICE WITHOUT DELAY!
RETAIL PRICE £25
ORDER NOW FOR £20+p&p

This final installment of the 4-volume 800-page history of the Thames Valley Traction Co. Ltd. brings the story to its conclusion on the last day of 1971.

All route developments and changes to the fleet are fully detailed, along with special appendices for the service vehicle fleet, garages and out-stations, a route map, garage allocations and working arrangements.

Profusely illustrated with 548 monochrome half-tone illustrations and a full-colour section of 45 photos, this provides a very comprehensive history of this interesting decade, including the numerous secondhand vehicles acquired during those years. Demand will be high, so

order now from: Paul Lacey, 17 Sparrow Close Woosehill, Wokingham, Berkshire, RG41 3HT

If you are local and wish to collect please call me on 0118 979 4097 and arrange a suitable time, but no casual callers please!

Other volumes still available while stocks last at half price-

A History of the Thames Valley Traction Co. Ltd., 1920-1930	(£15) £7.50 ☐
A History of the Thames Valley Traction Co. Ltd., 1931-1945	(£25) £12.50 ☐
A History of the Thames Valley Traction Co. Ltd., 1946-1960	(£25) £12.50 ☐
The Newbury & District Motor Services Story (new in 2011)	(£25) £12.50 ☐
50 Years of South Midland 1921-1970 (by David Flitton)	(£11) £5.50 ☐
Thackray's Way – A Family in Road Transport	(£10) £5.00 ☐

Please add the appropriate postage and packing contribution as below –
1 book £3   2 books £5   3 books £7   4 or more books £9

Please make your cheque payable to Paul Lacey – thank you for your order

The Newbury area routes reached out in all four directions to Swindon, Basingstoke, Oxford and Maidenhead. Graham Low caught this scene at East Ilsley pond as Guy 'Arab' MkIII 6LW Car H16 (HOT 394) in at 12.44 met with one of the Reading-based LL5G buses on the 12.45 Route 102 to West Ilsley. Such connections enabled easy transfers between the Reading and Newbury services. The Guy's crew take a rest before setting off again at 1.05pm.

Philip Wallis saw Bristol KSW6B Car 743 (JRX 818) as it passed by Kingsclere Square on the 122 from Basingstoke. Note the coach seating and rear platform door, this bus having originally covered the London Route B, and been transferred to Newbury in 1961 in exchange for 'Lodekkas' taken for London Route A double-decking. A Wilts & Dorset-style bus stop can be seen to the left of the bus, and to the right is a very short 30mph sign!

The coach–seated LD-types were also the usual performers on Route 112 to Oxford, and Car 763 (MBL 844) is seen turning into Gloucester Green Bus Station. This bus had also seen use on Route B when new, but transferred to Newbury for use on the longer routes later on. The platform doors, saloon heaters and 6-cylinder Gardner engine made for a smooth warm journey over the Berkshire Downs, and these buses were well liked by the crews.

Another regular issue for the Traffic Office was road closures, whether for just a few days or much longer term, calling for frequent re-routing of bus services. When Robin Hood Lane at Winnersh was closed for some 6 months from 12th November for a reconstruction of the railway bridge adjacent to Winnersh Station, at least parallel Watmore Lane was then available as an alternative way for Route 1b from Reading – Hurst – Shurlock Row.

Didcot was only directly served by *Thames Valley* buses on Sundays, since rail replacement Route 129 (Newbury – Hampstead Norris - Compton – Didcot) had been put on by agreement after trains on that line had ceased to operate on that day in May 1953. It was now proposed to completely withdraw the passenger service, so talks took place between *British Railways* and *TV* on 1st December. Slightly earlier, notice was tendered on the Lambourn – Didcot (ROF) contract on 24th November, as the Company no longer found it worthwhile retaining a vehicle for that purpose.

Some alterations took place to Route 110 (Newbury – Thatcham – Tadley) from 2nd December, with a new relief working to convey schoolchildren between Thatcham (Broadway) and the Winchcombe School at Shaw, whilst other changes reflected working patterns at Cropper's Factory and the Thatcham Depot.

On that same date the journeys on Route 27 (High Wycombe – Great Missenden) travelling via Little Kingshill were designated as 27a. At Maidenhead Route 24 was reduced to an hourly operation, to run as Maidenhead – Cookham Station – Cookham Dean, and still covered by single-deckers, whilst a new 24a was provided with double-deckers and ran to Cookham Rise (Westwood Green) via Whyteladyes Lane and Cookham Station. The established extra journeys on Route 24 between Cookham Dean (Quarry Wood Road) and Cookham Rise (Westwood Green) continued to be covered by double-deck buses as before. Also at Maidenhead the Company learnt that workers at the Anti Attrition Works on White Waltham airfield were to be provided with contract coaches instead from 11th December, and there is no doubt that the recent staff shortages had caused some concern over workers reaching that site on time.

The close of 1961 was notable for the retirements of two pioneering employees. One of the very first crew at the local *British* branch, Charlie Hampton, ceased his driving duties after 46 years in December. He had been born at Bampton in Oxfordshire in 1895 and had started with *British* at the small Banbury operation in October 1914. That venture was cut short by the Great War, with the buses being requisitioned, so Charlie and his driver Owen Fox, were transferred to assist in establishing the Reading-based operations when they commenced in July 1915. Charlie was the only male conductor during the war years, though he went over to driving as soon as he was old enough. However, he did not leave the *'Valley's* employment entirely, as he took the place of Driver Wyeth on the newspaper duty now that the latter was fit enough to return to the cab. The author recalls interviewing Charlie a few years later, when still engaged on those duties, in full uniform and as a very polite and tall man, well known and respected by his colleagues.

Charlie Hampton leans on the mudguard of British Leyland bus (HE 9) ready for the Swallowfield route in the Winter of 1915. His lady conductor May Hatch would duly become his wife, whilst Owen Fox would later marry Charlie's sister Maud!

The other pioneer was Arthur ('Nobby') Clarke, who had joined as a driver at Maidenhead in November 1919. When a crew was required for outstationing at Ascot from November 1920 Nobby had volunteered, along with conductor Percy Stubbles, the pair sleeping in the hayloft of the barn at Englemere Farm in Blythewood Lane, where the bus was kept, until suitable accommodation in the farmhouse was negotiated! Nobby transferred to the new Ascot garage at Course Road in 1924, and in due course was made up to Local Supervisor, acting as Inspector at Windsor Central Station, where he kept the diverse services operating through there on track. Following his retirement on 29th December the Bracknell elements of his duties were covered by Inspector Strong, whilst supervision at Windsor was transferred to Maidenhead instead.

The final day of the year was marked by heavy snow, which disrupted services in general, and in the Reading area an LS-type saloon on Woodley Route 1c ended up in a front garden at Culver Lane, Earley, whilst the 7am Route 11 (Reading – Bucklebury) had to turn back after failing to ascend Buscot Hill.

1962

The snowy weather of late December 1961 carried on into the first two days of January, with services being badly disrupted and 40 vehicles out of service with burst radiators, rising by a further 20 by the close of 2nd January. All available staff were put to work on resolving these problems, and all buses were back in use by 4th January, by which time services returned to normal working.

At Bracknell one driver encountered a coal lorry stuck on the ascent of Station Hill towards the Bagshot Road and, after the drivers of both vehicles attempted to put coal under the wheels, the bus driver treated his passengers to towing the lorry up the hill before their journey continued! One *South Midland* driver had managed to get out onto the road on 1st January, but his journey was cut short after a collision with a *London Transport* Routemaster, putting Bristol LS6B Car 91 (TWL 56) out of service until 1st July. In all some 29,000 miles were lost in that period, but that figure would pale into insignificance by the standards of the following Winter!

The rising cost of fuel also resulted in a fares increase on the *South Midland* express services between Worcester, Oxford and London, which had a 8.3% rise applied from 1st January. On the tours front, planning was well underway for the annual Agent's Conference, which was held on 14th February at Victoria Coach Station, accompanied by traditional musical entertainment provided by the Tourist Boards of Scotland, Wales, Southern Ireland and Ulster, along with two coaches for inspection. In support of the Irish tours programme, General Manager Tom Pruett also visited Southern Ireland on 1st February to discuss arrangements for servicing the coach during the season.

Bedford SB8 coach 865 (519 ABL) was brought out of store for a series of static displays, starting with the Conference, then Maidenhead from 23rd February, followed by Reading (as seen here) from 8th March, Newbury from 15th March, Slough from 27th March, then finally at Swindon from 17th April, with pages from the latest brochure displayed in the windows.

During January public disquiet over parking in the High Street at Bracknell was joined by a call from *TV* to have reserved stopping areas, as in those days there were vehicles parked on both sides of the two-way road. The Easthampstead RDC blamed traders who parked there all day, adding that it lacked the powers to create reserved spaces. The author also recalls the old Warfield farmer Ted Gale, who would drive his grey tractor into town and leave it with the engine running in the middle of the street whilst he went into the Post Office, harking back to a somewhat quieter period of time!

South Midland's AEC 'Regal' MkIV coach 85 (SFC 571) had been up-seated from 37 to 39 by January, whilst *Thames Valley* transferred Bristol LS6B coach 691 (HMO 837) to the Oxford fleet in January, plus Bristol LS6G coach 671 (HBL 73) and fully-fronted Bristol LWL6B coach 610 (GBL 874) in February.

1951 Bristol LWL6B coach 610 (GBL 874) is seen after transfer to South Midland, though with a common livery, only a change of fleetname was required.

Unfortunately, another *South Midland* coach was involved in a fatal accident at Nuneham Courtenay on 10th February, when it collided with a private car, both occupants of which died. Bristol LS6B Car 692 (HMO 838) was de-licensed and its place taken by the reinstatement of stored Bristol LL6B Car 77 (FRP 834), acquired from *United Counties* in 1952.

In the meantime, arrangements were made to extend Route 1c (Reading – Earley – Loddon Bridge – Woodley Roundabout) to take in the new housing in the Silverdale Road area. This took effect from 1st February, but the operation was restricted to 7ft 6ins-wide buses until all the adopted roads were made up to full 18ft width throughout, this restriction duly being removed from 21st July, after which Bristol LS-types were the usual performers for the meantime. At Maidenhead the frequency of Route 18 (Maidenhead – Marlow) was reduced from 24th February, with the section between Summerleaze Road and the town centre being transferred to Route 18b instead.

Jim Vockings worked at Wycombe Marsh from 1960 and enjoyed the wide variety of operations in the area. He is seen here with 1949 Bristol K6B Car 506 (EJB 228) on Route 42 at Loudwater Station, complete with a siding full of goods wagons. Jim was recalled as a bit of a lad, but in due course he was made up to Inspector in 1969, staying on for a few more years before trying his hand at some coach operation and then high-class tour driving, taking in the sights of Britain.

Apart from the intensive Local Services, there were many other routes taking the Wycombe-based buses to various points up into the Chilterns. One such route was the once sleepy Route 31 (to Lacey Green or Walters Ash), which had become much busier with the establishment of RAF camps. Bristol LS6G Car 679 (HBL 81) of 1953 is seen by the camp gateway at Naphill headed back to High Wycombe.

Wycombe was also notable for having lots of female conductors in post-war years, due to high employment locally. Jim soon met Ann Dutton, who became his wife, and she is seen here at Cadmore End laid over with 1952 Bristol LWL6B Car 622 (GJB 260) after working there on Route 36. Once they had a child, the couple managed to keep working by gaining shift patterns that dove-tailed with friends who also had a child and were on the 'Valley, covering baby-sitting etc.

Another old employee was lost on 17th February, when Conductor P.R. Terry of High Wycombe died, having started at the 'Marsh in June 1925, when the allocation consisted of Thornycroft J-types. A few days later a different type of ticket machine was tried out, this being the Almex, as favoured by a number of other large bus operators, but evidently it did not impress, as a further batch of Setright machines were ordered, whilst the Reading diver-conductors were issued with individual machines from 31st March.

Another recent Wycombe recruit was Jim Vockings, who had applied as a driver after serving in the Military Police in Hong Kong. He recalled how he was sent along from the Frogmoor Office to see Frank Stacey at the 'Marsh garage for his assessment. There was no actual training, just a run-through of the controls and the need to double de-clutch when gear-changing on the Bristol K6B (Car 506 or 507), before taking in a circuit out to town and back! As with many others of his time, Jim had driven various vehicles in the Army, so he got along alright, before Frank asked him to back the bus into position in the garage. What he didn't know was that a 'failed' driver was always told to stop on the forecourt so, although he had to wait for a confirmation letter, he had already passed.

Jim also recalled many amusing episodes from his days on the buses, saying whoever had written the scripts for the TV series 'On the Buses' must have studied Wycombe Marsh and its characters. He also recalled that on Sundays the 'Marsh covered the routes in the Stokenchurch area, as the Dormy Shed crews worked a 6-day week, and on one occasion he and Ann took a bus on the run out to Radnage, where passengers picked up through Stokenchurch attended a service at the chapel. This was an easy duty with a nice lay-over in the village before the return trip, except that day one Easter it started to snow, and they were lucky to get back to the town.

Another view of one of Wycombe's many Bristol K6B's, with Car 507 (EJB 229) on Local Service 26a.

Also working out of Fingest then was Bristol LWL6B Car 579 (FMO 961), shown at High Wycombe station about to depart for Lane End on Route 37, its days of service now drawing to a close.

Another contract operation with its roots in the old *Newbury & District* wartime era was the Lambourn – Didcot (Royal Ordnance Factory), but with effect from 27th March this was cancelled by *Thames Valley*, allowing disposal of another coach retained only for very limited use, whilst changes in workings over at Maidenhead reduced the allocation there by 3 buses. There had also been a number of coaches in store for the Winter awaiting delivery of new vehicles. So, in January Bristol LL6B coach 825 (FRP 840) was sold, followed in February by Bristol LWL6B saloons Cars 581/5 (FMO 963/7), the first of that type to be withdrawn. March saw further LL6B coaches sold, with the departure of Cars 822/4/7 (FRP 837/9/42), all these LL6B's having 8ft-wide bodies and originating with *United Counties*.

From 1st March the recent fares rise on the *South Midland* express routes was also applied to the RAF camp services from Abingdon and Benson to London.

Housing developments at Woodley continued apace, and from 10th March certain peak journeys on Route 1a from Colemans Moor Road were allocated a double-decker, and a measure of how quickly the local population increased is that within a short time the service became the province of 70-seaters.

In order to accommodate more girls travelling on Route 2 to Windsor County Grammar School for Girls there was a short-working from Ascot (Horse & Groom) each morning. However, from 12th March this was changed to a dedicated contract journey, with the bus now running direct to the school over-looking the Long Walk. This was situated in a row of assorted old buildings, bearing some resemblance to the image of the infamous 'St. Trininan's' which around that time was the subject of a number of films, one of which featured several old coaches bought by the studio from *Gough's Coaches* of Bracknell.

From 26th March the terminal arrangements of a number of High Wycombe services was amended to Frogmoor Bus Station, as opposed to in the roadway in Frogmoor, these being Routes 27/27a (Great Missenden), 31 (from Lacey Green or Walters Ash), 34 (Speen) and 80 (from Aylesbury 'the pretty way'). Certain journeys on Route 34 that extended to the rail station set down at the Salvation Army Hall in Frogmoor, as did the Castle Street projections of Route 80. These changes removed the need for buses to circle the block, saving a total of 11,284 miles p.a.

Bristol FLF6G Car 849 (WJB 233) enters Queen Victoria Street in Reading on route to Basingstoke on the 6 via Spencers Wood, Riseley and Sherfield-on-Loddon. Note the parade of cafes stretching round the corner from the Southern railway station.

A new bus station was under construction for *Wilts & Dorset* at Wote Street in Basingstoke, and a meeting was held with Mr. Carruthers from that Company on 18th March regarding arrangements for Routes 6 and 122 to be accommodated there.

In the meantime the Company had tendered notice on the AERE contract runs starting from the Hungerford area, the two outstationed coaches covering Chilton Foliat – Harwell and Great Bedwyn – Harwell. Also surrendered was the contract from Ramsbury and Lambourn, covered by a coach based at the latter, all set to end on 30th April with the saving of 3 coaches and the part-time drivers who also worked at AERE.

As previously noted, *Thames Valley* often responded favourably to requests from Local Authorities and large employers regarding the re-timing of services, and from 26th March Route 27/27a (High Wycombe – Great Missenden) had timings amended to suit the revised train trains at Great Missenden. At Bracknell, another large employer on the Western Road was a branch the AERE, which had a non-nuclear scientific establishment there and was seeking better links to the town centre, particular at lunchtimes for shopping and visits to the banks and post office.

Car 446 (DBL 154) seen in April after its rebuild and now allocated to Newbury. There seems little doubt that this rebuild was instrumental in this bus lasting to later be preserved as a reminder of the once large fleet of K-types with the 'Valley.

We have already seen how a number of the older K-types had been thoroughly rebuilt by the crew at The Colonnade bodyshops, and in December 1961 Car 446 (DBL 154) had been taken out of service after someone's foot went through the gangway in the upper deck. After being store at Stokenchurch for a while it was decided to give this bus the treatment, and it returned to service in January, minus the upper-deck beading, but otherwise of original appearance. This was followed by another K6A-type Car 450 (DBL 158) and then by similar Car 439 (CRX 548), the oldest native bus in the fleet, during April. All lost the upper-deck beading but retained the original front destination apertures at that time.

A number of services were becoming unrenumerative, despite one-man working, including Route 114 to East Woodhay. Bristol LS6G Car 683 (HBL 85) is seen at The Wharf in Newbury on the service that had been started by Denham Bros. in the early 1920's, and duly inherited with the transfer of Newbury & District in January 1950.

All in all the Company now found that 43 of its bus services were not paying their way, these being in the Reading and Bracknell area Routes 1b, 2a, 2b, 2c, 3a, 5a, 5b, 6, 6a, 6b, 9a, 11, 53, 53a, 54, 54a and 102, in the Newbury area Routes 101, 101a, 103, 104, 105, 106, 106a, 108, 110, 111, 113, 114, 114a, 115, 116, 120, 120a, 121, 126 and 129, with Routes 17, 17, 18, 19, 21 and 23 in the Maidenhead area. A general fares increase on these services was therefore lodged with the Traffic Commissioners in early April.

One of the recently departed Bristol LWL6B's, Car 585 (FMO 967) is seen on Route 9a, originally taken over in 1937 from J. Spratley & Son (Blue Star Service) of Mortimer, and now regarded as not covering the cost of operation.

On 6th April Her Majesty The Queen undertook a tour of Buckinghamshire, though not using the *Thames Valley* services, and this resulted in a number of delays throughout her progress from Marlow to High Wycombe and Aylesbury during the morning, with similar restrictions in Slough in the afternoon.

Yet another meeting took place on 9th April regarding the possible use of the station yard at Camberley as a bus terminus. I say 'yet another' because this topic had regularly surfaced since the 1920's, not even being resolved when the Southern Railway held interests in *Thames Valley* and *Aldershot & District,* and the two shared Directors. The Frimley & Camberley UDC also sought such a solution regularly, but the various services of the two concerns carried on without shared termini in that border agreement town.

From 12th April a number of school contract workings in the Newbury area on behalf of Berkshire and Hampshire County Councils were cancelled in order to release poorly utilised vehicles, though such action soon drew angry responses from parents and meetings with the local MP.

The effects of the weather on ridership at Easter had always been a very unpredictable factor, and the Traffic Diary for 1962 records that Good Friday was poor weather, whilst Saturday was 'foul', but the weekend was saved by a good Sunday and Monday!

The South Midland touring coaches always received special attention, and here we see Car 859 (WRX 774) all polished ready for the new East Anglia tour, which included a visit to Royal Sandringham Estate.

For 1962 the *South Midland* extended tours had a couple of changes, with the Irish tours re-named as Ireland (Western & Northern Counties) and Donegal & Northern Ireland. The only new tour was one for 6 days based in East Anglia, though this did not attract many bookings and was dropped for 1963. The new coaches had been received into store a few months earlier, and these were prepared, along with others taken from hibernation, the new ones being licensed from 1st May. It is also interesting to note that an additional agent from 1962 in Maidenhead was the proprietors of *Alpha Coaches*, the Carter family also establishing a Travel Agency business.

Most of the new deliveries were Leyland-engined Bedford SB8 chassis with Duple 'Bella Vega' C37F bodies. One was to 7ft 6ins, Car 862 (516 ABL), replacing the sold Bristol LL6B on the Wye Valley tours. The others were Cars 863-5 (517-9 ABL), and these were 8-footers, all the Bedfords being ordered through Great Western Motors of Reading.

Martin Shaw took many excellent photos of South Midland at Oxford, but he also managed to catch this Duple-bodied Bedford SB6, Car 864 (518 ABL) in less familiar surroundings and covering the Wales tour based on Llandrindod Wells. Note the Tesco shop in the background before they spread like a rash.

31

During April further examples of the 1951 Bristol LWL6B saloons were disposed off, with Cars 577-80 and 583 (FMO 959-62/5) all departing, in favour of further rebuilt 1946 Bristol K-types.

However, yet another K-type found itself scheduled for an urgent rebuild when, on Wednesday 25th April, the low bridge at Wokingham claimed its second bus! 1948 Bristol K6B Car 471 (DMO 675) was actually on that driver's second trip of the day on Route 3, when he reverted to the old route, heading straight on the Finchampstead Road rather than turning left into Molly Millars Lane. Damage to the upper top deck was extensive, but fortunately there were no serious injuries, and indeed only one person required hospital treatment, as there were few passengers on the upper deck and the conductor had just gone back downstairs. As the bus was in otherwise sound order, it went to The Colonnade, where it was rebuilt and re-emerged in October to be re-allocated to Bracknell to cover a school special, of which we shall hear more of in due course.

This interior view, looking rearwards inside Car 866 shows the airy appearance given by the glazed roof panels. This style of body was already some way towards that developed for the new RE chassis, with the 3-window rear window arrangement, though still with opening side windows of the hopper variety. Car 866 always seemed well cared for by Reading garage.

Bristol MW6G coach 866 (520 ABL) was the only example with TV to bear the revised style of Eastern Coach Works body. In earlier years this was generally used on excursions and private hire work.

Two Bristol coaches had also been ordered for the 1962 season, though only one would be received that year. The original order called for a pair of MW6G's with ECW C39F bodies, but in the meantime one of these was altered to be of the new 36ft-long 'MWL', a description which duly changed as the engine was re-positioned under development to the rear of the chassis, the resultant vehicle becoming the high-floor version prototype of the RE-type. However, delivery of this was much delayed, so in the meantime the other from the order arrived as Car 866 (520 ABL), which was licensed from 1st May.

Outgoing vehicles in May were the first of the 1951 fully-fronted Bristol LWL6B coaches 612 (GBL 876), along with the first of the secondhand Bristol K-types acquired in 1969/60. The latter was Car 438 (HTT 980), a K5G from the *Bristol OC* fleet, though actually new to *Western National* in 1946.

Mention has already been made in earlier volumes of how the Thames valley was regarded as an area for days out and short breaks, and it is interesting to note that the *'Valley* continued the practice of issuing a guide book to possibilities for travelling by bus, as well as links to steamer cruises. This was regularly updated to take account of service changes, and was supported by extensive advertising, which meant it was free of charge. The front cover for 1962 featured a coloured sketch of a Bristol LS speeding along a riverside setting towards Oxford.

A little earlier the Company had cancelled a number of contracts to the Harwell AERE site, which evidently caused the management there to reconsider its options, as the nearby population was insufficient to draw a full workforce. As it was, *Thames Valley, Reliance Motor Services* and other local operators met regularly to discuss (i.e. fix) the rates for contracts to that destination. The AERE management then ended 3 contracts from Abingdon and Oxford which had been covered by *South Midland* with effect from 27th April, and after that built up its own fleet of buses instead.

Various changes took place during the Summer in order to make better use of the licensed fleet whilst, in view of the recent redundancies, it was also decided to close the Enquiry Office at Reading Stations Square on Sundays from 29th April. Bus running plates were introduced at Reading from 5th May, followed by High Wycombe on 9th June. However, the Inspectors soon found problems with these arrangements, having to intervene as the day progressed, so all spare plates were kept by the Inspectors to allocated to best effect.

The Royal Windsor Horse Show was a popular annual event held in the Great Park, so from 10th-12th May extra late journeys were provided on routes starting from that town. Up at Wycombe it transpired that some standing passengers had recently been carried on Route 35 (High Wycombe – Downley), contrary to a restriction that none should be taken when running up or down Plomer Hill, so all single-deck buses on the allocation there were given temporary notices from 26th May until permanent signs were prepared.

Over at Maidenhead there were once again staff shortages, so from 5th May some revisions were brought in on Routes 18a (Maidenhead – Pinkneys Green), 24 (M'head – Cookham Dean), 24a (M'head – Cookham Rise) and 60/60a (M'head – Slough via Main Road or Trading Estate), which allowed one double-decker to be saved. However, that was not enough, and by 2nd June, enforced reductions were losing 3,883 miles per week, amounting to 6.93% of the garage's workings, with 10 crew lines having to be omitted and 3 double-deckers delicensed.

David Howard, who was Traffic Assistant involved with the Maidenhead operations at that time, recalled the rather astute Union Shop Steward realised that more pressure could be put on Management by overtime bans, which at the same time did not affect the crews too badly. This was, unfortunately, a time when the traditional *Thames Valley* management was not used to having such regular labour disputes, whilst Unions were often uncompromising and automatically viewed the management as the enemy. This was a particularly difficult time for the Inspectors, a body of men who knew the job inside out, but due to promotion were now to be regarded as taking the Company side. Similarly, the Traffic Office staff was constantly having to prepare passenger notices for displaying in the buses or at the stops, all very time-consuming work. In hindsight, neither side emerges with much credit, as demands were invariably met in the end, but often for the wrong reasons.

To the west, many routes in the Newbury area were now losing money, so a number of changes were made from 16th June in order to reduce layover times and reduce the allocation. Routes 106 (Newbury – Lambourn), 109 (Newbury – Thatcham – Cold Ash), 111 (N'bury – Thatcham – Bucklebury) and 121 (Shaw – Newbury – Camp Close or Newtown or Penwood) were all converted to one-man-operation.

Increasingly the Newbury area routes had been made over to o-m-o in order to reduce costs, and Bristol LS6B Car 710 (HMO 856) is seen at The Wharf ready for the run to Hungerford on Route 116 via the A4.

As part of these changes Route 111 gained some Thursdays-only journeys onto Stanford Dingley, whilst Route 121 now had the southward journeys calling into The Wharf, and Route 127 (Shaw – Wash Common) was extended northwards to start from new housing on the Love Lane Estate. The Wednesdays-only Route 106a (Lambourn – Hungerford Newtown – Hungerford) had proved impractical, as it had been covered by one of the contract coaches now cancelled, so it was withdrawn in that form. In order to partially compensate local residents, and as a result of Parish Council correspondence, some Wednesdays-only journeys were operated by buses from Route 116 (Newbury – Hungerford via Bath Road) between Hungerford and Hungerford Newtown and known as the 116a.

At the same time Route 126 (Newbury – Greenham – Crookham Common), as seen here covered by LL6B one-manner Car 566 (FMO 948) ceased to operate. It was basically replaced by altering Route 103 (N'bury – Ecchinswell) via Boundary Road – York Road – Greenham Road - Pile Hill, then as before through Pinchington Lane and Bishops Green.

The Lambourn outstation had recently lost its contract coaches, but under the changes of June 1962, actually gained more service buses. Graham Low visited the site on a damp Sunday to record the scene above, with one of the lowbridge Guy 'Arab' MkIII 6LW Cars 170 or 171 (FMO 516/7) in the corner, then Bristol LL6B Car 564 (FMO 946) and Bristol LS5G Car 707 (HMO 853), both on Route 106, whilst Bristol KS6B Car 586 (FMO 968) is to the left with some roof damage.

Detailed changes to the timetables for Routes 106 (Newbury – Boxford – Lambourn) and 108 (Newbury – Wickham – Lambourn – Lambourn Woodlands or Hungerford Newtown) resulted in a double-decker being outstationed to cover the schooldays journey from Boxford to Newbury on the 106, plus the extra runs on Thursdays and Saturdays. The other double-decker covered the 108 journeys emanating from Lambourn Woodlands (Hare & Hounds), the positioning journeys of which were shown as 106, plus continuing the Thursdays and Saturdays link to Newbury from Hungerford Newtown. In all four buses were now allocated to Lambourn, usually the saloons being LL6B Cars 546/6 (FMO 946/8), whilst the double-deckers were one of the lowbridge Guys and usually a Bristol K6B, KS6B or another Guy.

The only service to totally disappear in the June changes was the Sundays-only Route 129 (Newbury – Hampstead Norris – Didcot), which had been put on to replace trains on that day. However, other factors would soon see this re-appear in modified form in order to provide some compensation following the end of passenger trains. At the same time all Newbury conductors were issued with individual ticket machines, thereby saving considerable time, and leaving only Reading garage to be fully equipped.

From 17th June changes were also made to the stands used by *Thames Valley* and *London Transport* buses at Mackenzie Street, to the front of Slough Station. This saw *TV* buses using Stand 8 for Routes 64 (to Salt Hill – Britwell) and 70 (to Salt Hill – Farnham Road – Burnham Village – Lent Rise – Taplow – Maidenhead), Stand 9 for Route 65 (to Salt Hill – Trading Estate (main and west gates) - Burnham Village – Lent Rise – Taplow – M'head), 66 (to Salt Hill – Trading Estate (main and west gates) Burnham (Hogfield Lane) – Lent Rise – Taplow – Maidenhead) and 67 (to Salt Hill – Trading Estate (main and west gates) – Priory Estate), whereas all Routes with 'a' journeys through the Trading Estate now used Stand 10. In order to achieve this, incoming buses now ran via The Crown – William Street – Station Approach.

Still going strong was K5G Car 475 (FLJ 978), seen swinging into the Weldale Road entrance of Reading garage after a relief working to Theale on Route 1.

34

On 24th June another visit by The Queen, this time to Wokingham, disrupted buses on Routes 3 (Reading – Wokingham – Crowthorne – Camberley), 3a (Reading – Wokingham – Barkham – Finchampstead) and 4a (Reading – Shinfield – Arborfield – Barkham – Wokingham) during the morning. On the following day she toured Bracknell, where delays were minimal, then in the afternoon progressed through Maidenhead, where buses were held in side roads for a time.

The new Bus Station at Basingstoke came into use on 28th June, and the terminus for Routes 6 (Reading – Spencers Wood – Riseley – Sherfield-on-Loddon - Basingstoke) and 122 (Newbury – Kingsclere – Basingstoke) was moved there from The Barge Inn. The new station was largely open air, with saw-tooth stands which buses reversed out of, and *Wilts & Dorset* had set a charge of 4d per departure on Route 6, though it waived charges on joint Route 122.

Coach-seated Bristol KSW6B Car 741 (JRX 816) leaves the new Bus Station at Basingstoke on Route 122 to Newbury via Knightsbridge and Headley.

At Bracknell Driver F.H. Deacon was made up to Inspector from 30th June, which was again in preparation for an impending retirement. From 2nd July the bus stands in Henley at the Market Place were slightly re-arranged, that month also seeing the busy Royal Regatta from 4th – 7th of the month, with extra buses laid on as usual for that annual event.

It was noted on 5th July that *Reading Corporation* had objected to changes on Route 1c in order to serve the estate around Silverdale Road. This boiled down to issues over protective fares for the Corporation buses, even though the area was <u>outside</u> the town boundary. As such, the Corporation argued that because *Thames Valley* issued Season Tickets (which it did not), it was abstracting passengers. When the matter went to the Traffic Commissioners on 13th July they saw through this argument. At the same hearing there was an application by the taxi-cum-coach operator *Cooper's Car Hire* of Bracknell, which *TV* objected to.

Another bus seen on a short-working of Route 1 was Bristol KSW6B Car 654 (HBL 56), leaving Reading's Queen Victoria Street for Hare Hatch on the A4 just east of Twyford and Ruscombe, where it turned back.

The latter item referred to a proposed express service between Easthampstead (South Hill Road) to Messrs. Aerosol's factory in Downmill Road on the Western Industrial Estate. That employer had many women working on a part-time basis, claiming that the current bus service did not suit their working hours, as many had to fit in with school hours. However, no one came from *Coopers* to support the application, so it was refused, the Commissioner adding that *Thames Valley* should consider meeting the need by amendments to its existing service.

Some of the 70-seater Bristol FLF's had started work on Route 28 (Reading – Wargrave - Henley – Marlow – High Wycombe), but the Union raised concerns over reversing them onto the stand at Quoiting Square, so after 15th July the buses ran straight along West Street instead.

The Royal Ascot Race Week in June 1962 was blessed with sunny weather, and Bristol KSW6B Car 702 (HMO 848) is seen on the stands at The Grange park. TV later received a complaint from the Course Authority that posts left behind damaged its mowers!

Another anecdotal item relating to Ascot concerns David Howard, from when he was Schedules Assistant at Bracknell garage. He recalls that he would often take the bus to Windsor when out for the evening, as it had good live music venues, a theatre and the cinema, and he noticed that many of the conductors (who had been transferred from the old Ascot garage) rather resented having to pass their homes and continue onto Bracknell. If the conductor wanted to drop off en route, David would take his ticket machine and sort out with him the next day – all highly unofficial, but much appreciated by some.

Despite the two earlier failed attempts to demolish the low railway bridge on the Finchampstead Road, a third Reading-based driver decided to try the rather more substantial Bristol LDL6G-type Car 779 (NBL 736)! It occurred on Saturday 11th August, and yet again this involved a driver who had already successfully followed the correct route on the outward route. This time three passengers needed to be taken to hospital, but thankfully only for cuts and bruises, but the roof was badly smashed to halfway back. It would be true to say that Car 779 earned something of a reputation as an unlucky vehicle, and indeed another low-bridge collision elsewhere would finally end its career in 1973. After the August crash it went into the body shops, returning to service on 1st December with re-allocation to Bracknell instead, where the extra 2ft 6ins in length often led to drivers clipping parked cars on housing estate roads!

'Big Bertha' Car 779 (NBL 736) working on Route 2 (Reading – Ascot – Windsor) prior to its altercation at Wokingham. Note the offside emergency door that was required due to its 30ft length. This body can also be compared with the standard 'Lodekka' on the right.

Further urgent Staff Notices were issued regarding the bridge hazard, and as a further precaution, the stop opposite to Two Poplars pub was moved to the kerb edge and fitted with an additional warning sign reminding all *Thames Valley* drivers to turn left.

A new timetable book was issued on 4th August in order to take into account the various recent changes, but it no longer had a rail section, featured since 1931.

On the excursions front, a very similar programme to the previous season was repeated, with the Heathrow guided tour still proving very popular.

In respect of plans for a new Bus Station as part of the redevelopment on the south side of Reading's Station Hill on railway-owned land, *TV* officials attended a meeting towards the end of August.

From 27th August a one-way flow of traffic through the village of East Ilsley, at that time still situated on the busy A34, meant that the buses on Routes 101 (Newbury – East Ilsley – Harwell), 102 (Reading – East Ilsley – West Ilsley) and 112 (Newbury – East Ilsley – Rowstock Corner – Oxford) were re-routed accordingly.

1957 Bristol LD6G Car 786 (NBL 743) was one of the 60-seaters to be found on Route 25 from September, seen here at Frogmoor Bus Station.

Over to the north-east, enough buses were now free to allow the double-decking of Route 25 (High Wycombe – Loudwater – Flackwell Heath) with effect from 1st September, which saved some 3000 miles per week of single-deck relief journeys. Across Treadaway Hill on the descent from Flackwell Heath was a railway level crossing, which gave passengers and crews an unpleasant bump, whilst any driver who got caught by the crossing gates on the ascent had a difficult task starting off again with a full load. Indeed that crossing was attributed by Fred Sugg, the owner of the *Penn Bus Company*, with cracking the chassis of his 1928 Leyland 'Lion' PLSC1 bus No.16 (PP 9657), which had been assigned to that service!

The Service Vehicle fleet saw a number of changes during the Summer, with the GM's Wolseley 6/90 car (MMO 731) of 1956 replaced by a Wolseley 6/110 (457 BMO) in July, when the Newbury Inspector's Ford 'Popular' (JRD 479) and similar 1954 car (JRD 982) used by the Assistant Traffic Manager were sold. The recently damaged Traffic Manager's Vauxhall 'Velox' (LBL 331) also departed in July, along with

Morris 'Oxford' MkII car (XFC 888) of 1955 as used by the Traffic Superintendent at Oxford, along with 1956 Ford 'Popular' staff car (MRX 116). The incoming replacements were a Ford 'Anglia' car (764 BJB), Vauxhall 'Velox' car (460 BMO), and No.49, a Ford Thames 307E van (165 BJB), all received during July. These were followed by an Austin A40 car (592 BMO), for the TS at Reading, his old Morris 'Oxford' car (WMO 279) being cascaded for pool use.

Bristol FLF6B Car 868 (536 BBL) is seen above shortly after delivery in Lower Thorn Street yard at Reading. Cars 868-72 also had offside illuminated advert panels, and Car 872 (540 BBL) is seen below at St. Mary's Butts in Reading on the long Route 1 (Maidenhead – Reading – Newbury). Note the revised radiator grille fitted to deliveries from 1962.

September saw the arrival of 6 further Bristol FLF's, though this time fitted with the Bristol 6-cylinder BVW engines, and with ECW H38/32F bodies. These were Cars 868-74 (536-42 BBL), and 868/9 went to Reading and were licensed from 1st September, which allowed Woodley Local Service 1a to go over to 70-seater working. Cars 870-4 were licensed later that month, with 870/3/4 going to Wycombe Marsh, 871 to Maidenhead and 872 to Newbury.

K5G Car 465 (FPU 513) had just arrived back on Station Hill from a relief working on Route 5 as far as Pangbourne.

The only outgoing vehicle in September was another 1951 Bristol LWL6B saloon, Car 584 (FMO 966), but that was followed in October by a number of Bristol K-types cascaded out of service. From the ranks of native buses were 1946 K6A-type Cars 442 (CRX 551), 444/9/51 (DBL 152/7/9) and the 1947 examples 466/7 (DMO 670/1). Also ousted were the first of the former *United Counties* K5G's to depart, Cars 465 (FPU 513) and 477 (GNO 698), both of which carried 7ft 6ins wide bodies. Of interest is the fact that these, along with similar bus 476 (GNO 688) had actually received 8ft wide bodies in 1952, but those had been switched with 1947/8 bodies of the narrower width just before delivery to *Thames Valley*, something that had annoyed Chief Engineer Ian Campbell so much that he took Graham Low down the pit to show him the evidence their underhand body-swapping!

Cars 466/7 (DMO 670/1) were both converted for grit-spreading by Berkshire CC, with 466 being based at Wokingham and 467 at Reading. These looked like a ghostly L-type viewed on a snow-bound road at night, both being finally scrapped in March 1969.

37

Re-bodied Bristol LL5G Car 820 (FMO 24) crosses from West Street into St. Mary's Butts on Route 6b for Bramley via Beech Hill and Stratfieldsaye, a nice rural run for the driver but some tight corners too!

Throughout the Summer and into early 1963, the front destination boxes on the re-bodied LL-types were first reduced by paint to show a single line display, then re-panelled to the same effect. These were Cars 794-9 (DMO 664-9) and 817-20 (FMO 21-4), and the same treatment was also given to the Bristol SC Cars 774-8 (NBL 731-5). Curiously, afterwards some double-line displays were fitted into the reduced space, examples being Route 9a to Aldermaston (Soke Corner), 24a to Cookham Dean (Quarry Wood Road) and, in due course, new Route 19 to Long Lane (via Overdown Road), which poses the question why change them?

From 2nd September the late-night short-working on Route 28 from High Wycombe to Danesfield RAF Camp finally ceased, having its origins in the wartime era. On 8th of that month the passenger service on the Didcot-Newbury railway line ceased, and it had been agreed that *Thames Valley* would provide a weekdays service. This re-used the route number 129, as previously taken by the Sundays-only facility between Newbury and Didcot withdrawn in June. The bus followed the same route, but deviated via Hampstead Norris and went only as far northwards as Compton, taking in some journeys previously on the Route 5b timetable. This was another o-m-o working and began on Monday 10th September.

A new school contract started on 11th September, when Berkshire CC paid the Company £5 2shillings per day to provide a double-decker taking children from Earley, Woodley and Sonning to Maidenhead Grammar School. This was a time of a general shortage of secondary school places for the many baby-boomers passing their 11-plus exam and being allocated to Grammar Schools. It was through this process that the author, who then lived at Priestwood in Bracknell found himself rather surprisingly allotted a place at Windsor County Grammar School for Boys, an 8-mile journey from his home!

There was already an established morning 'special', which started from Jocks Lane on the Binfield Road at 7.50am, quite a shock to the system after having lived only 5 minutes walk from Sandy Lane Junior School. The bus basically followed Route 2 to Windsor, but it omitted the loop down to Ascot High Street, instead turning into Fernbank Road, North Ascot. Boys could join at any public bus stop and most stops were used right through to The Squirrel at Winkfield, so the journey took almost as long as the service bus, but the vehicle did at least deliver us to the side entrance of the school in Vansittart Road.

Bristol K6B Car 471 (DMO 675) is seen in Bracknell garage yard recovering from a school journey on the Windsor Boy's special, a regular duty when returning to service in October 1962 after its bridge collision.

Another daily sight at Windsor was Bracknell Cars 766/7 (MBL 847/8) on the circular Local Services 51a and 51b, and Car 766 is shown in the Central Station on that duty. Always a difficult place to photograph buses due to the light, it was here that the author started his Thames Valley apprenticeship, sitting on one of the window ledges seen on the right.

When I started at Windsor a 55-seater would suffice for the special from Bracknell, with a similar size bus also starting out from South Ascot, which was more traditional catchment for the school. These tended to be the older buses, so apart from K6B Car 471 there were also ex-*Hants & Dorset* K5G Car 475 (FLJ 978) when it was a Bracknell, or more likely ex-*United Counties* K5G Cars 462-4 (FPU 515, 517 and 511), although the latter had 8ft-wide 1952 bodies on their 1937 chassis. However, Car 475 still had its 6-bay Brush body, heavily rebuilt with rubber-moulded windows by its former owners. As the strangest bus in the fleet, we soon dubbed it the 'Stone Age Flyer'!

In due course the special was increased to 60-seaters, after which the pair of Bracknell-based LD5G Cars 766/7 (MBL 847/8) were taken off the Windsor Local Services for that duty, or sometimes we would get Car 779 (NBL 736) the 70-seater Bristol LDL6G, which was noticeably faster than the Gardner 5-cylinder examples. Kneeling on the front rearward-facing seats we would watch the speedometer as the bus raced down Highstanding Hill from Winkfield to Windsor, though some of the old K-types would struggle with the upward journey on that hill.

Bracknell had two Bristol LWL6B's at the time, Cars 624/31 (GJB 262/9), of which the latter is seen in Reading garage. These often appeared on Route 53/53a relief workings, passing both the mysteriously named Mushroom Castle (a nursery) and Carnation Factory (another nursery specialising in flowers for button-holes). A ride in the front seat on a wet day was an atmospheric experience, with the engine sounds and water splashing up the mudguards.

In the afternoons the boys had to return by service bus, which was partly designed to take account of after school sports etc., so those of us from Bracknell could choose between Route 2 (Windsor – Winkfield – Ascot – Bracknell – Reading) or the single-decked Route 53/53a (Windsor – Winkfield – Chavey Down – Bracknell – Crowthorne – Camberley), the latter making a nice rural alternative to the main line route. From the school we walked up Maidenhead Road and the cobbled Goswell Hill, past old railway arches up to the bus stands at the Central Station. Segregation prevailed then as well, as originally the Girl's School used the bus stop outside the King George V Hospital, so the only way to meet them was to run along to the Prince Albert stop further up St. Leonards Road. I once did that, only to find that the noise of 50 girls easily overshadowed any social possibilities!

And then there was the Grand Tour, the day I set off to see the other *Thames Valley* garages. Bracknell I saw on a daily basis, whilst Reading I went to about every fortnight, so I set off one Saturday morning with my Day Ticket on Route 2 into Reading, then onto Newbury on Route 1, visiting Mill Lane garage. From there I took the 112 up to Oxford, had a look at Botley Road garage and then found a friendly *South Midland* driver, who took me onto Wycombe (ticket not valid on the coach), even dropping me outside Desborough Road garage. Then onto Frogmoor, followed by a 26a to Wycombe Marsh for a good look around, before a 20 down to Maidenhead and along to the garage there. On another 20 I reached Windsor, then Route 2 again back to Bracknell, a total of some 118 miles!

Above is LD5G Car 783 (NBL 740) in Bridge Avenue on Route 18a, and below LL5G Car 818 (FMO 22) at High Wycombe Station on Route 32 to Bledlow Ridge.

39

Far to the western reaches, the terminus of Route 106 (Newbury – Lambourn – Swindon) was altered from Clarence Street to Regent Circus from 16th September, so arrangements were made for buses to proceed to the *Bristol OC* garage in Eastcott Hill for layovers.

At Oxford Inspector Morgan retired at the close of the month, so Driver N.H.R. Deacon was made up from 21st December. Another notable retirement occurred on 31st October, when Frank Williams left the post of Depot Inspector at Bracknell after 40 years service. He had joined as a conductor at the Ascot Dormy Shed in Blythewood Lane in July 1922, and his place was taken by the transfer of Inspector E.J. Terry from Reading. The latter was replaced there by Inspector Peedell, one time driver at Stoke Row Dormy Shed, whilst at Maidenhead Driver S.H. Spicer was also made up to Inspector in October.

The driver situation at Maidenhead had improved to the point that services were back to normal from 22nd September, but some routes were revised to make better use of duties. Route 21 (M'head – Woodlands Park – White Waltham – Waltham St. Lawrence – Shurlock Row – Binfield – Wokingham) was joined end-on with buses working through on Routes 65/65a and 66/66a from Slough. Double-deckers were now used throughout from 10th November, the 60-group service numbers replacing the 21. At the same time some journeys on Route 63 (M'head – Cliveden – Dropmore – Burnham – Slough) were routed via Taplow Common and known as Route 68. Route 70 (Maidenhead – Burnham – Britwell – Slough) now had peak time journeys via the Trading Estate at Slough, shown as 70a, these changes saving one single-decker, 1,324 miles per week and £9,607 annually in wages.

An increase in pupils attending Windsor County Grammar School for Girls, meant a special was laid on starting from The Regal Cinema at Bracknell and taking the same route as the boy's bus but to Osborne Road for the school. This started from 11th October, and the girls caught service journeys home. Also due to the shortage of places at Bracknell secondary schools at that time, pupils from the Long Hill Road and Bullbrook areas were allocated Borough Green Secondary Modern School in Rectory Lane. Although not far in distance, the walk was acknowledged as hazardous, so after a campaign by parents special short-workings were laid on as Route 53 between those points from 12th November. In the Wokingham area, adjustments were also made from 24th November to Route 4a (Reading – Arborfield – Barkham – Wokingham) to run onto Norreys Avenue, for the benefit of primary children attending the school, along with secondary pupils at nearby St. Crispins School.

In the meantime talks had taken place with *London Transport* regarding the use of the Frogmoor Bus Station by its services, which used slightly different points to *TV*. Over at Newbury, co-operation also saw certain journeys on Route 106 from the Lambourn direction terminating at Newbury Station in order to afford better train connections from 1st December.

The valley of the River Thames was covered by a thick blanket of fog, which persisted from 3rd-7th December, badly affecting services and seeing both London routes from Reading abandoned. The bus on which the Traffic Superintendent for High Wycombe was travelling overturned at Hare Hatch on the first day, whilst 13,500 route miles were lost in total. On the Oxford route *City of Oxford* started using a 36ft AEC 'Reliance' from 5th December, though *TV* was still using Bristol LS-types, there having been no single-deckers delivered since the MW6G's in 1960.

The only other rebuild for the year was 1948 Bristol K6B Car 469 (DMO 673), which out-shopped from The Colonnade in December, minus the upper-deck beading and with the front destinations rebuilt to a T. The only vehicle departing in December was ex-*United Counties* Bristol LL6B coach 75 (FRP 832).

K6B Car 469 (DMO 673) is seen on Route 110 (Newbury – Thatcham – Tadley) after being rebuilt.

From 19th December the rest of the Reading conductors were equipped with individual ticket machines, completing the process Company-wide, whilst Assistant Engineer Brian Hancock resigned to become the Engineer at the Isle-of Wight-based *Southern Vectis* from 31st of that month.

Many will recall the exceptional 'Big Freeze' of 1962/3, which began with snow on 27th December, badly affecting services, with 30 burst radiators. Half of those were at Newbury, so the town routes were taken off to cover other services. In 3 days 1,894 miles were lost, then the whole South was blanketed in snow, causing 32,320 miles to be lost between 30th December and 5th January, and more was yet to come!

1963

The Transport Act 1962 came into effect from the 1st January 1963, setting up the public authorities of the British Railways Board, the London Transport Board, the British Transport Docks Board, the British Waterways Board, and in respect of State-owned passenger road transport interests, the Transport Holding Company, though no immediate changes affected the daily operations of *Thames Valley*. However, on that same day the Traffic Manager's Vauxhall 'Velox' car (460 BMO) went missing from Vincent's Garage, and was found 3 days later by the Police and returned.

A further pair of Bristol FLF6G's with ECW H38/32F bodies were licensed from 1st January, as Cars 875/6 (543/4 BBL), allocated to Maidenhead just as that town was put on a flood alert due to a thaw.

Graham Low was in Wellington Road, Wokingham when Bristol KSW6B Car 654 (HBL 56) passed by in blizzard conditions on Route 3 to Camberley.

After a journey lasting twice as long as normal the Windsor Boy's special finally arrived at the school to find it closed due to the heating having no water after many pipes in the town froze. The following day our special, which was one of the FPU-registered K5G's, came across the Route 2 service bus at The Splash (so called because of its tendency to flood), where the Winkfield and North Ascot roads parted. As the buses approached, each rose up on the nearside due to packed snow and the roofs came into contact. So we were all turfed off whilst the drivers struggled back and forth, adding flakes of red paint to the snow, until at last they were parted. By then, totally frozen, the author jumped the service bus and went back home!

In the meantime passenger service on the rail line from Princes Risborough ceased, so from 7th January travellers would need to catch Route 20/20a buses to High Wycombe, then a *South Midland* coach to reach Oxford, in place of the more direct rail link.

Another dedicated enthusiast recoding the scene in the Winter of 1962/3 was Philip Wallis, who caught Bristol LL5G Car 818 (FMO 22) and former Hants & Dorset Bristol K5G Car 474 (JT 9360) in the yard at Reading Stations between duties.

The sight that greeted Peter Wilks in the Lower Thorn Street yard when he turned up for work one morning, with Bristol K5G Car 474 (JT 9360) and K6A Car 450 (DBL 158) amongst the frozen ranks outside at night.

Indeed, it was the continuing freezing weather that dominated everyday life throughout the whole of the first month, and by 6th January a number of services had to be suspended due to icy roads. 4694 service miles were lost that first week, and a further 5270 in the following one. Of particular significance was that fresh snow repeatedly fell over packed snow and ice, causing badly rutted roads which contorted suspension and caused many broken spring leaves, and these took quite a bit of time to rectify.

Over at Maidenhead, the rather exposed Coach Station site soon became like an ice rink and too large to clear, so all services using it stopped in the adjacent York Road between 10th January and 5th February. On 8th January even the River Thames froze at Windsor, just as the author returned to school after Christmas.

During January Driver A.V. Hawes and Conductor G.E. Wyatt were made up to Inspector at Reading, whilst from 10th of that month the Parcel's Office of *Reading Corporation* was transferred to 15 London Street, although the cycle link was still maintained with the *TV* buses at Stations Square.

However, a rather more serious alteration was the closure of the historic suspension bridge carrying the road over the Thames at Marlow to all vehicular use from 10th January, anticipated to be for 4 months. After then Route 18 (Maidenhead – Marlow) deposited its passengers on the Bisham (Berkshire) side at Quarry Wood Road, before they walked over the bridge into Buckinghamshire to board a shuttle bus along the High Street to the Quoiting Square terminus, that bus being driven each day via Bourne End and also seeing use on the short-workings to Marlow Bottom or Chisbridge Cross as Route 18b.

Issues with school places led to children from the east of Sandhurst having to attend St. Michael's School in Little Sandhurst, so a short-working on Route 53 from the Wellington Arms in Sandhurst was put on from 14th January, and duly extended to start from the Jolly Farmer at College Town from 23rd September.

C403 (833 CRX) was one of the new touring coaches, and is seen at Victoria Coach Station for the extended tour to Scotland in original livery of all lower panels in maroon, though this was changed to cream with the mid-ships area in maroon from the following season.

The season's new coaches were received as Cars C401-3 (831-3 CRX), these being Bedford SB8-types with a revised style of Duple 'Bella Vega' C37F body, and all in *South Midland* livery. They had Leyland 0350 engines and the bodywork was 8ft 2.5ins wide and 30ft 4ins in length, also featuring 45-gallon fuel tanks rather than the 26-gallon tanks of previous examples. C401 was licensed in advance of the season at put on display at Burnham from 5th February, moving to Maidenhead on the 15th, then to Frogmoor Bus Station on 28th. About this time Bristol MW6G coach 800 (ORX 631) was re-seated from 34 to 38.

These were the first vehicles in a new numbering scheme, which segregated vehicles as D1-300 for double-deckers, S301-400 for single-deckers and C401-500 for the coach fleet.

Bristol FLF6G Car 878 (546 BBL) is seen on Station Hill soon after delivery on the busy Route 4 through Shinfield, Arborfield, Eversley, Yateley to Camberley.

The latter part of January remained bitterly cold, and during the last week over 7000 route miles were lost, though the first week of February saw that reduced to only some 2000. Maintenance inevitably suffered due to the weather conditions, leading to the first ever recorded instance of a complaint from the Union over vehicle condition in respect of Maidenhead garage.

Another pair of Bristol FLF6G's with ECW H38/32F bodies were licensed from mid-February, with Car 877 (545 BBL) going to Maidenhead and Reading receiving Car 878 (546 BBL). As these buses were part of an outstanding order they retained their earlier allocated fleet numbers, as did similar Cars 879/80 (547/8 BBL) which arrived in March and were sent to Maidenhead and High Wycombe. The final bus of that order and the old numbering scheme was Car 881 (549 BBL), which arrived in April for Reading's use.

Car 881 (549 BBL) awaits service on Route 1a out to the growing housing estates of the Woodley area.

Car 443 (DBL 151) at Newbury Wharf was one of those not to be selected for a body rebuild.

The only vehicle to depart during February was 1947 Bristol K6B Car 453 (DBL 161), as a number of older double-deckers received a temporary reprieve to cover buses damaged on the icy roads. During March former *United Counties* 1951 Bristol LL6B coach 78 (FRP 836) was sold, along with 1947 ex-*Bristol OC* K6A-type Car 456 (KHW 633). These were followed in April by 1946 Bristol K6A Cars 443/5 (DBL 151/3) and K6B Car 470 (DMO 674) of 1948, as well as ex-*Bristol OC* 1947 K6A Car 458 (KHU 606) and former *United Counties* K5G Car 476 (GNO 688) new in 1938 but bearing a 1948 ECW body.

Entering Maidenhead Bus Station is Car 879 (547 BBL), returning from Langley on Route 60. Note how many conductors set the blinds slightly high due to the angle they viewed them from the step, though older hands knew to compensate for that.

In order to keep up vehicle numbers during February two *South Midland* Bristol LS6G coaches were taken out of store and sent to Reading, these being Cars 672/5 (HBL 74/7) and used on relief workings.

A number of other *South Midland* coaches were re-licensed earlier than planned to cover shortages at Oxford, whilst *City of Oxford* was forced to hire from that fleet in order to maintain services. Between 1 and 4 coaches were used as required from 22nd January to 8th March, being taken to Gloucester Green each day. Those involved were AEC 'Regal' MkIV Car 85 (SFC 571), Bristol LL6B Car 76 (FRP 833), Bristol LWL6B Cars 608/10 (GBL 872/4), Bristol LS6B Cars 93 (TWL 58) and 688 (HMO 834) and Bristol LS6G's 79-83 (SFC 565-9) and 671/3 (HBL 73/5). The latter pair was put onto the joint Oxford-Reading service, *City of Oxford* Route 34, covering that duty for over a month and regularly seen on Station Hill in Reading.

South Midland Bristol LWL6B coach 610 (GBL 874) is seen at Gloucester Green Bus Station in Oxford whilst on hire to City of Oxford. Note the paper sticker and the chalk board destination, along with the icy conditions prevalent at that time.

An interesting request was received from the Rank Organisation, proprietors of the Majestic Ballroom in Reading, for a special late bus from the town to Bracknell to leave at 11.35pm after the cessation of 'bingo' sessions. This was arranged experimentally for one month, with Rank repaying any shortfall in fares receipts, but in the first week no one used it, then only 2 passengers travelled as far as Winnersh in the second and third week, followed by none in the fourth, so the journey was dropped. However, despite this experience the 'bingo craze' would develop, and we shall hear more of it soon. The author recalls one female colleague who went along regularly taking her unopened weekly wage packet as a place stake!

From 13th February changes at Windsor saw Peascod Street closed to traffic between Victoria Street and Oxford Road, so buses on Local Services 51/51a/51b were diverted via William Street. From 1st March a one-way system meant that Peascod Street could only be used for outward journeys, so buses coming into the town centre from St. Leonards Road did so by way of Victoria Street – Sheet Street – High Street, which added a further 400 miles per week, whilst the weather lost some 900 miles each week in February.

South Midland Bristol LS6G coach 671 (HBL 73) at Gloucester Green on hire to City of Oxford in March.

Following on from the severe weather a number of urgent road repairs were soon found to be necessary, and from 7th March the usual road used by Route 32 (High Wycombe – Chinnor) was closed, so it ran on from Bledlow Ridge only to Chinnor Hill (Woodlands Farm) until service could be resumed on 22nd March. From 18th March the narrow stone arched bridge on the Wargrave to Henley road, known as Conway's Bridge, was completely closed due to frost damage. An inspection had revealed that it actually lacked any proper foundations, having been constructed as a folly for viewing from the riverside lawn below. Of course, it had been taking quite a pounding recently, with the closure of Marlow bridge and the weight restriction imposed on Sonning bridge in the other direction. Due to this Route 28 (High Wycombe – Marlow – Henley – Reading) was diverted to run via the Shiplake and Binfield Heath road until 31st March, whilst a shuttle bus ran between Reading and Wargrave, leaving the sparsely populated section between Wargrave and Henley left un-served for that period.

Bristol LWL6B Car 629 (GJB 267) was caught by Philip Wallis amongst the melting ice in February on Route 5a to Streatley, Chilton and Wantage. Due to the high number of deliveries during 1950-2, many of those buses could still be found on all-day turns.

Over in the Newbury area a weight restriction was also placed on the Iron Bridge, so Route 121 (Shaw – Newbury – Newtown Common – Penwood) deviated at Newtown Common via Oxdrove and the Carpenters Arms in both directions from 2nd April. Also in that area, an earlier short-working on Route 1 at 5.30am was put on to Colthrop Board Mills from March, the bus turning on the forecourt of the North Board Mill.

A notable trio of retirements took place on 31st March, when Elmet Abberfield, John Giles and Alexander Pack left after a total of 111 years of service. 'Abber' had been born on the last day of 1894 at Chelmsford in Essex, training as an engineer fitter before war service with the Royal Engineers in France from 1914 to 1919. His older brother Tomo was apprenticed at the Crompton Electrical Works, where he worked with Theodore Graham Homer, the future General Manager of *Thames Valley*. Through this connection came the marriage of the latter to Elmet's sister Lily, which no doubt had something to do with him joining the Company later on 25th February 1924, and also explains the relative freedom under which he is recalled as operating. His tasks as Clerk of Works included the erection of dormy sheds, garage maintenance, bus stops and shelter sites, along with tree-lopping, and various jobs at the GM's home!

Elmet Abberfield is shown in the centre, fronted by Jimmy Lewington, with High Wycombe area Traffic Superintendent Ernest Jeffries at the rear on the test-run of the open-top riverside service in 1957.

John ('Jack') Giles had joined the Maidenhead garage as Chargehand on 23rd June 1926, also having served in the Royal Engineers from 1909 and on through the Great War, rising to Company Sargeant Major. He was amongst the first in the town to volunteer for ARP training in 1938, thereafter serving in the Local Defence Volunteers (Home Guard) during World War 2, and succeeded Mr. Stephens as Garage Foreman. His successor from 1st April was W.E. Lee, who joined the '*Valley*' in 1927 as Tilling B9A's arrived.

The third of the retirees worked on the office side at Reading, and he was 'Alec' Pack. Born in 1897 in Paddington he had joined the Company shortly before the first Leyland 'Titans' arrived on 7th February 1928. By the early 1960's he was a most welcomed sight each week, as it was his job to hand out the wage packets! All three were joined by their colleagues, some from the past, for a celebratory dinner at the Caversham Bridge Hotel on Thursday 28th March, where each was presented with a gold watch by the General Manager Tom Pruett.

There were of course still many long-serving employees in evidence in 1963, another Maidenhead example being Inspector John Harris, whose father had sold his *Pixey Bus Service* to *Thames Valley* in April 1933 on condition that young Harris was employed. One other unplanned personnel change on 4th April was caused by the untimely death of Inspector Charlie Seagrave at the age of 55.

The Bristol REX6G coach 867 (521 ABL) was caught on camera leaving The Colonnade by Graham Low. The slightly old-fashioned stepped waistrail was not continued on the production models, which also had less but longer side windows. The Lodekka-style grille suited the twin headlamp layout.

However, the real star delivery on 25th April was the long-awaited prototype high-floor Bristol REX, which retained its reserved fleet and registration numbers despite being delayed by a year. In fact it had already been at the Bristol Commercial Vehicle works for a month before being received for evaluation on express workings by *South Midland*. This carried an Eastern Coach Works C47F body, which apart from being the first received to the full permitted dimensions of 36ft x 8ft 2.5ins, also introduced a new system of forced-air ventilation, with air intakes under the front dome, from which air was channelled to individual nozzles over each seat. In its earliest form this system was often found to be insufficient in very hot weather, so the three lifting roof vents were then required, there being no opening side windows. With its Gardner 6HLX engine of 10.45 litres this coach proved popular with drivers, though as with all prototypes it was absent at times for modifications and testing.

This rear end shot of Car 867 (521 ABL) as it turns into London Road from The Colonnade shows the neat window arrangement. There was even a boot area as the engine was set some 3ft forward of the rear.

Also concerning *South Midland* vehicles, the Head Postmaster at Oxford met with the Assistant Traffic Manager in April concerning the hiring of some coaches to carry the Christmas mail, something which continued for a number of years, and the coaches chosen were usually due for re-seating or repaints.

Car 867 (521 ABL) is seen later at Victoria Coach Station on the service to Oxford via Maidenhead and after the rather vulnerable fog lamps had been taken off, these being damaged by kerbs or flying gravel. It had a long life of service, so it is regrettable that 867 did not survive into preservation as the first of many.

In the meantime the 9th April saw the opening of the Slough By-pass, part of the M4 motorway, by the Minister of Transport, though there were no immediate effects on *Thames Valley* operations. Good Friday on 12th April was the start of another Ban the Bomb March from Aldermaston, so Route 9 carried some 800 extra passengers from Reading Stations, but otherwise that weekend suffered from poor weather which affected takings in general.

Some Thames Valley High Wycombe Area Personalities of the 1960's

Ann Vockings and Reg Cubbage.

*Above: Charlie Maun.
Below: Harry Kercher.*

Top: Les Dearlove. Above: Michael Dearlove and Harry Hooper. Below: Ann Vockings and Tom Gomme.

Eddie Edwards (on the right).

*Above: Bob Ditch.
Below: Ted Tapper.*

Above: Arnold Jones and Jock Pusey. Below: Driver Rose.

46

Some further changes took place on services in the High Wycombe area, with Routes 25 (High Wycombe – Wycombe Marsh – Loudwater – Flackwell Heath) and 28 ('Wycombe – Marlow – Henley – Reading) now terminating at Frogmoor Bus Station from 22nd April. From that same date Route 81 (High Wycombe – Desborough Avenue – Booker) also had its terminus changed to the Bus Station, though it still departed from the street stand in Frogmoor. Also affected at that time was Route 20/20a (Aylesbury – 'Wycombe – Maidenhead – Windsor), which now ran through the Bus Station at Frogmoor, also calling at the Rex Cinema in Oxford Street in both directions. From then all journeys on Route 38 (High Wycombe – Sands – Booker) which had previously started from the Guildhall were now transferred to the Bus Station.

Desborough Road-based Bristol K6B Car 506 (EJB 228) is seen at the Turnpike Corner terminus of Route 81 at Booker. Close examination of this photo shows the bus to be in fine order for its 1949 vintage.

There were many old-stagers at High Wycombe, with a number of instances of generations following on, the Dearlove family being an example. Les Dearlove had started as age 17 as a conductor with *House Bros.* of Watlington on the service to High Wycombe, duly becoming a driver. Later he went to drive for Booker-based *Fred Crook*, who in turn sold his bus services to *Thames Valley* in June 1937, after which Les worked from Wycombe Marsh until his retirement in 1976. In the meantime his son Michael joined as a conductor on the *'Valley* in 1963 with driver John Ashby or at times with his father. He passed as a driver in 1968 and his first service run was with Bristol KSW6B Car 695 (HMO 841) on Route 42 (Loudwater – High Wycombe – West Wycombe – Booker Hill Estate) in company with regular conductor Harry Hooper. In 1971 he went over to one-manners, though he reckons the years 'on the back' were the best, and continued until retiring in 2008. His cousin Trevor was also on *TV* from the Marsh during the late 1950's, usually paired with conductor Jim Tanner.

There were several long-service men at the Dormy Sheds in the Wycombe area, one of whom was Bryn Essias, who had a wooden leg after war service and drove out of the 'Risborough shed. The other was Charlie Maun at Stokenchurch shed, who had been born in 1909 and saw service in the RAF and as a chauffeur prior to joining *City of Oxford* in June 1934, when he was living at Chinnor. The family moved to Ipswich later that year, so he drove for *Eastern Counties* out of Saxmundham before returning to his old haunts to marry the following year. He re-joined *COMS* at Stokenchurch, passing with the services transferred to *Thames Valley* in July 1937, thereafter settling down to the 6-day shed workings on Routes 39/40/41. When one-manners were introduced there in September 1971 he instead transferred to Wycombe Marsh as a driver until retiring in March 1975.

In the Wokingham area further housing developments in Emmbrook saw the need for children to travel across to the eastern side of the town to attend the Keep Hatch Primary School. This commenced from 23rd April 1963, but as this duly required a double-decker from the start of the Autumn term arrangements were made to lop the trees along Commons Road – Matthewsgreen Road – Milton Road – Broad Street – London Road – Norreys Avenue during July, with Wokingham BC footing half the cost. At the same time for the Autumn term the existing short-working between Emmbrook and Wokingham (Broad Street) on Route 3a (Reading – Wokingham – Barkham – Finchampstead) was run onto Seaford Road for the benefit of Secondary pupils at St Crispins School on the London Road.

Over at Maidenhead a new school was opened at Furze Platt to replace the Cookham Secondary School, and from 23rd April a link between Cookham Rise (Westwood Green) and the new site was added to Route 24a.

Buses on school workings often went unrecorded, but ex-Hants & Dorset Bristol K5G Car 475 (FLJ 978) was caught by Graham Low in Milton Road on its way to the junction of Lowther Road and Forest Road.

To the east of Maidenhead more housing had been built, so Route 15 was extended from 16th April on from the Curls Lane Estate to Norden Road – Altwood Road – the junction of Highfield Road and Cannon Lane, with some journeys running slightly further to the Black & Decker factory on the White Waltham airfield at peak times on Mondays to Fridays. Such was the demand for this service that further journeys were added from 17th June.

As the Easthampstead estate in Bracknell developed it was possible to eliminate the need to reverse at South Hill Road, as the buses on Route 52 ran by way of Manston Drive – Longwater Road – Heathmoors from 29th April, though no stops were included en route.

The route from Maidenhead through Binfield and to Wokingham had a complicated history, but after linking with the Slough services it warranted 70-seat double-deckers at times. Bristol FLF6B Car 871 (539 BBL) is seen at Wokingham Station on Route 66.

May 1963 saw the strangest acquisition of vehicles by *Thames Valley*, when it decided to purchase 5 1948 Bristol L6A's from *Crosville Motor Services*, a type it had eliminated previously back in 1959! However, as *Thames Valley* had been busily selling their rear-entrance examples, so *Crosville* had been converting them to front entrance for one-man-operation on rural services in North Wales. This feature, along with their 7ft 6ins wide ECW B35F bodies, made them useful on certain services.

Car S303 (GFM 884) at Bracknell in July 1964.

A close up of the front end of Car S302 (GFM 882) showing the angled window, swivelling seat for the driver and ticket machine to make these one-manners.

These buses became Cars S301-5 (GFM 881/2/4/7/8), having been *Crosville* SLA 72/3/5/7/8, and the author recalls their comfortable green moquette seating and the lively performance of the AEC 7.7 litre engines. All had been repainted into red and cream at Chester Works before coming south, and during that time they had flashers added of the 'orange segment' type then appearing throughout the fleet. Car S302 (GFM 882) was the first to be licensed from 2nd May, but S304 (GFM 887) languished at The Colonnade and was not licensed until March 1964, after which it was mainly to be seen on driver-training duties. Surprisingly there were also some instances when they appeared on the 28.5-mile Route 75 (Reading – Bracknell – Bagshot – Guildford)! All were initially based at Reading, but Car S305 (GFM 888) went over to Newbury in May, being joined by S303 (GFM 884) in July. The latter transferred towards the end of the year to Bracknell, where it was joined by S304 (GFM 887) in April 1964, then also by S301 (GFM 881) in July 1964.

Car S301 (GFM 881) on the Woodley service which would be renumbered from 1c to 10 later during 1963.

48

The only outgoing vehicle in May was a further ex-*United Counties* Bristol LL6B fully-fronted coach 76 (FRP 833), the remaining members of this type being used on contracts to Harwell. There was also a slight reduction in vehicle requirements at Maidenhead as a result of recent changes in working arrangements in respect of Borlase School specials to Marlow by one bus, with only 1 bus in the mornings and 2 in the afternoons now needed.

The Royal Windsor Horse Show in the Great Park again saw extra buses added from 9th to 11th May, on all routes into the town, whilst the usual facilities for combining travel by bus and Salter's Steamers during the Summer was offered as had long been the case.

The excursions programmes were very similar to previous years, though Maidenhead now lacked any allocated coaches, people in the town being only offered the London Airport tour (ex-Reading) and the Southsea express service (ex-High Wycombe), both of which called into Maidenhead Coach Station. On the *South Midland* extended tours, the success of the tour of Scotland resulted in two versions of 9 or 11 days duration now being offered. The Donegal & Northern Ireland tour was re-named as Donegal & Ulster Coast, whilst the East Anglia tour was discontinued. In respect of the London outstation for *South Midland*, the venue was changed from the Gillingham Street (Victoria) garage of *London Transport* in favour of *Samuelson's* from 16th May.

Bristol KSW6B Car 637 (GJB 275) after its rebuild, which included loss of the upper deck beading and a T destination layout, as seen in Reading Stations yard.

A start was made on the next series of rebuilds, this time the 1951 trio of coach-seated 53-seaters, and Car 637 (GJB 275) went to The Colonnade on 1st July and re-emerged in November with cut-down seats. After an unfortunate accident when a Bracknell conductor was thrown off the stairs and onto the road whilst changing a rear destination blind, the Union insisted the use of these was discontinued on buses without rear doors, which led to a general painting over or full removal of such apertures, the space providing further advertising revenue, as already seen on o-m-o buses.

Bristol LS6G Car 682 (HBL 84) is seen after rebuild to a T frontal display on Route 116 to Hungerford.

A campaign of rebuilding front screens to a T layout started, though it lasted several years and is best described as piecemeal, being done mainly when body rebuilds or accidents occurred. Of those done in 1963, Bristol LS6G Car 684 (HBL 86) emerged in October, followed by similar bus 682 (HBL 84), Bristol LWL6B Cars 623/5/6/8 (GJB 261/3/4/6) and KSW6B Car 695 (HMO 841) and even 1947 Bristol K6B Car 454 (DBL 162) during November, all also receiving flashers of the 'orange segment' type. December saw K6B Cars 450 (DBL 158), 469 (DMO 673), 506 (EJB 228) and 528 (FBL 30) done, as well as LWL6B Car 613 (GJB 251), the latter receiving the rear gear taken from Bristol LS6B Car 714 (HMO 860), now o-m-o-worked at Bracknell.

The methods for conversions to T blind layouts varied from those retaining the old box outline to those with a smooth outline. This greatly changed the overall appearance of some types more notably than others, and 1952 Bristol LWL6B Car 628 (GJB 266) is seen at Frogmoor Bus Station on Route 31 to Lacey Green.

In the meantime operating costs rose further after a recommendation in May by the National Council for the Omnibus Industry for an increase of 8shillings and 6pence to the basic weekly rate. At that time the rates, after completion of 12 month's service and for a 44-hour week, were £9 10s 6d for drivers and slightly less for conductors. Most crews relied on regular over time working, which was paid at an enhanced rate up to reaching 46 hours, then time-and-a-half above that or for Sunday and Bank Holiday working. Due to this the Company submitted a general fares increase of 8.3% application to the Traffic Commissioners to be implemented with the Winter timetable. As an interim measure a minimum fare was introduced of 3d for adults or 2d for children from 6th July, which drew a lot of complaints from Local Authorities.

At High Wycombe Driver Burridge was promoted to Inspector from 8th June, whilst a few days later the Traffic Manager met with Oxford City Council regarding proposed one-way traffic and its affects on the Company's services, similar meetings in other towns becoming a regular feature of the Traffic Diary. There were also regular contacts with *British Railway* officers regarding proposed branch line closure under the infamous Beeching Report.

Despite some of the pressures on operations, Royal Ascot Race Week still drew the crowds in June, and 1956 Bristol LD5G Car 769 (MBL 850), newly out from repaint was pressed into service as a relief.

In Bracknell the Company made some adjustments to Local Service 52 in order to meet the pressure for better lunchtime journeys into the town centre from Western Road commencing on 22nd June.

Over in Newbury, the main north-south traffic route still passed through Northbrook Street and via the arched stone bridge over the Kennet & Avon canal, so on 18th July a railway engine mounted on a low-loader held up traffic for much of the afternoon after blocking the road, causing severe disruption to buses.

From July Bristol LS6G coach 674 (HBL 76) was transferred to *South Midland* to take the place of Car 823 (FRP 838), a former *United Counties* full-fronted LL6B which was sold. However the surprising disposal of July was one of the 1957 Bristol SC4LK's, Car 778 (NBL 735), which then became the first of its type with an independent operator. This withdrawal is attributed to vehicle reductions caused by re-working of Routes 16 (Maidenhead – Warren Row – Henley), 17 (Maidenhead – Hurley – Henley) and 18 (M'head – Marlow) a little earlier in the year.

Bristol LD6B Car 810 (PRX 928) was later based at Stokenchurch Dormy Shed and is seen at 'Wycombe Station on Route 39 to Watlington, in company with Bristol LWL6B Car 613 (GJB 251), a Fingest-based bus on the 37 to Henley. The 'Lodekka' was one of a small number rebuilt with T front destination screens, whilst the single-decker now has the intermediate box disused but not yet over-painted in red.

One-way traffic schemes not only affected large towns and busy through roads, and at Watlington this resulted in buses changing terminal point from the Hare & Hounds to Love Lane from 9th August. Buses coming in still dropped at the pub, but outgoing ones started from outside The Aces Café, whilst those with a layover would proceed to the *City of Oxford* garage in Couching Street.

The first meeting took place with Mr. Palmer, who was the Assistant Organisation & Methods Officer at *London Transport* during late August, with a view to the computerisation of scheduling. Other meetings took place with *British Railways* regarding bus service provision in the light of station or line closures during July and August as decision were in progress. Amongst the proposals was a plan to completely close the Reading – Guildford line to passengers, whilst on the Berks & Hants line Aldermaston Station was to be closed, and it was concluded in both cases that the bus services were already adequate. From 9th September the Abingdon – Radley branch line closed, so timings were adjusted on Route 50 (Reading – Abingdon) to facilitate better connections to the London – Oxford trains at Culham Station. In respect of the large site close by occupied by the UKAEA Culham Laboratory peak journeys were diverted via the main gate from 3rd November, but these were discontinued a week later as no one actually made use of them.

Lowbridge Duple-bodied Guy 'Arab' MkIII 6LW Car 171 (FMO 516) is seen laid over at the Bristol OC garage on Route 106 in Swindon. Flashers are now fitted, and the front destination screen reduced by black paint, though the latter would duly be made a single-line display only and rather less informative.

Mention has been made of the established protective fares within Reading Borough, introduced originally in order to protect the Corporation trams from 'unfair' competition from buses, so it is interesting to note that such an understanding was also reached with *Swindon Corporation*, whereby buses on Route 106 (Newbury – Lambourn – Baydon – Swindon) had a higher fare than the municipal buses between Regents Circus and Coate Water.

It will be recalled that *Wilts & Dorset* kept one bus at the *Thames Valley* Newbury garage for its workings on Route 135, but it also had quite a network of services in the Tadley and Baughurst area inherited from *Venture*, with buses outstationed at the latter's old Dormy Shed at Heath End, aided by others from Basingstoke, and these and types used in 1963 were:

132 (Baughurst - Tadley – Bramley Camp) LS6G
133 (Baughurst – Silchester – Bramley Camp) KSW5G
134 (Basingstoke – Silchester – Baughurst) KSW5G, LS6G
135 (Newbury – Whitway – Whitchurch) LS6G
136 (Basingstoke – Baughurst – Beenham) LS, LWL, KSW
137 (Basingstoke – Tadley – Baughurst) KSW5G, KSW6B

On his wanderings in the above area Philip Wallis noted that where *Thames Valley* routes traversed the same roads, along the main road through Tadley and Baughurst between Allen's Garage and via Tadley Hill, Mulfords Hill and on past The Falcon Inn to Heath End, the bus stops were of metal poles with a small square flag on top and bearing no operator's name. However, after *TV* had diverted Route 9 via Rowan Road and Pamber Heath, it soon discovered that *Wilts & Dorset* had never bothered erecting posts for its Wednesdays/Saturdays-only 134 (Baughurst – Pamber Heath – Slichester – Little London – Bramley – Basingstoke), so the '*Valley*' had put up its own bus stops with concrete posts. On one occasion Philip decided to try out the 134 by boarding at the New Inn at Tadley, but the driver was so surprised to find someone waiting there that it took him some way to bring his ex-*Venture* AEC 'Regent' to a halt!

It is also worth noting that after the closure of the Tadley Dormy Shed, the *TV* bus now outstationed at the *Wilts & Dorset* Baughurst Shed had about a 2.5-mile dead run to the Tadley (Allen's Garage) terminus, being the first bus to leave at 6.45am, and not returning until 11.39pm Mondays to Saturdays.

Philip Wallis caught Bristol FLF6G Car 881 (549 BBL) at Heath End by a Wilts & Dorset-type bus stop.

Royal Blue Bristol LS coach 1293 (OTT 92) of the type outstationed at High Wycombe, actually seen at The Wharf in Newbury on the service to Southampton.

The other instance of outstationing concerning *TV* was that of a *Royal Blue* coach, which had started in 1955, and had been kept at Desborough Road since 1957, an arrangement which continued through until 1973. Over the years the ultimate destination of the service varied between Paignton, Brixham and Totnes, though all were reached by a routing through Reading –

Newbury – Andover – Salisbury – Yeovil – Honiton – Exeter. This was a weekend service, with the coach working down one day and back the next over two return journeys, and seems largely to have been aimed at the personnel at RAF Naphill and the nearby Strike Command Headquarters at Walters Ash, both of which were a 3-mile bus ride from 'Wycombe on Route 31. For many years this duty was covered by Roy Dean, a former *Greenslades Tours* of Exeter driver, who also did some driving for *Thames Valley* on other days. The allocation was invariably one of the 1952/3 Bristol LS-types with the ECW coach body incorporating the roof-mounted luggage carrier with cat-walk access via rear steps, and before setting off south he would take his charge along to the 'Marsh garage for fuel, water and a run through the bus wash.

As noted earlier, Car 695 (HMO 841) was the first of the Bristol KSW6B's to be altered to T-style frontal destination display, and it is seen at Frogmoor Bus Station on Route 27 bound for Great Missenden.

Also in the High Wycombe about this time there was an unfortunate accident involving one of the LD-types on Route 20/20a as it approached Princes Risborough. Several boys had already crossed the road from a farm track to the field opposite, where a funfair was pitched, when their younger sibling rushed straight out and under the front of the bus. Driver Jim Tilbury could do nothing to avoid him, the boy being killed outright, and the poor driver was so shocked he never drove a bus again.

Another fatal accident befell Bristol FLF6G Car 849 (WJB 233) in August as it ran along London Road in Earley, and the damage was so extensive that the bus did not return to service until December 1964.

The other significant event of August was on the 29th, when the Company Secretary John Pearmain retired after 32 year's service. He is recalled as invariably polite and dedicated to his responsibilities, and his role was then taken by Gerald Brook, who at the time was stated to be the youngest holding such a post.

Reading-based Bristol KSW6B Car 648 (GJB 286) is seen heading eastwards along Wokingham Road for a school special working. Note the over-head wires for the Corporation trolleybuses and the Austin Mini car.

The issue of finding enough school places for the post-war baby-boomers resulted in further workings for *Thames Valley* from the Autumn term 1963, with Routes 15 (Maidenhead – Curls Lane – Cannon Lane) and 17 (Maidenhead – Hurley – Henley) gaining extra journeys to cater for pupils attending the new Altwood School on the east side of Maidenhead. There was also a new contract run for Berkshire CC taking pupils from the Woodley area to Maidenhead High School for Girls. At the same time Route 65 (Wokingham – Maidenhead – Slough) had some journeys diverted via Taplow School for the benefit of schoolchildren.

Bristol FLF6G Car 876 (544 BBL) is seen on the forecourt of Maidenhead garage with the special side advert commemorating 48 year's of service for when it appeared in the town's carnival on 21st September. Strangely, the 50th anniversary saw no such actions.

Another new contract from 20th September came from the 'bingo craze', when TV was asked to run special journeys from Bracknell and Ascot on Friday and Saturday evenings to the Windsor Bingo Club set up in a former cinema, a commonplace situation at that time. This was paid for by the proprietors, though in due course both the Windsor and Slough venues made arrangements with cheaper operators for that purpose.

On the 21st September the Newbury Show was held for the last time at Elcot Park, on the Bath Road halfway between Newbury and Hungerford, and the usual enhanced service was provided from both directions by Route 116.

With the publication of the new timetable booklet of 28th September the opportunity was taken to re-number several areas of services where the variants had become complex. The Route 9 workings had long contained various short-workings and projections, but these were now better defined as:

Route 9 Reading – Burghfield Common – Mortimer – Tadley or Baughurst;
Route 9b Reading – Burghfield (ROF) - Burghfield Common – Mortimer Station;
Route 9c Reading – Burghfield Common – Padworth – Aldermaston (Soke Corner) – Baughurst.

The re-numbering of the Woodley area services was accompanied by this leaflet in red on a yellow paper, which diagrammatically shows the various different routes which had developed as the population grew.

For the first time all the *South Midland* and *Thames Valley* express coach services were shown, complete with route numbers, though these were not displayed on the vehicles other than Route A and B at that time:

Route A Reading – Ascot – Staines – London;
Route B Reading – Maidenhead – Slough – London;
Route C Oxford – Henley – Maidenhead – London;
Route D Oxford – High Wycombe – London;
Route E Worcester – Oxford – Henley – London;
Route F Worcester – Oxford – Newbury – Southsea;
Route G High Wycombe – Maidenhead – Southsea;
Route H Booker – High Wycombe – Bournemouth;
Route J Booker – 'Wycombe – Eastbourne – Hastings.

Also included in a special section were the services operating on certain days to hospitals and churches:

Reading – Fair Mile Hospital (Moulsford), every Thursday and Sunday;
Newbury - Fair Mile Hospital (Moulsford), 1st and 3rd Thursdays and 2nd and 4th Sundays each month;
Reading – Borocourt Hospital (Kingwood Common), 1st Sunday each month;
Cippenham – Lower Britwell RC Church (Burnham), 4 journeys each Sunday for service times;
Britwell – Lower Britwell RC Church (Burnham), 4 journeys each Sunday for service times.

From 1st November some of the journeys on Route D were operated non-stop between Headington and the Odeon Cinema (Shepherds Bush), reducing the running time by 29 minutes to 2 hours 15 minutes.

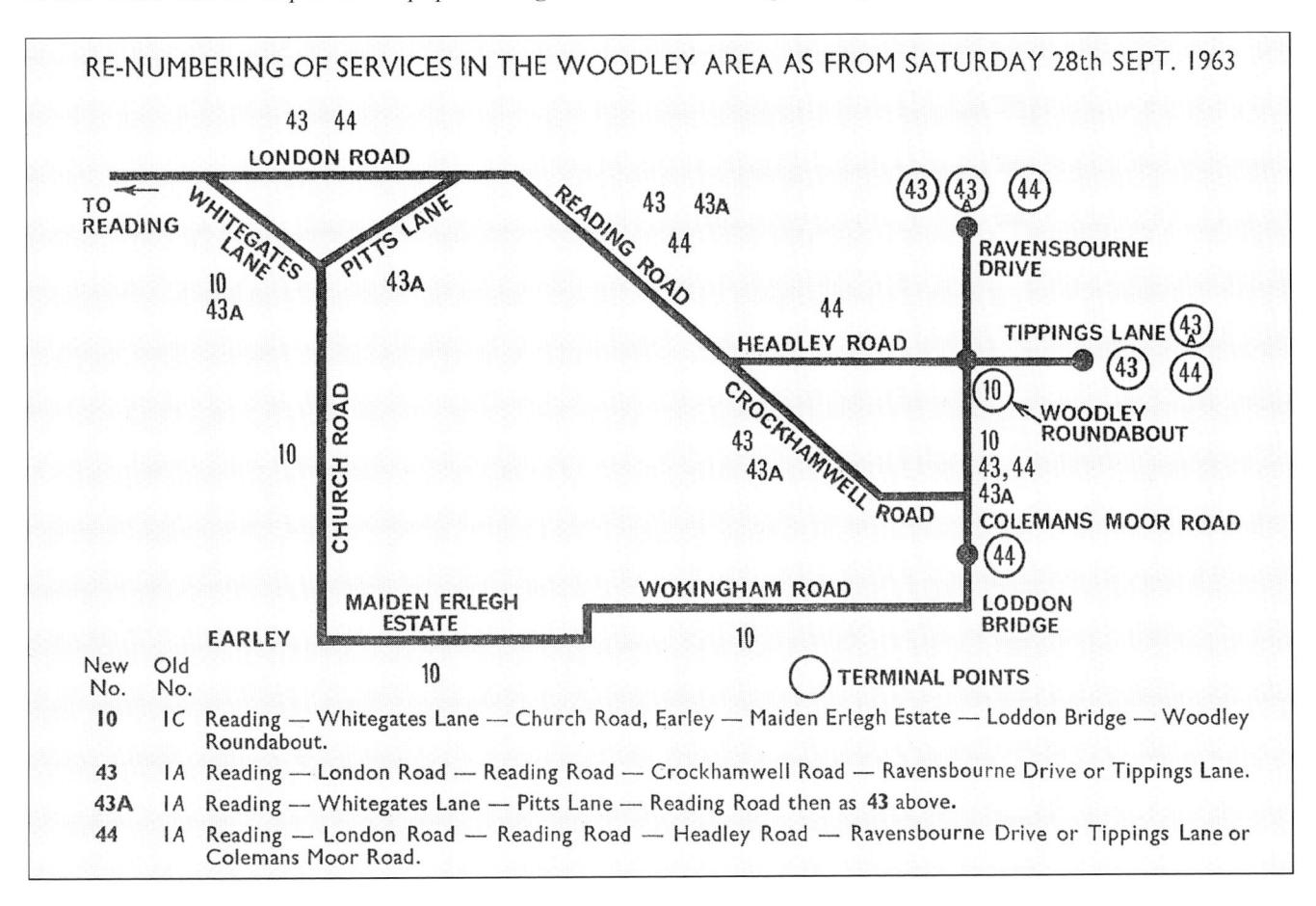

RE-NUMBERING OF SERVICES IN THE WOODLEY AREA AS FROM SATURDAY 28th SEPT. 1963

New No.	Old No.	
10	1C	Reading — Whitegates Lane — Church Road, Earley — Maiden Erlegh Estate — Loddon Bridge — Woodley Roundabout.
43	1A	Reading — London Road — Reading Road — Crockhamwell Road — Ravensbourne Drive or Tippings Lane.
43A	1A	Reading — Whitegates Lane — Pitts Lane — Reading Road then as **43** above.
44	1A	Reading — London Road — Reading Road — Headley Road — Ravensbourne Drive or Tippings Lane or Colemans Moor Road.

With a 'Non Stop Express' board in the front nearside windscreen, 1952 Bristol LS6G coach 82 (SFC 568) arrives at Gloucester Green in Oxford from London.

There were relatively few new buses arriving in 1963, but in October the first double-deckers in the new D-series came as Cars D1-3 (839-41 CRX), all being Bristol FLF6G's with ECW H38/32F bodies. Unlike previous examples of that type, these featured the heating system developed by Commander T.R. Cave-Browne-Cave, latterly as Professor of Engineering at Southampton University, which utilised engine heat and required the fitting of air intake grilles. Of this trio only Cars D1/2 also had illuminated offside advert panels, and all featured green PVC seating, which was less comfortable than earlier examples and easy to slip off. D1 was allocated to Maidenhead, D2 to Reading and D3 to Wycombe Marsh.

Bristol FLF6G Car D1 (839 CRX) is seen on the stands at Mackenzie Street in Slough working Route 65 as far as Maidenhead. It is interesting to note that a number of the illuminated panels were used for bus travel ads, suggesting that advertisers did not wish to pay a premium for that innovation.

Additional housing in the Cox Green area, south-west of Maidenhead town centre, resulted in extra shorts operating on Route 65 between there and Northumbria Road with effect from 5th October, a situation also made possible by improved staffing at Maidenhead.

An interesting application went before the Traffic Commissioner in early October, wherein both *Thames Valley* and *Reading Corporation* sought to amend existing services in order to serve new housing at West Wood Housing Estate between Tilehurst and Purley. The *Corporation* intended to extend its existing route to Overdown Road, whilst *TV* proposed diverting buses on Route 5b (Reading – Pangbourne – Yattendon – Newbury). However, the Commissioner felt these proposals were somewhat half-baked, and sent both parties away to talk further! After several meetings this did develop into a proper joint venture, so a new application was submitted, whilst in the meantime the *Corporation* made a short extension on from Overdown Road to the junction of Dark Lane and Long Lane from 16th December as an interim measure, and *TV* erected the bus stops along that road.

Wycombe Car D3 (841 CRX) leaves Aylesbury on the 35-mile Route 20a through to Windsor. The intake grilles for the C-B-C heaters are either side of the front destination screen.

In the meantime over at Bracknell, further housing development and new roads in the Harmans Water area resulted in a new service starting from 12th October. This was Route 56 (High Street – Bullbrook – Broad Lane – Ralphs Ride – Harmans Water Shops – Primrose Walk), the terminus actually being only some 300 yards from the South Hill Road Route 52, which it was earmarked for combining with in future.

From 9th November further changes to working arrangements at Maidenhead saw Routes 60 (Slough – Bath Road – Maidenhead), 18a (Maidenhead – Halifax Road or Pinkneys Green) and 19 (Maidenhead – Crauford Arch – Sealey's Stores) combined to form revised Routes 60 (Slough – Bath Road – Maidenhead – Halifax Road or Pinkneys Green) and 69 (Slough – Bath Road – Maidenhead – Sealey's Stores). The opportunity was also taken to eliminate the reversal at Sealey's Stores, the bus running around Courthouse Road – St. Marks Road – All Saints Avenue. A number of other long-standing reverses were removed in similar fashion due to safety issues over o-m-o.

54

There were quite a number of minor changes on the Maidenhead area services from the same date, whilst Route 15 (Maidenhead – Curls Lane – Cannon Lane) was given some extra journeys to suit the employees of the publishing firm McGraw Hill at Cox Green.

Reading-based Car D2 (840 CRX) was put to work on the recently renumbered Woodley service 43 through to Ravensbourne Drive. Also note than many of the FLF's carried the same advert for South Midland extended tours on the offside panel backing onto the staircase.

Many of the Newbury services were affected by the complete closure of the railway bridge in Cheap Street for rebuilding from 17th November. The inward journeys diverted via Bartholomew Street – Market Street – Cheap Street – Market Place - Wharf Street, whilst the outgoing buses ran via Wharf Road – Black Bear Lane – Market Place – Mansion House Street – Bartholomew Street. The bridge took some time to complete, and in the meantime advantages were found with the revised routing, so most services were kept like that and Road Services Licenses duly amended.

There was also an issue with Arborfield Bridge, which carried the road between Shinfield (School Green) and Arborfield Cross over the River Loddon, so a meeting was held on 26th November with the County Surveyor, at which it was agreed that buses could continue to pass over it but at walking pace only, otherwise Routes 4 (Reading – Shinfield – Eversley – Yateley – Camberley) and 4a (Reading – Shinfield – Barkham – Wokingham) might have had a long diversion.

Reading-based Bristol LS6B Car 722 (HMO 868) was badly damaged in an accident at Aldermaston whilst working Route 9a (Reading – Grazeley – Padworth – Aldermaston – Tadley) on 8th November, but duly returned to service. Wycombe-based Bristol LL5G Car 797 (DMO 667) also sustained frontal damage and re-emerged during November rebuilt with an LD-type radiator grille, which improved its appearance.

Car 797 (DMO 667) at Frogmoor Bus Station on Route 34 to Speen soon after its front end rebuild. It is unclear whether all the changes of similar nature to the LL5G's were as a result of accidents, or perhaps someone else felt it overcame the rather 'grumpy' look of that style of body, but in due course Cars 795/8/9 (DMO 665/8/9), along with 820 (FMO 24) would be treated, though the latter was after damage.

Further improvements to Bracknell Local Service 52 resulted in former *Crosville* Bristol L6A Car S303 (GFM 884) being sent to that garage to cover additional journeys from 19th November, whilst it also made appearances on relief duties on Routes 53/53a out of Windsor at times. Also on the one-man front, 1953 Bristol LS6G Car 682 (HBL 84) was finally re-seated to B41F and fitted out for one-man-operation.

An end of year clearout saw the demise in December of 1946 Bristol K6A Car 440 (CRX 549), 1948/9 K6B Cars 492 and 501 (EJB 214/23), along with ex-*Bristol OC* 1947 K6B Cars 437 and 455 (KHU 601/4). On the coaching side, 1951 full-fronted Bristol LWL6B's 607/11 (GBL 871/5) also went after the Harwell contract from Wash Common had been cancelled by the UKAEA from 29th November.

The hiring of *South Midland* caches to the Post Office saw Bristol LS6B Cars 93 (TWL 58) and 689/91 (HMO 835/7), along with MW6G Car 802 (ORX 633) hired from 16th-24th December for £227 16s 6d.

Car 455 (KHU 604) on Route 4 in St. Marys Butts.

Bristol L6A Car S302 (GFM 882) passing the Reading branch of glass merchants James Clark & Eaton on the Basingstoke Road en route to Bramley Station on Route 6b, a service originally bought from Blue Star Service of Mortimer. The over-large branch was built before WW2 for use as a glass store out of the vulnerable Blackfriars area in view of the anticipated air raids, but did well out of housing developments post-war, and saved a lot of mileage.

After the diversions for avoiding the closed rail bridge in Newbury, Guy 'Arab' MkIII 6LW Car 170 (FMO 516) was seen by Philip Wallis emerging from Black Bear Lane for the Market Place working Route 113 to Inkpen. That service had come into the Newbury & District fold through the amalgamation of Burt & Greenwood, one of many routes with its origins as a Country Carrier's service from the numerous villages and hamlets focussed on the market town of Newbury.

A route pioneered by Reading & District was the original version of the 5b, which ran only as far as Tidmarsh. Thames Valley still had a few shorts to that spot, though most journeys were either through to Newbury or other short-workings to Pangbourne or those from Newbury to Hampstead Norris. Bristol KSW6B Car 634 (GJB 272) is seen on Station Hill in Reading, with the old Frame Clothing factory and the yard of Vincent's behind.

1964

From 1st January George Shaw joined the Company as Assistant Engineer, whilst J. Sanders became Foreman at Oxford. However, on the following day the Traffic Manager was annoyed to learn that Black & Decker had made other arrangements for transport for its large workforce to the factory on the Cannon Lane side of White Waltham airfield. Transport from Maidenhead was now contracted to *Walwyn's Coaches,* whilst it was also known that *Alpha Coaches* of that town had been asked to provide 5 coaches on contracts, with 1 coach each from Reading, Henley and Bracknell, plus 2 from Maidenhead. This left *Thames Valley* with only the extra scheduled journeys from Tittle Row, and there is little doubt that the employer's decision had to some degree been forced by unreliability of bus services locally resulting from staff shortages. Indeed, although new crews were regularly recruited, some from outside areas, once they were established they often moved onto better paid employment.

Bristol MW6G coach 807 (PRX 933) is seen acting as the official Oxford United Football Club transport on a murky day at Gloucester Green Bus Station. Drivers who followed the club were no doubt happy to volunteer for this particular duty!

Over at Burghfield some additional journeys were put on Routes 9/9b from Reading to serve the WREN's shore-base HMS Dauntless from 4th January. From 6th January the bus stands at Henley Market Place were re-arranged, with the Wycombe-bound Route 28 from Reading, along with Route 37 buses both to and from High Wycombe, were assigned the stop outside the Lovibond's Wine Store, whilst the Reading-bound 28 used The Argyll pub stop. Over at Camberley the new Town Centre Plan envisaged moving the terminus for buses from Princess Street to (yes, you guessed it) the yard at the railway station, though nothing ever came of this oft-discussed relocation. At the end of January there was a meeting with British Railways concerning bus services in light of proposals to close the station at Crowthorne, from which it was concluded that existing routes could cope or be amended.

The ECW bodies by for the Bristol RELH6G coaches now lacked the stepped waistrail and had less side windows. C404 (834 CRX) is seen soon after delivery at Gloucester Green, the fog lights still positioned under the bumper, which would soon be moved up.

The new coaches for 1964 were all received during January, though those for touring were not licensed until required. However, the pair of Bristol RELH6G coaches were for express duties and had ECW C47F bodies, as Cars C404/5 (834/5 CRX) for the *South Midland* fleet. The other quartet consisted of Bedford SB13's with Leyland 0370 engines and Duple 'Super Vega' C37F bodies. C406 (836 CRX) was for the *TV* fleet and based at Reading, whilst C407-9 (837/8/42 CRX) were *South Midland* vehicles for touring work.

Bedford SB13 coach C408 (838 CRX) shows the revised livery for this batch of Duple deliveries, which was also applied to the trio of the previous year for 1964, and it is seen on Watlington Hill.

Although the suffix letter system for registrations had been introduced in some areas from 1963, Berkshire did not start until 1st February 1964, so these coaches retained part of a batch of numbers already issued to the Company back in 1963. *Thames Valley* example C406 (836 CRX) was licensed from 1st March, but it suffered from a fire to the bodywork just one week later, though it was soon repaired! After that it could be found on private hire and excursions.

C406 (836 CRX) is seen later in the Summer on a dull day excursion to the popular resort of Southsea, a venue specially developed around the needs of the early charabanc trippers, with its large coach park, funfair and direct access to the seafront.

The sole AEC 'Regal' MkIV coach 85 (SFC 571) had its seating increased from 37 to 39. Over the Winter months the opening windscreens on the 1952 Bristol LS6G coaches 79-83 (SFC 565-9) were replaced by fixed screens, as they had started to rattle and leak. Interestingly, Car 83 re-appeared with a 'C' prefix to its fleet number in January, along with Bristol MW6G-types 805/7 (PRX 931/3), whilst LS-type coach 671 (HBL 73) had the same in July, so someone at the garage evidently thought the new system also applied to existing vehicles!

On the touring front, Bristol MW6G Car 804 (PRX 930) was the Irish Tour coach for the season, and it was noted carrying *Ulster Transport Authority* plate number 3158, as all vehicles operating in the province were technically sold to it whilst there. The *South Midland* tour drivers were issued with a black blazer and dark grey trousers for this season. On the tours themselves, the Scottish Tour was offered at 9 and 12-days duration, whilst the Wye Valley Tour was discontinued, despite having once been the most popular on offer during the *Red & White* era.

Although a number of Bristol LS buses had been one-man-operated for some years, in January it was decided to put notices on the front offside bulkhead stating 'No standing forward of this partition', and the 1960 Bristol MW saloons were similarly treated.

Expansion at Heathrow Airport saw the opening of a new British European Airway's Catering Building on the Great West Road, so *Thames Valley* added a stop on its Route B (Reading – Slough – London) from 29th January, though only passengers boarding west of Salt Hill in Slough could be carried on easterly journeys in order to protect *London Transport* services.

Reading Central Works had responsibility for all major dockings, and it is interesting to note throughput for the month of January, with Bristol K6B Cars 500/6/16 (EJB 222/8/38), Bristol KSW6B Car 653 (HBL 55), Bristol LS6B Cars 712/23 (HMO 858/69), Bristol LD6G Car 761 (MBL 842) and Bedford SB8 coach 862 (516 ABL). Body repairs and repainting was handled at the Colonnade Works, and during the same period, body repairs took place on K6B Car 518 (EJB 240), Bristol LWL6B Car 633 (GJB 271) and Bristol FLF6G Car 837 (UJB 203), whilst repaints were undertaken on K6B Car 529 (FBL 31), KSW6B Cars 601 (FMO 983) and 650 (GJB 288), LWL6B Car 629 (GJB 267), Bristol LL5G Car 819 (FMO 23) and 1963 delivery FLF6G Car 879 (547 BBL), the latter after an accident. The REX6G coach 867 (521 ABL) also spent several weeks away that month down at Brislington for modifications.

Above is D5 (ABL 117B) at Victoria Coach Station, and below is D4 (ABL 116B) outside Samuelson's Garage off Eccleston Place, Victoria. The black-on-white plates will be discussed later in this chapter.

Production at both Bristol Commercial Vehicles and Eastern Coach Works was rather stretched at the time, and amongst those vehicles overdue for the 'Valley' were 5 coach-seated FLF-types, and 4 of these finally arrived for licensing from 1st February, becoming Cars D4-7 (ABL 116-9B). These had been planned to take registrations 842-5 CRX, along with D8/9 due to have been 846/7 CRX, though only 842 CRX was actually used on Bedford coach C409 due to the new suffixes.

The ECW CH37/28F bodies had red and white interiors, and red leatherette upholstery with headrests which looked very smart, whilst their chassis had the Bristol BVW engine. The relatively low seating on the lower deck was due to an extra full-height luggage rack on the front offside, whilst these buses also had C-B-C heaters, as fitted to all subsequent deliveries of FLF's to *Thames Valley*. All were nominally allocated to Reading for the London services, though two were outstationed at Samuelson's on a rota with the earlier coach-seated examples. However, D6 (ABL 118B) did stray further afield in June, when it deputised for a *Bristol Greyhound* coach after an accident. Back on 28th February Bristol SC4LK Car 774 (NBL 731) also did a similar cover from Maidenhead, certainly the first time it had visited Bristol since being built!

Bristol LWL6B Car 616 (GJB 254) is seen on Route 35 to Downley at High Wycombe Station following rebuilding of its front destination screen to a T layout.

The rebuilding of front indicators to the T layout sped up during 1964, with Bristol KSW6B Cars 601 (FMO 983) and 647 (GJB 285) in January, Bristol LWL6B Cars 616/27/9 (GJB 254/65/7) in February, then KSW Car 650 (GJB 288) by May. When KSW Car 601 was in the bodyshops it also lost the upper-deck beading and luggage racks, whilst KSW6B Car 748 (JRX 823) was rebuilt to T at an unrecorded date in 1964. Many other buses with 3-piece apertures had their intermediate boxes over-painted in red, and those recorded were KSW6B Car 729 (JRX 804) in March and Fingest-based LWL6B Car 630 (GJB 268) by April, some also passing through that phase until being converted to the T format. Also from March the unused rear apertures on saloons started to be used for adverts, the first noted being Bracknell-based Bristol LS6B Car 714 (HMO 860) in that month.

The official allocation for 1st February showed that Bracknell had 32 vehicles, Maidenhead 70, Wycombe Marsh and Desborough Road a combined 68, Oxford 18, Newbury 48 and Reading 110, the un-licensed fleet being 33, which of course included a number of coaches yet to be licensed for the season. An overtime ban came into effect from 15th-19th February, though it only affected Reading, Maidenhead and High Wycombe garages. At the latter location the dispute was not lifted until 29th February, being over the time taken to implement the recent wage award.

Bristol LWL6B Car 630 (GJB 268) is seen on the same day as 616 (opposite) and still sports all three destination boxes in use on Route 36 to Cadmore End from High Wycombe Station.

Due to industrial action at Reading it was necessary to get *Smith's Luxury Coaches* to cover some private hire bookings and the afternoon journeys on UKAEA contracts from Harwell. The latter situation further damaged the Company's standing with that employer, leading to contracts going elsewhere or being covered by Harwell's own increasing fleet of buses.

In fact the National Council for the Omnibus Industry had agreed a further wage rise from 3rd March, with drivers and skilled maintenance staff getting a rise of 14 shillings per week, whilst conductors gained 10s and 6d. This came into force from 7th March, putting more pressure on the viability of services, though the Union's claim for a shorter working week was rejected.

The rear of Bristol LS6B Car 714 (HMO 860) shows the advert over the old destination aperture, along with the reversing light fitted to o-m-o conversions.

59

Bristol LD6G Car 753 (MBL 834) was photographed by Philip Wallis at Boundary Hill in Tadley, fresh out of a repaint on Route 9 to Reading in March 1964.

In the meantime at Maidenhead certain shorts on Route 17 (Maidenhead – Hurley – Henley) were transferred from 4th January to Route 15, as they provided school journeys between Tittle Row and Altwood School. From Reading the Route 6 entered Basingstoke via Reading Road – Gashouse Road – Basing Road with effect from 21st January, whilst over at Newbury there were some adjustments from 22nd February, with the journeys previously on Route 121 between Shaw (Factory Gates) and Newbury (The Wharf or Regal Cinema) now transferred to Local Service 127, leaving the 121 as The Wharf - Penwood only. On Route 111 (Newbury – Bucklebury – Stanford Dingley) the long-established layover at The Blade Bone at Bucklebury Common was amended to around the corner in Hatch Lane from 24th February.

A bus washer was installed at Frogmoor Bus Station in due course, and buses outstationed were done during layovers. Stokenchurch-based Bristol LD6B Car 811 (PRX 929) had worked in on Route 41 from Ibstone.

The Service Vehicle fleet saw the departure of 1958 Morris 'Minor' 1000cc car (RBL 109) in February, along with the arrival of Ford Thames 307E van No.51 (32 GBL), whilst in April a Ford 'Zephyr' car (ARX 554B) was delivered.

On the train front, services no longer stopped after 8.10pm at Winnersh Halt, so arrangements were made to accept rail tickets for passengers completing their journey by bus to Winnersh Crossroads and claimed back from British Railways from 2nd March onwards.

March 1964 saw the Union pressing for the early replacement of buses without heaters and doors, and in the meantime the Company undertook to schedule those so equipped as effectively as possible. March also featured a notable transfer to Bracknell of the sole Bristol LDL6G in the fleet, Car 779 (NBL 736), which took the place of Bristol KS6B Car 588 (FMO 970), which had been there since December 1961. The additional 2ft 6ins in length soon saw it in (literally) frequent scrapes on the narrow estate roads when out on Local Services with unwitting drivers! However, it spent most time on Routes 2 (Reading – Bracknell – Ascot – Windsor) or 3 (Reading – Wokingham – Crowthorne – Camberley), finally returning to Reading's allocation in March 1967.

The 105 route to Wantage, and extension to Childrey Ridgeway was under threat of withdrawal when Peter Wilks took a ride out to the very rural terminus in February 1964 on Bristol LL6B Car 564 (FMO 946).

The Company gave notice that it intended to surrender the licenses on Route 105, as well as the 6b (Reading – Grazeley – Bramley) during March, though in each case there were protests from Local Councils.

Easter was a bitterly cold affair, with Good Friday on 27th March, also dull and wet over the weekend, so takings were adversely affected, whilst only 25 of the 30 coaches planned for re-licensing were placed in service at that time.

On the personnel front, the Management Trainee Mr. A.S. Rolls, who had been on secondment to *Thames Valley* since 1st October 1963, now went from the Schedules Office to the Traffic Office from 5th April, whilst Peter Wilks did the opposite, then Rolls went onto the Engineer's Office from 22nd June.

Another rumour of joint operation by *TV* and *Reading Corporation* was sparked when the Route Servicing team took Bristol K5G No.43 (BRX 921) to Whitley Wood Road and erected 3 pairs of TV-flagged posts along there on 10th April. However, these were for use by schoolchildren directed from the RAF houses to the Shinfield School at School Green, which was a short-working on Route 4.

With the Transport & Road Research Laboratory over by Pinewood Crossroads, the buses of the Company had already taken part in a number of experiments on the private tracks on that site. There were also strips buried in the road at Pinewood Crossroads, which gave preferential traffic light changes to approaching vehicles, something the drivers on Routes 53/53a soon cottoned onto, as they cruised up to the junction at the appropriate pace. In April a new style of reflective registration plate was fitted to buses usually on the London express routes, which could be observed by TR&RL staff at various points throughout the day. These were fitted to Bristol LD Cars 752/3 (MBL 833/4) and FLF Cars D4-7 (ABL 116-9B), and as these plates did not conform to the then current legislation, each bus carried a certificate from the Ministry of Transport permitting their use on the road.

Bristol LD6G Car 752 (MBL 833) is seen at Reading Stations, on this occasion covering Route 1 between Newbury and Maidenhead, when caught by Philip Wallis with the new plates. These were removed at times for examination, the old plates returning to use at such times. This style of plate was finally developed to be introduced in the UK from December 1967, by then with black-on-yellow used at the rear as well.

At High Wycombe the contingent of 1950/1 Bristol LL6B's were still putting in full-day turns on the busy Local Service 33, conductor assistance in loading also helping with timekeeping. Car 571 (FMO 953) still had another 3 year's of service ahead of it when seen in Newland Street loading on front of an LT 326 bus.

Philip Wallis saw Bristol L6A Car S304 (GFM 887) in the Southern yard when engaged on the threatened 6b service to Bramley Station.

A new timetable book was issued from 11th April, and the absence of both Routes 6b (Reading – Grazeley – Padworth – Bramley Station) and 105 (Newbury – Wantage – Childrey Ridgeway) caused quite a stir! It transpired that both had been prematurely deleted, as plans to provide some residual services had yet to be finalised, and we shall hear more of these soon.

A number of changes affected the High Wycombe area, where Route 42 (Loudwater – High Wycombe – West Wycombe – Booker Hill Estate) was reduced to operate as Wycombe Marsh (Post Office) – High Street – Downley Turning – Booker Hill (Field Road). At the same time some extra journeys were added to Route 81 (High Wycombe – Desborough Avenue – Booker) to operate between Wycombe Marsh (Post Office) to Booker (Turnpike Corner) as Route 81a, all buses on this and the 42 now running via Desborough Road and Newland Street rather than the previous routing along West Wycombe Road.

Bristol K6B Car 533 (FMO 8) of 1950 is seen on new working 33a at Frogmoor Bus Station. Note the advert for Milwards, one of a series going back many years on the buses of the 'Valley and painted on.

Additional journeys were also added to Route 33 (High Wycombe – Desborough Castle Estate) from Newland Street (Car Park) to Desborough Castle Estate (Link Road), double-deck operated and known as Route 33a. The area also saw a number of extra buses laid on at schooltimes for pupils at Castlefields School at the request of the Education Authority. The service to Downley on Route 35 was improved with timings better suited to connect with trains, whilst the Henley – Hambleden shorts on Route 37 were now part of Route 28, with buses working through from Reading just twice a day on weekdays.

Many other Wycombe area services were slightly modified, whilst Route 25 to Flackwell Heath gained 4 weekday extensions via Blind Lane to Bourne End (Post Office) for connections with Route 20 buses to Maidenhead and Windsor. However, another change in that area was the final removal of the 'lamp time' allowance for Dormy Shed crews, something going back to the days of acetylene lighting!

Mention has already been made of buses appearing in service with part-painted adverts, and Bristol FLF6G Car D1 (839 CRX) is seen laid over in Maidenhead Coach Station with only the base areas prepared for a 'Maidenhead Autos for Ford' advert, as it awaits further duties on Route 69 (Slough – Sealey's Stores).

Over in the Bracknell area Routes 55/55a had timings amended from 13th April at the request of ICI Jealotts Hill, and journeys now started from Bracknell Station. On the following day a new school journey was added at the request of the Education Authority, taking pupils from Binfield (The Roebuck) to Bull Lane for Wick Hill School. It is worth noting the continued role of requests from larger employers in that town, with a number of short-workings on Route 2 either from Ascot or Binfield to Fluidrive in Broad Lane, Kent's Engineering at Brants Bridge and Castrol Laboratories in London Road, all three sites being very close by off the Running Horse crossroads. The author also recalls from this period some notable characters on the one-manners out of Bracknell, known as 'Ginger' (who drove around with his left foot up on the front dash of the LS's) and 'Oscar' (famous for introducing his own form of unofficial half-fare scheme)!

As already noted, a number of the ex-Crosville Bristol L6A's worked for Bracknell at some point, and Car S305 (GFM 888) is seen in the garage yard disabled by a loose nearside flasher between 53 relief duties.

In Reading the effects on services by proposed one-way schemes were discussed with Reading BC during April. Elsewhere, as more roundabouts replaced once sleepy junctions, a number of longstanding bus stops had to be relocated. One example at this time was that for Routes 2 (Reading – Wokingham – Bracknell – Ascot – Windsor) and the London A, which had used the stop outside the Royal Ascot Hotel for many years. This was move across the roundabout to a point further east and opposite the entrance to Heatherwood Hospital. Similarly, the westbound stop was relocated opposite that, also handy for the hospital, though under changes made later on an alternative stop also had to be reinstated westbound close to the old site. Not long after these changes the hotel burnt down, but at least new shelters were duly provided on what could be a rather windswept location backed by the open expanse of the race course.

During April ex-*Crosville* Bristol L6A Car S304 (GFM 887) was sent to Bracknell, where it stayed for about a month before being replaced there by S305 (GFM 888), meaning that only Car S303 (GFM 882) did not serve at that location at some point.

The long-established Newbury – Moulsford (Fair Mile Hospital) service ceased *Thames Valley* operation on Sunday 26th April, having originated with *Durnford Bros.* back in October 1933. This was due to the need to reduce buses at Newbury, as the recent loss of some contracts had left that bus under-utilised, though *Reliance* had already agreed to take over the license.

Although some of the earlier coach-seated Bristol double-deckers were now being re-seated as buses, the 1954 examples were to be found on longer routes such as Car 740 (JRX 815) seen by Philip Wallis on Route 12 at Aldershot Bus Station.

Another sign of the economic pressures on the Company was the ending of return fares with effect from Saturday 2nd May, which also coincided with a general fares increase. The exceptions to this change were certain long-distance fares on the London A and B services, along with those affecting joint workings with *City of Oxford,* though Routes 5, 50 and 112 were adjusted in due course.

On 15th May there were late journeys operated on all routes out of Windsor following the flood-lit finale to the Royal Windsor Horse Show, and the Whit weekend of 16th-18th was blessed with very warm sunny weather. Shortly afterwards, on 22nd May, the Tilling Association borrowed Bristol MW6G coach 866 (520 ABL) and the REX6G coach 867 (521 ABL) for a film on coach travel, with shooting taking place at Reading garage, Maidenhead bus station and out on the roads north of Basingstoke.

In the meantime, a number of older types had been disposed of, with further inroads into the ranks of the Bristol K's, with 1946 K6A-type Car 439 (CRX 548) going in March, along with ex-*Hants & Dorset* 1949-bodied 1938 K5G Cars 472/3 (JT 9354/5). April saw the sale of a further pair of fully-fronted Bristol LWL6B coaches, Cars 608/10 (GBL 872/4), followed by the last of that type Car 609 (GBL 873) in May, as well as LWL6B-type saloon 623 (GJB 261).

Philip also managed to catch Bristol LWL6B coach 609 (GBL 873) at Harwell in March before its sale.

However, during Spring rumours had started about 'something special' due for service on the single-deck front, which on the face it could have referred to the trio of 36-foot Bristol RELL6G's then overdue for delivery. As this gradually centred on whatever was going on at The Colonnade Works, the author spent several Saturday mornings staking out the site, as that day was traditional for transfers between there and the Central Works, but the big green doors stayed shut!

When the 'new' buses were finally revealed, it was a surprise to find former South Midland Bristol LS6B coaches rebuilt to their new guise as Cars S309-11 (HMO 835-7). The virtually all-red livery and extra brite-work gave them a distinctive appearance which would have looked more at home with Red & White.

The trio of rebuilt buses were for the new joint service with *Reading Corporation* as Route 19 (Stations – Overdown Road – Long Lane – Highfield Road) from Saturday 23rd May. The arrangements saw 27 journeys operated on weekdays, of which *RCT* covered 18 and *TV* the other third, with fares pooled on a mileage basis. Sundays had the first 3 journeys by *TV,* then *RCT* buses for the remaining 6 throughout the day.

Graham Low caught Car S310 (HMO 836) at the Highfield Road terminus on the first day of operation. The narrow nature of some sections of the roads traversed is evident behind the bus, as are the trees.

Reading Corporation fielded its latest AEC 'Reliance' 2MU3RV-types with East Lancs B34D bodies and 26 standees, Nos.47-50 (5147-50 DP), whereas the LS Cars S309-11 (HMO 835-7, formerly Cars 689-91) used by *Thames Valley* seated only 41 plus the standard standing compliment of 8. Even on the first day, though mainly due to the presence of enthusiasts, some reliefs were necessary, the *TV* Inspector having to resort to Bristol K6B Car 471 (DMO 675), even though the trees had not been cut in anticipation of double-decks along that road! Its driver had to steer carefully along the appropriately-named Oak Tree Road, whilst the narrow section there also needed some slight re-timings to avoid buses meeting there.

We have already seen how the Reading-based o-m-o workings were largely inter-worked, and that affected this trio of converted LS-types, resulting in all three appearing during the day, whereas the *Corporation* assigned one bus throughout that duty. For the same reasons, other types would also sometimes appear, and apart from one-manners Bristol L6A Car S304 (GFM 887) and LL5G-type Car 794 (DMO 664), with only 35 or 39 seats, there were instances of two-man Bristol LWL6B saloon 620 (GJB 258) and even LS6G coach 675 (HBL 77), the latter with its hinged door!

However, despite the above, the service settled down, apart from a lingering suspicion on the part of some residents that using the *TV* bus would cost more, a hangover from the protective fares still enjoyed by the *Corporation* elsewhere in the Borough. Indeed, the only difference was that *TV* season tickets were not accepted on that route. Another facet of co-operation saw *TV* providing buses to cover for rail services between Reading and Basingstoke on Friday 22nd May, Bristol LS Car 686 (HBL 88) working alongside *Wilts & Dorset* Bristol FLF6G No.660 (469 BMR).

From 23rd May a further Bristol LS saloon was sent to Bracknell to cope with loadings on Route 52 (High Street – Bullbrook – Harmans Water), whilst from 25th May it was necessary to lay on a bus to take primary school pupils from South Hill Road (Golden Farmer) to Wellington Drive for the new Harmans Water School. Over at Maidenhead another cycle of staff shortages saw 5 double-deckers de-licensed with effect from 30th May, along with much work for the Schedules Office in re-arranging duties and producing window bills to inform the public.

During May two of the pioneering coach-seated Bristol KS6B's went through the body-shops, having their seats cut down and re-upholstered, along with front screens rebuilt to T layout and upper-deck beading removed. Cars 595/7 (FMO 977/9) were dealt with, and the latter seen in Reading garage.

Nearing the end of its Thames Valley days was former Hants & Dorset Bristol K5G Car 474 (JT 9360), but still in good shape when seen at Cemetery Junction in June on an Ascot Race Week relief on Route 2.

Excursions continued from all the previous locations throughout the 1964 season, with the London Airport tour still attracting a high level of interest.

Despite further inroads into the K-type ranks, many could still be found working all day on routes such as the 4a (Reading – Arborfield – Wokingham), and Car 526 (FBL 28) also displays the central route number in an otherwise unmodified lower destination box.

From 13th June a number of detail changes were made to Routes 27 (High Wycombe – Great Missenden), 31 (High Wycombe – Naphill – Lacey Green), 33 (High Wycombe – Desborough Castle Estate) and 80 (High Wycombe – Lacey Green – Aylesbury) to allow them to serve High Wycombe Station, which gave better connections, along with removing a reversal for o-m-o buses in Castle Street as requested by the Union.

Over at Windsor the Maidenhead garage still fielded one bus daily for the Local Service 51 workings, and 1953 Bristol KSW6B Car 661 (HBL 63) was typical.

The Royal Ascot Race Week of 16th-19th June was beset with wet weather, and on the last two days even the course was flooded. As the ground softened, the sloping field at Turner's Farm (formerly Englemere Farm, where *TV's* Ascot Dormy Shed had been), got saturated by the end of the card, causing a number of coaches to become bogged down. The Police called out the local breakdown firms, and even the Army, to extricate the muddy coaches – Gough's of Bracknell being allowed to use single trade plates per vehicle in order to maximise availability! As the *Thames Valley* buses still used The Grange Car Park they were not adversely affected.

On 16th June there was another notable retirement, when H.F. ('Frank') Robinson, manager of the Traffic Office departed after 40 years of service. Several weeks later Mr. A.H. Maddealoccus, a Director and Traffic Manager of the United Bus Service of Mauritious had visited to study the methods used for scheduling as part of his research tour.

Peter Wilks also took this rear view of Bristol LL6B Car 564 (FMO 946) on the windswept junction up at Childrey Ridgeway in February 1964, there being no houses around that point.

A leaflet had been produced in respect of Route 105 (Newbury – Wantage – Childrey Ridgeway) after its omission from the timetable booklet, but from 4th July the service was further cut to operate as one daily return journey, leaving Newbury at 1pm and departing Wantage at 3.40pm, giving just 1 hour 40 minutes in Wantage on Wednesdays (market day) and Saturdays only. The Wantage to Childrey Ridgeway section was cut altogether, though it had been useful for walkers in order to reach the terminal point where the ancient Ridge Way track crossed the B4001 road to Lambourn, as it was only some 3 miles east of White Horse Hill and other points of early historic interest.

By July a number of Bristol LS saloons had been re-seated to B41F and equipped for one-man-operation, these being Cars 684 (HBL 86) and 710/6/8/20 (HMO 856/62/4/6). Also later that month the author was on a family holiday when a visit to ECW at Lowestoft was made, and one of the RELL's was being bodied.

On 8th August *Wilts & Dorset* introduced a Day Out Ticket, which could also be used on *Thames Valley* journeys on joint Route 122 (Newbury – Kingsclere – Basingstoke). Over at Bracknell increasing congestion in the High Street was eased by routing some services along The Broadway for eastbound journeys, with Routes A (to London), 2 (to Ascot and Windsor), 53/53a (to Winkfield and Windsor), 55/55a (Warfield, Jealotts Hill and Hawthorn Hill) and 56 (to Bullbrook and Harmans Water) being provided with two stops, one outside Fine Fare supermarket, and the other at the eastern end opposite the large Reading Co-Op. All westbound buses still used the High Street, whilst Route 75 (to and from Guildford) used the stop in Station Road, these arrangements coming into effect from 8th July. Ten days later, over at Worcester, the parking accommodation for *South Midland* coaches was amended from the open Croft Road car park to the *Midland Red* garage at Padmore Street.

There was a further incident at Wokingham at 5.30pm on 21st August where a double-decker caused embarrassment to the Company. However, this time it was not a low-bridge collision, as the unrecorded bus on Route 3 failed on the level crossing by the station, causing a complete stoppage on both lines for nearly an hour, backing up both freight and passenger trains!

On 29th August a further alteration to the Watlington terminal point saw the buses on Route 39 from High Wycombe now laying over in the side road at Gorwell, which meant they no longer needed to go to the *City of Oxford* garage. From that same date Route 81 (High Wycombe – Desborough Avenue – Booker) used Frogmoor Bus Station rather than the Palace Cinema stop. It is also interesting to note that at that time the designated replacement buses for 'Wycombe buses away for engineering purposes were Bristol LL5G rebuild Cars 817/20 (FMO 21/4), along with Bristol KS6B Car 590 (FMO 972) and KSW6B-type Car 697 (HMO 843).

The outstanding coach-seated Bristol FLF finally arrived in August as Car D8 (BRX 141B), and was photographed by the author's school friend Andy Goddard at Victoria Coach Station on Route A shortly after entering service from Reading garage.

Two views of Bristol FLF Car D9 (BRX 142B) outside Bracknell garage in Market Street, the top one with it just in from a double-deck working on Route 53, and the rear shot shows the T-type indicators, along with some evident damage by a driver more used to 27ft 6ins models!

D8/9 (BRX 141/2B) arrived during August, the former having an ECW CH37/28F body, and the latter fitted with standard H38/32F bodywork, both of these powered by Gardner 6LW engines. D9 was licensed for 1st September and allocated to Bracknell garage.

Only one 1951 Bristol LWL6B saloon departed during August, that being Car 614 (GJB 252), and it was followed in September by another ex-*Hants & Dorset* Bristol K5G Car 474 (JT 9360) of 1938 vintage, but now carrying a 1949 ECW L55R body. Also withdrawn at the end of that month was another acquired K5G, being Car 460 (FPU 510), originally as *Eastern National*, passing into *United Counties*, where it received an 8ft-wide ECW L55R body in 1952. But even this was not the end of its career, as *TV* selected it to replace 1939 Bristol K5G No.43 (BRX 921) as the Route Servicing Vehicle. It then went into the body-shop for conversion, and re-appeared painted all-over green on 18th November, converted to open-top, along with other alterations for its new role as ED53. The old faithful former Car 405, which had been converted in October 1956 was then broken up.

ED53 (FPU 510) was seen in the Southern yard by Graham Low, with the old station canopy and the buildings of Walter Parsons Corn Stores, the Reading Mercury and the Prudential all visible behind.

The Annual Horticultural Show still featured on the *Thames Valley* social calendar, and on 22nd August part of the Central Works was cleared for the displays. One week later the first of the famous Steam Fairs took place at Shottesbrook Park, near White Waltham and organised by enthusiast John Carter. *TV* laid on extra buses on Routes 65/66 between Maidenhead and the site, though a few years later this popular event moved a couple of miles north to Knowl Hill, taking that title and still continuing as a large crowd-puller. The Newbury Agricultural Show had also switched to a new location off the Bath Road between Newbury and Thatcham, so on 19th September extra buses ran from The Wharf and Thatcham throughout the day.

At Bracknell an increased use of buses by scholars at Windsor County Grammar School for Boys resulted in an additional single-decker being allocated from 24th September, this being ex-*Crosville* Bristol L6A Car S305 (GFM 888). From the start of the Autumn term there were further shorts put on Route 17 from Tittle Row or Lee's Gardens to serve Altwood School and Maidenhead Girl's School, whilst a short-working on Route 65 brought pupils to Maidenhead schools from Waltham St. Lawrence and Woodlands Park.

The large yard once forming part of the Vincent's site off Station Hill in Reading had latterly been used as a public car park, but that closed on 26th September as a start to the redevelopment of that site, which would also include the new Bus Station for *Thames Valley*.

The Traffic Office noted on 1st October that *Aldershot & District* was now using its 68-seater Weymann-bodied Dennis 'Loline' MkIII Nos.484/5 (484/5 KOT) on the joint Route 12 (Reading – Aldershot), so in an effort not to be upstaged it allocated a coach-seated Bristol FLF from the 834-8 (UJB 200-4) batch to the duty in place of the coach-seated Bristol KSW6B's then in use on that service.

Route 12 now became the province of sliding-door double-deckers, with the Aldershot & District Dennis Loline No.485 (485 KOT) above, matched by Thames Valley coach-seated FLF6G Car 837 (UJB 203).

The long-awaited Bristol RELL6G saloons arrived in September, entering service as Cars S306/7 (CBL 355/6B) on 3rd October, followed by Car S308 (CBL 357B) on the 11th. All had ECW B54F bodies for crew operation and weighed in at 7tons 12cwt 2qtr, and had a step-less ramped floor rising towards the rear, along with dark green PVC seating. As 36-footers they were fitted with two emergency exits, one positioned in the last full-size bay rearwards on the offside, whilst they also echoed 1930's practice in having a centre door in the rear end. Due to their length and high seating capacity they were nick-named by the Engineering Office as 'trams', their overall appearance being heightened by the fitting of high peaked domes front and rear for destination boxes.

S308 (CBL 357B) is seen above at Gloucester Green on Route 5, whilst below we see S307 (CBL 356B) on a short-working to Borocourt Hospital on Route 7.

These buses were the first new saloons for the fleet since the Bristol MW6G's of 1960, and they were primarily intended for the joint Route 5 (Reading – Wallingford – Oxford), to work alongside *City of Oxford's* 36ft AEC 'Reliances'. However, that duty only required two buses, so the third was placed onto Route 7 (Reading – Peppard – Nettlebed), the choice being influenced by good turning facilities there.

Due to projected delays for Bristol-ECW vehicles, it had been decided that Lowestoft would take no further orders for coach bodies until the backlog had been addressed, leaving TV needing to consider alternative suppliers for the 1965 programme. The choice of the Bedford SB13 was not unexpected, but the body order went to Harringtons of Hove. A trio of coaches were ordered in good time to ensure no disappointments in delivery, but they actually arrived in October, so were stored until Spring 1965, when they would become C410-2 (EMO 551-3C) for the *South Midland* fleet. The latter had of course taken bodies from that source many years before, and indeed *Thames Valley* had 10 coaches by them on Leyland 'Tiger' TS8 chassis just before WW2, but the order was notable as being the first for a Tilling Group operator since *United Auto* took 6 Bristol L6B's for its Tyne-Tees-Thames route in 1950. The trio were of the 'Crusader' MkIV style and were 30ft 5ins long and 8ft 2.5ins wide. Fitted with 45-gallon fuel tanks and public-address systems they were intended for extended tours.

The style of *Thames Valley* ticket had remained the same for some time, but from 1st October 1964 it was altered to have the Company name at the top only, whilst at the bottom was stated 'Issued subject to the Company's published conditions', the rear now available for adverts instead of conditions. It is also interesting to note the anomaly whereby a passenger travelling to Reading Stations who boarded Routes 1b, 2, 3, 3a or 75 (i.e. from Wokingham Road) had a fare from Cemetery Junction of 7d, whereas those using Routes 1, 10, 28, 43, 43a and 44 (i.e. from Bath Road) paid only 6d. This originated in the protective fare for the *Reading Corporation Tramways* service terminating in Wokingham Road, which was extended to the Three Tuns when the trolleybuses took over. In October the Corporation agreed that this could now be standardised at 6d regardless of route for *TV* buses.

From 3rd October the staffing situation at Maidenhead had again improved, so all journeys cancelled from 30th May were fully reinstated. Over at Thatcham buses no longer used the High Street from that date, instead taking the new relief road to The Broadway. The now familiar 24-hour clock made its first appearance in the timetables for *South Midland* from 18th October, whilst from then 3 journeys on Route C (Oxford – Henley – London) proceeded non-stop via the M4 motorway, omitting Maidenhead and Slough.

As already noted, the license for Route 6b to Bramley Station was due to expire on 30th October, though the proposal drew complaints from Local Councils. From the following day it was arranged for 3 daily journeys on Route 6 (Reading – Riseley – Basingstoke) to turn off the main road at Three Mile Cross for Grazeley – Beech Hill – Stratfieldsaye – Stratfield Turgis, where they re-joined the route into Basingstoke, these journeys once again being designated as 6b, with an additional journey on Saturdays, but none on Sunday.

Bristol LWL6B Car 631 (GJB 269) is seen on the new version of Route 6b in the following year, having transferred from Bracknell to Reading in the changes to operations from 31st October.

From 31st October the Sunday service on Route 9a (Reading – Grazeley – Padworth – Tadley) was also withdrawn. Woodley was still expanding, so Route 10 projections to Tippings Lane were now curtailed at Woodley Roundabout, with 6 buses an hour in place of the previous 5 on services 43 and 44, including a new variant via Beechwood Avenue to serve housing on the Bulmershe Estate, shown with a 'b' suffix.

The new timetable book of 31st October, though not in the 24-hour format, was a bumper issue of 216 pages, and brought with it some major re-organisations on services worked by Reading and Bracknell garages.

Bristol LS6B Car 722 (HMO 868) now has a T-type front destination screen and is seen on new Route 46 to Shurlock Row.

Route 1b (Reading – Winnersh – Hurst – Shurlock Row), along with short-workings on Route 1 between Reading and Twyford, were revamped as new Routes 46 (Reading – Twyford – Ruscombe – Waltham St. Lawrence (The Bell) – Shurlock Row Church) and 47 (Reading – Winnersh – Hurst – Twyford Station), both operated by one-manners. At the same time the journeys on Route 1 operating via Sonning Village were now designated as 1a.

Also replaced was Route 3a (Reading – Wokingham – Barkham – Finchampstead), along with certain shorts on Route 2 from Bullbrook and Binfield to Bracknell or Reading to Wokingham, covered by new Route 49 (Reading or Bracknell – Wokingham – Barkham – Finchampstead – Yateley – Camberley). This also included schooldays journeys from Eversley (Mill End Turn) through California Crossroads to serve St. Crispins School in Wokingham. At times the route also continued southwards from Finchampstead onto Eversley – Yateley – Camberley. Worker's journeys from Binfield (Royal Standard) to the Castrol, Kent's and Fluidrive area off the Running Horse crossroads were also included, and these were further extended to start from the Shoulder of Mutton end of Terrace Road in Binfield from 15th May 1965. The Reading – Emmbrook – Wokingham section of the old 3a would also be covered by other changes as we will see soon.

Route 49 was run operated by Bracknell and Bristol LS6B Car 719 (HMO 865) is seen at that garage with blinds set for Finchampstead.

Routes 55/55a (Bracknell – Warfield – Jealotts Hill – Hawthorn Hill) were reduced, leaving only work-related peak journeys all week, plus some shopper's timings on Tuesdays, Thursdays and Saturdays.

The long-established Route 2 (Reading – Wokingham – Bracknell – Ascot – Windsor), and its subsidiary links through from Ascot to South Ascot, Sunninghill and Sunningdale, were all revised and re-numbered in the changes of 31st October. The basic 2 route operated with alternate journeys via Binfield, though nothing in the service number gave any indication of which route was taken, whilst the Ascot 'local services' had remained virtually unaltered since pre-1960 when operated from the Ascot garage. Other changes within the corridor from Reading – Wokingham also replaced elements of the old 3a, giving three variations between Reading and Windsor:

<u>Route 90</u> - Reading – Wokingham – Bracknell – North Ascot – Windsor;
<u>Route 91</u> – Reading – Emmbrook Village – W'ham – Bracknell – North Ascot – Windsor;
<u>Route 92</u> – Reading – Wokingham – Binfield Village – Bracknell – North Ascot – Windsor.

Bristol LL5G Car 796 (DMO 666) on new Route 47.

Bristol LS5G Car 706 (HMO 852) on new Route 57a.

These three variants turned left off the London Road at Fernbank Road to proceed through North Ascot without serving Heatherwood Hospital or Ascot High Street, but certain journeys did undertake the loop down that road and back, and they had an 'a' suffix, actually penetrating further onto Ascot (Station), Sunninghill (Schools) and Sunningdale (Station) at peak times. Whereas the old 3a service had entered Emmbrook past the Rifle Volunteer and under the railway bridge, the double-decked service 91 turned into Forest Road then via Commons Road, and gave a steady headway between Reading and Wokingham by these services and Route 3 journeys to Camberley.

The Ascot Local Routes 2a/2b/2c were recast to include short-workings on Route 53 from Bullbrook to Bracknell, and to operate from Bracknell to serve Heatherwood Hospital. These were as follows:

<u>Route 57</u> – Bracknell – Ascot (Horse & Groom) – Ascot (Station) – Sunninghill (Schools) – Sunningdale (The Rise) – Sunningdale (Station);
<u>Route 57a</u> – Bracknell – Ascot (Horse & Groom) – Sunninghill (Schools) – Sunningdale Park – S'dale (Schools) – S'dale (Larch Avenue) – S'dale (Station);
<u>Route 57c</u> – Bracknell – Ascot (Horse & Groom) – Cheapside (Post Office) – Cannon Corner;
<u>Route 58</u> – Bracknell – Bullbrook (Shops) – Long Hill - Ascot (Horse & Groom) – Ascot (Station) – S'hill (Schools) – Sunningdale (The Rise), S'dale (Schools) – Bedford Lane – Sunningdale (Station);
<u>Route 58a</u> – Bracknell – Bullbrook (Shops) – Long Hill – Ascot (Horse & Groom) – Ascot (Station) – Sunninghill (Schools) – Sunningdale (Schools) – Sunningdale (Larch Avenue) – Sunningdale (Station);
<u>Route 59</u> – North Ascot (Brookside PO) – Fernbank Corner – Ascot (H&G) – S'hill (Schools) – S'dale (The Rise) – Sunningdale (Station);
<u>Route 59a</u> – North Ascot (Brookside PO) – Fernbank Corner – Ascot (H&G) – Ascot (Station) – S'hill (Schools) – S'dale Park – S'dale (Schools) – S'dale (Larch Avenue) – Sunningdale (Station).

All of these services were one-man-operated, and complex composite timetables of these with the 90-group services were provided, along with exchange tickets for those wishing to alight at Fernbank Corner for connections to Ascot and beyond.

Ex-United Counties K5G Car 463 (FPU 517) is seen at Bracknell garage in 1964 set up for Route 90.

In respect of the Bracknell Local Services, Routes 52 and 56 were joined together from 31st October to form a circular route, with the new 52 running Broadway - London Rd. – Broad Ln. – Ralphs Ride – Harmans Water Rd. – South Hill Rd. – Reeds Hill – Crowthorne Road – Rectory Ln. – Bagshot Road – Station Rd. – High Street – Wokingham Rd. (or via Western Rd. on 'a' journeys) – Moordale Avenue – Binfield Rd. – Shepherds Ln. – Horsneille Ln. – Bull Lane – By-pass – Broadway, whilst Route 56 ran the same in reverse. It was still possible then to exit Bull Lane and cross the By-pass, though this frequent accident black-spot was later blocked off.

Routes 52/56 were now double-decked, and Bristol KSW6B Car 642 (GJB 280) is seen by the Prince of Wales pub on a snowbound Horsneille Lane. Note the faded '2', the bus having worked the route since new!

As a result of these changes the Bracknell allocation rose by 4 buses, meaning that the same number was now parked outside in the yard at night. Drafted in where Bristol KSW6B Cars 659 (HBL 61) and 732 (JRX 807) from Maidenhead, along with similar Car 646 (GJB 284) from Reading, whilst the extra saloons were Bristol LS5G Car 708 (HMO 854) and LS6B-type Car 716 (HMO 862). Bracknell lost both its Bristol LWL6B Cars 624/31 (GJB 262/9) to Wycombe and Reading, leaving that garage with 36 buses as follows – Bristol K5G Cars 462-4 (FPU 515, 517, 511), Bristol KSW6B Cars 640-6 (GJB 278-84), 701-3 (HMO 847-9) and 732/44-7 (JRX 807/19-22), Bristol LD5G Cars 766/7 (MBL 847/8), Bristol LDL 6G Car 779 (NBL 736), Bristol FLF6G Cars 843/7 (WJB 227/31) and D9 (BRX 142B), Bristol L6A Car S305 (GFM 888), Bristol LS5G Cars 706/8/9 (HMO 852/4/5) and Bristol LS6B Cars 711-3, 716/8/9 and 721/4 (HMO 857-9/62/4/5/7/70).

Some fortnight after these changes old Ascot hand and Bracknell Inspector H.E. ('Bert') Woods retired, and over at Maidenhead the following month saw H.M. Owens and J. McMahon promoted to Inspectors.

D12 (CMO 835B) at the Henley Market Place stop.

Delays had affected further double-deckers until 4 arrived for licensing from 1st November as Cars D10-3 (CMO 833-6B), all Bristol FLF6G's with green PVC-seated ECW H38/32F bodies. D10/1 went over to Maidenhead, D12 to Wycombe Marsh and D13 to Reading. Disposed of during November were Bristol L6A Cars S301/3 (GFM 881/4), though they remained in the area as staff buses for builders Collier & Catley in full red and cream livery. Indeed, this small batch had been moved about between garages so much that the casual observer would have thought there must be more of them! Even Maidenhead, which officially never had any, did use Car S301 on Route 16, though probably as a short-term engineering loan. However, the star disposal that month was former *Hants & Dorset* 1942 Bristol K5G Car 475 (FLJ 978) with its much-rebuilt Brush 6-bay body which only seated 54, having only a double seat at the rear of the top deck.

D13 (CMO 836B) working the Woodley service 44b.

The Crowthorne Road was closed to traffic in Bracknell for some 6 months as new roads were linked to it, so Routes 53/53a had to be diverted via South Hill Road – Bagshot Road – Downshire Way, and at the latter junction with Old Bracknell Lane a stop was erected to serve that side of Easthampstead. In Reading a large number of red (compulsory) stop flags were changed for black (request) flags in an effort to aid traffic flows on routes through the town.

A local football derby between Reading and Aldershot saw extra buses to the latter town on 5th December, as well as advertised excursion coaches. Over at Newbury a variant of Route 128 (Shaw – Newbury P.O. – Valley Road Estate) was introduced from 21st December, operating as Valley Road Estate (Garford Crescent) – Bartlemy Close for the benefit of school – children, in addition to the existing shorts between Bartlemy Close and Broadway, all of which were shown as 128a. The subject of bus stations occupied a number of talks, with *London Transport* seeking greater use of Frogmoor, and the Aylesbury Town Plan had a new facility to replace Kingsbury Square.

4 coaches were hired to Oxford P.O. for Christmas, Bristol LS Cars 81/2 (SFC 567/8) and 692/3 (HMO 838/9), the latter part-converted for its new role as a service bus, as seen in this photo by Martin Shaw!

Another varied selection of photos by Philip Wallis, with coach-seated Bristol KSW6B Car 743 (JRX 818) on Route 122 from Newbury to Basingstoke on a short-working at Kingsclere on 1st March 1964. This bus was one of a pair based at Newbury to be found on the longer services, having been relegated from the London route B for which it had originally been ordered. Also note the style of road signs, along with the three wheeler invalid car parked in the far left background.

The much-reduced Route 105 saw the Thames Valley bus laying over at Wantage for 100 minutes on every Wednesday and Saturday, so arrangement was made for it to proceed to the Wantage garage of City of Oxford in Grove Street. Bristol MW6G Car 855 (VJB 946) is seen on the duty at that location, with City of Oxford's AEC saloon 743 (743 HFC) on its Route 25 (Uffington – Wantage – Didcot), in the maroon, red and duck egg blue livery unique to them.

Christmas Day 1964, and all the Thames Valley fleet is having a rest. Note how crowded the yard on the Lower Thorn Street side was by then, though more room would be duly made by further demolitions in Weldale Street. 'Lodekkas' predominate in this scene, with (left to right) LD6G Car 762 (MBL 843), FLF 6G Car 849 (WJB 233) and FLF6G Car 836 (UJB 202), the latter with sliding door and coach seating for London Routes A and B, plus a few flakes of seasonal snow.

72

1965

Apart from some light snow over the Christmas period, the Winter of 1964/5 was without disruption to services caused by adverse weather. After a while the use of the on-road *London Transport* stop on the A30, opposite Halfpenny's Garage at Sunningdale, was found to impede traffic flow, so the layover for Route 57 (Bracknell – Ascot – Sunningdale) was moved a short distance to a quieter spot in Broomhall Lane. It is also interesting to note that there were a number of places in that area where both *LT* and *TV* bus stops existed within sight of each other for historical reasons, though from 22nd January the two concerns agreed to merge into one stop that outside the Wells Hotel, just east of Ascot High Street.

The second new bus of the year was Bristol FLF6G Car D15 (DJB 530C), which is seen on Station Hill in Reading on Route 28 to High Wycombe.

However, of more lasting concern was the news that a recent survey of Marlow's historic suspension bridge, designed by William Tierney Clark and completed in 1832, would be closed for up to 2 years for rebuilding. As a result of this the arrangements whereby Marlow passengers were dropped at the junction of Bisham Road and Quarry Wood Road were reconsidered, and a bus layover point was constructed in Quarry Wood Road. The passengers still alighted in Bisham Road and walked over the bridge to the waiting shuttle bus, the revised layover being in use from 5th January.

Over at Wokingham the Berkshire CC Education Department asked *TV* to operate a new contract route known as SS1 from 7th January, to cater for primary school children travelling from the new housing in the California Crossroads area of Finchampstead to the schools at St. Paul's (Shute End), Palmer (Rectory Road), Emmbrook (Matthews Green), Keep Hatch (Norreys Avenue) and Westcott Road, this bus starting from Kingsmere Crossroads. Similarly, extra housing in the Crowthorne, Sandhurst and College Town areas saw Route 53 now very busy at school times with pupils attending Bracknell's Ranelagh School, so from 18th January double-deck shorts were put on between Camberley and Bracknell.

One of the usual performers on the reduced Route 80 was Bristol LL5G Car 819 (FMO 23).

In the meantime some services in the High Wycombe area were revised, with Routes 20/20a (Aylesbury – High Wycombe – Maidenhead – Windsor), 32 (Wycombe – Bledlow Ridge – Chinnor) and 34 (High Wycombe – North Dean – Speen) amended to save 3,260 p.a. from 16th January. At the same time the 22-mile long Route 80 (High Wycombe – Lacey Green – Princes Risborough – Aylesbury) was revised, losing 60% of its weekday journeys and all Sunday workings, saving 34,392 miles p.a.

Further south at Maidenhead, there was another staff shortage, which resulted in 8 duty lines being deleted from the rota and 4 double-deckers de-licensed from 30th January. As an economy of mileage, the shorts to Cox Green from Maidenhead were replaced by buses being diverted on Routes 65/66 through Wessex Way and Highfield Lane from 30th January. Another route extension saw Service 4a (Reading – Arborfield – Barkham – Wokingham) extended onwards from the southern edge of Norreys Avenue through to Ashridge Road and Warren House Road junction from that date.

Now nearing the end of its service with Thames Valley, former Bristol OC K6B-type Car 459 (KHU 622) is seen at Maidenhead Bus Station on the 18a.

73

Baughurst-based Car D17 is seen with Jack Lambden at the wheel on Route 9b to Mortimer Station. The purpose of the strange adverts will be revealed soon.

Unfortunately the popular Newbury Depot Inspector Les Mercer died suddenly aged 60 on the last day of January. His place was taken by Bill Phillips from 20th March, and N.W. Fox took his role as Inspector from 17th April.

On the vehicle front a further pair of Bristol FLF6G buses with ECW H38/32F bodies were licensed in January as Cars D14/5 (DJB 529/30C), and these were followed by similar Cars D16/7 (DRX 120/1C) in February and D18 (DRX 122C) in March. D17 was sent to the Baughurst outstation in the care of long-serving Driver Walter ('Jack') Lambden, or 'Tadley Jack' as most people still knew him as, after his service at that Dormy Shed from 1924-1960. Cars D14/5 both went to Wycombe Marsh, whilst D16 was at Maidenhead and D18 went to Newbury.

D18 (DRX 122C) was only the second 70-seater at the Newbury garage, and is seen at The Wharf on the 31-mile run through to Maidenhead. It is parked by the traditional stopping place for Thames Valley buses, and its driver heads to the staff canteen.

January saw the departure of Bristol K5G Car 462 (FPU 515), a former *United Counties* 1937 chassis with an 8ft-wide ECW L55R body of 1952, the demise of which was hastened by a skidding accident on 21st January. Other secondhand buses sold in February were Bristol K6A Cars 457/9 (KHU 605/22), both formerly *Bristol OC*, leaving only K6B Car 436 (KHU 624) from that source still active. In fact the latter was sent to Bracknell in place of 462 for a few months before its place was taken by another K6B Car 471 (DMO 675). Native Bristol K6A Car 446 (DBL 154) was also withdrawn and subsequently sold following an altercation with the jib of a mobile crane in the Newbury area.

The sorry state of the rear upper deck on Car 446 (DBL 154) after the accident. However, despite this it was sold for further service, repaired by the new owners, and survives to this day in preservation.

Single-deck departures for February were ex-*Crosville* Bristol L6A Car S304 (GFM 887), along with a pair of Bristol LWL6B's, Cars 617/8 (GJB 255/6).

Another change to the garaging arrangements for the London-based *South Midland* coaches was required due to overcrowding at Samuelson's Garage, so from 12th February they transferred to the Walworth Garage of *London Transport* in Camberwell New Road.

Sharp-eyed viewers of 1960's films such as the 'Carry On' series will often note *Thames Valley* buses in the background, as much filming was done in the area. In Windsor the upper floor of Barclay's Bank on the corner of Peascod Street and Thames Street was used, whilst at Maidenhead the Civic Offices in St. Ives Road became the 'District Hospital'. Some other Bray and Pinewood Films also show glimpses of *TV* buses, whilst a number of Norman Wisdom films used the old back streets of Windsor as London street-scenes, and we Windsor Boy's soon got to hear of such events. In later years the author came across one of the Bristol RESL6G's parked at Holyport, part of filming with Jenny Agutter, lucky Driver Alf Waterman being hired out just prior to his retirement!

As already noted, further conversions of Bristol LS6B coaches for bus work were in hand over the Winter months, with Cars 692/3 (HMO 838/9) tucked away at The Colonnade. However, the progress of these subsequent conversions often seemed to be interrupted by more urgent work, whilst the quality also varied. The first of the new examples was Car S313 (HMO 839), which emerged in February still fitted with 39 coach seats and luggage racks, sporting a new dual-purpose livery, along with a jack-knife door and bus indicators.

Andy Goddard caught S313 (HMO 839) on the West Ilsley 102, this bus being allocated to Reading garage.

Another run of industrial action occurred during February, due to the slowness of the Company over a wage demand put forward by the Transport & General Worker's Union, with Bracknell and Maidenhead out all day on 13th February, followed by other one-day stoppages at Reading, Bracknell, Maidenhead and High Wycombe on 20th, 27th February and 6th March, though both Newbury and Oxford were unaffected.

The Parcels Service was still being used, though to a lesser extent, and from 1st March the charges rose to 1 shilling and 6 pence for up to 7lbs, 2s for up to 14lbs, and 3s for the maximum 28lbs. The Company itself had a good system of pouches between Head Office and the garages etc., whilst smaller spare parts for garages were also sent by bus if a van run was not soon enough. Indeed, the enamelled Parcel Agent signs could still be seen widely, the author particularly recalling those on the walls of Mr. I. Zaradi's tobacco shop in Ascot High Street and Mrs. Christmas, the hairdresser in North Street, Winkfield. At Marlow the former *Marlow & District* booking office at Market Square was still the local parcel agency, though now rented out as a shop. The April 1965 timetable book lists 177 such agents throughout the Company's area.

Work started on re-configuring the Maidenhead Bus Station with saw-tooth stands on the western side and built into the former flower beds, so from 1st March buses used temporary stands in York Road, with spare buses parked over in the Coach Station.

Damaged Car 622 (GJB 260) in Weldale Street yard.

Another bad collision occurred on 8th March, when Bristol LWL6B Car 622 (GJB 260) was hit by a lorry at Park Lane in Lane End whilst working Route 36 to Cadmore End. This bus did not return to service, the body being dismantled for spares, whilst the chassis was subsequently seen in Weldale Street yard on 3rd June. Disposals of a more routine nature during March saw the departure of a further ex-*Crosville* Bristol L6A Car S302 (GFM 882), along with Bristol K6B-type Car 468 (DMO 672).

In the meantime there had been criticism regarding the arrangements for passengers needing to transfer from Reading-bound 90/91/92 services for onward travel to Ascot High Street and points beyond. Timetables were therefore revised from 7th March to improve matters, whilst the opportunity was also provided to run more journeys past the popular Marie Louise Social Club in South Ascot. In Bracknell the Traffic Manager meet with the Development Corporation to discuss future bus services in line with further housing expansion.

Another collision during February resulted in Car 820 (FMO 24) receiving an LD-type radiator grille when the front end was repaired. It is seen at Reading Stations on Woodley route 10.

The next of the coach-to-bus conversions was S312 (HMO 838), which is seen at Wokingham Town Hall stand for the Route 49 on a through journey to Camberley, a distance of just over 12 miles away.

On 19th March former coach 692 (HMO 838) turned out as saloon S312, though this time in all-over red livery and with bus seating. The latter had somewhat pock-marked metalwork, having come from *Smith's Luxury Coaches* out of one of their ex-*City of Oxford* AEC 'Regents'! So this introduced further variety within these conversions, and it was allocated to Bracknell in place of former *Crosville* Bristol L6A Car S305 (GFM 888), that garage now having all LS-type saloons operating as one-manners.

Further rebuilding of former London service coach-seated double-deckers continued, with 1951 Bristol KSW6B Car 638 (GJB 276) having its luggage racks removed and seats cut down to bus-style during February, followed by identical Car 639 (GJB 277) in March.

Car 639 is seen after being rebuilt, now without the upper deck beading and with a T-type destination box at the front. However, this photo taken several years later also shows the slippage in standards sometimes evident, with two incomplete adverts on the nearside.

Route 65 (Slough – Maidenhead – The Walthams – Binfield - Wokingham) was diverted from 20th March to run through the Ashridge and Norreys Estates on the approach to Wokingham town centre, also linking them to the railway station. At Windsor, traffic flows now used the island setting of the *London Transport* garage in St. Leonards Road as a roundabout, with *TV* Routes 53/53a from Camberley, the 90-group services from Reading, along with Local Services 51/51a/51b all affected from 22nd March.

During March the Company became aware that two local operators were running unauthorised services, these being *Pangbourne Coaches* between Reading and Pangbourne on behalf of Concert Entertainments, and at Bracknell once again was *Cooper Car Hire,* on an unlicensed service from Western Road to the town. Both were reported to the Traffic Commissioners, who took action and had them fined under the Road Traffic Act 1930.

A surprising find at Victoria Coach Station was 1950 Bristol LL6B Car 569 (FMO 951), which had worked in from High Wycombe in place of a South Midland coach taken into Desborough Road with a problem!

For many years, in fact originating from 1916, buses had served the Arborfield Camp, originally a Cavalry Remount Depot, but latterly the Army Apprentices School of the Royal Electrical & Mechanical Engineers. On late night services on Fridays and Saturdays up to 4 double-deck reliefs could be required, the Duty Inspector having discretion to turn out incoming service buses onto that route as required. However, from April the Camp Authorities agreed to operate a pre-booking system in order that only those buses required were made available.

During the early months of the year the 1952 batch of Bristol LS6G coaches 671-6 (HBL 73-8) had their front windscreens replaced by fixed units, whilst Car 672 was given *South Midland* fleetnames from April and placed on contract duties. In its place at Reading former *South Midland* Bedford SB8 coach 863 (517 ABL) got *Thames Valley* fleetnames in exchange, and the 'extended tours' legend on the rear waistrail panel was over-painted in maroon, its duties now being for private hire and excursions.

The Easter weekend over 16th-18th April was rather cold with sleet and snow showers, and did not tempt many passengers out, whilst at Oxford there was a one-day strike on 27th April regarding the pay claim. In respect of tours for *South Midland* for the season, the full listing, duration and costs was as follows:

Tour Title	Duration	£	s.	d.
Donegal & Ulster Coast	10 days	38	15	0
Southern Ireland	10 days	42	00	0
Scotland (on tour)	12 days	47	15	0
Scotland (from hotel base)	9 days	35	00	0
English Lakes	8 days	32	00	0
Welsh Coast	8 days	29	10	0
North Wales	8 days	29	15	0
Mid Wales	8 days	23	15	0
West Wales (a new tour)	5 days	20	15	0
North Devon	8 days	27	15	0
South Devon	8 days	24	15	0
Cornwall	8 days	30	10	0

1963 Bedford SB8 Cars C401/2 (831/2 CRX) were chosen for residency in Ireland that year, whilst the trio of Bedford SB13's with C37F Harrington 'Crusader' MkIV bodies were taken out of store during April and registered as Cars C410-2 (EMO 551-3C). They were primarily intended for touring work though, like all members of that fleet, would also see some use on express services at other times.

The Harrington-bodied Bedfords were quite unlike anything else in the South Midland fleet. Car C410 (EMO 551C) is seen above at Gloucester Green later in the year when helping out on express reliefs, whilst below we see Car C412 (EMO 553C) showing the sliding door fitted to this body type.

Highbridge Duple-bodied Guy 'Arab' MkIII 6LW Car H15 (HOT 393) is seen at The Wharf in its final form.

Several unusual workings had led to sightings of the former *Newbury & District* 1950 Guy 'Arab' buses at Reading during the early months of 1965, so it was pleasing to note that the purpose in running them over via Route 5b from Newbury was for a thorough overhaul. Indeed, their future was further assured by the acquisition of the chassis remains of *United Welsh* Guy 'Arab' No.676 (DWN 378) for spare parts. Also put through the shops in the early part of the year was the batch of Bristol SC4LK Cars 774-7 (NBL 731-4), thereby dispelling rumours that the closure of Marlow bridge had made these lightweight buses superfluous.

Flashing trafficators continued to appear on buses, including those as old as the early K-types, whilst a new type of temporary bus stop was now introduced, using an old brake-drum as a sturdy base, fitted with a handle for ease of movement. By May having two bus stops in The Broadway at Bracknell was found to be rather time-consuming, so the one opposite the Co-op was discontinued from 13th of that month. Of course, at that time the road had two-way traffic and parking in long lay-bys on both sides, a recipe for accidents!

Peter Wilks made a further move within the Company when, following the resignation of L. Holdsworth as Assistant Traffic Superintendent at High Wycombe, he took his place from 17th May, at the sum of £850 p.a. The office was at the rear of 37 Frogmoor, part of the site originating from the days of the *Penn Bus Company*, and the Traffic Superintendent was then Gilbert E. ('Joe') Morris. The latter had worked in the Accounts Office at Lower Thorn Street, but had been off sick for some time, his return to work coinciding with the retirement of Ernest Jefferies as TS for the 'Wycombe area. Although he was a good organiser, the often protracted dealings with the Union Reps left him somewhat in despair, as they certainly knew their rights and, at times, led the local management a fair old song-and-dance over relatively trivial issues.

Joe had not driven before then, but was allocated an Austin A40 'Farina' car (WMO 52), and it is recalled that he drove it rather erratically, even once turning it over. Another local problem was keeping up staffing levels, and Peter went on a recruiting trip to Inverness and Aberdeen with Ken Rogerson (TS at Maidenhead) without much success. He also noted that when there were disputes halting services, it was the Depot Inspectors who felt real frustration, as they knew the job inside out, and at that time they were Chief Inspector Percy Hounslow, with DI's George Grant, Ron Nash and Harry Hope at the Marsh, and Travers looking after Desborough Road. Peter also had to keep the Frogmoor Canteen open weekdays 6.30am to 11pm (less on a Sunday), not an easy task at 3s 3d per hour in a town with good employment prospects!

A good example of how effective the Union Shop Stewards were is the allowance for travel granted to High Wycombe crews, which originated with the 1946 opening of Desborough Road Garage. The Union argued that ever since the Wycombe Marsh Garage had opened in 1924, crews had based their accommodation on that east-of-town location. With the opening of Desborough Road the original plan was to rota crews between the garages, though this was duly changed to fixed locations. In the meantime the Union claimed, and were successful, in gaining a 20-minute daily allowance for travel time, based on the relocation of their workplace by just 2.2 miles!

The other odd vehicle in the fleet at that time also had its origins in the Red & White era, though delivered to Thames Valley, who had it bodied by ECW as shown. However, despite looking like a Bristol LS, it was in fact an AEC 'Regal' MkIV! Car 85 (SFC 571) could usually be found on the London expresses and, despite being a one-off, led a full career with South Midland, and it is seen outside the café at Gloucester Green.

The usual working pattern at the time was for a 6-day rota of between 6hrs 20mins for a straight shift or 7hrs 20mins for a spread-over. The whole working day was covered by a combination of duties known as 'earlies, middles, early-finish lates and lates', and there was a high reliance on overtime working by both the crews (in respect of earnings) and the Company (in order to fully cover the duty rota). Holiday leave was also allocated by the Company, with 'swops' possible.

About this time the Marsh Garage suffered from a flash flood, no doubt due to recent development of the old allotment plots on the other side of Micklefield Road. Water poured down the slope and into the garage, before exiting via the front doors onto the A40. This photo shows staff reaching for their wellies!

Another sign of those times was discussions over the used of 'coloured' staff, as the Shop Stewards at High Wycombe had been asked to consider letting some of the conductors train for driving duties. Apparently, there was already an agreement limiting the number of 'coloureds' employed to 19, and it was agreed on 18th May that some could train as drivers, but 'only for limited duties'. Over at Maidenhead, and in a move to address the chronic staffing position there, it was also agreed that garage staff holding PSV licenses could undertake driving duties on rest days. Indeed, the Maidenhead advertiser carried a piece stating that out of 500 journeys in a 3-day period, *Thames Valley* had failed to operate 194 of those due to crew shortages.

By June the pair of coach-seated Bristol MW6G Cars 852/3 (VJB 943/4) had been repainted in the dual-purpose livery, and Car 853 is seen working the 6a to Odiham from Reading's Station Square.

David Nicholls caught Bristol K6B Car 526 (FBL 28) when it was allocated to Bracknell, now rebuilt with a T front box. It's has those odd adverts again – can you tell what it is yet (with apologies to Rolf Harris)?

A general fares increase came into effect from Whit Sunday 5th June, the 12th in only 10 years, but at least the weekend was warm and sunny, tempting many out to local beauty spots by bus. However, from that date the Sunday runs on Route 75 (Reading – Bracknell – Bagshot – Guildford) were discontinued, though lack of patronage played a large part in that decision. On Route B (Reading – Maidenhead – Slough – London), a change in its status to a Stage Carriage Service, attracted fuel relief with effect from 10th June.

During May two further Bristol K-types departed, as 1946 K6A Car 448 (DBL 156), along with ex- *United Counties* 1937 K5G Car 464 (FPU 511), though now carrying a 1951 ECW L55R body, the latter's place at Bracknell being taken by K6B-type Car 526.

Incoming buses in June were a further trio of Bristol FLF6G's with Eastern Coach Works H38/32F bodies, as Cars D19-21 (FBL 483-5C), the first being sent to Bracknell and the other pair allocated to Maidenhead. At that point in time the official allocation of 70-seat buses was Bracknell 5 (including the LDL Car 779), Maidenhead 14, Newbury 2, Reading 12 and High Wycombe 11. On 24th June another foreign visitor was touring THC operators, when Miss Kygo came to Lower Thorn Street from Yugoslavia.

About this time some rather curious adverts started to appear on double-deckers throughout the *TV* area, with swirling yellow patterns on a black background. As an advertising campaign it was certainly successful in making people wonder what it was all about, as the patterns gradually morphed to form the word 'Post'. Words such as 'colour' or 'coming soon' were duly added, this heralding the publication of the Evening Post, a new daily paper for the Thames valley region, and effective replacement for the defunct Reading Standard. It used the latest web-offset printing process which included the use of colour throughout, and the first edition appeared on 14th September 1965.

Another facet of operation at that time was the need to re-time many long-established journeys due to traffic congestion and to ensure they reached places of work and schools at the appropriate times.

Bristol FLF6G Car D19 (FBL 483C) is seen above outside the Regal Cinema in Bracknell High Street on the 52a Local Service, whilst similar Car D20 (FBL 484C) has just come into Maidenhead Bus Station on Route 24a from Cookham Rise (Westwood Green). To its right an Inspector emerges from the his office.

The author witnessed an amusing event on 11th June, as Bristol K6B Car 471 (DMO 675) appeared round the top of Bracknell High Street, headlamps on full and towing Bristol LS6B Car 714 (HMO 860), which had evidently failed on a 53a journey from Windsor!

From 16th June yet another school journey was required to take Bracknell girls to a neighbouring town, with a special from Long Hill Road in Chavey Down through Bracknell and Binfield to Wokingham (St. Paul's Church) for the Holt School. Westwards over at Newbury, there was also a considerable daily movement of schoolchildren, as the main girl's school was located just north of the town at Shaw, whilst many boys attended Park House School at the other end of town. In addition there was the County High School for Girls and St. Bartholomew's Grammar School for Boys, these situated on the Andover and Enborne Roads and drawing from a wide area including parts of north Hampshire. There was also St. Gabriel's Convent School as favoured by Catholics, whilst other parents might opt for the Kennet School at Thatcham, all adding to the daily pattern of travel.

At Maidenhead it was necessary to cut 8 duty lines from the rota from 3rd July, and 6 double-deckers were de-licensed, these being Bristol K6A Car 441 (CRX 550), K6B Cars 500/2/3/14 (EJB 222/4/5/36), along with KS6B-type Car 598 (FMO 980).

Also not needed at Maidenhead at that time was KS-type Car 587 (FMO 969), which was transferred for a couple of months to Bracknell, and it had worked the morning Camberley – Bracknell short on Route 53 to cater for Ranelagh School pupils.

A new timetable book was issued from Saturday 3rd July, which included some re-arrangements on Routes 63 (Maidenhead – Cliveden – Dropmore – Burnham – Slough) and 68 (M'head – Cliveden – Hitcham Park – Slough) in order to reflect reduced duty lines worked by the Maidenhead Garage.

There were counter-campaigns by other newspapers due to the new Evening Post, as seen on Bristol K6B Car 532 (FMO 7), still in mostly original condition when caught by Philip Wallis at Maidenhead.

The new timetable also heralded a number of other more significant changes, as well as being the first in the now familiar 24-hour format. The Sunday service on Route 19 (Reading Stations – Long Lane) had been only sparsely used and was discontinued, as were the Sunday journeys on Windsor Local Service 51, which was Maidenhead's share of those routes on that day. Other services had also been earmarked for total withdrawal on selected dates, the final journeys being:

7th July - Route 105 (Newbury – Wantage);
8th July - Route 101a (Newbury – Peasemore):
8th July - Route 114a (Newbury – West Woodhay);
8th July - Route 120 (Newbury – Aldworth);
9th July - Route 46 (Reading – Shurlock Row);
9th July - Route 54 (Wokingham – Gardeners Green – Crowthorne - Bracknell).

Notes – Route 105 operated on Wednesdays and Saturdays only, Routes 101a, 114a and 120a operated on Thursdays and Saturdays only, whilst Routes 46 and 54 ran on Mondays to Saturdays.

Graham Low saw Bristol LS Car 709 (HMO 855) on Route 54 on 9th July, though the final journey was worked by similar Car 718 (HMO 864).

80

The final Route 46 journey was worked by Bristol MW6G Car 865 (VJB 947), usually a Newbury bus, but at Reading temporarily. All of the above deletions saved a grand total of 61,282 miles p.a.

July saw 1953 Bristol LS6B coach 688 (HMO 834) re-emerge as S314, once again rebuilt only with a jack-knife door and bus indicator, though retaining 39 coach seats. It was also in the dual-purpose livery and was allocated to Reading. Outgoing buses that month were further K-types, as K6A Car 447 (DBL 155) and K6B Cars 496/8 (EJB 218/20). Also withdrawn was Bristol LWL6B Car 616 (GJB 254), though this was reserved for a non-PSV role.

As reconstruction of Maidenhead Bus Station entered its next phase, Bristol LWL Car 616 (GJB 254) was parked in the 'out' lane of the Coach Station for use as an Inspector's Office. Note the phone bell mid-way on the offside, the bus being wired to the nearby pole.

Another curious incident spotted at Bracknell on 5th July was the unscheduled appearance of coach-seated Bristol FLF-type Car D4 (ABL 116B), which came into town on the 18.00 departure from Victoria on Route A, drove over the pit with passengers still seated, then left again after about 10 minutes! Of course there were times when Bracknell-based buses were sent out to cover for failed London service buses, whilst on Sunday nights the Duty Inspector might have to add a further relief to the 19.04 from The Broadway to Victoria. Another unexpected event was the arrival of Maidenhead Car 777 (NBL 734), one of the Bristol SC's, deputising for a failed *South Midland* coach through to Victoria on 24th July.

At Reading Inspector R.E. Lansdowne retired on 23rd July, and his place was taken by Driver Bayton from the following month. Also concerning staff, the canteen at Wycombe Marsh was closed on 12th August, the canteen at Frogmoor now meeting most needs. Over at Newbury there was some excitement on 30th July, when it was discovered that a single-deck bus parked on the side at The Wharf had disappeared! This was about 10.30pm, and shortly after that a lorry driver reported to the Police a near collision with it south of Newbury. The bus was later found in a ditch at Kingsclere, and a man was imprisoned for a year and banned from driving for 3 years. This was one of a number of incidents where someone took a bus home (literally) after probably drinking too much, and where cuts in services may have even been a factor?

The rest of the 1951 coach-seated Bristol KS6B-types, Cars 596/8-600 (FMO 978/80-82) were next to be rebuilt, losing their luggage racks and having seats cut down to bus type. Each was done by the end of August, though exact dates are not known for all.

Rebuilt KS6B Car 596 (FMO 978) is seen above at Maidenhead after losing its upper deck beading and receiving a T-type destination screen, whilst Car 599 (FMO 981) is seen below after allocation to Bracknell out of shops in August in exchange for Car 587. Note the lower deck emergency door fitted to these, opening from the platform out of the rear nearside.

With the increasing spread of the M4 motorway, *TV* was asked to a meeting in late July to consider how it could assist *Bristol Greyhound,* as the latter proposed running some journeys non-stop between Reading and London. It was agreed that the coaches would also call at Reading Stations Square, where passengers for any intermediate points through Maidenhead, Slough and the Great West Road could transfer to buses on Route B (Reading – Maidenhead – Slough – London), and these facilities were introduced from 17th October. Also, due to the lack of excursions from Maidenhead, adverts suggested using Route B for day outings.

Early August had also seen a meeting with *Reading CT* over the latter's proposal to introduce a concessionary fares scheme for OAP's. Also on 22nd of that month The Company had played host to the Brighton Bus Enthusiast's Club, who visited Reading and Newbury Garages. On that same day the Sunday operations on Route 102 (Reading – East Ilsley – West Ilsley) ceased, saving 7858 miles p.a.

D22 (FJB 738C) takes shape at Lowestoft, as the ECW electricians wire up its body. The author was on another family holiday when this opportunity arose.

During August a further pair of Bristol FLF6G's with ECW H38/32F bodies were received as Cars D22/3 (FJB 738/9C), and both were sent to Maidenhead. Due to their arrival and the loss of more Black & Decker journeys to private contracts, the double-deckers at that garage were reduced by 3, leading to the sales of 1948/9 Bristol K6B Cars 493-5 and 503 (EJB 215-7/25) that month. Also departing from that allocation was former *United Counties* 1937 Bristol K5G Car 461 (FPU 509), now carrying a 1952 ECW L55R body, which was sold. That left only similar Car 463 (FPU 517) still active at Bracknell, the latter being by far the best of the batch.

Another significant change occurred at Reading from 4th September, with the closure of the separate station originally for the *Southern Railway* trains.

Bristol K5G Car 461 (FPU 509) spent its TV career at Maidenhead Garage, and is seen approaching town along Braywick Road on a relief 20a from Windsor.

The use of Dormy Sheds and other Outstations may have declined compared with the peak activity of the 1930's, but in such a wide operating area they still had an important role. A survey of them in August showed the following allocations:

Baughurst (Wilts & Dorset) – Bristol FLF Car D17;
Fingest Dormy Shed – 2 Bristol LWL6B in rotation;
Kingsclere Outstation – Bristol KSW6B Car 741;
Lambourn Outstation – Guy 'Arab' Cars 170/1 and Bristol LL6B Cars 564/6;
Princes Risborough Dormy Shed – 2 FLF on rotation;
Stokenchurch Dormy Shed – 2 KSW6B on rotation;
Victoria (Samuelsons) – 2 Bristol FLF on rotation;
Walworth (LT Garage) – 2 *South Midland* coaches;
Worcester (Midland Red) – 2 *South Midland* coaches.

Bristol FLF6G Car D23 (FJB 739C) is seen in Mackenzie Street at Slough on the 65 to Maidenhead. For some reason this bus had a darker radiator grille than others of that type, which was quite distinctive.

The evolution of the bus station off Frogmoor in High Wycombe took place over some 15 years, with almost annual extensions to the area occupied, along with several major re-arrangements of stands and the facilities for staff catering and public toilets. Fortunately, Driver Jim Vockings took his camera to record the scene as it was in 1965/6. This top view shows the toilet block on the right, along with the two-way entrance and a central island.

This view pans round to the left, showing the bus stands where they loaded before exiting onto Frogmoor. LD-type Car 812 (SMO 78) waits ready for a short-working on Route 28 to Marlow. An Inspector walks towards the staff canteen and the rear bus parking area. The arrangement of white-painted walls shows the piecemeal nature of the demolition of buildings in order to maximise use of the site, the Company having obtained most of the leases over the years.

Still further to the left and now looking north to the railway embankment is the staff canteen. On the right FLF-type Car 848 (WJB 232) is about to unload passengers before turning right into the parking area. On the left can be seen rebuilt LL-type Car 799 (DMO 669), doing a common duty for a pair of these, i.e. spare buses kept on hand for emergencies. The different shades of tarmac add further clues to recent layout changes.

As the Evening Post advert campaign reached its climax, extra strap-line words started to appear on the buses, with Bristol KSW6B Car 727 (JRX 802) seen above at the Allen's Garage terminus of Route 110 at Fairlawn Road in Tadley with 'New for Reading' added, whilst below is Bristol LD6B Car 815 (SMO 81) with 'Colour' added, as it leaves York Road on Route 69 for Slough Station.

All journeys on Routes 20/20a (Aylesbury – High Wycombe – Maidenhead – Windsor) switched to run via Frogmoor Bus Station, rather than some from the Rex Cinema from 10th September. From the following day all services through South Ascot now used All Souls Road instead of Church Road, which avoided reversing on short-workings or standing on the road.

On 16th September the Assistant Traffic Manager met with officials from RAF Benson, who were seeking better bus links between the base, Benson Village and Wallingford on Route 5 (Reading – Oxford).

Coaching levels at Oxford had been reduced by the loss of some contracts, whilst the poor Easter weather had only seen 25 out of the anticipated 28 vehicles re-licensed that Summer. So, by September 1952 Bristol LS6G coaches 79-83 (SFC 565-9) were available for disposal, as was similar Car 675 (HBL 77) from the following month. When these appeared in Weldale Street yard, it seemed that they were to be the next coach-to-bus conversions, but the narrower front entrance on these ruled that out. Also disposed of in October were 1946 Bristol K6A Car 450 (DBL 158) and 1947 K6B-type Car 454 (DBL 162).

South Midland's Austin 'Gypsy' recovery van No.59 (GBL 227C) at Gloucester Green Bus Station in the maroon and cream livery.

Few changes had occurred in the ranks of the Service Vehicle fleet, but in October a number of departures and arrivals took place. At Oxford the 1951 Bedford 10/12cwt depot van No.27 (RWL 71) was replaced by the Austin 'Gypsy' shown above, which was fitted with a front winch and other equipment for recovery work. A similar vintage Bedford van No.31 (GJB 552) had been new to Reading Garage, passing to Ascot in 1957, then transferring to the new Bracknell Garage in 1960, and this was replaced by the transfer of No.39 (MRX 114), a 1956 Commer 'Cob' transferred from Reading. Also going that month was 1956 Bedford CA5 van No.41 (MRX 115) from Reading, whilst 1960 High Wycombe depot van No.47 (UJB 299) was repainted as the new publicity van in place of withdrawn 1951 Austin A40 van No.33 (GMO 943). New Leyland 15cwt depot vans arrived in July as No.55 (FMO 831C) for Reading and No.57 (GMO 760C) for High Wycombe in October.

Advertising was still an important source of income for bus operators, brochures and rate-cards being produced by British Transport Advertising and double-fronts were £1 8s a pair for 12 months display.

Thames Valley used the double-front advert facility to a greater extent than some other THC operators, and Bristol KSW6B Car 653 (HBL 55) rests at Reading.

Only one new bus arrived during September as Car D24 (FJB 740C), another Bristol FLF6G with ECW H38/32F body allocated to Reading, and in October it was followed by similar bus D25 (GBL 907C) which was allocated to Wycombe Marsh from 4th November.

Bristol FLF6G Car D25 (GBL 907C) parked in Micklefield Road outside the 'Marsh Garage.

During October to November 1965 each of the coach-seated Bristol FLF6B Cars D4-7 (ABL 116-9B) was off the road receiving modifications to their heating systems, resulting in the re-appearance of LD-types on Routes A and B between Reading and London.

Mention has already been made that the former Tadley Dormy Shed workings on Routes 9/9b/9c still terminated adjacent to the old location in Fairlawn Road (Allen's Garage), resulting in dead mileage to the *Wilts & Dorset* Baughurst Dormy Shed. However, from 2nd October this situation was rectified by buses working through via Pamber Heath Road – Rowan Road – Mulfords Hill – Baughurst (Woodlands Road), also taking in recent new housing in that area. From the same date the Sunday services on Routes 6 (Reading – Basingstoke) and 47 (Reading – Winnersh – Hurst – Twyford) ceased, saving 9615 and 2825 miles each year respectively.

At Maidenhead the staffing situation had improved to the extent that 2 double-deckers could be re-licensed from 23rd October, with some 1250 route miles being reinstated weekly, and leaving only Bristol K6A Car 441 (CRX 550), K6B Car 502 (EJB 223) and KS6B-type Car 600 (FMO 982) delicensed in the yard there.

However, traffic congestion was now making it not possible to keep to time at busy periods on the 35 mile long Routes 20/20a (Aylesbury – High Wycombe – Maidenhead – Windsor), so in order to address this the route was split at High Wycombe on 23rd October to form the following services:

Route 20 - (High Wycombe – Maidenhead – Fifield – Windsor);
Route 20a – (High Wycombe – Maidenhead – Hatch Bridge – Windsor);
Route 21 – (High Wycombe – Princes Risborough – Butlers Cross – Aylesbury);
Route 21a – (High Wycombe – Princes Risborough – Little Kimble – Aylesbury.

From 25th October the school workings from College Town (Jolly Farmer) to St. Michael's School in Little Sandhurst ended, releasing a double-decker from Bracknell to Reading, where it replaced Bristol LS-type coach 675 (HBL 77), which had been helping out on relief duties. However, on 31st October another accident befell the fleet, when Bristol LS6B saloon 715 (HMO 861) was lost in a fire caused by a sleeping vagrant whilst it was parked in Maidenhead's yard. The LS coach was quickly sent over to stand in until a more suitable replacement could be arranged, whilst what little of the bus remained was towed to The Colonnade and finally scrapped on 8th February 1966.

Bristol LD6G Car 761 (MBL 842) waits for Route 21a at Kingsbury Square in Aylesbury.

During the reconstruction of the Maidenhead Bus Station, buses used either York Road or the Coach Station instead. Bristol FLF6G Car 876 (544 BBL) is seen in the latter, with Bridge Avenue in the background, working a short on Route 66a from Slough, running via the Trading Estate, through Maidenhead, Cox Green, Woodlands Park, White Waltham and Waltham St. Lawrence to terminate at Shurlock Row, reversing to turn at the church.

At Camberley decades of discussions on a new site for terminating TV buses had come to nothing, so the traditional stops along Princess Street continued in use for Routes 3, 4, 49 and 53/53a. Bracknell-based Bristol LS6B Car 718 (HMO 864) was seen loading there by Philip Wallis on a 53a to Windsor. The whole route was 22.2 miles long and took 1 hour 22 minutes to complete, though the run through the back-roads made for a pleasant ride in the daylight.

The newest bus in the fleet was Bristol FLF6G Car D26 (GJB 874C), which was allocated to Bracknell and is seen outside on the stop at the Regal Cinema. 70-seaters were not the usual buses on the 52/56 Local Services due to the sometimes narrow roads. Note the No Waiting sign at the bus stop, whilst the film Tom Jones features Albert Finney. Nothing in this scene now survives, swept away through re-development of the High Street area shortly after.

From 1st November recent new allocations allowed the replacement of the Bristol KSW6B's assigned to the Stokenchurch Dormy Shed, usually two of Cars 729-31 (JRX 804-6), by 60-seaters fitted with heaters and rear doors, the usual performers being Bristol LD6B Cars 810/1 (PRX 928/9).

Car 810 (PRX 928) is seen just prior to transferring to Stokenchurch duties, working what was then still the 20 to Aylesbury, and passing through the Hughenden valley. Note the counter adverts by other evening papers, including the double-use of the word reading.

One week later the Reading one-way traffic scheme came into effect, so TV buses needed revised routings in a number of cases, using Caversham Road for northbound journeys and Greyfriars Road for southbound buses. Incoming buses on Routes 1, 4, 4a, 6, 6a, 6b, 9, 9a, 9b, 9c, 11 and 12 were all diverted via West Street – Friar Street – Lower Thorn Street (where a bus stop was erected outside the Head Office for the first time ever) – Caversham Road – Tudor Road. Routes 5, 5a, 5b, 50, and 102 entered via Chatham Street, and then via Lower Thorn Street. Outgoing buses on Routes 7 and 8 ran via Greyfriars Road – Stanshawe Road – Caversham Road.

Work at Maidenhead Bus Station was completed for the revised layout to come into full use from 21st November, with most services now working out of saw-tooth stands on the western edge of the site, a situation was took away the old character of the bus station, and was pretty useless for photography! In the Slough area the early-morning church specials to the Roman Catholic Church at Burnham were deleted from 28th November due to lack of use, though later journeys were continued.

One further Bristol FLF6G with ECW H38/32F body arrived in November as Car D26 (GJB 874C), which was allocated to Bracknell, whilst during December similar buses D27/8 (GMO 827/8C), were sent to Wycombe Marsh and Maidenhead. Also received were four Bedford VAM14 coaches with Duple 'Bella Venture' C41F bodies, as Cars C413-6, which were placed in store. Redundant 1949 K6B Cars 500/2/3/5 (EJB 222/4/5/7) all departed during December.

Bristol FLF6G Car D28 (GMO 828C) is seen at the Maidenhead Bus Station soon after delivery, working Route 69 to Sealey's Stores in Courthouse Road.

In Bracknell another stage in the major road changes saw the Crowthorne Road closed from west of Church Hill House Hospital towards Crowthorne for the redevelopment of Mill Lane from a narrow lane to dual-carriageway, and this was only a pedestrian route after that, so buses on Routes 53/53a diverted via Reeds Hill and South Hill Road from 4th December.

As the vehicles of Bristol Commercial Vehicles could now be supplied outside of the State-owned operators, there was a flurry of activity at Reading Garage over 10th-13th December in order to prepare demonstrators visiting *Reading Corporation*, who sampled *Central SMT* FLF6G-type BL278 (EGM 278C) and RELL6G SRG15 (HWU 641C) from *West Yorkshire*, as well as inspecting an FLF6G in chassis form only.

Only 2 *South Midland* coaches were hired by the GPO at Oxford for Christmas post, and these are likely to be Bristol LS6B Cars 90/1 (TWL 55/6), next in line for conversion to o-m-o buses. At the end of 1965 Chief Engineer P.A. Robinson took up a similar post at *Bristol OC,* and his place was taken by Mr. Albert Baker, who had been the Assistant Engineer there.

The last of the former Bristol OC buses was Car 436 (KHU 624), seen in June 1965 as relief on Route 7.

Buses lined up along York Road during the first phase of Maidenhead Bus Station changes. Philip Wallis caught Bristol LL5G Car 819 (FMO 23) on Route 18 to Marlow Bridge only, whilst SC4LK Car 776 (NBL 733) is set to travel to Marlow via the Bourne End road. In the background are Bristol LS Car 677 (HBL 79) on the 24 to Cookham Dean and LD-type Car 750 (MBL 832) is on a Local Service. The Civic Offices on the hill were used in Carry On Nurse as a hospital.

A number of services had been lost in the Newbury area, though many places still had bus routes which could be traced back to a Country Carrier origin. The route to Ecchinswell had come to Newbury & District through Tom Holman, and in this photo Bristol LL6B one-manner is seen on a Wednesdays and Saturdays-only short working to Bishops Green on Route 103, as it passes the Thames Valley enquiry office at The Wharf Bus Station by the canal.

Another Newbury view taken in April 1965 shows a typical line up of types, with Bristol KS6B Car 595 (FMO 977) through from Reading on Route 5b via Yattendon, then Bristol MW6G Car 855 (VJB 946) on the Ashford Hill and Kingsclere Route 104, with coach-seated Bristol LD6G Car 764 (MBL 845) working the 30-mile Route 112 to Oxford. The latter service had been started as a joint venture with City of Oxford when N&D was part of Red & White.

1966

Yet another fares increase came into effect from January, though this related to child fares, which were raised to 75% of the adult equivalent. This, along with cuts to services relied upon by schoolchildren, would result in a rise in the number of contracted services by County Councils, such operations generally going to other providers. Indeed, such was the general feeling by passengers over recent fares rises, that in Bracknell there was the threat of a boycott of the bus services!

Now nearing the end of its service was 1946 Bristol K6A Car 441 (CRX 550), seen above at Stations Square in Reading on a short-working to Twyford on Route 1. In the same position was similar Car 452 (DBL 160) on Route 11 to Bucklebury seen below at that terminus on a rather more dismal day.

During January three accident victims from December 1965 returned to service, these being Car 694 (HMO 840), a 1953 Bristol KSW6B bus, and Car 752 (MBL 833), a 1956 coach-seated Bristol LD6G, both of which were damaged in separate accidents at Aldermaston, along with coach-seated Bristol FLF6G Car 838 (UJB 204), which was hit by a crane jib when in Crowthorne on a rare outing on Route 3 (Reading – Wokingham – Crowthorne – Camberley). Also from January o-m-o buses started to receive a transfer on the nearside stating 'Please tender exact fare'.

On 6th January the Traffic Manager was alerted to the proposal by Oxfordshire CC to relocate bus stands in Henley Market Place to the Kings Road Car Park, but it must be assumed that counter-arguments won, as the change did not occur. However, at Windsor there were further route changes within the town following the rather spectacular main sewer collapse, which took out much of the width of Sheet Street. After this buses once again ran both ways along Peascod Street from 14th January through to 2nd April, including those on Routes 53/53a and the 90-group services.

Nearby, at Slough, there were discussions with the Borough Council and *London Transport* regarding new links between Langley and the Bath Road, with joint operation in mind. In response *Thames Valley* extended its Routes 60 (Pinkneys Green/Halifax Road – Maidenhead – Slough) and 69 (Sealey's Stores – Maidenhead – Slough) onto Langley Village, though these through journeys omitted Slough Station, whilst *LT* extended its Route 407 with 407a journeys from Mercian Way in Cippenham. This resulted in each service operating on an hourly basis to give a roughly 30-minute headway, with effect from 22nd January. There was no sharing of revenue from these services, and some journeys on Routes 61/61a (Cippenham – Slough, with 'a' journeys via the Trading Estate) were discontinued, whilst neither operator provided a Sunday service. It is also worth noting that at that time Slough was served by green-liveried *LT* buses from the garages at Amersham (MA), Garston (GR), Staines (ST) and Windsor (WR), with red-liveried buses on Route 81 from Hounslow (AV).

New Bristol FLF6G Car D29 (GRX 129D), caught on Local Service Route 15 at Maidenhead Bus Station.

January saw a further trio of Bristol FLF6G buses with ECW H38/32F bodies, as Cars D29-31 (GRX 129-31D) and, like D19 (FBL 483C) beforehand, these had inverted T rear destination apertures, whilst the upper-deck cream band and its associated beading was discontinued. Adjustable blanking-off plates were fitted to the C-B-C heater grilles at the front, and these were also fitted to other buses with such equipment in the light of operational experience. D29 was allocated to Maidenhead and the other pair went to Reading.

The arrival of these displaced the two K-types illustrated on the previous page, 1946 Cars 441 (CRX 550) and 452 (DBL 160), the last of the K6A-types, which left ex-*Crosville* Bristol L6A Car S305 (GFM 888) as the sole vertically-engined AEC-powered bus in the fleet. However, during January this was mainly used on driver-training duties, where its layout was particularly useful, as most training buses required the removal of the window to the rear of the cab in order for instructions to be given. The only change to the Service Vehicle fleet during January saw the arrival of an Austin 1100 car (HBL 297D).

The Bristol L6A one-manner's had been a surprise addition to the Thames Valley fleet, and Car S305 (GFM 888) is seen after it returned to Reading depot, coming in on a Relief working to Stations Square and passing the Art Deco car showrooms of Vincent's of Reading and the old Jolly Porter pub.

Due to recurrent bouts of seasonal weather throughout January and February, there were a number of unusual sightings, with high-bridge Duple-bodied Guy 'Arab' MkIII 6LW Car H13 (HOT 391) turning up on Route 1 (Reading – Newbury – Maidenhead), though only as far as Reading from its Newbury base, whilst 36-foot long Bristol RELL6G Car S307 (CBL 356B) was a less than suitable choice for Route 4a from Reading and through Arborfield and Barkham to Wokingham! Bristol KSW6B Car 749 (JRX 824) hit a tree on 20th January at Burghfield, which likely dates when it was rebuilt with a T front indicator, whilst Bristol LS6G coach 671 (HBL 73) slid into a ditch at Hermitage on a contract run on the morning of 27th January, and Bristol L6A Car S305 (GFM 888) suffered damage on driver-training on the 21st of that month.

Coach-seated 1960 Bristol FLF6G Car 835 (UJB 201) is seen at Maidenhead Bus Station in the maroon and cream scheme, working Route B to London's Victoria Coach Station, a service started by Thackray's Way back in 1929.

The old mansion at Lily Hill Park, on the eastern outskirts of Bracknell, became the new headquarters of International Computers & Tabulators Ltd., (or ICL as it soon became known), so *TV* was asked to provide Monday to Friday lunchtimes journeys from Lily Hill Road to the town centre from 24th January.

However, something of a surprise from early February was the out-shopping of the coach-seated Bristol FLF buses in the maroon and cream livery already found on the coaches, especially as the other dual-purpose types had recently received the half-and-half red and cream livery. Car D7 (ABL 119B) was the first done, and the rest of the 1964 deliveries followed in March (D6, ABL 118B), April (D4/5, ABL 116/7B) and in September (D8, BRX 141B). The 1960 batch of Cars 834-8 (UJB 200-4) was dealt with in March (838), May (836/7), June (834) and August (835), and all of the repaints had the centre of the roof in grey.

All the repaints to maroon featured a painted advert for the extended tours on the offside staircase panel, but only the 1964 batch was also provided with new fleetnames in blue lettering on an illuminated yellow panel in the between decks cream band, the 1960 examples having a sliding front entrance doors.

The appearance of these buses in the maroon scheme gave rise to a rumour that the express services were to be operated under the *South Midland* banner, though the work on the fleetname panels showed otherwise. Alternative theories were that this made them not confused with the red buses of *London Transport,* but of course they could now be mistaken for those of *Reading Corporation!* Black rear wheel discs were also fitted, and front ones later followed, though the latter were short-lived and prone to damage.

By coincidence, there was also a change to the routing of buses on the A and B services from 15th February, as a one-way system saw incoming buses turning from Sloane Square via Holbein Place and Pimlico Road, though outgoing buses continued directly to Sloane Square. Of course, as all enthusiasts of that era will recall, laid-over express coaches could be found in many of the surrounding streets, whilst those for night services etc. would either be cared for at Samuelson's or the nearby *London Transport* Gillingham Street, or parked on flattened bomb-sites in the Battersea area.

1949 Bristol K6B Car 509 (EJB 231) was nearing its departure when caught by Philip Wallis on Route 101 at The Wharf in Newbury, in from Harwell.

In the meantime, February saw *Bristol Greyhound* in discussions on how it might co-ordinate its intensions to make more use of the growing motorway network with *South Midland* services through Oxford, whilst nearer to home their was a meeting with *Bert Cole* of *Blue Bus Services* regarding the sale of his bus service covering Maidenhead – Eton – Windsor.

Traffic congestion in general caused many start times of services to be put back by up to 15 minutes in order to maintain arrival times for work and schools, whilst from 19th February Route 7 (Reading – Nettlebed) was diverted to enter Reading via Caversham Road and Tudor Road in place of its old routing of Vastern Road and Blagrave Street due to peak-hour delays.

The irony of delays and adjustments was that they made the buses less reliable than had been the case for the preceding 4 decades, leading to a spiral of higher car ownership and even more traffic chaos!

Bristol FLF6G Car D33 (GRX 133D) is seen at Slough on Route 62 to Cippenham (The Green) in this 1970 view by Philip Wallis with damaged mudguards.

February saw another pair of Bristol FLF6G's with ECW H38/32F bodies arriving as Cars D32/3 (GRX 132/3D), the first of which went to Wycombe Marsh, and the latter to Maidenhead. This resulted in the demise of the last of the ex-*United Counties* Bristol K5G, 1937 Car 463 (FPU 517) now carrying a 1951 ECW L55R body, along with Bristol K6B Car 515 (EJB 237), these being followed in March by similar K6B Car 509 (EJB 231), both new in 1949 and with standard ECW L55R bodies, as well as 1951 LWL6B Car 582 (FMO 964). From about then the older Bristol FLF's lost their pale olive green interior paintwork for a darker shade, making them look rather drab.

A further Bristol LS6B coach-to-bus conversion was completed during February, when former *SM* coach 90 (TWL 55) re-appeared as Car S315, now fitted out with 41 bus seats and allocated to Reading.

Car S315 (TWL 55) just in from Odiham on Route 6a.

A trio of views seen through the lens of Philip Wallis and exploring some less photographed places in the Thames Valley area. Bristol KSW6B Car 749 (JRX 824) turns by The Crown at Silchester on Route 9 to Baughurst. The bus had recently received accident repairs and had its front screen rebuilt to a T layout. The shelter was one of many provided by Local Councils in rural locations, whilst this type of road junction, with its central grassed area, was still commonplace then.

Seen outside Stratfieldsaye Schools on a relief 6b working is 1953 converted Bristol LS6B Car S314 (HMO 834), alongside a bus shelter of a different design and similar to those erected by Thames Valley at various places. The otherwise rural nature of the area is evident, with the footway only reaching the cottages, the village being on the edge of the large estate once owned by the Duke of Wellington, hero of Waterloo and often commemorated by pub names locally.

Another old scene, now largely gone is of Cheap Street in Newbury, as Bristol LD5G Car 782 (NBL 739) takes the turn into Market Street on the Local Service Route 127 towards Wash Common. The New Market Inn was a Wethered's house, though a long way from Marlow, whilst all those buildings on that corner are now the site of the Kennet Centre and new cinema complex. The no entry signs also show that traffic levels in Newbury were increasing.

Those familiar with the Newbury area will already know of *Reliance Motor Services* and how its coach and contract work had expanded greatly after the Second World War. Lesser known though are the bus services between Brightwalton, Wantage and Newbury, along with the Cold Ash service acquired after the sudden death of *Bert Austin* in 1948. Those to Newbury and Wantage from the Brightwalton base could trace their origins back to before 1919, when young *George Hedges* returned from war service and took over the carrier's route his father had covered during the war. However, these services were now running at a loss, and the Hedges' family hoped that if *Thames Valley* took over, the latter might be able to work them in with other local operations, the parties meeting to talk over the matter on 25th February.

The Blue Bus fleet was an eclectic collection which included this 1953 Dennis 'Lancet' UF demonstrator, originally with its Strachan body having a rear entrance, though subsequently altered for o-m-o use. KOT 600 passes Windsor Guildhall for Maidenhead.

Negotiations also continued with *Bert Cole (Blus Bus Services)* regarding the transfer of his service, though he had actually acquired another route from *Bray Transport*, who rather confusingly was originally known as *Blue Bus!* This service was originally from Maidenhead (Station) – Bray, but had been extended southwards onto Holyport – Moneyrow Green (Wheel of Fortune) – Foxley Corner – Touchen End - Paley Street (Sheepcote Lane), taking it over on 1st March.

The quartet of Bedford VAM14 coaches with Duple 'Bella Venture' C41F bodywork, Cars C413-6 (GRX 413-6D) was licensed from 1st March and were generally intended for *South Midland* express duties. No other coaches for that fleet were added that year, though Reading-based Bristol MW6G Car 866 (520 ABL) was sent to Oxford on loan from May 1966, but it retained *Thames Valley* lettering. From 27th March fares on *South Midland* Oxford – London services rose by 8.33%, though those on Worcester – Oxford – Southsea only increased by 5%. On the tours front the West Wales tour was not repeated, whilst the Donegal & Ulster Coast bookings had faded due to the troubles in the Province, and it was also discontinued for 1966. Of the Bristol MW6G coaches, Cars 805/7 (PRX 931/3), 830-3 (UJB 196-9) and 858-60 (WRX 773-5) had all remained as 34-seaters for the 1965 season, but are believed to have been up-seated to 38 around this time for more general duties.

Bedford VAM14 Car C415 (GRX 415D) is seen above at Didcot Station on a rail replacement working, and the nearside of Car C414 (GRX 414D) is shown below at Gloucester Green in Oxford on express duties.

Over the Winter of 1965/6 the Company had come in for complaints in the local press regarding the high number of its buses without heaters, and indeed at March 1966 the only vehicles so equipped were the Guys 170/1, H10/3-6, Bristol LL-types 564-8, 794-9 and 817-20, Bristol LWL's 582, 613/5/9-21/4-33, KS-types 595-600, KSW's 637-9, 738-49, LS-types 677-87, 706-14/6-24 and S309-15, LD-types 750-4/60-4 and 808-15, then all buses from FLF Car 834 of 1960. This situation was acknowledged as being worse than in many comparable fleets due to the unusually high intake of vehicles during 1950-3 as replacements for pre-war and former *Newbury & District* vehicles.

From 1st April the *Thames Valley* General Manager, Tom Pruett, was also Director of *Hants & Dorset, Wilts & Dorset and Venture Ltd.*, the latter still being registered, although no longer in the public view. Even so, no further attempts at joint operation with these companies was forthcoming, though surely the 18-mile long Reading – Basingstoke service was a good candidate? However, a meeting did take place with *Reading Corporation* over possible co-operation, as it too was feeling the pinch of additional costs.

93

Indeed, from 1st June, the Parcels Office in London Street was closed, so any parcels arriving in Reading on *Thames Valley* buses now had to be collected from the Station Square Enquiry Office. At the Head Office the Saturday morning opening ceased, as Office Staff worked only a 40-hour week from 2nd April.

At Bracknell Route 49 (Reading/Bracknell – Earley – Wokingham – Finchampstead – Eversley – Yateley – Camberley) saw some reductions from 14th May, as some of the longer journeys were poorly patronised, and the author recalls that he never travelled the full route even once! The Local Services 52/52a/56/56a had extra journeys added, necessitating the allocation of a further double-decker there, whilst also from 14th May Route 38 from High Wycombe was extended half a mile on from Booker (Limmer Lane) to serve the Clayhill Estate.

Bristol KSW6B Car 647 (GJB 285) displays the new extended destination on Route 38, its front boxes rebuilt to the T format when seen at Frogmoor. In the background is the large and unsightly multi-storey car park constructed at the rear of the site.

Over at Swindon the terminal point of Route 106 (Newbury – Lambourn – Baydon – Swindon) changed from Regent Circus to Horsell Street from 22nd May, whilst from 25th the buses passing through East Ilsley now made use of the new slip road on the re-aligned A34, which now returned that village to the quieter ways of former days.

Also on 22nd May discussions with *Bristol Greyhound* were concluded, so passengers from Bristol, Bath and Faringdon wishing to alight at intermediate points between Oxford and London would transfer to *South Midland* services from 15th October, as the service would now proceed non-stop. However, the *'Valley's* seasonal coastal express services from Booker, High Wycombe and Maidenhead to Southsea, Hastings and Eastbourne, were discontinued, having operated since being acquired from *Fred Crook* of Booker in 1937.

Former United Welsh Bristol LS-type Car S322 (KWN 795) is seen at Newbury Wharf on Route 129 to Hampstead Norreys and Compton in later days.

During May a number of buses from other THC fleets appeared in the Weldale Street yard at Reading, these being a pair of Bristol LS's as *United Welsh* Nos. 1263/4 (KWN 794/5) and some high-bridge bodied K-types from the *Bristol OC* as Nos. C3439, C3453 and 3679 (LHY 928/45 and JHT 128), though some reports say there were 5 of the latter at one point. On the face of it, these looked to have been acquired, but as it turned out the double-deckers had only been left temporarily by drivers of scrapyard owner North's of Leeds, and these duly moved on.

However, the saloons had indeed been acquired, and that was therefore an interesting reverse journey in respect of the many *Thames Valley* L-series buses which went to Swansea some years before. These became Cars S321/2 (KWN 794/5), both being LS6B-types new in 1955. As with subsequent purchases the seating was reduced for o-m-o working, a luggage pen being added on the nearside, to give a B41F layout. However, Car S322 had been built with a 2-and-3 seat layout for 54 passengers, and an emergency exit in the centre of the rear end, so with *TV* it was down-seated from its later layout of 44 to seat 40.

Both of the LS's from United Welsh were initially allocated to Maidenhead, also receiving the thin MW-type front strip in place of the original heavy bumper. S321 is seen in Park Street, Windsor on Route 22 acquired from Blue Bus shortly after it arrived.

Also seen on Route 22 at Maidenhead Bus Station is converted LS6B Car S316 (TWL 56) fresh out of the paintshop, with the author's fellow bus spotter David Nicholls resting after both had cycled from Bracknell.

Also completed in May was coach-to-bus conversion S316 (TWL 56), though once again it retained the 39 coach seats and roof-mounted luggage racks, being allocated to Maidenhead. Another of the author's old favourites departed that month in the shape of 1948 Bristol K6B Car 471 (DMO 675).

1948 Bristol K6B Car 469 (DMO 673), now the oldest native 'decker in the fleet, is seen heading towards Tadley on Route 110 from Newbury.

On 4th June Conductor A.C. Porter and Driver V.J.D. Mortimer were both made up to Inspectors at Reading along with Driver Swindler of Newbury on 23rd July.

From Saturday 4th June the services to Woodley were once again increased, with additional journeys on Route 45 between Reading and Woodley Roundabout via Reading Road – Western Avenue – Butts Hill Road, and returning by way of Loddon Bridge Road – Crockhamwell Road – Reading Road, whilst journeys to Ravensbourne Drive were extended up Butts Hill Road and Western Avenue. From 6th June certain peak-time runs on Route 43 ran along Butts Hill Road and to Twyford (Station) for commuter connections with the train services.

With effect from Saturday 18th June through journeys on Routes 65/65a/66/66a between Wokingham and Slough were de-linked at Maidenhead in order to overcome delays caused by traffic at peak times, whilst from the same date the evening service on the 67 was discontinued in favour of diverting buses on Route 70 (Maidenhead – Burnham – Britwell – Slough) to serve the Priory Estate. A number of other Slough area services were reduced to 30-minute headway, with some only 2-hourly on Sundays, once again in reflection of the staffing situation at Maidenhead.

From early June overhauled Bristol LS saloons had their original front bumper replaced by the thin strip used on the MW bodies, which was intended to update their appearance, though it actually made the front end even more prone to accidental damage. Those noted were Cars 677/85/7 (HBL 79/87/9) and 707/20/2/3 (HMO 853/66/8/9), and after June many more were done, including secondhand examples, though full dates are not available.

However, the big news for June was that of takeovers! The Maidenhead – Dorney – Eton – Windsor service of *Blue Bus Services* went to *Thames Valley* on 4th June, and *Bert Cole* retired, though he passed on the Maidenhead – Paley Street route to his son Ron, who was then the third generation of the family business. Indeed, Bert had actually driven for *TV* from 1928-33, before going to assist his father (also Bert). The last bus of theirs' on the Windsor service was 1954 Duple (Midland) B41F-bodied Bedford SBO (VPJ 750). *TV* numbered the service as Route 22, and although 2 of the *Blue Bus* drivers opted to work for them, no buses were involved in the deal. The terminus in Windsor was at the junction of Park Street and St. Albans Street, and this and the original timings were retained.

The other takeover of June involved the small network of bus services covered by *Reliance Motor Services*, which transferred to *Thames Valley* on 25th June.

Bristol LS6G Car 682 (HBL 84) was sent to Newbury to cover the former Reliance service to Brightwalton, a place not on the blinds, hence the window board!

The services taken over from *Reliance* became Routes 107 (Newbury – Brightwalton) and 119 (Newbury – Cold Ash), requiring 3 o-m-o saloons with a weekly mileage of 800 and 527 miles respectively, which continued to operate to the inherited timetables. There was also a 7.50 am departure from The Wharf to Hambridge Road (Opperman's Gears), though this was put under Route 103 instead. *Reliance* had also included the license for the Wantage service, though *Thames Valley* surrendered this without operation.

Following the sale, Reliance disposed of its quartet of Bedford SB-type buses Nos.73 (NTH 690), 75 (NUY 331) and 80/2 (SX 8901/2), and 80 is seen at Newbury Wharf on the Cold Ash service.

In the meantime there had been no improvement in the staffing situation at Maidenhead, and the changes outlined above saw the 3 double-deckers de-licensed in October 1965 put up for disposal.

In fact, staffing issues were now starting to affect the Reading garage as well, so it was decided that from 20th June no new Private Hire work would be taken on, along with the cancellation of the usual excursions programme, effectively ending a tradition of coaching work going back to 1919. Indeed, the only coaches to still bear the *Thames Valley* name were now Bristol LS6G's 674-6 (HBL 76-8), which were on contract duties from Newbury, along with Bristol MW6G Car 866 (520 ABL), already on loan to *South Midland*, leaving only Bedford SB-type coaches 862/3 (516/7 ABL) and C406 (836 CRX) allocated to Reading.

From 26th June the Sunday service on Route 50 from Reading to Abingdon ceased, though intending passengers could still catch Route 5 for Oxford and change onto the *City of Oxford* bus at Wallingford to reach those points, this saving 6302 miles per year. Excellent weather for Henley Regatta from 29th June to 2nd July tempted large crowds out, many of them by bus, but the increased traffic through the town also disrupted services. With increasing traffic also in mind, the Company met with *London Transport* over plans for a new off-road bus station at Slough on 25th June, whilst on 8th August the first meeting took place at Paddington regarding a Rail-Air coach service.

Bristol FLF6G Car D35 (GRX 135D) at Maidenhead.

New buses for June were a trio of Bristol FLF6G's with ECW H38/32F as Cars D34-6 (GRX 134-6D), allocated to Reading, Maidenhead and Wycombe. Also arriving during June was a pair of 1955 Bristol LD6B's with ECW LD33/37RD bodywork, formerly Nos.1257/8 with *United Welsh,* which became Cars 770/1 (LWN 52/3). As with a number of double-deck buses from that fleet, they were put into use without being repainted, temporarily re-introducing the upper deck cream band, some with black lining out! These were followed by similar buses (but without rear doors) as Cars 772-5 (LWN 48-51) during July, formerly Nos.1253-6 with *United Welsh*. All had been delivered with the full-length style of 'Lodekka' grille, but all had received shorter ones by then.

Ex-United Welsh Car 770 (LWN 52) is seen outside The Regal Cinema at Bracknell in original livery.

It will be noticed that some of the above had taken the fleet numbers of the Bristol SC4LK's, causing another rumour of their departure, though in fact they were soon noted as renumbered to S301-4! This, combined with the numbers previously used by the open-top Bristol K5G's from 1957-60, freed up the sequence of 770-8 for re-use on incoming LD's.

The fleet was actually down by a 70-seater for a month from 7th June, as FLF6G Car 878 (546 BBL) was away for accident repairs. During that same month former *Thames Valley* Car 336 (ABL 766), a Leyland 'Titan' TD4 of 1937, returned to the area after being a mobile caravan since 1953! The author recalls coming across it in the Norfolk Broads, still in full red and cream livery, a surreal sight. It was hoped that it would be restored, but unfortunately this did not materialise.

Former United Welsh Bristol LD6B Car 774 (LWN 50) is seen above in Reading on Route 45 to Woodley, whilst below is the upper deck interior looking towards the rear on Car 775 (LWN 51), showing the dark green seating and generally good condition of these buses.

During July two further LS6B-type coaches returned as Cars S317/8 (TWL 57/8), both retaining 39 coach seats and wearing the dual-purpose livery for service at Bracknell and Maidenhead. The ranks of LS6B's in the fleet were further swelled that month through the acquisition of 1955 examples formerly *United Welsh* Nos.1265/6/67, which became Cars S323-5(KWN 796/7 and MCY 39), the first two went to Newbury and the last one to Reading.

These arrivals displaced 1949 Bristol K6B Cars 497, 504/17-9 (EJB 219/26/39-41), similar 1949 Car 525 (FBL 27) and the final ex-*Bristol OC* K6B Car 436 (KHU 624). On the single-deck front Bristol LWL6B Car 619 (GJB 257) also departed that month.

Frank Ranscomb happened to be on hand to record Car 846 'at rest' in the graveyard.

There were some red faces at *Thames Valley* on 26th June, when Bristol FLF6G Car 846 (WJB 230) left the Bath Road at the junction with All Saints Avenue in Maidenhead and came to rest in the graveyard of the church! The incident occurred at 5.30pm, as the bus travelled empty to London to form a relief bus for Route B, when it was involved in a collision with two cars, resulting in its off-road deviation to the route.

The AEC content of the Oxford coach fleet doubled during August, when *Timpson's* Duple C41F-bodied 'Reliance' coach (JJD 568D) was exchanged for a month with *South Midland's* Bedford VAM14 C416 (GRX 416D) for comparative trials.

On 10th August it was noted that *Cooper's Car Hire* was once again trying for a license service from the Western Road to Bracknell town centre, though the matter was adjourned at the Hearing in Aldershot, and *TV* successfully countered the application by providing suitable extra journeys from 14th October.

One of the incoming LS6B buses from United Welsh was Car S325 (MCY 39), seen in Wantage on the 5a.

Two further Bristol FLF6G buses with ECW H38/32F bodies arrived in August as Cars D37/8 (GRX 137/8D), which were initially allocated to Wycombe and Reading, though the latter went to Maidenhead soon afterwards as originally intended. Outgoing that month were 1949 Bristol K6B Cars 506/8/16 (EJB 228/30/8), along with 1952 Bristol LS6G coach 672 (HBL 74) off of contract work from Newbury.

The coach seats on Car S318 (TWL 58) seem wasted on the 5-mile trip out to Speen on Route 34, though the service was usually worked by LS-type saloons.

Bristol FLF6G Car D38 (GRX 138D) was working Route 60 to Halifax Road in Maidenhead when seen at the Mackenzie Street Slough terminus.

A considerable number of changes to services in the Newbury area came into effect from Saturday 3rd September, to reduce the annual mileage by 274,981!

Route	Served	Changes	Miles
1	N'b – Maidenhead	Reduced service	66,685
5a	Newbury – Wantage	None onto Chilton	12,943
5b	Newbury – Reading	Sundays now only	30,742
		N'b – Hampstead Norreys	
101	Newbury – Harwell	No Stanmore loop	2,569
102	Reading – Ilsleys	To East Ilsley only	29,968
103	N'b – Ecchinswell	Reduced service	3,458
104	N'b – Kingsclere	Ashford Hill only	5,138
106	Newbury – Swindon	No Sunday service	6,183
		Lambourn – Swindon	
108	N'b – Hungerford Newtown/Shefford Woodlands		
	Now as far as Hungerford Newtown only	31,283
110	Newbury– Tadley	Reduced service	15,980
111	N'b – Bucklebury/Stanford Dingley	10,436
	No Bucklebury (Slade) or Sunday service	
112	Newbury - Oxford	2-hourly on Sunday	9,313
113	Newbury – Inkpen – Hungerford	6,256
	Considerably reduced and none via Olive Branch
114	N'b – East Woodhay	No Sunday service	8,237
115	Newbury – Highclere	No Sunday service	20,732
	Section from Woolton Hill – Highclere withdrawn
116	N'b – Hungerford – Hungerford Newtown	*
	General reductions but some via Stockcross now
120	Newbury – Frilsham/Curridge	3,515
	Curridge journeys now on new Route 105
121	Newbury – Penwood	No Sunday service	11,544
126/7/8/8a	Newbury Local Services (see below)	N/A

August saw a rash of breakdowns, resulting in *City of Oxford* lending 1955 Willowbrook-bodied AEC 'Reliance' No.741 (WJO 741) for *Thames Valley* crew working on Route 5 (Reading – Oxford), whilst *Wilts & Dorset* sent out a 'Lodekka' to Reading on Route 6 from Basingstoke one day, then a Bristol L-type bus on the 6b (Basingstoke – Stratfieldsaye- Reading) on another occasion!

* Journeys onto Hungerford Newtown were covered by bus on Route 108, mileage included under that heading.

The Newbury Local Services were re-organised as:

126 Wash Common – Valley Rd. – Wharf – Shaw Estate;
127 Wash Cmn. – Andover Rd. – Wharf – Turnpike Est.;
128 Wash Common – Valley Road – Wharf – Shaw Estate or Turnpike Estate;
128a – This designation no longer in use.

Recently acquired S323 (KWN 796) is seen at The Wharf in Newbury on Route 115 to Woolton Hill.

It should be noted that the condition of the incoming Bristol LS-types varied quite a lot, and on one visit to Newbury Garage the author was taken down the pit by Reg Hibbert, who proceeded to poke a large file through the rather dubious under-side of an example he described as 'just bloody rubbish'!

98

One of the services to see a large decrease in mileage was Route 108, which also had inter-workings with Route 116 journeys serving Hungerford Newtown, and Bristol LL6B one-manner Car 568 (FMO 950) is seen at Newbury Wharf ready for a departure to that point via Stockcross.

At the same time the routing of the 5b was amended so that all journeys on from Upper Basildon ran via Kiln Corner, and then followed Route 102 through to Compton Road – Ashampstead Woods – Yattendon, whilst Route 1 (Maidenhead – Reading – Newbury) was diverted via new houses at Meadow Way, Theale.

September saw another trio of Bristol FLF6G buses with standard ECW H38/32F bodies arrive as Cars D39-41 (GRX 139-41D), the first pair being allocated to Maidenhead and the last to Newbury. Similar Cars D42-4 (GRX 142-4D) followed in October, with D42 at Wycombe Marsh and D43/4 at Reading. These led to the departure of 1948/9 Bristol K6B Cars 469 (DMO 673) and 524 (FBL 26) during October.

Brand new Bristol FLF6G Car D41 (GRX 141D) is seen shortly after delivery on the Newbury – Oxford Route 112 at Gloucester Green Bus Station.

The last week of September was not a good one for *Thames Valley* buses, with 'Big Bertha' Bristol LDL-type Car 779 (NBL 736) in trouble once again! This time it was working the morning journey of the Windsor Boy's Special, when it rounded into Fernbank Road from Bracknell, clipped the kerb and ending up with the front end down the nearside ditch, taking out an electric distribution pole and the power supply to around 100 homes! No one was injured in this event on Friday 23rd September, though to the Company's embarrassment someone took a photo which appeared in the local rag.

The author clears brushwood from the front of Car 837 (UJB 203) after it landed on the roundabout.

The second event occurred on Sunday 25th September, as the author watched the 7.04pm departure on Route A towards London progressing up The Broadway, as it appeared to jump up in the air! Leaping on his bike, he was soon on the scene, to assist Conductor Bryn Wells, who was somewhat shaken, get the passengers off the bus. The Driver Reg Cox managed to get out of the cab alright, whilst with the Police Station only yards down the hill, officers were quickly on the scene and directing traffic around the rear of the bus as it was still in the road of the Eastern Roundabout (a.k.a. Met Office Roundabout). The bus itself came to rest between a pair of fir trees only 8ft 6ins apart, so it was a fortunate escape from a possibly worse accident. The bus had brushwood in front, though at that time the roundabout was much smaller and just a shallow mound, with the later subways not yet constructed.

Various theories, such as brake failure, were duly examined whilst the bus was impounded at the Police Station, though what actually happened was that the offside front wheel clipped the kerb of the triangular island approaching the roundabout, being steered over the bollards and straight towards the roundabout, the driver fighting to bring it to a safe halt, and fortunately only one passenger was slightly injured.

After Car 837 (UJB 203) was 'released', it went to Bracknell Garage before being driven back to Reading, though it was not too badly damaged.

Work on the Marlow Bridge was completed, so the through service was reinstated from 15th October, and the Route 18 table also now included the various short workings and extensions to cover Chisbridge Cross, Marlow Bottom, Danesfield and Bourne End, which had previously been designated Route 18b. However, the 15-passenger limit still applied for buses over the bridge, which could be embarrassing for the driver if not enough volunteers came forward to walk over!

From that same date drivers had reported difficulties caused by indiscriminate parking around the village hall at Downley, so the Company informed Wycombe RDC that its buses on Route 35 in the evenings would run only as far as Littleworth Road, in order to ensure a safe turning place for the o-m-o bus. The former *Blue Bus* Route 22 (Maidenhead – Eton – Windsor) was a given a revised timetable, which evened out weekly workings to the same each day, but reduced evening journeys to save 34,500 miles per annum.

Ex-United Welsh Bristol LS Car S324 (KWN 797) is seen at Newbury Wharf on Route 104 to Ashford Hill.

Road changes occupied much time in the Traffic Office at the end of October, with the closure of the section of Crowthorne Road between South Hill Road and Nine Mile Ride for an indefinite period during the completion of Mill Lane and the feeder roads to new housing estates at Great Hollands. Camberley-bound Routes 53/53a were therefore diverted from 31st October by turning left at The Golden Farmer onto South Hill Road, then via the Bagshot Road and Nine Mile Ride, before re-joining the old route at the crossroads with Crowthorne Road. Also affecting Bracknell services was a reduction in poorly-used off-peak journeys on Routes 55/55a (Bracknell – Warfield – Hawthorn Hill) from 31st October, although this was also to release the bus for other duties.

At High Wycombe, developments in the town centre resulted in numerous changes to stopping places, often upsetting arrangements going back to early days, with return stops now located in a different road, whilst at Wokingham discussions took place in November over the proposed one-way traffic scheme due in 1967.

Former coach-seated Bristol KSW6B Car 738 (JRX 813) is seen shortly after its rebuild as L27/26RD.

The next vehicles to go through rebuilding were former London service Bristol KSW6B Cars 738/9 (JRX 813/4), which had their luggage racks removed, coach seats cut down and were re-panelled without the top-deck beading, also gaining T-type destinations, both being completed during November. A start was also made in replacing the engines in LD-type buses which had originally received reconditioned Gardner 5LW units taken from wartime Guy 'Arabs', with Car 782 (NBL 739) receiving the Bristol AVW unit taken from departing K6B Car 469 (DMO 673), during November, similar engines being fitted to Cars 784/91 (NBL 741/8) in December. Around this time it was decided to transfer 1956 Bristol LD5G Cars 766/7 (MBL 847/8) to High Wycombe, but as soon as their power source was noted, the Company was reminded that only 6-cylinder 'deckers were acceptable there!

With the re-opening of Marlow Bridge, Route 18 now ran through to Quoiting Square once again. Bristol SC4LK Car S304 (NBL 734) was caught by Graham Low coming over the bridge towards Maidenhead.

Unfortunately, there were two further bad accidents affecting the Reading-based fleet in the latter months of the year. On Saturday 5th November Bristol KSW6B Car 660 (HBL 62) was in collision with a lorry in Burghfield Road at Southcote, as it worked the 9 towards Baughurst. The front offside and cab were badly damaged, and Driver Les Jarvis had a lucky escape with only cuts and bruises. His full bus of passengers were also fortunate, and after this the bus spent some months tucked behind the door in the Weldale Street entrance of Reading Garage before it eventually returned to service.

In the second incident, disaster was again narrowly avoided, when recently transferred Bristol LD5G Car 766 (MBL 847) mounted the kerb as it entered the bus lay-by near Alfred Sutton School on the Wokingham Road whilst working Route 90a into Reading. This was on the morning of 9th December, and the stop was a busy one, though fortunately a *Reading Corporation* trolleybus on Route 17 had just cleared the queue! The bus demolished the bus shelter and suffered much frontal damage, returning to service with front screens rebuilt to a T format.

As noted from photos of recent deliveries, rear wheel discs had now become a standard fitment, but from late 1966 the coach-seated FLF's were noted also with front discs, though only as a short-lived feature.

November saw just one more Bristol FLF6G with ECW H38/32F body arrive as Car D45 (GRX 145D), which went to Bracknell, being joined there in December by similar Car D46 (GRX 146D).

Also during November a number of changes occurred in the Service Vehicle fleet, with the disposal of the former Publicity Van, 1951 Austin A40 No.33 (GMO 943), along with the replacement of 1954 Ford Thames 4D Stores Lorry No.35 (KBL 963). The latter was replaced by No.63 (KRX 563D), a Bedford KDL C1 with drop-side open body, which came in October, along with Bedford CALV30 Van No.61 (KRX 261D).

Recently delivered Bristol FLF6G Car D43 (GRX 143D) is seen on lay-over in the old Southern yard at Reading Station between duties on the busy Route 9 to Baughurst.

Another bus parked in the Southern yard was former United Welsh Car S326 (JCY 997), still with original heavy front bumper and awaiting relief duty on Route 102, though probably only as far as Pangbourne.

The other incoming vehicles for November were all secondhand, and included some intriguing additions! A trio of Bristol LS's was an expected choice, with ex-*United Welsh* 1953 LS6B Car S326 (JCY 997) and 1957 LS5G Cars S327/8 (OCY 947/8) joining their old friends from that fleet, having previously been Nos.1250 and 107/8, all being allocated to Reading.

However, the other arrivals from that stable were quite unexpected, being a pair of Bristol KSW6G buses with ECW L55R bodies and dating from 1953 as *United Welsh* Nos.1242/3! These took the vacant fleet numbers 672/3 (JCY 989/90), appropriate to their age, though before entering service their engines were replaced by Bristol AVW 6-cylinder types, their 6LW engines no doubt duly being re-issued into LD-types.

Both the KSW's were allocated to Newbury and were in very good condition. Car 672 (JCY 989) is seen on Route 110 to Thatcham and Tadley soon after arrival.

As a result of these incoming buses, November saw the disposal of 1949/50 Bristol K6B Cars 507 (EJB 229) and 530 (FBL 32), along with 1952 Bristol LS6G coach 674 (HBL 76) and the first pair of rebuilt Bristol LL5G Cars 798/9 (DMO 668/9), the latter only going to *A. Moore & Son,* operators of *Imperial Bus Service,* who ran Windsor Local Services. The only outgoing bus in December was the last of the former *Crosville* Bristol L6A one-manners, Car S305 (GFM 888), which was also the last vertically-engined AEC-powered bus in the fleet, a type evident since 1945. When Car 463 (FPU 517) left earlier in the year, the K5G ceased to feature for the first time since 1939.

As already noted, the sole *Thames Valley* Bristol MW6G coach, Car 866 (520 ABL), had been on loan to Oxford Garage since May, but during December it returned to Reading, with its place now taken by 1952 Bristol LS6G coach 675 (HBL 77). Also at Oxford, work had started on converting 1953 Bristol LS6B coach 95 (TWL 60) to its new role as dual-purpose 39-seater S320. However, it was still in progress when hired minus seats to the Oxford GPO for Christmas mail duties, before completion and allocation from 1st January to Bracknell. The work on 94 (TWL 59) had also commenced, but was not completed until later.

This view of S328 (OCY 948) shows how the front end details of the Bristol LS-types varied, this bus also having lost the old heavy bumper for an MW-type thin strip – but note the dented front nearside corner!

By the close of 1966 the following buses had been rebuilt with T-type front destination screens (the list includes some buses sold in the meantime):

K's 450, 454, 469, 471, 497, 506, 517, 526, 528, 529, 530;
KS's 588, 593, 595, 596, 597, 598, 599 and 600;
KSW's 601, 637, 638, 639, 640, 642, 644, 646, 647, 650, 695, 698, 700, 738, 739, 742, 746, 748 and 749;
LD's 766 and 810;
FLF's 837 and 838;
LWL's 582, 616, 623, 624, 625, 626, 627, 628 and 629;
LS's 682, 684, 687, 708, 713, 719, 722, 723 and 725.
Total number of buses converted 60.

1967

Changes in High Wycombe town centre saw the closure of Newland Street from 2nd January, so the Local Services 33/33a now used Link Road instead. New housing north of Winnersh Crossroads led to an additional short-working on Route 47 from 4th of that month in order to facilitate a link to from Robin Hood Lane and Watmore Lane to Bearwood School, and this was extended further east to start from Emmbrook (Rifle Volunteer) from 23rd January. Also from that date the situation at Maidenhead had eased to the extent that two of the de-licensed double-deckers were reinstated.

Recently delivered Bristol FLF6G Car D46 (GRX 146D) was based at Bracknell, and is seen emerging into the sun from the shade of Windsor Central Station on Local Service Route 51a.

On 23rd January Reading Garage played host to several demonstrators, though not officially visiting the Company, both being cleaned prior to driving for inspection at Mill Lane by *Reading Corporation*. One was an AEC 'Regent' MkV with 70-seater East Lancs bodywork, as *Southampton Corporation* No.392 (JCR 392E), and the other was a Bristol VRLS6G prototype with ECW 80-seater body and in *Bristol OC* livery (HHW 933D), though this did not actually enter that fleet. As it was, *Reading CT* did order Bristol VRT-types, and no doubt *Thames Valley* officers also took the opportunity to sample it whilst there. The author also had a chance to ride on this prototype over the hilly terrain around Bristol and was impressed with it.

January saw the entry into service of a pair of Bristol FLF6G buses with ECW H38/32F bodies as Cars D47/8 (LBL 847/8E), being allocated to Bracknell and Reading. All FLF deliveries from these onwards had formica-backed seating of a light grey mottled pattern, which helped to lighten up their interiors.

D47 (LBL 847E) is shown outside the Red Lion, the opposite side from the Regal Cinema, at the western end of Bracknell High Street, as it awaits a crew change on Route 92 to Windsor, this point being a short walk from the Market Street garage.

The other vehicles received on 10th January were a quartet of Bedford VAM14 coaches with Duple C41F 'Viceroy' bodies as Cars C417-20 (LJB 417-20E), though these were placed in store at The Colonnade. Outgoing vehicles for that month were further Bristol K6B Cars 513/4 (EJB 235/6) and 526-8 (FBL 28-30), along with Bristol LL5G rebuild Car 795 (DMO 665), which joined others already at *Imperial* of Windsor.

On the services front, the importance of early-morning links between Newbury and the industries at Colthrop is highlighted by variations in timings made to Route 110 from 4th February to suit Cropper's Factory, with buses being extended to turn at Field's Factory. From 25th February there were alterations to Route 7 in order to provide better links between Reading and the Borocourt Hospital at Kingwood Common.

Despite the new FLF deliveries, the large fleet of Bristol KSW's were still the daily workhorses of many routes, and 1953 Car 663 (HBL 65) is seen in the Southern yard on Route 3 during the Summer of 1967.

The Traffic Manager John Stevenson took up a new post as Deputy General Manager with the *Midland General* Company from 1st March, and his place was taken by Spencer Gwinnell, who transferred from the Exeter headquarters of *Southern/Western National*.

The Bedford coaches mentioned above had been specially ordered for a new joint venture with *British Railways (Western Region)*, which would provide a link between trains at Reading and Heathrow Airport, and would replace the less convenient facility already operated by *Charles Rickards* on the railway's behalf between Slough Station and the airport. As the matter required the usual deliberation by the Traffic Court, the standing operator fought hard to take on the new link, though obviously *Thames Valley* felt confident enough to buy the specially modified coaches for the service. Indeed, it was implied at the time that the new Reading-based facility was a 'done deal' from the outset, as both parties were State-controlled, which was no doubt true.

Following the outcome of the hearing a trade press conference was held in the newly-completed Western Tower headquarters of the railway in Reading in 14th February, and then another with representatives of the British Airports Authority at Heathrow on 2nd March. In the meantime, a trial run for invited guests took place on 22nd February, when Assistant Engineer George Shaw showed Bedford Car C417 (LJB 417E) off.

In time-honoured tradition Bedford coach C417 (LJB 417E) was posed at the Thames-side Promenade, seen here with Assistant Engineer George Shaw.

The public service commenced on 6th March, using the 4 Bedford coaches C417-20 (LJB 417-20E), fitted with two-way radios in touch with the control centre in the 16-story high Western Tower, and was manned by a special rota of hand-picked drivers. At the same time Reading-based Bedford SB13 coach C406 (836 CRX) and Bristol MW6G coach 866 (520 ABL) were also fitted with radios as reserve coaches for the new service.

Bedford coach C419 (LJB 419E) is seen at Heathrow on the 'Air Road Rail Service – Heathrow to South Wales, Bristol and the West', as the service was first advertised. This photo is the only found of one of these coaches with front fleetname.

No route number was displayed on the coaches, or in the initial timetables, but by May 1968 the letter H had been allocated, now a vacant designation and an obvious choice for Heathrow. The adult fare was £1 whether single or a day return, and this was shared as 15 shillings to *Thames Valley* and the rest to *British Railways*. As such this was quite a money-spinner for the Company, as the comparable journey on Route B (Reading – Great West Road – London) would have been 7 shillings, then a 4-penny bus ride on *London Transport* into the airport. However, most passengers were paying for this element within rail fares, so such a comparison was not readily apparent. Non-rail travel on the coach could also be made by purchasing a ticket at Reading Station or from the airport.

The service had 24 journeys on weekdays and 13 on Sundays, with an hour allowed on the timetable for a journey usually taking some 45 minutes, the difference being noted as taking account of possible late-running of trains and traffic delays. It was stated that some 80 long-distance trains would be met by the service, and passengers arriving by train at Reading were directed to a Rail-Air lounge on Platform 5, where hostesses in rail-blue uniforms greeted them and directed them to the coaches waiting outside the front entrance of the old *Great Western* station. After leaving Reading the coaches all called at the No.1 (Europa) Building and the No.3 (Oceanic) Building, as the terminals were then known. As some travellers might be staying overnight before flying, request stops could also be made at the Ariel, Excelsior and Skyway Hotels just outside the airport by prior request to the hostesses.

At the Heathrow end, similar hostesses were stationed at the BOAC information desk, where tickets could also be purchased. The first coach left Reading at 6am and returned from the airport at 7am, all coaches being Reading based. They had also been fitted with additional side lockers in anticipation of higher levels of passenger luggage, though apparently the Bedford rep nearly had a fit when he heard the hard-running these coaches were intended for! However, there is no doubt the improvement the service brought, although at the time it was intended as a stop-gap until trains from the west would be diverted direct to the airport!

Also on the theme of railway co-operation was the extension of inter-availability of tickets from 6th March between Reading and Newbury in response to a reduction of stopping trains on that service. Indeed, at the time it was anticipated that a number of the stations along that line would be completely closed.

Further pairs of Bristol FLF6G buses with ECW H38/32F bodies arrived in February as Cars D49/50 (LBL 849/50E), followed by Cars D51/2 (LBL 851/2E) in March, and all these went to Reading except Car D51 which went to Wycombe Marsh. Disposals were of 1950 Bristol K6B Cars 529/31 (FBL 31/3) during March, along with 1950 rear-entrance Bristol LL6B Car 559 (FMO 941) and front-entrance rebuilt LL5G Cars 794/7 (DMO 664/7).

New Bristol FLF6G Car D49 (LBL 849E) working on Route 12 to Aldershot. Note to the right the now closed Southern rail station about to be demolished.

In respect of Car 794, not long before its sale it had been involved in a bizarre failure when running towards West Ilsley in the care of Driver Maurice Smith and with half a load on board as recounted to Dave Wilder. As he reached the hill the bus glided to a halt for no apparent reason, the Gardner engine was ticking over and the clutch and gear selection worked alright. He visually inspected the prop shaft was in place before walking into West Ilsley to call Newbury Garage. A short while afterwards Reg Hibbert's right-hand man 'Ginger' arrived with 'towing bus' Bristol LL6B Car 565 (FMO 947) and a fitter. In the meantime the remaining passengers had taken the short walk home, so the empty bus was towed back by 565, which started away up the 1-in-7 gradient without complaint, before the 65ft-long convoy took the narrow lanes across to reach the Wantage road. Back at the garage the differential had been found to have shattered, something not previously experienced!

In February a further pair of Bristol LS6G buses was acquired from *United Welsh* as Cars S329/30 (JCY 995/6), new in 1953 as Nos.1248/9. The former received a 6-cylinder Bristol engine before going to Newbury, whilst the latter was sent to Wycombe and retained the Gardner unit, becoming a regular on Routes 36 (High Wycombe – Cadmore End) and 37 (Wycombe – Fingest – Henley), when based at the Fingest Dormy Shed.

Bristol FLF6G Car D50 is seen is these two views in Reading, above on Route 4 to Camberley, and below on the 12 to Aldershot, also showing the emergency doors provided on both decks on these bodies.

The Service Vehicle fleet saw a number of changes, with a pair of incoming Austin 1100cc cars in January (LJB 229/30E), along with Bedford CALV30 Vans No.65 (LRX 865E) and 67 (MMO 367E). These took the places of Bracknell's 1956 Commer 'Cob' Van No.39 (MRX 114) and the 1960 Austin A40 car used by the Traffic Superintendent at High Wycombe (WMO 52), whilst the General Manager's Wolseley 6/110 of 1962 (457 BMO) was replaced by an updated version of that model (LRX 475E) during February.

105

Bristol LS6G Car 684 (HBL 86) was caught by Robin Symons as it waited for the level crossing to be opened, showing Private on the blind. Note the old Wokingham Electro-heat Works which occupied the corner with Wellington Road, along with the cars in this 1967 view. The style of barriers have since changed, though the busy crossing still causes regular complaints from motorists, the first of which was noted in the Borough Council minutes in the early 1900's, when very few cars were in use!

Another Bracknell scene since gone completely has Bristol KSW6B Car 642 (GJB 280) emerging from Station Road and from the garage for a short on the 92 to Binfield. This bus had operated on the old 2 out of Ascot garage since new, hence the faded blind on that number. The Times newspaper office replaced the wool shop on the left of the Regal Cinema, whilst the Southern Electricity Board had a large showroom on the opposite corner.

One scene not really changed is Wallingford Bridge between Berkshire and Oxford and over the River Thames. 36ft-long Bristol RELL6G Car S307 (CBL 356B) leaves the town on Route 5 towards Oxford. The riverside attracted lots visitors in the Summer months, with Salter's Steamer boat trips and a children's paddling pool on offer, along with attractive walks, pubs and well-kept parks, buses also connecting with City of Oxford to Abingdon etc.

Bristol LD6B Car 789 was also notable in being the last of its type to have the upper-deck cream band when it finally lost it in April.

With further new 70-seaters now at Bracknell, the Bristol LDL6G-type Car 779 (NBL 736) was transferred to Reading in March 1967. However, on 3rd April it was in trouble once again, being involved in a nasty head-on collision near the Sutton's Seed Trial Grounds on the A4 whilst heading to Woodley on Route 43. The collision involved a big Ford 'Zephyr' car, which badly damaged the front offside wheel and suspension, and it took the rescue crew 3 hours to get it fit to tow back to the garage.

Even before Thames Valley started to acquire second-hand Bristol LS-types, quite a variety of frontal details had changed due to the vulnerability from accidental damage, with some losing the Bristol-ECW badges or receiving thin MW-type strips in place of original bumpers. In the view above at Newbury Wharf on Route 103 to Ecchinswell ex-United Welsh Car S329 (JCY 994) had lost its badge, but gained an MW strip. Below we see its twin as Car S330 (JCY 996), still with original bumper and panelled-over former fog-light in the centre, and retaining its badge but having lost the nearside dumb-iron panel. It was awaiting a turn on Route 36 to Cadmore End at Frogmoor.

Fitters work on Car 779 (NBL 736), whilst the Police sweep debris from the road after extricating the badly damaged car.

1954 coach-seated Bristol KSW6B Cars 740/2 (JRX 815/7) were put through the bodyshops during April and March respectively, emerging with seats cut down and luggage racks removed as L27/26RD, and both had T-type destination indicators, though retaining the upper-deck beading. It should be noted that similar former London service Cars 741/3 (JRX 816/8) did not receive the same treatment, as both were allocated to Newbury and still being used on longer routes.

During the first half of 1967 the re-engining of Bristol LD-types with Gardner 5LW units continued, and all received the Bristol AVW 6-cylinder engines reconditioned from sold buses, with the exception of Car 765, which received a Gardner 6LW. These were dealt with in January Car 767 (MBL 848), February Car 768 (MBL 849) and 781/9 (NBL 738/46), March Car 769 (MBL 850), in April Cars 765/6 (MBL 846/7) and 785 (NBL 742), and Car 783 (NBL 740) in May.

Also noted in April was that those Bristol MW6G coaches still reserved for touring work had received chrome-plated wheel discs both front and rear, these being Cars 833 (UJB 199) and 858-60 (WRX 773-5), whilst the Irish tour coach for the season was C416 (GRX 416D), a Bedford VAM14 with Duple 'Bella Venture' 41-seater body. The *South Midland* tours were still holding up quite well, despite the rise of the package holiday to Spain etc., though they did actually attract quite a few clients from the USA and Canada from brochures sent to agents there. For 1967 some hotels were changed, with the South Devon tour relocating to the Linscombe Hall Hotel in Torquay and the Llandrindod Wells-based Mid Wales tour now using the Commodore Hotel. Also added for the first time was another 'foreign' destination, in the shape of a 9-day holiday based at the Grand Island Hotel in Ramsey and covering the interesting Isle of Man.

April saw the first of a trio of Bristol RELH6G coaches intended for *South Midland* express duties arrive as Car C421 (LJB 421E), which had a 47-seat ECW body, and this was followed in May by similar Cars C422/3 (LJB 422/3E). Evidently the Bedford VAM14 Cars C413-6 (GRX 413-6D) had not been found entirely robust enough for such work, and certainly the drivers recall these RELH's for their power and good handling. They also featured larger front destination screens and jack-knife doors, the idea being to speed up loading and to make them easy to later re-assign to bus work.

From the Spring of 1967 adverts started to appear on the sides of saloon buses, and in the case of Bristol LS, MW, SC and RE-types the fleetnames were brought further forward, those on the SC's being split into two lines. However, in respect of the LWL-types, such adverts were placed over the fleetname, whilst the original broad area over the windows (intended for adverts) remained unused. Car 627 (GJB 265) is seen on a lay-over on Route 33 at High Wycombe.

Over at Bracknell, development of the Southern Industrial Area went hand-in-hand with the new dual-carriageway Mill Lane, and led to a new service for workers at the Rowney's artist materials factory there. This was provided by new Route 54, though it also incorporated some established short-workings from Bracknell to Crowthorne on Route 53, which were now diverted via the same factory, then onto Peacock Lane, past Easthampstead Park Teacher's Training College and along Lower Wokingham Road to regain the old route from Pinewood Crossroads and past the Transport & Road Research Laboratory to the Iron Duke at Crowthorne. These arrangements started on Monday 3rd April, and the route left Bracknell (Regal Cinema) and ran as Skimped Hill Lane – Downshire Way – Mill Lane – Ellesfield Avenue (Rowney's). As the area received more employers, the route took the right turn off the lower roundabout in order to circle Doncastle Road and reach the side of Rowney's, this being effective from 6th November. Nearby, housing estates at Wildridings and Great Hollands were under construction, so further changes would follow.

From mid-April a 5-ton weight limit was placed on the railway bridge at Chinnor, so buses on Route 32 (High Wycombe – Bledlow Ridge – Chinnor) had to turn just short of that point at Chinnor Hill (Woodlands Farm). Also concerning railway matters, the Company received notice that the passenger service of trains to South Aylesbury Halt would cease from 5th June, leaving the buses of Route 21 (High Wycombe – Princess Risborough – Aylesbury) as the only link. This was still a time of many closures of railway stations or the abandonment of entire branch lines throughout the *Thames Valley* operating area.

Car C422 (LJB 422E) is seen above at Oxford, having worked in on Route C via Maidenhead from London, whilst Car C423 (LJB 423E) arrives at Maidenhead from London on Route E to Worcester, where it was based overnight.

May saw the last pair of Bristol K6B-types eliminated from the fleet, and they were the final examples bought new as Cars 532/3 (FMO 7/8). Also departing that month was the first of the front-entrance Bristol LL6B one-manners, Car 564 (FMO 946), which left only similar Cars 565-8 (FMO 947-50) in use at Newbury, and rear-entrance examples Cars 560/71/4 (FMO 942/53/6) up at High Wycombe.

Although work on the new Bus Station off Station Hill at Reading was progressing well, the old Enquiry Office required demolition before the new one was completed, so a suitably-painted red and cream caravan was situated at Stations Square from 1st May.

The last of the conversions of Bristol LS6B coaches was finally completed in June, when former *South Midland* coach 94 (TWL 59) re-appeared as Car S319, retaining 39 coach seats and in dual-purpose livery.

Car S319 (TWL 59) was allocated to Newbury and is seen in these two views at The Wharf Bus Station. The upper photo shows it working former Reliance Route 107 to Brightwalton. These were quite attractive-looking buses, though this example was to have the shortest career of all the conversions, being retired in December 1968.

A number of route changes occurred in June due to traffic management schemes, with Route A (Reading – Ascot – London) being diverted from 3rd June away from Highfield Terrace at Chiswick to run via Turnham Green instead, whereas at High Wycombe a one-way scheme was introduced on 17th of the month and affected services in general. The latter, when taken along with the one-way working introduced at Maidenhead from 8th November, needed re-timing of journeys on Routes 20/20a (High Wycombe – Maidenhead – Windsor).

During June Peter Wilks came to the conclusion that *Thames Valley* was entering a terminal decline, so he took a position with the High Wycombe division of Bucks County Council, with responsibility for school transport and manual staff at schools. It has already been noted that reductions in bus services resulted in an increase in contract operations from the late 1960's and of course many of those contracts went to other operators. Peter already possessed the local knowledge essential for the task, though as the author can personally confirm, school transport is not for the faint-hearted! His place was taken by the transfer of the former Cashier at Wycombe Marsh, John ('Mac') McCrindle, who lived at Bourne End.

On the excursions front, Newbury remained the only *Thames Valley* garage still offering such facilities, but these had now been reduced to just the London Airport tour, along with the Hythe and Beaulieu trip which included the 2-hour cruise around Southampton Water. The same tours would also feature for 1968, after which the excursions programme finally ceased, leaving *Reliance Motor Services* a clear field. The latter had for many years maintained a booking office at The Wharf, along with licences permitting pick-ups there. Newburians could, however, still use the *South Midland* service to Southsea for day trips or longer.

June saw just one further Bristol FLF6G bus with ECW H38/32F bodywork arrive as Car D53 (LBL 853E), and this was allocated to Maidenhead Garage. Another pair of secondhand Bristol LD6G's was also acquired as Cars 776/7 (JCY 993/4), being new in 1954 as *United Welsh* Nos.1246/7 and carrying ECW LD33/25R bodies. Both were allocated to Reading, and as with other examples from that fleet they had already had their original full-length radiators grilles replaced by the shorter type.

Car 777 (JCY 994) is seen in the old Southern yard at Reading awaiting service on Route 9b to Mortimer Station. The intermediate destination screen has been over-painted in red, whilst the ends of the ultimate box have been painted black to take a narrower blind. Note that the old Southern Station is now a car park.

109

Another Bracknell scene in which nothing now remains shows Bristol LS6B Car S320 (TWL 60) at the Station Road stop by the car park of the Regal Cinema, with the Southern Electricity showroom behind it. Also note the coal lorry turning from the High Street in front of Cyril H. Lovegrove, the local undertaker's shop front. Only half a dozen of the old buildings in the High Street would survive the re-development that soon followed this 1967 photo by Graham Low.

Another of Graham's shots shows 1952 Bristol LWL6B Car 625 (GJB 263) on the steam-cleaning ramp at Reading Garage, such attention being undertaken prior to major dockings. This photo is taken over the remains of cottages in Weldale Street which have just been demolished to make way for a new Staff Canteen and general increase in yard space. The bus sports one of the side adverts then in vogue and a T-type front box.

A number of short-workings on Route 53 used the Iron Duke stop in Crowthorne High Street as a turning point, and 1951 Bristol KSW6B Car 642 (GJB 280) is seen there. Increased housing, along with large numbers of children travelling to Bracknell schools, saw an increase in double-deck operations. The pub was one of a number in the area named after the Duke of Wellington, and the College founded by Queen Victoria in his honour is just beyond the trees.

At this time a number of buses were prepared at The Colonnade for full repaints which took place at Reading Central Works, and during July Bristol KSW6B Cars 651/5/68 (HBL 53/7/70) were all noted in flat red paint traversing Reading between those two points. On 26th July recently acquired former *United Welsh* Bristol LS6B Car S329 (JCY 995) was also noted on suspended tow with extensive front end damage and blinds set for the ex-*Reliance* Cold Ash Route 119.

Over at Swindon a new Bus Station was opened at Fleming Way on 6th August, so *Thames Valley* Route 106 (Newbury – Lambourn – Swindon) transferred there from Regent Circus. Work on the Reading Bus Station was now nearing completion, and the Enquiry Office was ready for occupation from early August.

Although coaching work from Reading had declined to very little, an exceptional private hire saw 8 Bristol FLF's used on 12th August to convey American students from Reading University to Caversham Court for a Sedimentalogical Conference, which ironically was a journey wholly within the Reading Borough.

The new Bus Station at Reading was constructed on a large site between Station Hill and Garrard Street, part of the once extensive area of Vincent's Garage, and was built in a semi-underground position beneath the Top Rank Ballroom. The official opening took place on Friday 1st September, when Minister of Transport Stephen Swingler cut the ribbon to allow the longest-serving *Thames Valley* driver, Walter ('Tadley Jack') Lambden to drive the newest bus Car D53 in.

Jack Lambden proudly displays his array of long-service and safe-driving badges. He had joined in 1925 and soon transferred to Tadley Dormy Shed.

Graham Low caught D49 (LBL 849E) on the stand for Route 4 at the new Bus Station, the inadequate level of lighting being clearly demonstrated.

He was joined that day by Jack Bowles, his regular conductor of some three decades, whilst the official guests were transported by Bedford VAM14 coach C420 (LJB 420E), taking time off from Rail-Air duty.

Bristol RELL6G Car S308 (CBL 357B) is seen from the Staff Canteen as it turns in from Garrard Street on a Route 5 journey from Oxford. This style of ECW body, with the wrap-round windscreens and peaked domes was only built for a few operators. Note also the parking area to the right for spare buses.

The new facility was heralded as an improvement, though the poor lighting and bare concrete did little to make passengers feel they were appreciated. Indeed, many made a point of boarding at other places in the town rather than go there. The saw-tooth stands were laid out to the eastern side of the site, with a sub-way connection to Reading General Station, whilst the Enquiry & Booking Office faced onto Station Hill, where parcels were also handled. At the Garrard Street end was the Inspector's Office on the ground floor, with a Staff Canteen above that.

The new Bus Station as seen from Station Hill, with the Reading Traffic Superintendent's Austin A40 car (592 BMO) parked on the slope, a feature that would prove difficult when Winter set in! To the left is the Enquiry Office, whilst the large ballroom is nearing completion above. Further to the left is Western Tower, with the offices of BR (Western Region).

The public use of the new facility started on Sunday 3rd September, and the saw-tooth stands were allocated as follows:

Bay	Route Nos.	Destination
A	4	Eversley and Camberley
	4a	Arborfield and Wokingham
	6a	Riseley, Hook and Odiham
B	6	Sherfield and Basingstoke
	12	Hartley Row and Aldershot
C	9	Mortimer and Baughurst
	9a	Padworth and Tadley
	9b	Mortimer Station
	9c	Tadley and Baughurst
D	5/34*	Wallingford and Oxford
	5a	Harwell and Wantage
	5b	Yattendon and Newbury
	50/40*	Wallingford and Abingdon
	102	Compton and East Ilsley
E	7	Stoke Row and Nettlebed
F	1	Thatcham and Newbury
	1a	Thatcham and Newbury
	28	Henley and High Wycombe
G	8	Binfield Heath and Henley
	11	Bradfield and Bucklebury
H	1	Twyford and Maidenhead
	1a	Sonning and Maidenhead

*Route numbers used by City of Oxford journeys

Bay	Route Nos.	Destination
I	10	Earley and Woodley
	47	Hurst and Twyford
	49	Wokingham and Camberley
	75	Bracknell and Guildford
J	3	Crowthorne and Camberley
K	90/90a	Wokingham and Windsor
	91/91a	Windsor via Emmbrook
	92/92a	Windsor via Binfield
	(90-group 'a' journeys operated via Ascot)
L	Spare bay

Bays M to S were arranged longitudinally along the western edge of the site and were for express services, with *Thames Valley* Routes A (to London via Ascot) and B (to London via Maidenhead) on Bay M. *Bristol Greyhound* services used Bay N, and Bays O to S were reserved for the other express coach services which would transfer from The Colonnade in October.

The exceptions to the use of the Bus Station were the Woodley Local Services 43/44/45 (and variants), which took the former 9-group stands on the north side of Station Hill, whilst the joint Route 19 (to Long Lane) with *Reading Corporation* continued to use the stop towards the top end of Station Hill. It should also be noted that this was *Thames Valley's* Bus Station and was not used by any Corporation buses. It was of course built on land originally owned by the *Great Western Railway* and leased to Vincents. All buses entered from Garrard Street and departed via the front slope onto Station Hill.

<u>Please note</u> - This chapter continues on page 129 following the Colour Section.

Philip Wallis lived in the Baughurst and Tadley areas since childhood. As his interest in buses, and more particularly routes and networks developed, he travelled extensively by bus across Thames Valley territory, reaching places as varied as Sunningdale and Swindon, Oxford and Odiham. He recalls travel on the open top service in 1957 and trips on the A and B express routes to London. In 1971, the final year of Thames Valley, he travelled on the Rail Air coach service to Heathrow Airport. He usually had his camera with him, so enabling him to capture the buses and coaches over a wide area.

Top – The Duple-bodied Guy 'Arab' MkIII 6LW double-deckers new to Newbury & District were still very much part of the scene in that area, and low-bridge Car 170 (FMO 515) waits at The Wharf for service to Inkpen in July 1963.

Middle – The high-bridge Guys had Duple 57-seater bodies and fleet numbers in the H series, and Car H13 (HOT 391) is seen at the terminus of Route 110 at Allen's Garage in Tadley in June 1963.

Bottom – The other oddity still in evidence from the vehicles inherited from the Red & White ownership of South Midland was Car 85 (SFC 571), the only AEC 'Regal' MkIV delivered after Thames Valley took over. Originally intended for a Duple 'Ambassador' body, this was duly changed to the type of body then being supplied on Bristol LS chassis. It is seen at Gloucester Green.

113

Reading Stations Square and Station Hill offered a good variety of Thames Valley buses in the 1960's ranging from secondhand Bristol K's to the latest models.

Top – Always something of a local favourite was Car 475 (FLJ 978), a K5G-type new in 1942 and fitted with a 6-bay body by Brush, though rebuilt by its original owner Hants & Dorset, who fitted the PV2-type radiator. This bus could always easily be distinguished from native examples from a distance. It is seen on Station Hill in May 1963 between trips on Route 1a to Woodley.

Middle – Most numerous of the K-types were the 6-cylinder Bristol engined examples, and Car 497 (EJB 219) of 1949 is also seen on the 1a in May 1963, still working full-day turns. Note the variety of other PSV's in the shot, with a Smith's Bedford in front of the Station, an AEC 'Reliance' of Aldershot & District on joint Route 75, along with Reading Corporation AEC 'Regent' and 'Reliance'.

Bottom – The Reading saloon duties covered a wide variety of short and long runs to diverse places, and 1954 Bristol LS6B Car 716 (HMO 862) is seen in May 1963 on the 1b to Twyford via Hurst route. Note the painted base area on the roof side for the Job's Better Milk advert, the signwriter still to add the lettering next time the bus is idle for long enough. For many years the Station clock was set several minutes in front of GMT, the Reading time of pre-railway days.

Thames Valley services at Slough were varied, with Local Services reaching out to the large housing estates at Cippenham, Chalvey, Langley, Britwell and Burnham. Workings to the Trading Estate also featured on many routes, plus through journeys to link with Maidenhead via the Bath Road or Taplow and Cliveden.

Top – Known locally as 'the Archer's bus' Bristol KSW6B Car 699 (HMO 845) did indeed have every advert space used for that one advertiser. As Slough-based stationers and printers, its use on Route 61 to St. Andrews Way was appropriate.

Middle – Indeed, many of the Maidenhead double-deckers spent the whole day working services in the Slough area. Bristol KSW6B Car 655 (HBL 57) was working Route 64 to Britwell. Notice the lack of intermediate destination display and the painting out of the upper deck cream band, typical features of the period. All three of these photos were taken in April 1963.

Bottom – On the stands at Mackenzie Street, and in front of the Archer's bus, is Bristol FLF6G Car 850 (WJB 234) of 1961, in use on Route 60 via the 'Main Road' to Maidenhead. New deliveries still had an upper deck cream band, and this was one of the batch with cream rubbers on the window surrounds and destination apertures. It also has the illuminated advert panel on the offside which was fitted to some of Thames Valley's FLF's of the 1961–1963 batches, and eye-catching at night.

A trio of quite different types of buses on varied duties, all photographed in April and July 1963.

Top – The bulk of the Bristol MW6G saloons had gone to Newbury as replacements for the AEC 'Regals' of the Red & White era. Car 855 (VJB 946) is seen laid over at The Wharf after an April shower, evidently in from Penwood or Newtown on Route 121. Note the front nearside damage and dented side panel, which Reg Hibbert will have something to say about!

Middle – When London Route A was converted to double-deck operation in 1961 Newbury lost a pair of coach-seated LD-types, and one was Car 751 (MBL 832), which had in earlier years covered the B Route between Reading and London. Note the side advert for biscuits made by Huntley & Palmer, as often painted onto the vehicles used on London express routes for some years. Bristol KSW6B Car 646 (GJB 284) awaits its journey to Basingstoke.

Bottom – In 1958/9 some of the out-dated Bristol L-type coaches were rebuilt as LL5G's and re-bodied with ECW FB39F bodies for one-man-operation. Car 794 (DMO 664) was one of those and is seen at Newbury Wharf awaiting departure to Wantage on the Wednesday/Saturday-only Route 105. The bright yellow roundel reminds passengers that this is a one-manner bus, though older generations would in fact have recalled that many of the early services operated on that basis on the country roads

A further selection of the variety to be found at Reading and Newbury in the Summer of 1963.

Top – *The 1951 Bristol KS6B's were still very active, and Car 595 (FMO 977) had travelled to Newbury Wharf on Route 1 from Maidenhead. It is parked at the site of the original Thames Valley shelter from when only the service from Reading was in operation. It is notable how few double-deckers carried front upper-deck adverts at that time.*

Middle – *Also at Newbury in July was 1956 Bristol LD6G Car 764 (MBL 845) on the long Route 112 to Oxford, where its heaters, platform door and coach seating would be enjoyed by the passengers. This bus, along with identical vehicle 763, would be the last buses still with the upper-deck cream band and lined in black, due to Newbury garage doing its own repaints.*

Bottom – *In the last of the Philip Wallis colour shots we see a varied line up of Reading-based single-deck buses. On the left is Car 796 (DMO 666), a Bristol LL5G on the 1c Woodley route, and in the centre is Bristol LS6B Car 720 (HMO 866) on a Route 9a journey to Aldermaston (Soke Corner). To the right is the final LWL6B-type delivered as Car 633 (GJB 271) working on a relief journey on Route 5, though only through as far as Pangbourne. The Reading saloon workings were so arranged to give crews variety and to make up a working duty, and the buses also covered varied routes within the day.*

117

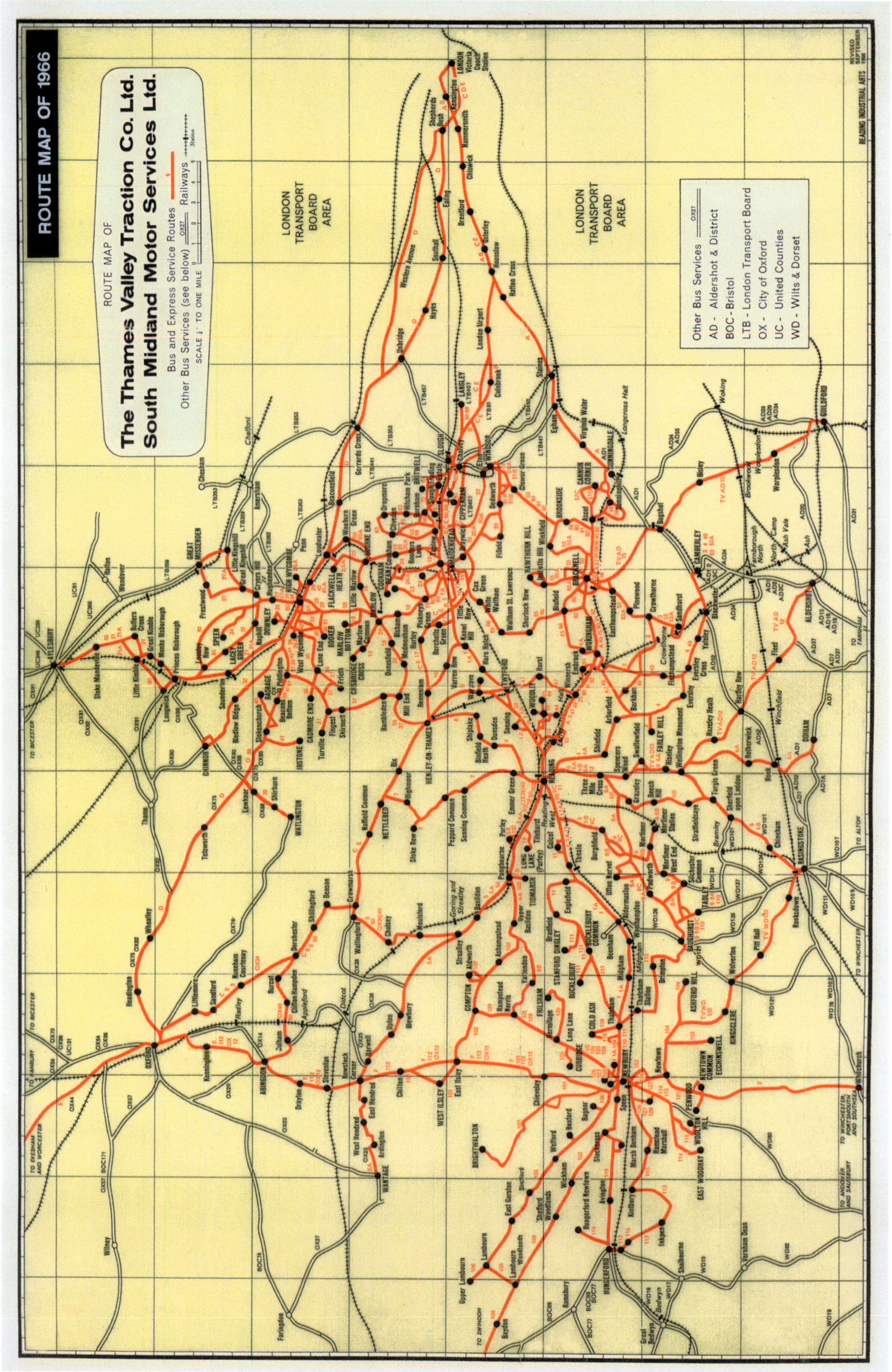
ROUTE MAP OF 1966
ROUTE MAP OF
The Thames Valley Traction Co. Ltd.
South Midland Motor Services Ltd.
Bus and Express Service Routes
Other Bus Services (see below)
Railways
Station
SCALE ½" TO ONE MILE
LONDON TRANSPORT BOARD AREA
LONDON TRANSPORT BOARD AREA
Other Bus Services
AD - Aldershot & District
BOC - Bristol
LTB - London Transport Board
OX - City of Oxford
UC - United Counties
WD - Wilts & Dorset
REVISED SEPTEMBER 1966
READING INDUSTRIAL ARTS

The Bristol K-type was still to be found widely in use by Thames Valley in the mid-1960's.

Top – Maidenhead's Bus Station was well laid out and had good passenger facilities. 1946 K6A-type Car 440 (CRX 549) was on Route 23 to Cookham Dean (Church) and still in good condition, other than its buckled blind. These 49-inch blinds were prone to damage, as over the years new destinations had been sewn into place, each garage having its own blind, usually with the main town name repeated at intervals throughout.

Middle – Also dating from 1946, K6A Car 450 (DBL 158) was one of those rebuilt at The Colonnade in 1961/2, when it lost its upper-deck beading and had the front destination aperture rebuilt to the T layout. It waits at Stations Square for duty on Route 43a to Woodley sometime after September 1963, the date the routes in that area were re-numbered.

Bottom – Another of the K-types to be rebuilt was former Bristol Omnibus Co. K6B Car 436 (KHU 624), though its selection was determined by the low railway bridge on Route 3 on Finchampstead Road in Wokingham! The bus was certainly one of the best in the fleet, as can be seen from this view taken in the Southern Yard parking area by the author in 1965. After it was sold in July 1966 in turned up in Canada, where it was used as a 'London' bus, with the old TV blind display of Loddon Bridge no doubt going unnoticed by most of those who saw it there!

The High Wycombe and Maidenhead operations also featured a variety of types.

Top – High Wycombe town had built up along the valley of the River Wye and later spread up the hillsides in all directions, resulting in a network of Local Services linking them together. Bristol KSW6B Car 731 (JRX 806) is seen at Oxford Road on the busy 42 service from Loudwater to West Wycombe or Booker Hill Estate in the mid-1960's

Middle – Several of the High Wycombe Local Services used rear-entrance Bristol single-deckers for many years, and LWL6B-type Car 621 (GJB 259) is shown on the 33 route emerging from Bridge Street and turning right into Desborough Road. Buses on this route stopped at virtually every stop between Newland Street and Desborough Castle Estate, plus some journeys extended onto High Wycombe Station.

Bottom – On the route to Marlow special light bus types had been employed for many years, and from 1957 this was met by five Bristol SC4LK-types with ECW B35F bodies. Cars 775/6 (NBL 732/3) were photographed in their usual position at the Bus Station in Maidenhead. One is on Route 18 to Marlow and the other on a short-working to Tittle Row on Route 17, this batch also covering some duties on Routes 16 and 17. Drivers recall that these buses were under-powered for the steep climb up Bisham Hill!

120

Thames Valley took small batches of the Bristol RE between 1964 and 1971, so each batch represented different body styles.

Top – The original buses on the RE chassis for TV were a trio of RELL6G's delivered in 1964 and used for crew operation from Reading garage on Route 5 (to Oxford) and some duties on Route 7 (to Stoke Row or Nettlebed), the latter having space to turn a 36-footer. The 54-seater bodies featured the peaked domes and wrap-round windscreen of that year, and Car S307 (CBL 356B) turns on Station Hill to the service stand.

Middle – The second batch of RESL6G buses were intended as crush-loaders, but Union opposition saw them re-figured for normal use, albeit retaining the dual-doorway layout. By 1967 the body style had a flatter front and restyled destination area. Car S338 (LJB 338F) entered service at Bracknell, and is seen parked in Market Street outside the garage, but was not the usual choice for Route 49 to Finchampstead.

Bottom – The body style had changed one again by the 1971 deliveries of RELL6G's, and the ECW body seated 49 for o-m-o working. Car 231 (CMO 649J) is seen at Oxford's Gloucester Green Bus Station on Route 5 for Wallingford and Reading, a route generally covered by 36ft-long RE buses from 1964 onwards, the initial batch of S306-8 (CBL 355-7B) duly being down-seated to 51 with a luggage pen for o-m-o.

Bristol FLF-types were purchased by Thames Valley from 1960 to 1968.

Top – Far from the usual format for the FLF were the five coach-seated 65-seaters ordered for the London express service B, which were also virtually unique in having power-operated sliding doors. Car 837 (UJB 203) is seen after being repainted into maroon and cream coach livery, and also having had its front destination screens rebuilt to T layout.

Middle – 1967 FLF6G Car D47 (LBL 847E) went as new to Bracknell, and is seen when two-way traffic used The Broadway and outside the Fine Fare Supermarket soon after entering service, heading for Windsor on a Sunday. The painted advert for Guilloud's Sports Stores in Slough always made this bus easy to spot. Note the total lack of cars, as no shops then opened on Sunday in Bracknell other than newsagents in the mornings and the 'open all hours' Mrs. Murphy's!

Bottom – There was less call in general for the 70-seater in the Newbury area, due to numerous narrow roads, but they were used on Route 1/1a to Maidenhead and in due course the 112 to Oxford and 122 to Basingstoke, and Car D18 (DRX 122C) of 1965 waits in the parking area of The Wharf for duty on Route 1a. The grilles set either side of the destination aperture are for the Cave-Browne-Cave heating system that made these buses nice and warm during the Winter, although they reduced potential advert spaces.

The distinctive maroon and cream livery of South Midland coaches started to be applied in varied proportions with differing body styles.

Top – The Bristol MW6G coaches were the first to wear the new livery, with other existing coaches and Thames Valley examples following that. 1959 Car 807 (PRX 933) had an ECW C34F body with quarter light panels for touring work. The rather neat integrated fleetname and radiator grille made these easy to spot, and the coach is on the Wales tour based at Llandrindod Wells. The maroon and cream theme continued on the interior scheme.

Middle – A shortage of body-building capacity for the 1965 season led to an order for Harrington-bodied Bedford SB13's, with 'Crusader' C37F bodies. Car C411 (EMO 552C) was the middle of the trio, which had cream and maroon in roughly equal amounts. These also had forced air ventilation, hence only a couple of opening windows on each side.

Bottom – The next batch of Bedfords used the VAM 14 chassis with a front overhang, and had bodies by Duple of the 'Bella Venture' style with seats for 41. These were mainly for excursions and private hire work, but also could sometimes be found on the London express services. Car C414 (GRX 414D) was new in 1966 and is seen at Gloucester Green Bus Station at Oxford on express duties. The livery has once again been fitted to the existing beading.

Small batches of Bristol MW6G's were purchased for the Thames Valley and South Midland fleets between 1958 and 1962.

Top – The pair of coach-seated MW's were always allocated to Reading and originally worked Route A to London (Victoria) and the 75 to Guildford. From 1965 these were in the new 'dual-purpose' livery as shown here, when Cars 852/3 (VJB 943/4) were parked at the Reading Bus Station yard. Note how the front ends vary in detail, with Car 853 in original condition, whilst Car 852 has evidently been rebuilt following an accident.

Middle – The only MW6G coach delivered new to TV was Car 866 (520 ABL), as the other of a pair ordered was duly changed to become the REX coach prototype. It was delivered in 1962, and was also the only one with the revised style of coach body with TV or SM. Originally used on excursions and private hire work, it was later on loan to South Midland, returning to Reading as a spare coach for the Rail Air Link from 1967.

Bottom – Although TV had only taken 6 saloons on MW6G chassis, it duly created a further 9 from former South Midland coaches during 1969/70. These followed on from similar conversions of LS coaches, with a jacknife door, bus-style indicators on the front dome and bus seats. The retention of the glazed quarter-lights gave them an airy interior, and former coach 800 is seen after re-emerging as Car 159 (ORX 631) in Lower Thorn Street yard.

The single-deck fleet was still quite varied, often responding to local needs, plus the increased use of one-man-operated buses.

Top – In the Newbury area the half-cab Bristol LL6B's were found to be more suitable for narrow roads, so the trio 564-6 remained there until 1968. Car 565 (FMO 947) was also fitted with a tow-bar and was used to recover breakdowns when needed. It is seen parked by the old stone building of the Kennet & Avon Canal.

Middle – Further variety came when Thames Valley created more LS-type buses out of some coaches from 1964. The original trio were prepared for the start of the joint Route 19 (Stations – Long Lane) with Reading Corporation and Car S310 (HMO 836) was one of those. As the Reading-based one-man duties worked over a variety of routes, these also took turns on other services, and in this case it had just worked in from Odiham on Route 6a.

Bottom – Marlow Bridge had influenced the single-deck fleet since the 1920's due to its weight limit. By late 1969 the Bristol SC4LK buses were in need of replacement, so after a trial with a loaned Bristol SUS4A it was decided to source 5 of that type from Bristol Omnibus and the Western National fleets, and Car 158 (845 THY) is seen inside Maidenhead garage. These buses had 30 seats and were used on Routes 16/17/18, but could even occasionally be found on Route 55 to Bracknell via Jealotts Hill and Warfield.

Thames Valley took the Bristol LS-type bus in good numbers, but later purchased a further 50 secondhand examples.

Top – The largest number of acquisitions came from United Welsh, and Car S330 (JCY 996) is shown turning out from Thames Side in Henley into Hart Street, having worked in from High Wycombe via Lane End and Hambleden on Route 37. The LS-types varied widely in condition but this was one of the better ones.

Middle – Only a quartet of LS's came from Bristol OC, easily distinguished by their single destination aperture. Car S345 (PHW 932) went to Newbury and is seen covering the ex-Reliance MS Route 107 to Brightwalton. Note the absence of a front fleet number, along with the position of the nearside one (and matching one on the offside), this occurring because BOC had painted the buses on behalf of TV.

Bottom – Another bus in from Route 37 and on the stand at Henley Market Place is Car 126 (966 ARA), one of a sizeable number from the Midland General fleet. Built in 1956, it was an LS6G and has the front destination display typical of that operator. This body style was quite unlike the native examples, as these had been new as dual-purpose vehicles, most re-seated as service saloons before sale to Thames Valley. They had interiors finished in blue and red and were in good condition, arriving at Reading in their blue and cream livery, and two retained coach seating.

126

A large number of 'Lodekkas' were also purchased from other THC fleets in order to speed up withdrawals of older models.

Top – Many of the earlier LD's had been built with the larger style of radiator grille, though most had received newer types over the years. However, Car 625 (THW 743) retained the old unit when acquired by Thames Valley. It was an LD6B new in 1955 and is seen coming in from Woodley on Route 1a into Stations Square, Reading.

Middle – Most of the ex-United Welsh LD's were placed into service still in original livery, which re-introduced the upper deck cream band and black lining previously lost from the native fleet. Car 797 (NCY 636) was new in 1956 and was an LD6G-type with ECW H33/27R body. It is parked on the forecourt of Maidenhead garage, lacking the oval Bristol badge on the top of the radiator grille, but with the scroll badge set centrally.

Bottom – Another source for LD's was Lincolnshire Road Car Co., but these varied in condition a lot. Car 607 (NBE 133) was an LD6B new in 1955 and is seen soon after repaint, coming into Reading Bus Station from Garrard Street and working in on Route 7 from Nettlebed. A couple of LRCC examples languished in the Weldale Street yard for some time prior to use, whilst buses from that source saw the shortest periods of use by TV, not even managing to put in a full year with their new owners!

The Rail Air Coach Link between Reading Station and Heathrow Airport was a good earner for Thames Valley, and on this page we view the three batches of coaches bought for the service.

Top *– The initial coaches used were a quartet of Bedford VAM14's with Duple 'Viceroy' bodies, of which Car C417 (LJB 417E) is seen in Reading garage with the dedicated signage used. However, these coaches were soon found to be underpowered for the task, spending only a year on the route before cascading to other duties.*

Middle *– The replacement coaches were RELH6G-type Bristols with powerful 6LX engines and more luggage stowage space, 4 of which were delivered in 1968. Car C427 (RJB 427F) is seen in front of Reading General Station in the layby reserved for the service. Similar coach C424 duly became a total loss when it caught fire on the M4 when heading for Heathrow Airport in 1970.*

Bottom *– The final batch of coaches delivered to TV for the Rail Air service were a further 6 Bristol RELH6G chassis, but this time with Plaxton C51F 'Panorama Elite' bodies new in 1971. Car 400 (BJB 883J) awaits service in the reserved space at Reading General, and by this time relief coaches were required on many journeys, so the frequency was increased to every 30 minutes. Rail passengers were met by uniformed railway hostesses, in a dedicated lounge area, before being escorted over to the coach service.*

1967 continued

Although the newest bus had enjoyed the limelight of the opening of Reading Bus Station, the next newest Car D52 (LBL 852E) was away for all of September at Lowestoft after accident damage! Also joining it there was Bristol LDL6G Car 779 (NBL 736), which was having a manually-operated rear door fitted. This was in line with Union demands for heaters and doors to be fitted to those buses not already so equipped, and further Bristol LD-types took the 332-mile round trip for the same treatment, returning to service in:
September – Cars 792/3 (NBL 749/50);
October - Cars 783/6/9/90/1 (NBL 740/3/6/7/8);
November – 781/2/4/5/7/8 (NBL 738/9/41/2/4/5);
and lastly in December – Car 780 (NBL 737).
Each bus was typically away for 3 to 4 weeks and they were ferried to and forth by 2 drivers, who returned with completed buses.

The fitting of a platform door to Bristol LDL6G Car 779 (NBL 736) emphasised still further its additional length, and following this work it was found that it would not clear the sloped exit of the new Bus Station! After that it was banished to a life on the Woodley Local Services, and also got larger fleetname transfers to use up existing stock, as seen here.

On 6th September a lorry collided with the railway bridge in Palmer Park Avenue, so the *'Valley* provided a shuttle service of buses between Reading and Earley Stations using Bristol FLF Cars 839 (WJB 223) and 868 (536 BBL), along with Bristol LS Car 683 (HBL 85) until the line could be re-opened.

Overall the year was a quite one for service changes, other than those imposed by external factors, which also highlights the work put into organising the Rail-Air service and the opening of Reading Bus Station. However, at Maidenhead, the one-way traffic scheme affected many routes through the town centre in a westwards loop via King Street and Grenfell Road outwards, returning via Grenfell Road – Broadway – York Road on incoming journeys from 8th November.

The Broadway at Bracknell was given a further extension westwards, as can be seen behind Bristol KSW6B Car 700 (HMO 846), caught by the camera outside Fine Fare on a Route 91 journey to Windsor. The lack of traffic indicates that this was a Sunday, as at other times this was then a very busy place.

No further new buses entered service during 1967, though we shall hear more soon of the outstanding 8 Bristol RE-types. During August the last of the batch of Bristol L6B coaches rebuilt as LL5G's and re-bodied with ECW FB39F bodies in 1958 was sold as Car 796 (DMO 666), whilst October saw the end for 1952 Bristol LS6G coaches 671/5 (HBL 73/7), latterly on contract duties from Newbury. Also going was Car 85 (SFC 571), the sole AEC 'Regal' MkIV coach with ECW C39F body new in 1952 as a legacy from the *Red & White* ownership of *South Midland*. Bristol MW6G coaches 802/3 (ORX 633/4) were transferred to Newbury to take over the contract runs to Harwell.

The departure of the above LS coaches left only Car 676 (HBL 78) of that type still active. It spent a while on loan to Maidenhead, transferring to Reading in March for relief duties, and is seen on layover in the Southern yard during the Summer of 1967.

Seen in the front doorway of Bracknell Garage is Car D45 (GRX 145D) ready for Route 90 to Windsor. The fuel pumps can be seen on the right, with the Enquiry Office door behind the author's bike, the Staff Canteen being situated upstairs. The site was leased from Bracknell Development Corporation.

From 1st December a weight limit of 10 tons was imposed on Spencers Bridge, so Route 24a from Maidenhead to Cookham Dean was diverted to run via Harrow Lane – Queensway – Gardners Road. On 16th December the Sunday workings on Routes 16 (Maidenhead - Warren Row – Henley) and 17 (Maidenhead – Hurley – Henley) were reduced. Over at Bracknell the new Wildridings Estate was now taking shape, so a new o-m-o Route 98 was laid on from 18th December, which ran as Bracknell (Regal Cinema) – Bracknell (Station) – Crowthorne Road – Wildridings Road – Shops (Deepdale) – Easthampstead (Church) – Crowthorne Road (Green Man) – Bracknell (Station) - Bracknell (Regal). Bracknell Garage workings could actually be quite involved at that time, as the Duty Board for Duty 517 with bus B58 for 16th September 1967 demonstrates:

From Garage at 0758 dead to Station Road;
Depart 0800 Route 53 to Windsor arrive 0842;
Depart Windsor 0855 as 53a to Camberley arrive 1017;
Depart Camberley 1025 as Route 49 to Wokingham (Town Hall), arrive 1114;
Dead to Garage arrive 1128;
1208 dead to Broadway for 1210 Route 58a, arrive Sunningdale 1242 (connect with Route 92 ex-Windsor at Fernbank Corner);
Depart Sunningdale 1247 on 58a to Bracknell (Regal), arrive at 1321, then dead to Garage;
Dead to Broadway 1408, the as 58a at 1410, arrive Sunningdale 1442 (connect at Fernbank Corner with Route 92 ex-Windsor);
Depart Sunningdale 1447 to Bracknell (Regal) on Route 58a, arrive 1521, then dead to Garage;
Dead to Borough Green School (School Special) for 1605, arrive Bullbrook (Shops) 1609, then dead to Station Road;
1620 Route 53 to Crowthorne (Iron Duke), arrive 1635;
1640 Iron Duke Route 54 to Bracknell (Regal) arrive 1658.

December saw the demise of another rear-entrance 1951 Bristol LL6B Car 571 (FMO 953), along with the first Bristol KS6B to depart, as Car 591 (FMO 973), also new in 1951. A further pair of Bristol LD6G buses with ECW 58-seater bodies arrived that month, formally *United Welsh* Nos.1244/5, though the latter example had already been fitted with a platform door. These became *Thames Valley* Cars 778 and 794 (JCY 991/2), the fleet numbers recently vacated by the LL5G's now providing a useful batch for re-issue, and both buses were sent to High Wycombe.

Car 778 (JCY 991) is seen above on Route 38 to Booker, after a platform door was added, whilst Car 794 (JCY 992) works in on Route 39 from Watlington.

Mention has been made of the 8 Bristol RESL6G buses received during September/October, which had been built by ECW as B38D+27 standee passengers and intended for o-m-o working on the Slough crosstown Routes 62/63/68. However, these were blacked by the Union and placed in store pending further talks, which dragged on into the following year.

1968

This was a year of unprecedented changes within the fleet, with 59 departures and 63 buses and coaches entering service. The author, along with other local enthusiast never knew what they would find when at the Reading Garage, and having obtained a *United Welsh* fleet list, the next prediction was proved wrong by the surprise arrival of a quartet of Bristol KSW6B buses ex-*United Automobile Services* of Darlington! New in 1952 as *United* Nos.BGL76/8 (then with 5LW Gardner engines) and BBL66/7 (PHN 819/21/8/9) they now took vacated LS fleet numbers as Cars 691/90/88/89 respectively, all carrying standard ECW L27/28R bodies, and as with the KSW's from *United Welsh,* these all went to Newbury Garage.

The ex-United Auto Bristol KSW's were in good shape and were mostly used on the Newbury Local Services. Car 691 (PHN 819) is seen above on Route 128 at The Wharf, whilst the rear view of Car 698 (PHN 829) shows in on the 127. Note the car-height damage to the offside, many of the estate roads being narrow.

No doubt in response to the increasing raft of package holidays now starting to tempt people abroad, there were a number of adverts placed in various local newspapers for the *South Midland* extended tours from the start of January.

However, of more pressing concern was the heavy snowfall of early January, which soon revealed the folly of a sloped exit from the Reading Bus Station! Drivers struggled to get their charges up the slope and then onto Station Hill, whilst further afield a number of buses were involved in weather-related incidents.

Bristol 'Lodekka' Car 753 (MBL 834) attempts the climb out of Reading Bus Station as it sets off on Route 4 for the 17-mile journey to Camberley.

At Bracknell the steady slope of Station Road once again proved challenging, so drivers tended to take a good run up and hope they could just keep going to the top without having to stop. Also in that town, 22nd January saw the opening of new primary schools on Wildridings Estate at Netherton. A number of pupils were directed there from the housing at the RAF Staff College off Broad Lane, and others from the early stages of Great Hollands Estate, so a special journey was provided from the College (Birch Grove) to the schools on Route 53, whilst the service was also diverted via Great Hollands (Aysgarth) from that date.

Up in the Wycombe area another large employer asked for extra buses to Glory Mill, one of a number of paper mills then operating along the Wye valley at Wooburn Green. Extra journeys were provided from 27th January out of High Wycombe via Wycombe Marsh – Loudwater – Holtspur Lane – Holtspur Avenue – Glory Mill Lane, and these timings were shown under Route 20/20a and included mid-day times to suit the shift patterns at the mill.

Bristol KSW6B Car 735 (JRX 810) slid off the road and into a ditch at Binfield Heath whilst working Route 8 to Henley in the snow of 9th January.

The final batch of Bristol FLF's for *Thames Valley* entered service in February as Cars D54-60 (PBL 53/55-60F), all with Eastern Coach Works H38/32F bodies. They had Clayton Dewandre heating and also had Gardner 6LX engines of 10.45 litres instead of the 8.4-litre 6LW units previously used, which did improve their turn of speed. These were allocated to Bracknell (D59), Maidenhead (D58), Newbury (D55), Reading (D54/7/60) and Wycombe Marsh (D56). Another FLF absent from 30th November 1967 was Car D30 (GRX 130D), which was at ECW receiving repairs until 16th January after fire damage.

It will be noticed that D54 didn't have a matching registration number, as apparently this was issued in error to another user. It is seen helping out on Route B and passing Bowater House at Knightsbridge.

These double-deckers were amongst the last 30 Bristol FLF's built, and it was confirmed that a pair of the new Bristol VRT-type chassis had been ordered to take ECW bodies for evaluation later in the year.

Another form of traffic management then making an increased presence locally was the roundabout, usually replacing 4-way crossroads, though from 8th February the complicated junction at Shepherds House Lane was altered to form a large roundabout. This resulted in some changes to the Woodley Local Services, which were further affected by the placement of another one at Pitts Lane and London Road junction from 15th May.

Bracknell's Regal Cinema forms the back-drop for Bristol FLF6G Car D59 (PBL 59F) on Route 91 for Popeswood - Wokingham – Emmbrook – Reading.

The bus stop outside Heatherwood Hospital was given a nice wooden shelter by Sunninghill Parish Council in February, at a cost of £340. This was the homeward boarding place for the author, who then worked nearby in Kings Ride, and this could be a very wind-swept spot opposite the open ground of Ascot Race Course, so it was much appreciated. A similar shelter was erected on the opposite side a few months later. A number of other shelters were of course provided by other Local Councils throughout the large *Thames Valley* area, whilst some of the 1920's examples put up by the Company were still in evidence in the '60's.

There were further surprises in store in February, with the arrival of more buses from the *United Automobile* fleet, though this time they were Bristol LS5G saloon buses new in 1953 as Nos.BU38-40, they became Cars S339-41 (SHN 728-30). These were all initially at Maidenhead, though S340 was duly transferred to Newbury, and those were indeed interesting times, when every trip to a *Thames Valley* garage was rewarded with something unexpected!

Indeed, March saw the end of the road for a number of the Duple-bodied Guy 'Arab' MkIII 6LW buses, with highbridge examples Cars H10 (FMO 517) and H13/5/6 (HOT 391/3/4) all departing. Bristol types out that month were 1950 KS6B Car 586 (FMO 968) with ECW L27/28R body, LWL6B Cars 613/26 (GJB 251/64) of 1951/2 and with ECW B39R bodies, along with the first of the 1959 rebuilds to LL5G-type fitted with ECW FB39F body Car 820 (FMO 24). Bedford SB8 coach 861 (WRX 776), which had a 7ft 6ns-wide Duple 'Super Vega' C37F body and was new in 1961, went in February and was followed by similar 1962 Car 862 (516 ABL) during April.

In respect of the Service Vehicle fleet, February had seen the departure of a 1962 Vauxhall 'Velox' car (460 BMO), followed in April by a 1960 Morris 'Minor' 1000cc car (UMO 568), a 1960 Morris 'Oxford car (WMO 279), the 1956 Newbury Depot Commer 'Cob' Van No.37 (MRX 113) and 1960 Bedford CAV Van No.45 (UJB 298) latterly used as the Publicity Van. May saw the disposal of 1964 Ford Thames 307E Van No.49 (765 BJB), followed by 1961 Vauxhall 'Victor' car (YBL 283) in June. 1962 Austin A40 car (592 BMO) was also sold in August.

The vans were replaced by new ones taking their old numbers, with No.49 (PJB 349F), a Ford 7cwt during February, No.37 (RJB 37F) as a Bedford CAV 10/12cwt arriving in May, along with a 15/17cwt van of the same make as No.45 (RJB 45F). The cars were replaced by a Wolseley 18/85 car (PJB 98F) arriving in January, followed by a trio of Austin 1100 cars in February (PJB 421-3F), then an Austin 1300 car (RJB 934F) in May, and in November by an Austin 1300 estate (TJB 348G) to complete 1968's changes.

Ex-United Auto Bristol LS5G Car S341 (SHN 730) is seen above at Castle Hill in Windsor on a short-working of Route 22 to Eton, Eton Wick and Dorney Reach. On the same route Car S340 (SHN 729) is shown below as it comes into Maidenhead.

Yet another source provided a further 4 Bristol LS5G-type saloons during March, this time *Bristol Omnibus,* whose 1954 ECW-bodied Nos.2839-42 (PHW 929-32) became Cars S342-5. All of these went to work from Newbury garage, largely because they featured the single rectangular destination screen, which was painted down to single line and they were fitted with blinds taken from outgoing Guy 'Arab' double-decks.

Former Bristol OC Car S344 (PHW 931) is seen at The Wharf for Route 114 to East Woodhay. They were repainted into Thames Valley livery by their former owner, who then positioned the fleet numbers on each side of the body in accordance with its own practice.

Bristol LS5G Car S343 (PHW 930) is seen at The Wharf on Route 119 to Ashmore Green and Cold Ash.

In the meantime the negotiations had continued regarding operation of the 8 Bristol RESL6G saloons still in store. The Union would not budge on the idea of standee-type working, even though the Company pointed out that similar types of buses were in use with *Reading Corporation* and *London Transport*.

Once the octet of Bristol RESL6G's entered service they were allocated to a number of garages rather than being kept together. Car S331 (LJB 331F) is seen parked outside the Maidenhead garage with blinds set for Route 17, a service which at times could be busy with school children coming in from Tittle Row to Altwood and the Girl's schools.

Also with blinds set for the same service is S332 (LJB 332F), which would duly count young Jenny Agutter amongst its passengers, as it was hired for filming by Bray Studios of 'I Start Counting' in 1969. It is seen in the front yard of Maidenhead garage with a side advert, which looked odd because such items did not feature on the near side due to the dual-entrance layout.

The rear elevation of the batch was quite neat, with the triple windows in order to accommodate the centre rear emergency exit. Note the reversing light, something only then found on such vehicles as o-m-o buses. Car S332 (LJB 332F) is parked on the Maidenhead forecourt also showing the air scoop on the roof for engine cooling.

Reading's examples could be found on most single-deck duties, and Car S336 (LJB 336F) is seen leaving the Bus Station as it turns onto Station Hill for the 30-mile Route 50 through Pangbourne, Wallingford, Dorchester for Abingdon, a very pleasant outing on a nice day following the River Thames, which the bus crossed over twice.

These buses had been intended for the conversion of Routes 62 (Slough – Chalvey – Cippenham), 63 (Maidenhead – Cliveden – Dropmore – Burnham – Slough) and 68 (Maidenhead – Cliveden – Hitcham Park – Slough), and at one point the Management threatened to abandon those services completely, such was the level of frustration felt at Lower Thorn Street. Indeed, after a time the Union accepted in principle the conversion to one-man working, but would not approve their use in the format they were delivered.

As this became apparent, work started on altering the buses at The Colonnade to a B40D capacity plus the standard 8 standing passengers, though the centre exit was retained. Although the space opposite did prove useful for buggies and shopping trolleys, the stepped exit meant that passengers with such items found it easier to leave by the front door instead. Indeed, many drivers just ignored the centre door entirely, whilst the lack of suitable notices to passengers internally did nothing to encourage use of the dual-door facility.

The batch carried their allocated fleet numbers S331-8 but had been delivered with pre-booked registrations LJB 331-8E, though the licensing authority agreed to alter just the suffix of these to 'F' rather than issue a further set when they were finally licensed in March. The ECW bodies gave an overall length of 32ft 3.25ins, whilst internally they had green PVC seating with formica backing, the overall appearance being quite airy due to glazed roof panels.

The interior of Car S334 looking rearwards from behind the driver's cab and showing the centre exit, rear emergency door and luggage pen.

The driver's cab area shows the semi-automatic gear knob just to the left of the steering wheel, and also the holder for the Setright Ticket Machine. When new these were stated by the Company as intended for a 'sophisticated fare collection system', though obviously that part of the plan did not go ahead.

Car S335 (LJB 335F) is seen in Lower Thorn Street yard at Reading Garage with blinds set for Route 6a to Odiham, hardly warranting the dual-door layout.

As with the Bristol RE in general, these buses gave a good ride and were popular with those drivers who could get the best out of using the pre-selective (semi-automatic) gearing. The batch was divided up between Bracknell (S333/4/8), Maidenhead (S331/2), Newbury (S337) and Reading (S335/6), though in retrospect it was a pity they could not have been used in a manner more fitting to their layout on an intensive service.

Traffic delays were adversely affecting the reliability of many services, and from 2nd March the 7am Route B bus to London had to be re-timed at 6.45 in order to reach Kensington for 9am, a factor that also improved reliability for workers at the Mars chocolate factory in Slough, who used that journey. Also, as the M4 motorway progressed it initially worsened traffic on the A4 through Reading, causing more congestion!

Although there had been quite a variety of service buses coming in secondhand, it still came as quite a surprise to find three *Eastern National* coaches in The Colonnade during March. All had ECW C34F bodies and were new in 1957/8, so at first it was thought that these were going to be converted for service work. In fact the truth was even more unlikely, as all were repainted and lettered for *South Midland!* They had been new as Nos.428/9/32 (613/4/8 JPU), the first pair as Bristol LS6G chassis, whilst the latter was the first of the MW chassis built. These became Cars C432-4 and the MW even saw use on some touring work.

Former Eastern National Car C433 (614 JPU) is seen above at Oxford on express duties. Note the additional side beading, which included green plastic strips (retained when repainted), along with the glazed quarter-lights. Below we see Car 432 (613 JPU) emerging from a Winter in store at Stokenchurch.

During April further inroads were made into the ranks of rear-entrance Bristol saloons with 39-seater ECW bodies, with LL6B Car 560 (FMO 942) and LWL6B Car 624 (GJB 262) both departing, the latter being a favourite of the author when on Route 53. April also saw the end for the remaining Guy 'Arab' MkIII 6LW double-deckers with Duple bodies. Lowbridge L27/26RD-bodied Cars 170/1 (FMO 515/6) and high-bridge H31/26R-bodied Car H14 (HOT 392) were also the final vehicles owned by *Newbury & District*.

High-bridge Guy Car H14 (HOT 392) is seen on Route 113 to Inkpen in its latter days, with the new by-pass recently opened to the east of The Wharf.

The fitting of manually-operated platform doors on Bristol LD-type buses continued at Lowestoft throughout the first half of 1968, with the following vehicles returning in the months shown:

April – Cars 755/6 (MBL 836/7) and 767 (MBL 848);
May – Cars 757 (MBL 838) and 765 (MBL 846);
June – Cars 758/9/66/8 (MBL 839/40/47/9).

New vehicles for April were a quartet of 36ft-long Bristol RELH coaches as replacements for the Rail-Air Bedford VAM's C417-20 (LJB 417-20E). The latter's 6.17 litre engine had proven inadequate for the task, whilst the incoming coaches had 10.45 litres of Gardner 6HLX for power. These were fitted with Duple 'Commander MkIII' C49F bodies, which also provided improved luggage space. Cars C424-7 (RJB 424-7F) also followed railway tradition by being named as 'Western Pegasus, Western Mercury, Western Eros and Western Hermes', these being on a plaque situated inside above the windscreen.

The former Eastern National MW6G coach C434 (618 JPU) was the only vehicle of that chassis type to be acquired secondhand. The trio were all in good order but the use of this coach on extended tours was quite unexpected, and it is seen at Oxford ready for the Welsh Coast Tour based at Porthcawl.

136

The interior of Reading Garage as seen from the Weldale Street entrance, with the Engineering Offices to the rear and the Central Works over to the right of Bristol FLF6G Car D43 (GRX 134D). Rail-Air coach C426 (RJB 426F) is shown with the blind used for this service which incorporated the BR logo (also referred to at the time as 'the arrow of indecision'). The roof was the largest of its type when constructed in 1938 and required no supporting pillars, which left a large uninterrupted space.

The garage is again seen from the Lower Thorn Street entrance, with a variety of types in view of Bristol KSW, LD, LS and RE. This scene records the out-shopping of ex-United Automobile Services KSW Car 690 (PHN 821) amidst a cloud of exhaust. Note the trade plate (112 RD), one of a number in use at Thames Valley for un-licensed buses or on the recovery wagons. This yard could take a double row buses on the left and a single row on the right.

Another integral slice of Reading scenery was St. Mary's Butts, where the Company's buses had originally terminated. In this view we see converted Bristol LS6B Car S309 (HMO 835) with its front end rebuilt following an accident, coming in on Route 9a from Tadley and Grazeley. Note the shops off to the right, whilst behind the bus there is the toy shop, which included a 'doll's hospital' where such items could still be taken for repair!

Rail-Air coach C427 (RJB 427F) is seen parked at the Heathrow terminus.

As a result of the above new Rail-Air coaching stock, the Bedford VAM14 Cars C417-20 (LJB 417-20E) were displaced onto other duties. C417/8 were given *South Midland* fleetnames and allocated to Oxford, whilst the other pair was usually found at Reading. One was loaned to Maidenhead for a while, intended primarily for covering broken down coaches on the M4 between that town and London for associated companies, similar arrangements also existing at Reading, Newbury and High Wycombe. Indeed, prior to that it was the practice to send out a spare bus, usually an LS-type saloon, though on several occasions a Bristol SC had been the only option!

On the services front, Routes 58/58a (Bracknell – Bullbrook – Ascot – Sunningdale) were amended to run via Lily Hill Road – Long Hill Road – Priory Road, re-joining their original route on the London Road at the Royal Forester's crossroads, with effect from 20th April, which better served the residents of the Chavey Down area (where quite a few local bus crews still lived). In Reading there was a diversion on Route 4a (Reading – Shinfield – Arborfield – Barkham – Wokingham), with buses leaving the Bus Station from 21st April by way of Station Hill and Greyfriars Road as part of the one-way scheme.

Former United Welsh Bristol LD6G Car 795 (NCY 634) is seen in the Newbury Garage shortly after it was acquired. The intermediate destination box has been painted out in black, something of a speciality of that garage, whilst the paintwork is as received.

Despite other recent acquisitions from other operators, it transpired that the *United Welsh* source had not in fact dried up, and in April a further quartet of Bristol LD6G's with ECW LD33/27R bodies arrived, new in 1956 as Nos.301-3 (NCY 634-6) and in 1957 as No.307 (OCY 953). These became Cars 795-8 in the same order, and allocations were to Maidenhead (797), Newbury (795/6) and Wycombe (798).

Another ex-United Welsh LD6G in original paintwork is Car 798 (OCY 953), seen at Wycombe Marsh soon after arrival. It still had both cream bands and black lining. The author also noted that some of these buses appeared a slightly lighter shade of red – was this due to United Welsh using a different supply, or just long-term exposure to the sea air of Oystermouth Bay?

The use of the size of adverts from the sides of double-deckers on saloons widened still further when they also appeared on the 36ft-long Bristol RELL6G Cars S306-8 (CBL 355-7B) during May, though generally this practice cheapened the appearance of the fleet. Other changes saw converted Bristol LS6B Cars S309 (HMO 835) and S315 (TWL 55) both with rebuilt front ends after accidents by May, each having a plainer style without the ECW-Bristol wings. Also during that month similar bus S310 (HMO 836) had its Bristol engine replaced by a Gardner 6HLW unit.

May saw further depletions of 7ft 6ins-wide Bristols, with the exit of rear-entrance 1951 LL6B Car 569 (FMO 951), 1951 KS6B double-decker Car 589 (FMO 971) and LL5G rebuild with 1959 ECW FB39F body Car 819 (FMO 23). Also sold that month was a further Bedford SB8 of 1962, though with an 8ft-wide Duple 'Super Vega' C37F body as Car 864 (518 ABL), whilst during June identical coaches 863/5 (517/9 ABL) were also cleared out. Another of the 1959 LL5G rebuilds with ECW FB39F bodies went in June as Car 818 (FMO 22), along with front-entrance ECW 39-seater LL6B Car 566 (FMO 948), which had spent some years on the Lambourn outstation. After that there was an eerily quite spell as no other changes in the fleet took place between July and September.

In the meantime the year's intake of new coaches for *South Midland* had finally arrived on 18th May, hence the retention of the Bedford SB8's just in case!. These were Cars C428-31 (RJB 428-31F), and they broke new ground by being based on the lightweight Bristol LH6L chassis, which used the Leyland 400/75 engine, and the unladen weight of these was 6tons 18cwts, exactly 2 tons less than the (slightly longer) RELH coaches carrying similar bodywork. These were again by Duple with 'Commander' MkIII bodies, though they were only 32ft 7ins long and seated 41.

No Bristol badges were evident on the LH6L coaches, and these two views show Car C431 (RJB 431F) above at Gloucester Green in Oxford on express work, though these were primarily touring coaches. Also seen below at the same location is Car C429 (RJB 429F), also awaiting an express run to London.

Although new arrivals were lacking for a few months, the public could have been forgiven for thinking there were some new double-deckers on the London Routes A and B, as the coach-seated buses received another re-paint, this time in a double-deck version of the dual-purpose livery. 1964 Bristol FLF Cars D5 (ABL 117B) and D8 (BRX 141B) re-appeared in May, followed by D6 (ABL 118B) in June and D4/7 (ABL 116/9B) in July. The 1960 batch of FLF's was also dealt with, and Cars 834-6/8 (UJB 200-2/4) were done by July, followed by Car 837 (UJB 203) in August.

Whilst on the subject of paintwork I am reminded that over the years the Company sold off surplus paint to its employees, and in the early days many lived in houses with green windows, fences and sheds. Ed Maun recalls that his parent's kitchen at Stokenchurch was for some years finished in maroon and cream!

Coach-seated Bristol FLF6G Car 838 (UJB 204) is seen after repainting to red and cream. However, this photo may not be what is seems, i.e. working the South Midland express from Oxford to London via High Wycombe, and is actually believed to be seen on a private hire, when the photographer decided on the mischief with the blinds!

From 25th May the Woodley Local Services were further altered to operate as follows:

Route 10 – Reading (Bus Station) – Church Road – Earley (Crossroads) – Silverdale Road – Earley Station Turn – Loddon Bridge – Colemans Moor Road – Wheelers Green – Woodley (Roundabout);
Route 43 – Reading (BS) – London Road – Reading Road – Crockhamwell Road – Loddon Bridge Road – Woodley (Roundabout) or Tippings Lane, some extended via Butts Hill Road to Twyford;
Route 43a – Reading (BS) – London Road – The Drive – Whiteknights Lane – Culver Lane – Church Road – Woodlands Avenue – Howth Drive – Beechwood Avenue – Crockhamwell Road – Loddon Bridge Road – Woodley (Roundabout) or Tippings Lane, with some via Butts Hill Road to Twyford;
Route 44 – Reading (BS) – London Road – Reading Road – Headley Road – Woodley (Roundabout), then either to Tippings Lane or via Loddon Bridge Road to Colemans Moor Lane and Colemans Moor Road;
Route 44a Reading (BS) – London Road – The Drive – Whitegates Lane – Culver Lane – Church Road – Woodlands Avenue – Howth Road – Beechwood Ave. – Headley Road – Woodley (Roundabout), then either to Tippings Lane or via Loddon Bridge Road to Colemans Moor Lane and Colemans Moor Road.
Route 45 Reading (BS) – London Road – Reading Road – Western Avenue – Butts Hill Road – Woodley (Roundabout).

Several Bristol FLF's were absent for attention up at Lowestoft after bad smashes, with Car D48 (LBL 848E) away for the whole of May, followed by coach-seated Car 835 (UJB 201) from mid-June for a month. Bristol KSW Car 746 (JRX 821) was also damaged front and rear when running empty at Winnersh on 10th July, but it was dealt with at The Colonnade.

139

A pair of the 1964 coach-seated Bristol FLF6B's are seen at Victoria Coach Station in the red and cream scheme, with Car D6 (ABL 118B) above for Reading, and the rear of Car D5 (ABL 117B) shown below. As the GM Tom Pruett came from Brighton, Hove & District perhaps that livery was the inspiration?

It was also intended to revise the services from Bracknell along the Sunningdale corridor from 25th May, as shown in the new timetable book, but the Union blacked these changes until finally agreeing to them from 30th November, and they were as follows:

Route 98 – Town Centre – Wildridings circular now discontinued as separate service;
Routes 57/57a/58/58a – Generally revised to provide better links between Bracknell and Heatherwood Hospital, with some journeys extended back from Bracknell (Regal) to Bracknell (Station) – Wildridings (Deepdale) – Easthampstead (Church) – Crowthorne Road (Green Man) – Bracknell (Station);
Routes 59/59a - (Brookside – Ascot – Sunningdale) now much reduced operation.

At Downley the issue of indiscriminate parking of cars around the village hall had become so chronic, that from 1st June all journeys on Route 35 (High Wycombe – Downley) were turned at Littleworth Road, returning via Plomers Green Road.

From 15th June some timings on Slough Local Services were altered in order to afford better connections with the *London Transport* buses reaching Wexham Park Hospital, some 2 miles north of the town centre, whilst from the following day the early morning journeys on Route 116 (Hungerford – Newbury) were re-timed to allow a good connection with the *Bristol Omnibus* service from Swindon.

Bracknell High Street, when buses ran both ways, with Bristol LS6B Car 712 (HMO 858) loading on Route 57a for Sunningdale outside the Post Office.

In Reading, the Kings Road one-way scheme came into effect from 16th June, with eastbound services still using Kings Road, whilst westbound buses were diverted via the A4 London Road and Watlington Street. This affected buses on Routes A and B (from London), 28 (from High Wycombe), 47 (from Hurst and Twyford), 3/49 (from Wokingham/Camberley), 75 (from Guildford) and the 90-group services (from the Windsor direction). This situation continued, despite *Reading Corporation* gaining permission to run its trolleybuses (and motorbuses) in a contra-flow lane westbound along Kings Road, such permission not being extended to *TV* buses until 12th April 1969.

Colin Routh spotted Bristol FLF6G Car D48 (LBL 848E) on its way to Lowestoft for rear-end repairs.

Bedford SB13 coach C406 (836 CRX) arrives at the front of Reading General Station from the garage in order to help out on the Rail-Air Service.

The small batch of Bristol MW6G saloons delivered in 1960 had remained at their original allocations, with coach-seated Cars 852/3 (VJB 943/4) at Reading and bus-seated Cars 854-7 (VJB 945-8) at Newbury. However, in June 1968 Car 856 crossed the Thames to High Wycombe, being joined there from July by Car 854 and then by Car 852 in December. Also in June the first of the 1954 Bristol LS-types to be re-engined saw Car 722 (HMO 868) lose its 6-cylinder Bristol unit in exchange for a Gardner 6HLW. Other detail changes affecting the LS fleet saw 1953 LS6G Cars 680/1 (HBL 82/3) finally reverting to B41F once again for one-man working from August.

The above changes were all integral to the departures of the same period, which resulted in High Wycombe losing its rear-entrance Bristol LL6B's, which were replaced by Bristol LS's released from Bracknell now the Bristol RESL6G's were available. Over at Newbury the old roles of the front-entrance LL6B's were taken by largely secondhand Bristol LS buses, which also allowed some transfers of MW's to High Wycombe where their power was appreciated, the character of operations at both Newbury and High Wycombe being quite altered by these changes.

Newbury Garage only got one of the Bristol RESL6G buses, Car S337 (LJB 337F), and in this shot taken at The Wharf it is seen having arrived in from Cold Ash and Thatcham on Route 109. North of Thatcham there were some narrow sections, so note the side damage!

The last of the Bristol LL5G rebuilds with 1959 ECW FB39F bodies was ousted in July as Car 817 (FMO 21), in company with the final 1952 Bristol LS6G coach 676 (HBL 78). July also saw the demise of 1950 Bristol KS6B Car 588 (FMO 970), with ECW L27/28R bodywork, and was followed by similar Cars 590/2/3 (FMO 972/4/5) in August. Departures continued with 1950 ECW B39F-bodied Bristol LL6B Cars 565/7/8 (FMO 947/9/50) in August, along with the final 1951 B39R-bodied example Car 574 (FMO 956) and 1952 ECW B39R-bodied Bristol LWL6B Car 615 (GJB 253).

Seven-and-a-half-footers were now dwindling in the fleet, and 1950 Bristol KS6B Car 597 (FMO 979) is seen traversing the temporary ramp erected over bridge works in Bridge Street during 1968. The use of such a vehicle on Route 6 through to Basingstoke was not usual at this point, whilst in the background can be seen the old Simond's brewery, which contributed one of Reading's then distinctive smells from its days as the town of the 3B's – beer, biscuits and bulbs!

From 12th August revisions were made to Route 54 (Bracknell (Regal Cinema) – Southern Industrial Area – Crowthorne), which added peak journeys starting out with a double-loop from the town centre to take in Priestwood (Moordale Avenue), then via Bracknell (Station) – Bullbrook (Castrol Laboratories) – Harmans Water (Shops) – Easthampstead (Church). Also at peak times there were through workings past Easthampstead Park College – Pinewood Crossroads – Crowthorne (Iron Duke), but for most of the day the operation covered the core runs between the town and the Rowney factory. Also in Bracknell, staff at the Dorothy Perkins head office on Wokingham Road sought better buses into town lunchtimes, so some additional Route 52/56 journeys were provided from the Bridge House stop from 7th October.

From the end of August the long-established special Sunday journeys on Routes 61 and 70 to serve Burnham RC Church ceased due to the lack of demand.

A trio of views from around the Thames Valley operating area, the first showing Bristol MW6G Car 856 (VJB 947) after its transfer to High Wycombe, ready for the former Penn Bus Co. Route 34 to Hughenden, North Dean and Speen. Bristol LWL6B Car 632 (GJB 270) is seen on Local Service 33, its days now numbered, and both buses are laid over at Frogmoor with the high railway embankment as the familiar backdrop to many Wycombe photos.

Thames Valley vehicles had run into London on a daily basis since May 1927, and 1964 Bristol FLF6B Car D5 (ABL 117B) is seen here after its repaint to red and cream in Kensington High Street. Note the lack of front fleet number and the newly-painted double yellow lines along this urban clearway. Note also the tall thin buildings in the Dutch style, so built for the same reason as those they imitate, in order to make maximum use of the expensive land locally.

Elsewhere, as in Bracknell New Town, land was made available for the laying out of new estates, each house with its own garden and some with garages. This view from the flats above the shops of Wildridings Square shows the turning circle, with former Red & White Bristol LS Car 356 (MAX 128), which would soon arrive to further boost such secondhand purchases. It is on the later Route 58B and bearing its subsequent fleet number 143.

142

The fitting of rear platform doors to Bristol LD-types continued, though few dates are known for those dealt with in-house. However, in July ex-*United Welsh* Car 797 (NCY 636) returned from Lowestoft, and this was followed by similar Cars 796 (NCY 635) in October and Cars 795 (NCY 634) and 798 (OCY 953) during November. The last of the 1956 batch of native 'Lodekkas' without a rear door, Car 769 (MBL 850) also returned from treatment at ECW in October.

Two of the former United Welsh LD-types are seen after being fitted with manually operated platform doors. Above we see Car 796 (NCY 635) at Newbury Wharf on Route 127 to the Turnpike Estate, whilst below there is a rear shot of Car 778 (JCY 991) seen in High Wycombe on Route 25a from Flackwell Heath (Rugwood Road), the latter modified in-house.

Only one bus was sold during September, that being a further 1950 Bristol KS6B Car 587 (FMO 969) with ECW L27/28R bodywork. Recent changes in the fleet make up saw more one-man-operation on Route 9c (Reading – Baughurst direct), though crew-operated double-deckers still covered peak-time journeys from 28th September. Also from that date the sometimes mixed operation by crew-operated saloons and one-manners on Route 50 (Reading – Abingdon) now went over fully to the latter as the Bristol LWL6B buses were becoming a rarity at Reading.

At Wokingham a partial one-way traffic scheme saw Peach Street with only westbound traffic, so from 30th September *Thames Valley* buses on Routes A (to London), 4a (to the Norreys and Ashridge Estates), northbound Routes 65/65a/66/66a (towards Slough), 75 (to Guildford) and the 90-group (towards Bracknell and Windsor) were routed from Broad Street via Rose Street and Wiltshire Road, before re-joining their old routes at The Ship junction. Also buses heading west to Emmbrook and Reading on Routes 91/91a could no longer enter Milton Road, so they were diverted down Rectory Road and Glebelands Road, though those in the easterly direction could still emerge from the now one-way section of Milton Road into Broad Street.

Whilst on the subject of entrances on 'Lodekkas', this close up of FLF6G Car D54 (PBL 53F) by Graham Low shows all the features very clearly.

From 1st October history repeated itself when Chief Engineer Baker informed Reg Hibbert, the Newbury Garage Foreman that he would once again be responsible for the maintenance of the *South Midland* fleet. In actual fact, although most major docking had been dealt with at Reading for many years, the garage staff at Oxford and Newbury had maintained close ties stemming back to their days under *Red & White*, often without the express knowledge of their Reading masters. Also during September one of the MW6G coaches used at Newbury was sent back to Oxford, its place being taken by Bedford SB13 coach C406 (836 CRX), which carried a Duple 'Super Vega' C37F body and had latterly been kept as a spare Rail-Air coach at Reading, now covered by the 1967 VAM's.

Over at Maidenhead garage further alterations to the working arrangements on Routes 60/60a (Maidenhead – Slough via the Bath Road, and Trading Estate on 'a' journeys) from 19th October saved two double-deckers on that allocation.

The latter, along with new deliveries, saw further inroads into the 1950 ECW-bodied Bristol KS6B's, with L27/28R Car 594 (FMO 976) and L27/26RD-bodied Cars 597/600 (FMO 979/82) all departing in October. Also ousted that month was the first Bristol KSW6B to depart, as Car 603 (FMO 985), with ECW L27/28R body new in late 1950, along with the first of the Bristol LS saloons, Car 686 (HBL 88), with 5HLW Gardner engine and ECW B41F bodywork new in 1953. This was joined by the first of the LS6B coaches converted to buses to be sold, ECW DP39F-bodied Car S313 (HMO 839), which didn't seem to have been in that form for long. Also out in October was another 1952 Bristol LWL6B with ECW B39R body as Car 632 (GJB 270) from Wycombe's stock.

The first of the Bristol LH-type saloons was Car 200 (RRX 991G), which is seen above passing the Gardeners Arms pub in Bridge Street, Maidenhead on a local working to Summerleaze Road on Route 18. Below we see Car 203 (RRX 994G) at Frogmoor Bus Station ready for Route 35 to Downley (Village Hall).

The incoming new buses for October were a batch of 8 Bristol LH6L chassis, which arrived fitted with standard ECW B45F bodies, though these were down-seated to 41 with a luggage pen before entering use. They were Cars 200-7 (RRX 991-8G) as part of a new fleet numbering scheme, with new saloons starting at 200 and new double-deckers at 500. The coaches would continue in the 400 series, though without the C prefix, whilst acquired saloons would also continue the 300 series, again losing the S prefix, whilst acquired double-deckers would gap-fill numbers in the 700's, then 600's and even 500's. However, at that point in time no existing vehicles were renumbered.

Newbury-based LH6L Car 206 (RRX 997G) waits at The Wharf for its next journey on Route 116 along the Bath Road to Hungerford.

The LH-type bus was a rather rugged affair, having been assembled from various bought-in units to create a new lightweight chassis for 30-ft bodywork, and in its original form it suffered from such severe vibration that fittings literally shock themselves off! Apart from the early Leyland 'Nationals' the author cannot recall a worse riding bus type. However, their simplicity did find particular favour at Newbury and High Wycombe though the initial batch was allocated as Bracknell (207), Maidenhead (200/1), Newbury (206) and High Wycombe (202-5).

The rear elevation of Car 201 (RRX 992G) is seen at Maidenhead Bus Station soon after delivery. The large single rear window suffered from the vibration.

A further pair of Bristol LD6G's with ECW LD33/27R bodies arrived from *United Welsh* in October and took the vacant fleet numbers 623/4 (NCY 637/8), being Nos.304/5 when new in 1956. The former went to Newbury, whilst the latter was allocated to Bracknell, making it the second vehicle of that number to reside at that garage. Unlike previous 'Lodekkas' from that source, these received full repaints at Reading before *Thames Valley* service.

Seen fresh out of the paint-shop is Car 623 (NCY 637) parked behind the Head Office building and awaiting delivery to Newbury. The significance of '295' on the blind in not known, as buses often displayed the fleet number in such situations, or were treated to such displays as 'London A' or 'Excursion'.

There were further secondhand buses arriving during October from South Wales, though this time they emanated from the Chepstow-based *Red & White!* All were 1954 ECW B45F-bodied Bristol LS6G's, with Cars 346-51 (MAX 116-9/22/3) arriving that month, followed in November by Cars 352-6 (MAX 126/7/1/5/8), these being part of a large batch and evidently allocated fleet numbers as they were ready, all being down-seated to 41 with a front luggage pen. MAX 116-9/21-3/5-8 had originally been *Red & White* Nos.U1654-1954/2154-2354/2554-2854, their fleet numbers being allocated in relation to the year, i.e. 154 followed by 254, with vehicle type prefix. Despite the large number of these buses they were shared between only Bracknell (354-6), Newbury (350/3) and Reading (346-9/51/2), working a wide variety of one-man services throughout those areas, and all had thin MW strips fitted during preparation

Another photo of the Bristol LH's shows Car 201 (RRX 992G) at Windsor on Route 22 to Maidenhead via Eton and Dorney, with the Royal Mews behind.

As these LS-types were in good order, their arrival spelt the end for various native saloons, with further crew-operated 1952 ECW B39R-bodied Bristol LWL6B Cars 628/33 (GJB 266/71) out in November, followed by similar Cars 620/30 (GJB 258/68) the following month. Also ousted were a number of Bristol LS-types, with 1953 ECW B41F-bodied LS5G Car 687 (HBL 89), similar LS6B Cars 710/23/5 (HMO 856/69/71) and former coach LS6B conversion Cars S309 (HMO 835) and S314 (HMO 834) all during November. These were followed in December by another converted Bristol LS6B, Car S319 (TWL 59), which had enjoyed a rather brief second career having only been rebuilt in June 1968!

Whereas Car 710 had 41 bus seats, Cars 723/5 were coach-seated and had worked high mileages when employed on Routes A and 75 in their heyday. S309 had been converted to B41F, whereas both S314/9 had retained their 39 coach seats when converted to buses, both having the dual-purpose livery, something never actually applied to Cars 723/5.

From December Bristol KSW6B Car 636 (GJB 274) became the Driver Training Bus, though it retained full livery and fleet number. It is seen on those duties passing under the railway bridge on the Oxford Road by Reading West Station.

Departures of the double-deck variety for December were 1951 ECW L27/28R-bodied Bristol KSW6B Car 634 (GJB 272), along with 1951 Bristol KS6B Car 595 (FMO 977), its ECW body being new with coach seating for the London Route B, but later modified as L27/26RD. This left the 7ft 6ins bus as a rarity in the fleet, with only Cars 596/8/9 (FMO 978/80/1) still in service, all three having been part of the same coach-seated batch which pioneered the *'Valley's* use of double-deckers of that enhanced standard on the London B service via Maidenhead and Slough.

These three views show the Thames Valley sites in Reading in use in 1968. This view shows the twin large sheds of the former Thackray's Way garage at The Colonnade to the right, with an express coach in the large yard. On the left-hand corner is the Granby Cinema, with the Crown Colonnade shops and the Marquis of Granby pub flanking the entrance to the site from London Road, just past the meeting point of the A4 and A329 at Cemetery Junction.

The Reading Garage and Central Works evolved on this site, between Lower Thorn Street on the edge of the upper triangle and Weldale Street at the base of this view. The central Works had spread through the three sheds on the right, with a Nissan hut for the Recreation Room in front. Some buses are parked in the yard by the Head Office building, whilst others are to be seen in the yard area recently extended by the demolition of cottages.

The new Bus Station looks no more appealing from the air, situated under the large Top Rank Ballroom, with the octagonal office for enquiries and parcels by the Station Hill exit ramp. The 16-storey block is Western Tower, where the radio control for the Rail-Air coaches was located. Also evident is much of the very large workshop area of Vincents of Reading, one-time important coachbuilders who had bodied some L6B Bristols for the 'Valley.

Former Red & White buses were no strangers at Newbury in an earlier era, and Bristol LS Car 350 (MAX 122) turns into Wharf Road on a Thursdays and Saturdays-only working to Curridge on Route 105.

A most notable event on the local transport scene was the final abandonment of trolleybuses by *Reading CT* on 3rd November after 32 years of operation. Despite the trolleys having been granted the use of the contra-flow lane along Kings Road from 16th June, the combination of more impending traffic flow changes and the high cost of obtaining new overhead wiring, had led to the decision to abandon electric traction. The decision was not without its critics, including the well-known local enthusiast Mike Dare, who wrote to the local press regarding the lack of pollution afforded by such vehicles, but it was to no avail.

Indeed, the traffic congestion in Reading had actually got worse since the partial opening of the M4 motorway and the Severn Bridge, as traffic that had previously used the A40 now focussed on the M4/A4 route instead, a situation yet to be resolved by a westwards extension of the motorway past Reading.

Another ex-Red & White LS, Car 355 (MAX 125) is seen laid over in Broomhall Lane, Sunningdale.

In the meantime Heathrow Airport had a third terminal building completed, so the Rail-Air coaches called at the renamed Terminals 1, 2 and 3 from 6th November. Also, the trio of Bristol RELL6G saloons Cars S306-8 (CBL 355-7B) were finally converted for one-man working, seating being reduced to 51, with a luggage pen built at the front nearside, the work being completed in October (S307), November (S308) and then S306 in December.

The year was notable for the news of two former *TV* double-deckers in far-flung locations, with ex-*Bristol OC* 1947 Bristol K6B Car 436 (KHU 624) discovered running as a 'London bus' in Canada, still in TV livery and displaying Loddon Bridge on the blinds, no doubt taken as being mistaken for the famous capitol landmark by most observers! On the other hand 1950 Bristol K6B Car 526 (FBL 28) had been driven overland to Turkey and back, by some students emulating the Cliff Richard film 'Summer Holiday', and it was later spotted in a Cheshire farmyard with Wokingham on the blind, both of these buses carrying standard ECW L27/28R bodies.

Bracknell received a trio of the former Red & White Bristol LS saloons, and Car 354 (MAX 121) is seen parked in the bus-washer at that garage.

Mention has already been made of the programme for fitting rear platform doors, which had started on the Union's insistence. However, as the number of buses so equipped rose, some invariably found themselves allocated to local routes where buses often called at almost every bus stop at busy times. The conductors soon found this to be a tiring matter, as the doors were all manually operated, also requiring frequent returns to the platform which interrupted the issuing of tickets. As a result of that it was often the case that the conductor would lock the door in the open position!

By now the old AEC 'Matador' breakdown wagon was getting pretty worn out, and it was not used unless unavoidable. Despite that, the Company was also obliged to rescue group vehicles broken down in the Reading area, so it was decided to fit tow-bars to some of the new Bristol LH's, Newbury of course having recently lost its old tow-bus Bristol LL6B Car 565 (FMO 947), and at Maidenhead Car 200 (RRX 991G) was the one selected for that task.

Car 353 (MAX 127) went to Newbury, and it is seen at The Wharf about to depart on Route 108 to Wickham Crossroads.

It is also worth noting that as the LH6L saloons had been fitted with T-type destination apertures, this resulted in the front windscreens being rather narrow. Drivers soon complained of poor visibility on these buses, particularly in respect of the nearside kerb, and they certainly compared badly to the Bristol LS-types. Due to this the subsequent batches received side-by-side boxes, which allowed the windscreens to be in line with the tops of the side windows.

Thames Valley was now experiencing a further spell of staffing problems, particularly in respect of garage workers, and frankly these difficulties started to show on the fleet. The most notable feature was caused by sloppy fuel-tank filling, which left buses stained with fuel that quickly attracted road dirt, several foregoing photos showing this issue. Also, torn adverts often showed parts of those underneath, which again looked tatty, whilst minor damage to panels etc. went unfixed for weeks at a time, whereas in previous eras such issues had been resolved at the earliest chance. The age of the fleet did not help matters either, as spare parts could be difficult to obtain.

However, the Company was not unique in respect of difficulties in recruitment for garage staff, and a similar crisis at *City of Oxford* saw *South Midland* providing coaches on loan for peak duties on a daily basis during early November, these being taken over to Gloucester Green and crewed by *COMS* staff:

1st - Bristol MW Cars 833 (UJB 199) and 858 (WRX 773);
4th – Bristol MW Cars 831/3 (UJB 197/9) and 858 (WRX 773) and Bedford SB13 Car C409 (842 CRX);
5th – Bristol MW Cars 831/2 (UJB 197/8) and 858 (WRX 773) and Bedford SB13 Car C411 (EMO 553C);
6th – Bristol MW Cars 832/3 (UJB 198/9) and 858 (WRX 773) and Bedford SB13 Car C411 (EMO 553C);
7th – Bristol MW Cars 831/3 and 858;
8th – Bristol MW Cars 831-3 and 858.

Also at Oxford, there was the usual hiring of *South Midland* de-seated coaches by the Post Master for the Christmas post, which included 1958 Bristol MW6G Car 801 (ORX 632), which of course came from the next batch earmarked for conversion to service buses.

Two of the buses entering service in 1968 are shown here, with the final Bristol FLF6G Car D60 (PBL 60F) seen above working on Route 4 to Camberley, whilst below we have one of Bracknell's trio of Bristol RESL6G dual-door saloons, Car S333 (LJB 333F) in the garage after arriving back from Sunningdale.

Mention was made earlier that no more Bristol FLF's were being ordered, and a pair of the new rear-engined double-decker chassis had been ordered for evaluation of the type. Although the prototypes had featured a longitudinally placed engine, it was the VRT with its transversal engine that *Thames Valley* took, and these were to receive ECW H41/29F bodywork. They were, however, delayed in delivery, with the first of the pair not arriving until the very last day of December 1968 as Car 501 (SRX 945G), its twin Car 500 (SRX 944G) having to await completion after the festivities, and both buses were earmarked for use of the London services to test performance.

1969

The other of the pair of Bristol VRT/SL6G buses with ECW H41/29F bodies was received in early January as Car 500 (SRX 944G), both of the type being allocated to Reading for operation on the London A and B express services. As new these had white fleet number transfers set centrally below the front windscreen, though the following examples had fleet number plates from new, and the initial pair had been fitted with the same by June.

Car 500 (SRX 944G) is seen above soon after delivery and in the Lower Thorn Street yard, whilst in the shot below it is seen entering Garrard Street for the 41-mile journey to London on Route A.

Over the winter months a start had been made on converting Bristol MW coaches 800-3 (ORX 631-4) for bus duties, though this would again prove to be a somewhat protracted project, with the resulting buses appearing out of sequence. Indeed, their bus fleet numbers had already been reserved in a new scheme to re-number the older saloons, and again this was not implemented overnight. Some of the buses were noted with new numbers as early as April, whilst others did not receive their new numbers until early in 1970! All very confusing at the time, especially once some numbers started to be re-issued. A full list of the 1969 scheme appears later in this chapter on page 163.

The interior of the lower deck on Car 501 (SRX 945G) looking forward to the entrance. The ECW bodies on these vehicles were neat and functional, though the use of ordinary bus seating for the London services was a retrograde step after the previous batches.

In the Wycombe area from 4th January Route 35 (to Downley) went over to one-man working, whilst Routes 36 (to Lane End and Cadmore End) and 37 (to Lane End and Henley) went partly that way. No doubt in connection with these changes, the last trio of crew-operated 1952/3 Bristol LS-type Cars 677-9 (HBL 79-81) were finally converted to B41F for one-man-operation during April and May. Otherwise, the year was a fairly quiet one for service changes.

One of the Bristol RESL6G dual-doorway saloons, Car S332 (LJB 332F), was away at ECW from 3rd February to 14th March for accident repairs, whilst not long afterwards one of the Bracknell-based trio of S333/4/8 (LJB 333/4/8F) disgraced itself when the engine caught fire on the Southern Industrial Estate, a not uncommon problem with earlier rear-engine types.

Further considerations for one-man working were the joint Routes 112 (Newbury – Oxford) and 5 (Reading – Oxford), both with *City of Oxford*. From 2nd March the schedules on the former were altered to allow for conversion in due course, and indeed from that date the Oxford Company did start using AEC 'Reliance' 36-footers experimentally on the route, though *TV* had no suitable vehicles to spare. On the service from Reading, the schedules also changed from the same date, with the '*Valley* continuing to use the trio of Bristol RELL6G Cars S306-8 (CBL 355-7B), which had recently been altered for such operation, whilst in that case *COMS* was not able to covert until 26th April. However, on Route 5 short-workings, buses were drawn from a variety of older types. Over at Bracknell, a suggestion came from the Union in order to improve timings on Sunday Local Services to better provide connections with the London-bound Route A.

Up in the Wycombe area the timetable on Route 41 (High Wycombe – Stokenchurch – Ibstone) was revised from 29th March to reduce mileage operated.

In the meantime just one disposal had occurred during February, this being 1950 Bristol KS6B Car 599 (FMO 981), carrying ECW L27/26RD bodywork, which was also Bracknell's last 7ft 6ins bus.

The MW's made quite stylish conversions, retaining the glazed roof panels. Car 159 (ORX 631) is seen in the layover bays at Reading Bus Station, though it was later transferred to Newbury, who used it from the Lambourn outstation for some time.

A number of alterations affected the older stock during the early months of 1969, with 1956 Bristol LD6G Car 750 (MBL 831) being re-seated to LD33/27RD in February, having previously been a 56-seater with coach seats, whilst converted Bristol LS6B Car S318 (TWL 58) and former *United Welsh* Bristol LS5G Car S328 (OCY 948) both received Gardner 6HLW units in March and April respectively.

Also noted in March were several vehicles lacking their former fleet number prefixes, with Bedford VAM14 coach C414 (GRX 414D) and Bristol SC4LK saloon S303 (NBL 733), the latter photographed by the author working Route 18 to Marlow as plain 303.

As already noted the first pair of Bristol VRT's was at work on the London express services, and another batch of 6 similar buses were due to join them, but they were slightly delayed in completion. Therefore, as it had already been decided to demote the Bristol FLF-types of 1960 and 1964 from such duties, it was necessary to make some temporary changes to vehicle availability. During January and February seven of the 1967/8 Bristol FLF's were altered by the replacement of the first pair of seats on the offside lower deck in order to provide additional luggage racking, leaving them as H38/30F. Those affected were FLF6G Cars D48/9/50/2 (LBL 848/9/50/2E) and D54/7/60 (PBL 53/7/60F).

Indeed, a start had already been made on repainting the older FLF's into standard bus livery, though no seating changes took place at that time, and these were turned out as follows:
March – Cars D4/5/7 (ABL 116/7/9B);
April – Cars D6 (ABL 118B) and 835 (UJB 201);
May – Car 834 (UJB 200);
June – Cars D8 (BRX 141B) and 836-8 (UJB 202-4).

During March former *South Midland* Bristol MW6G coach 800 (ORX 631) re-appeared in its new guise as Car 159 and was initially allocated to Reading.

March saw something of a clearout of redundant buses with the departure of 1951 Bristol KSW6B Cars 635/6 (GJB 273/4), both with ECW L27/28R bodies, along with an assortment of Bristol LS-types. The latter ranged from 1953 LS6G Car 680 (HBL 82) and 1954 LS6B Car 716 (HMO 862), both with ECW B41F bodies, to a trio of 1953 DP39F-bodied converted LS6B's S316/7/20 (TWL 56/7/60) and ex-*Bristol OC*

150

1954 LS5G Car S342 (PHW 929), which had an ECW B41F body, the first of the acquired buses to go.

Bristol KSW6B Car 640 (GJB 278) had been at the old Ascot Garage from new, working the long route between Windsor and Reading. It is seen at Bracknell still on that same duty near to the end of its days.

April continued the above trend, particularly as the new VRT's were now arriving, with the last of the 1950 Bristol KS6B buses with ECW L27/26RD bodies, and also the last 7-and-a-half-foot double-deckers in the fleet, Cars 596/8 (FMO 978/80), along with further Bristol KSW6B Cars 601 (FMO 983), new in 1950 and with an ECW L27/28R body, Cars 638/9 (GJB 276/7) with ECW L27/26RD bodies of 1951, and Car 640 (GJB 278) of similar vintage with ECW L27/28R bodywork.

The only saloon to go in April was 1952 Bristol LWL-type Car 616 (GJB 254), which had served as a temporary Enquiry Office, and then for some time as the Maidenhead Driver Training Bus in all-over red livery as seen below. With its departure only 5 of the ECW B39R-bodied buses of that type remained in service, as Cars 621/5/7/9/31 (GJB 259/63/5/7/9), all allocated to High Wycombe for use on Route 33.

The delayed Bristol VRT/SL6G buses started to arrive in April as Cars 502-5 (UBL 243-6G), and they were followed by Cars 506/7 (UBL 247/8G) in May. These all carried 70-seater ECW bodies, though the seating split was H39/31F as opposed to the H41/29F of the original pair, and like those they had semi-automatic transmission. They featured side-by-side destination boxes, with the place-name reduced to just a single line. Despite their evident suitability for o-m-o use, all of the Route A and B coverage remained crew-worked. As they entered service they displaced the Bristol FLF's recently converted for London services, though it was decided to retain Cars D50 (LBL 850E) and D54/7/60 (PBL 53/7/60) in that form as the regular relief vehicles, whilst the others returned to normal 70-seaters between May and August.

These two views taken at Victoria Coach Station show the VRT's soon after arrival, with the front nearside of Car 502 (UBL 243G) above, whilst Car 507 (UBL 248G) below shows the neat treatment of the ECW rear end.

From 12th April the Minister of Transport extended the Special Order in respect of the Kings Road contra-flow bus lane to include *Thames Valley* buses, with Routes A/B (from London), 1/1a (from Maidenhead), 10/43/44/45 (from Woodley), 28 (from Wycombe), 47 (from Twyford), 3/49 (from Wokingham/Camberley),

75 (from Guildford) and the 90/91/92 (from Ascot, Bracknell or Windsor) all making use of that facility.

April saw former *South Midland* 1958 Bristol MW6G coach 803 (ORX 634), now converted for bus work as Car 162 and allocated to Maidenhead.

The MW conversions also looked quite smart from the rear, with their polished aluminium strips. Car 162 (ORX 634) also has all the roof vents open at Maidenhead Bus Station on Route 17 to Henley.

Also at Maidenhead, the single-deck workings on Route 24 (to Cookham Dean) went over to one-man from 19th April, though the route remained diverted due to the rebuilding of Spencers Bridge. A number of other changes to workings took place from 26th April, when a number of journeys on Routes 6 (Reading – Basingstoke) and 8 (to Binfield Heath and Henley) were covered by o-m-o duties.

Over at Newbury from that date certain journeys on Route 113 (to Inkpen and Hungerford) went over to that mode, and most of the 5b (Reading – Yattendon – Newbury) was converted. Journeys on Route 102 (Reading – East Ilsley) via Ashampstead were also improved, whilst all buses on Newbury Local Services 126/7/8 now called at The Wharf. In respect of the latter, the expansion of housing both to the south and north of the town saw further scholar's timings added.

A further quartet of Bristol LH6L coaches for *South Midland* tours were licensed from 1st May as Cars 432-5 (UMO 688-91G), all bearing Duple 41-seater 'Commander' MkIV bodies. The sharp-eyed reader will of course note that these fleet numbers clashed with the former *Eastern National* Bristol LS and MW coaches, and it would seem from notes in the Vehicle Programme that these new coaches had been given the numbers following the previous new examples, whilst the acquired coaches were treated the same on arrival! Whatever the full reason, it was found less trouble to re-number the older coaches, which became Cars 440-2 (613/4/8 JPU) from April. Also, as the only post-1963 *South Midland* coach not now in the 400 series, it was decided to re-number Bristol REX6G Car 867 (521 ABL) as 403 with effect from July.

Due to further one-way flows in Reading from 4th May, Routes 4 (to Camberley), 6 (to Basingstoke), 6a (to Odiham), 6b (to Grazeley and Basingstoke) and 12 (to Aldershot) were all diverted on their outward journeys via London Street and Silver Street, though inward journeys continued to use Southampton Street.

The *South Midland* tours for the 1969 season still featured the usual destinations, though the costs had now risen with inflation and increased fuel duty:

Tour	Days	Base	Cost £-s-d
Scotland	12	Touring	56-7-6
Scotland	9	Arrochar	39-17-6
Isle of Man	9	Ramsey	39-17-6
English Lakes	8	Grange-over-Sands	38-17-6
Cornwall*	8	Newquay	36-17-6
Welsh Coast	8	Porthcawl	35-7-6
North Wales	8	Llanberis	35-7-6
Mid Wales	8	Llandrindod Wells	28-17-6
North Devon	8	Ilfracombe	34-7-6
South Devon*	8	Torquay	33-7-6

Costs were for full board, all sightseeing tours and meals en route, and all tours could be joined at London (Victoria), Slough, Maidenhead, Henley, High Wycombe and Oxford, whilst those marked * could also be joined at Newbury.

Bristol LH6L coach 433 (UMO 689G) is seen above at South Parade in Bath during a lunch break on the North Devon tour, whilst similar coach 434 (UMO 690G) arrives at Victoria to pick-up for the 12-day tour of Scotland, appropriately surrounded by Bristol REMH coaches of Eastern Scottish.

The job of preparing the *South Midland* brochure had fallen to Frank Robinson, though it was his final issue, as he retired in 1968 after 44 years of service. He had started back in 1924 when the *'Valley's* fleet consisted of almost all Thornycroft J-types, and his first task had been to make up the Bell Punch ticket racks for conductors, duly gaining responsibility for the Enquiries Office at Stations Square in Reading and generally increasing duties in the Traffic Office.

With the new coaches now safely in hand, the trio of 1963 Bedford SB8 coaches with Duple 'Bella Vega' C37F bodies, Cars C401-3 (831-3 CRX), which had been laid up since October 1968 were now sold.

The other incoming vehicles for May were a pair of 1957 Bristol LD6G's from *United Welsh*, formerly Nos.307/9 and with ECW LD33/27R bodies, which became Cars 632/3 (OCY 954/6) and both were sent to work from Wycombe Marsh.

Former United Welsh Car 632 (OCY 954) reverses onto the forecourt of Wycombe Marsh Garage, just in from working Local Service 81a out to Booker.

Further older types were cascaded out of the fleet, and the inroads into the ranks of the 1951 ECW L27/28R-bodied Bristol KSW6B's ran deeper with the departure of Cars 641-4/7/9 (GJB 279-82/5/7) in May, followed by similar Cars 645/6 (GJB 283/4) in June. On the last day of May converted Bristol LS6B Car S315 (TWL 55) was withdrawn, but it was not sold, becoming a source for spare parts until the next year.

Another Bristol KSW6B bus withdrawn from public service at the end of June was Car 670 (HBL 72) of 1953, which was modified as a Driver Training Bus. Former coach-seated 1956 Bristol 'Lodekka' LD6G Car 752 (MBL 833) returned to service in June re-seated as LD33/27RD, followed by similar Cars 753/60 (MBL 834/41) in October, all of these being 56-seater London cars when new. The high mileages of the latter services soon took their toll on the new VRT's, with Car 503 (UBL 243G) having to go to Lowestoft for accident repairs during May, and Car 505 (UBL 246G) from mid-August to 4th September.

Bristol VRT Car 501 (SRX 945G) is seen at the BCV works, alongside a RE-type chassis. Note that the blind has been set to Stratfieldsaye, somewhere not even known of outside of the immediate area!

Bristol MW6G Car 852 (VJB 943) was also away for 6 weeks from 18th July, whilst Cars 500/1 (SRX 944/5G) made a number of visits to the Brislington works of Bristol Commercial Vehicles for attention as various teething troubles were ironed out during 1969.

Incoming vehicles for June was limited to just one former *United Welsh* Bristol LD6G, new as No.310 in 1957 with ECW LD33/27R bodywork, which became Car 622 (OCY 957) allocated to Newbury. Also sent there that month was a further Bristol MW6G coach converted to bus work, as Car 161 (ORX 633). All of the MW conversions were to B41F, with jack-knife doors, though retaining the roof luggage racks.

Car 160 (ORX 632) followed in July, completing the converted 1958 MW's and was allocated to Reading.

153

Bristol MW6G Car 161 (ORX 633) is seen at Newbury Wharf on the former Reliance Motor Services Route 107 to Brightwalton, complete with sucker-board.

At Newbury converted MW Car 161 (ORX 633) was duly joined by similar Car 159 (ORX 631), and the pair spent some time outstationed at Lambourn.

A further Bristol VRT/SL6G with ECW H39/31F body arrived in July as Car 508 (VMO 223H), which was followed by similar Car 509 (VMO 224H) during August. Both of these were allocated to Bracknell Garage for the start of one-man double-deck operation in due course, and they featured illumination 'Pay As You Enter' signs at the front and nearside.

The interior view of the upper deck, looking towards the front, on Bristol VRT Car 508 (VMO 223H).

Despite these vehicles entering service there were no disposals during July or August, as the Company was experiencing problems returning defected buses to service due to staff shortages and the difficulties of obtaining spare parts for the ageing fleet.

From 2nd August some of the additional journeys on Bracknell Local Services 52/56 between Sperry's on Downshire Way and the town were discontinued due to declining patronage. Plans were also being made for a number of services from that garage to go over to double-deck one-man operation later in the year.

Of a more drastic nature was the curtailment of the long-established Route 50 (Reading – Abingdon) at Wallingford from 4th August, though passengers could still change onto the *City of Oxford* service there for onward travel. This was also effectively the end of joint-working over that route, as all journeys were now covered by *Thames Valley*. Also in the Reading area from that same date, the Route 7 journeys to Stoke Row were diverted via Borocourt Hospital in order to provide on a 2-hourly headway for visitors.

Although a number of Bracknell's operations were based on the expanding New Town, others took buses to some quieter locations. Bristol VRT Car 509 (VMO 224H) is seen ascending amongst the trees of The Rise at Sunningdale on Route 57a to Bracknell.

On the Service Vehicle front 1969 was a fairly quiet year, with the disposal of Wycombe Depot Van No.47 (UJB 299), a Bedford CAV new in 1960 and outgoing in March. Also that month, a 1961 Vauxhall 'Victor' car (YBL 284) departed, followed by 1964 Ford Thames 307E Van No.51 (32 GBL) comparatively early in July. The only incoming vehicle that year was a Ford 'Escort' Van No.69 (VBL 838H) in August.

One major event affecting the use of a number of bus services was the opening of Windsor Safari Park by the owners of Billy Smart's Circus in the Summer of 1969. The large site was based in the grounds of an old mansion off St. Leonards Hill, some three miles west of Windsor town centre, and also 0.75 miles from the circus Winter quarters off North Street in Winkfield, and in the early days it was not unusual to see a string of elephants walking between those sites! Most people went round the safari enclosures in their own cars, often coming out minus hubcaps, aerials or wing mirrors, removed by the monkeys, whilst foot passengers boarded special vehicles with guides. The attraction certainly boosted passenger numbers on Routes 53/53a and the 90-group services.

Further Bristol LH6L saloons arrived in August as Cars 208-11 (VMO 225-8H), all fitted with ECW B41F bodies and with an unladen weight of 5tons 10cwts, compared with the 6tons 11cwts of the MW-type. It was also pleasing to note that the excessive vibration of the earlier examples had now been dealt with, whilst the fitting of side-by-side destination boxes also improved the depth of the windscreen. The batch was allocated as Bracknell (211), Maidenhead (210), and Newbury (208/9).

Bristol LH6L Car 208 (VMO 225H) was seen by Graham Low on Route 105 to Curridge on a Thursday or Saturday at The Wharf in Newbury.

August also saw yet another ex-*United Welsh* Bristol LD6G with ECW LD33/27R body, new in 1957 as No.308, becoming Car 620 (OCY 955) and sent to work from Newbury.

Bristol LD Car 620 (OCY 955), ready for a run on Route 5b to East Ilsley, is seen after the fitting of a manually-operated platform door during 1970.

Also concerning Newbury operations, *South Midland* Bristol MW6G coach 805 (PRX 931) was sent there on contract duties in place of Bedford SB13 Car C406 (836 CRX) during August, the latter being earmarked for disposal. It should also be noted that when coaches were transferred from Oxford they generally retained *South Midland* fleetnames, as the legal owner was *TV*.

Car 501 (SRX 945G) is seen on Route 112 at Oxford's Gloucester Green Bus Station, by which time it had received the illuminated PAYE signs.

In connection with plans to convert Route 112 from Newbury to Oxford, Bristol VRT Cars 500/1 (SRX 944/5G) were sent on loan to Newbury during August for trial operation, though the project did not proceed because the *City of Oxford* Union would not approve such working on that service.

As noted above, a number of buses were in need of urgent attention, which led to 1953 Bristol LS5G Car 707 (HMO 853) being returned to service in September with a 6-cylinder Bristol engine instead.

Another trio of Bristol VRT/SL6G buses with ECW H39/31F bodies gradually arrived, with Car 510 (VMO 229H) in September, joined by 511 (VMO 230H) in October, then finally Car 512 (VMO 231H) to complete that year's order in November. All were allocated to Bracknell Garage, allowing further spread of o-m-o working there.

A number of older types departed during September, with the demise of further Bristol KSW6B's, as 1950 ECW L27/28R-bodied Car 602 (FMO 984), 1951 ECW L27/26RD-bodied Car 637 (GJB 275), along with 1953 Cars 659-61 (HBL 61-3), all with ECW L27/28R bodies. The only saloon to depart was 1954 Bristol LS6B Car S311 (HMO 837), one of the original coach-to-bus conversions done in 1964. Also by that month both of the coach-seated Bristol MW6G Cars 852/3 (VJB 943/4) were repainted in standard bus livery, losing their dual-purpose scheme, something which the coach-seated Bristol LS6B Cars 723/5 (HMO 869/71) had never received despite being generally regarded as the other pair of a quartet.

Also entering service in October was the first of the next batch of coach conversions, former *South Midland* 1959 Bristol MW6G coach 806 (PRX 932), now as B41F and Car 165, which was Bracknell's first bus of that chassis type.

155

Bristol VRT Car 501 (SRX 945G) was caught by Graham Low as it follows the new one-way diversion along Rose Street whilst working on Route A to London (Victoria). To the right is the old cake shop and café now demolished for road-widening. The old Midland Bank has also since gone, and Boots the chemist was then using the old Timothy White's shop. The new building on the left was for Milward's Shoes, whose adverts were a feature of Thames Valley buses from the 1930's on.

By 1969 the Bracknell allocation was fairly varied, with Bristol KS6B, KSW6B, LD and FLF-type double-deckers, and LS, MW and RE saloons, including some converted coaches. In this view we see LS Car S313 (HMO 839) on the 57a, ex-United Welsh LD Car 775 (LWN 51) on the 54 and LS Car 708 (HMO 854) on the 53. Nothing in this view now exists, even the houses of Skimped Hill Lane having been swept away by further expansion of the New Town.

This view of the steam-cleaning ramp at Reading Garage shows it after the new wall was built along the frontage of Weldale Street, where a line of cottages had stood. Steam-cleaning was the usual prelude to major overhaul and re-certification, and Bracknell-based Bristol LS Car 147 (HMO 870) was one of the last to physically receive its new number under the 1969 scheme, having been new in 1955 as Car 724 with an ECW B41F body.

First of the conversions from 1959 Bristol MW6G coaches was Car 165 (PRX 932), which is seen on the 49 at Bracknell Garage. This retained the original style of integrated radiator grille and fleetname panel, though for some reason the ECW-Bristol wings had been rather crudely altered.

The start of the Winter timetable was traditionally the point for introducing service changes, and from 4th October a number of alterations were made. The 31-mile Route 1/1a (Maidenhead – Reading – Newbury) was experiencing difficulties keeping to schedule due to delays entering and leaving the congested approach roads to Reading, so it was decided to de-link the route once again at that town. The Maidenhead part retained the route numbers 1 and 1a, the latter being those journeys through Sonning Village, whilst the western portion was given the vacant number 2. Also from Reading, extra short-workings were added to Route 8 between the Bus Station and new housing at Caversham Park, these being known as Route 8a and covered by one-manners.

Over at Bracknell double-deck one-man-operation was now expanding from the 52/56 Local Services to the routes of the Sunningdale corridor and the already established double-deck journeys on the 53. Car 512 (VMO 231H) is seen in Bracknell Garage yard.

At Maidenhead the Route 60 projections to Pinkneys Green (Wagon & Horses) were withdrawn from 4th October, though some journeys between Maidenhead and Sealey's Stores on Route 69 were extended to that point in compensation, town centre traffic once again being the cause of unreliability of the buses coming through from Slough. At the same time Route 23 (to Cookham Dean) went over to one-man working and marked the end of crew-operation of single-deckers at that garage.

On the subject of the saloon fleet, it will have been noticed that many of the Bristol LS-types had altered appearance over the years, due to various changes and often accident-related, so Car 684 (HBL 86) was still in remarkably original condition in 1969. The front destination box had of course been altered to a T layout, but even the plated-over original central position of the fog-light was evident, indicating that no front-end collisions had been suffered! It is seen at Frogmoor ready for Route 32 to Bledlow Ridge, one of the services taken over from Fred Crook in 1937.

Another interesting change from 4th October was the acquisition of the other *Cole* family *Blue Bus Service*, which ran between Maidenhead and Paley Street, and this took the vacant number 14 in the Maidenhead area series. No vehicles were involved in the purchase of the service, which actually had a number of variations. The core route ran as Maidenhead (Bus Station) – Maidenhead (Gregory's Garage, for Station) – Bray Village – Holyport (War Memorial) – Moneyrow Green (Wheel of Fortune) – Foxley Corner – Paley Street (Sheepcote Lane), with some journeys only between Maidenhead and Bray. Indeed, the first inward journey was to Maidenhead from that village, having been the base for the bus. Certain journeys ran at peak times omitting Moneyrow Green in favour of Stud Green Road junction, these affording commuter connections at Maidenhead Station, the point where the original (but not the same) *Blue Bus Service* of *West Bros.* of Bray terminated. No Sunday service was operated and, as we shall see in due course the penetration of this route would be duly reviewed with the future of the Bracknell – Hawthorn Hill Routes 55/55a, which terminated only some 1.75 miles away.

In the Slough area bus crews had been suffering from bad behaviour from youths in the evenings along the roads of the Britwell Estate, with shouts of abuse and stoning of the buses, so from 27th October Route 64 journeys after 7pm were curtailed at Farnham Road (The George), whilst passing Route 70 buses also avoided going through those roads. Although there is no record of a reinstatement of these journeys on the route history sheets, they evidently did return in due course following increased Police activity locally.

Mention was made earlier of the pair of Duple-bodied Bedford VAM14 coaches transferred from Rail-Air duties to the South Midland fleet, and Car C417 (LJB 417E) is seen passing the British Overseas Airways Corporation coach terminal as it swings into Victoria Coach Station from Oxford.

The general improvement to the service on Route 7 to Borocourt Hospital recently meant that the special runs on certain days were no longer required, the last such journey operating on 2nd November. From 17th of that month a new scholar's special was contracted by Berkshire CC running over Route 109 between Cold Ash (Hospital Crossroads) and the Kennet School at Thatcham, which ran mornings only, with pupils using any service run for the homeward journey.

Bristol LH6L Car 214 (VMO 234H) on the ex-Blue Bus Route 14, Paley Street not yet being on the blind!

November saw some new deliveries, plus some rather interesting vehicles on loan. In respect of the new buses, a further quartet of Bristol LH6L saloons with ECW B41F bodies were received as Cars 212-5 (VMO 232-5H), and they were allocated to Maidenhead (214), Newbury (213), Reading (212) and Wycombe (215).

However, another of that type, Wycombe-based Car 203 (RRX 994G), was a bad accident victim resulting in it being away at Lowestoft from 1st to 18th November. And that same road also saw a number of the Bristol VRT's going for heater improvements as the Winter set in and their system was found wanting. Whilst they were absent for 3 to 4 weeks at a time, the modified Bristol FLF6G's took over, their nice warm heaters being much more effective!

That month also saw a further Bristol MW6G coach-to-bus conversion, with former *South Midland* 804 (PRX 930) re-appearing as B41F and now Car 163, this being followed in December by coach 805 (PRX 931) in its new role as Car 164, the pair being allocated to Reading and Newbury respectively.

MW6G Car 164 (PRX 931) is seen at Newbury Wharf for Route 119, the Cold Ash circular service. Note the absence of a front fleetname in the beaded box.

During the previous Winter the Company had been publicly criticised for the high number of its buses not fitted with heaters, as in fact whereas most saloons did have them, only the doubles after 808 were all equipped, the exceptions being the batches selected for the London services and the last few Bristol KSW-types. Although this was probably not so unusual at that time, there is little doubt that the *'Valley'* had made no real effort to update such features, and the matter yet again came to a head when the Union backed crews at Bracknell who refused to take out such buses. Over the Winter months a total of 50 double-deckers were then fitted with heaters, at least 40 going for attention at *Smith's Luxury Coaches* at their Rose Kiln Lane garage off the Basingstoke Road in Reading. In all Bristol KSW Cars 665-7/94-6/8, 700-2/4/5/26-37, along with Bristol LD Cars 755-9/65-9/80-93, plus the LDL Car 779 were dealt with, some possibly by *TV* staff at Wycombe Marsh.

Some of the LS6B buses converted from coaches also went, including Car S311 (HMO 837), which is seen after the front-end rebuild following an accident. This bus was allotted the number 125 in the re-numbering.

This page shows some of the buses that left the fleet in 1969. Seen above is 1950 Bristol KSW6B Car 601 (FMO 983) on Route 9 to Baughurst. Below we see 1953 Bristol LS6G car 680 (HBL 82) working a short on the 28 from Marlow to High Wycombe.

One-man operation on Route 23 to the Spencers Estate at Cookham had ousted 1952 Bristol KSW6B Car 661 (HBL 63), seen here leaving Maidenhead.

Bristol KSW6B Car 637 (GJB 275) had been delivered with coach seats in 1951, but subsequently was rebuilt as L27/26RD. It is seen above in Stations Square on Route 3 to Camberley. Below 1954 Bristol LS6B Car 720 (HMO 866) passes along Oxford Road on Route 19 to Long Lane, having been modified with an MW front strip, also losing its maker's badge and one dumb-iron flap over time due to accidents.

Another of the November LH6L's was Car 212 (VMO 232H), allocated to Reading, and a regular bus for Route 75 to Guildford. It is seen returning to Reading along Kings Road past Greenslade's printing works on the south bank of the Kennet & Avon Canal.

Due to the Bracknell situation urgent action was required to cover for the blacked buses until heaters were installed, resulting in the surprise arrival of more Bristol LD buses from the *United Welsh* fleet, though this time on hire! The first three arrived at Bracknell Garage on 11th November, still in full livery and *UW* fleet numbers 313-5 (OCY 960-2), their Eastern Coach Works LD33/27R bodies of 1958 still sporting both cream bands and black-painted beading. They were joined by a fourth example of similar type but new in 1957, No.311 (OCY 958) from 1st December.

United Welsh No.315 (OCY 962) at Bracknell, from where these buses usually worked Routes 90/91/92.

In the meantime the Bristol SC4LK Cars S301-4 (NBL 731-4) were starting to exhibit signs of wear, as they were kept out at night in the yard at Maidenhead, and their lightweight bodies were suffering from water penetration. Clearly they were in need of replacement, once again raising the recurrent problem of obtaining a suitable type in their stead. One possibility had been to alter the Bedford SB8 coaches new in 1962, and Tom Pruett ordered one of these Duple-bodied vehicles, which weighed in at just over 5 tons to be stripped of all non-essential fittings. However, despite that, it was not a solution when passengers were also added due the 5-ton bridge limit.

Bristol Omnibus Company sent its 1964 Bristol SUS4A No.308 (AHW 227B) for trials as a possible solution to the Marlow Bridge problem.

This resulted in the other bus coming on loan from 22nd November, as seen above, this type with ECW B30F bodywork weighing in at 4 tons 3cwts. It was used on Route 18 between Maidenhead and Marlow in order to try out the type, which was fitted with the 4-cylinder Albion EN250 engine, whilst the bodywork was of 7ft 6ins width, as of course were the SC-types. This particular vehicle remained in use on the service through to early January 1970, and in the meantime an urgent memo went out to the few operators of that type in the hope that four such buses could be supplied. Indeed, apart from the *Bristol* fleet, only *Southern National* and *Western National* had taken the 25 examples of that type built.

Bristol Omnibus responded by supplying a pair of 1963 examples on 9th December, though only one was in use before the end of the year as Car 198 (844 THY), and it bore an ECW B30F body. This bus had been allocated to the subsidiary *Bath Tramways* fleet but was transferred via the main operator to provide this solution for *Thames Valley*, the third time buses from that fleet had been purchased since 1959. As this bus was prepared at short notice it received transfer fleet numbers, whereas subsequent examples all had fleet number plates. It has also been reported that the buses acquired early next year were initially used in their old green liveries for a short time until each could e repainted due to the withdrawal of the SC's.

Bristol SUS4A Car 198 (844 THY) after being painted in Thames Valley livery and on Route 18 to Marlow.

The re-numbering scheme for older saloons started in April was by no means fully implemented by the end of November, though the Bristol SC4LK Cars were included despite being earmarked for disposal. This batch had originally been Cars 774-7 (NBL 731-4), then S301-4, then minus the prefix, before finally becoming Cars 155-8! It is also evident that a number of buses in the course of disposal either had reserved numbers that were not officially issued, whilst some that did feature on the re-numbering list did not run under their new numbers.

Similarly, the surviving Bristol LWL6B saloons at High Wycombe were also re-numbered in order to make way for incoming secondhand 'Lodekkas', but again it is clear from photographic evidence that this was not physically completed until early in 1970. In their case they were given 2XX-series numbers in line with their registration numbers, so Cars 621/5/7/9/31 (GJB 259/63/5/7/9) duly appeared with those numbers in white transfers. Apart from the sheer confusion caused by having buses still bearing old numbers, and others running with new numbers, one of the staff also missed the point and turned out former *United Welsh* LS-type S326 (JCY 997) as S116!

Bristol LWL6B Car 267 (GJB 267) was photographed by Graham Low as it arrived in High Wycombe from Ibstone on Route 40, an unusual working for the type.

It should also be noted that as there was no Recovery Vehicle at Wycombe, Bristol LWL6B Car 265 had a towing bracket fitted under the rear end, and on one occasion the author saw it pulling in Bristol LS-type Car 146 (HMO 868), which had sustained front-end damage on Route 37 to Fingest.

November saw further disposals of 1952/3 Bristol KSW6B buses with ECW L27/28R bodies, as Cars 648 (GJB 286) and 653/6 (HBL 55/6), along with more from the ranks of the 1953/4 Bristol LS6B's with ECW B41F bodies, as Cars 707/20/1 (HMO 853/66/7). The latter trio had in theory become fleet numbers 109, 144 and 145, but there is no evidence they actually ran in that form. The same is true of former *Bristol OC* LS5G-type Car S345 (PHW 932), a 1954 bus with ECW B41F bodywork, which was to have been 132 but went in November still bearing its old number. A full re-numbering list for the 1969 scheme for saloons appears on page 163.

Bristol KSW6B Car 648 (GJB 286) is seen in earlier days at Maidenhead Bus Station on Route 18b.

At High Wycombe the town centre around the Newlands area was being completely redeveloped, and next to the new Octagon Shopping Precinct was the site for the new Bus Station. This was also to be the operating base for *Thames Valley,* replacing both the garages at Desborough Road and Wycombe Marsh, as well as the Frogmoor Bus Station and the old Enquiry Office at 37 Frogmoor. This was due for completion early in 1970, so the above other properties were duly advertised for disposal.

In the meantime the staffing crisis at Reading Garage was reflected in the number of buses not in use for lack of someone to fix them or due to a lack of spare parts. The fitting of heaters by *Smith's Luxury Coaches* has already been noted, but that firm also did other maintenance tasks at times, which was a situation most unusual for a Company of the *'Valley's* standing.

1965 Bristol FLF6G Car D17 (DRX 121C) receives a steam-clean at Smith's Rose Kiln Lane premises just off the Basingstoke Road to the south of Reading.

Bracknell-based Bristol VRT Car 508 (VMO 223H) is shown above at the crest of Crowthorne Road where it meets Reeds Hill in this photo by Graham Low, whilst below another photo from that source shows similar Car 509 (VMO 224H) on the 57a for Sunningdale.

Disposals for December were the first of the quartet of Bristol SC4LK's now displaced from Marlow Bridge duties, as Car 158 (NBL 734). Also sold was the first of the 1964 batch of Bedford SB13 coaches with Duple 'Super Vega' C37F bodies, Car C406 (836 CRX), also the only example with a *Thames Valley* fleetname. At the close of December the remaining SC's were withdrawn, with Cars 155-7 (NBL 731-3) being replaced by further Bristol SU's in the process of transfer, of which will shall hear more in the following chapter.

The Camberley terminus was finally relocated from Princess Street, though not to any bus station that had been proposed over the years, but to the roadside in Knoll Road, where Routes 3 and 4 (from Reading), 49 (from Wokingham) and 53/53a (from Windsor) transferred to from 1st December.

At Bracknell another phase of development in Great Hollands saw the introduction of temporary services 94/98 put on from 6th December, operated by one-man double-deckers on a circular route in opposite directions to cover Town Centre – Crowthorne Road – Ringmead – Great Hollands Road. In order to better serve Wildridings, Southern Industrial Estate and Great Hollands plans were being made for some bus-only slip roads, and the services would be revised again during the next year. Also in Bracknell, Station Road was now made one-way, in a northwards direction, so buses heading south now used Church Road, and also Northway if coming from the west, as the High Street was now one way only in a westwards direction, the latter also being earmarked for full re-development as a pedestrian area during 1970.

Re-numbering of older saloons scheme of 1969

New	Old	Reg. No.	Type	Year	Origins
100	677	HBL 79	LS	1952	New
101	678	HBL 80	LS	1952	New
102	679	HBL 81	LS	1953	New
103	681	HBL 83	LS	1953	New
104	682	HBL 84	LS	1953	New
105	683	HBL 85	LS	1953	New
106	684	HBL 86	LS	1953	New
107	685	HBL 87	LS	1953	New
108	706	HMO 852	LS	1953	New
109*	707	HMO 853	LS	1953	New
110	708	HMO 854	LS	1953	New
111	709	HMO 855	LS	1953	New
113	S318	TWL 58	LS	1953	New
114	S329	JCY 995	LS	1953	UW
115	S330	JCY 996	LS	1953	UW
116	S326	JCY 997	LS	1953	UW
117	711	HMO 857	LS	1954	New
118	712	HMO 858	LS	1954	New
119	713	HMO 859	LS	1954	New
120	714	HMO 869	LS	1954	New
121	717	HMO 863	LS	1954	New
122	718	HMO 864	LS	1954	New
123	719	HMO 865	LS	1954	New
124	S310	HMO 836	LS	1953	New
125	S311	HMO 837	LS	1954	New
126	S312	HMO 838	LS	1954	New
127	S339	SHN 728	LS	1953	UAS
128	S340	SHN 729	LS	1953	UAS
129	S341	SHN 730	LS	1953	UAS
130	S343	PHW 930	LS	1954	BOC
131	S344	PHW 931	LS	1954	BOC
132*	S345	PHW 932	LS	1954	BOC
133	346	MAX 116	LS	1954	R&W
134	347	MAX 117	LS	1954	R&W
135	348	MAX 118	LS	1954	R&W
136	349	MAX 119	LS	1954	R&W
137	350	MAX 122	LS	1954	R&W
138	351	MAX 123	LS	1954	R&W
139	352	MAX 126	LS	1954	R&W
140	353	MAX 127	LS	1954	R&W
141	354	MAX 121	LS	1954	R&W
142	355	MAX 125	LS	1954	R&W
143	356	MAX 128	LS	1954	R&W
144*	720	HMO 866	LS	1954	New
145*	721	HMO 867	LS	1954	New
146	722	HMO 868	LS	1954	New
147	724	HMO 870	LS	1955	New
148	S321	KWN 794	LS	1955	UW
149	S322	KWN 795	LS	1955	UW
150	S323	KWN 796	LS	1955	UW
151	S324	KWN 797	LS	1955	UW
152	S325	MCY 39	LS	1955	UW
153	S327	OCY 747	LS	1957	UW
154	S328	OCY 948	LS	1957	UW
155	S301	NBL 731	SC	1956	New
156	S302	NBL 732	SC	1956	New
157	S303	NBL 733	SC	1956	New
158	S304	NBL 734	SC	1957	New
159	800+	ORX 631	MW	1958	New
160	801+	ORX 632	MW	1958	New
161	802+	ORX 633	MW	1958	New
162	803+	ORX 634	MW	1958	New
163	804+	PRX 930	MW	1959	New
164	805+	PRX 931	MW	1959	New
165	806+	PRX 932	MW	1959	New
166	807+	PRX 933	MW	1959	New
179	852	VJB 943	MW	1960	New
180	853	VJB 944	MW	1960	New
181	854	VJB 945	MW	1960	New
182	855	VJB 946	MW	1960	New
183	856	VJB 947	MW	1960	New
184	857	VJB 948	MW	1960	New
185	S306	CBL 355B	RELL	1964	New
186	S307	CBL 356B	RELL	1964	New
187	S308	CBL 357B	RELL	1964	New
188	S331	LJB 331F	RESL	1968	New
189	S332	LJB 332F	RESL	1968	New
190	S333	LJB 333F	RESL	1968	New
191	S334	LJB 334F	RESL	1968	New
192	S335	LJB 335F	RESL	1968	New
193	S336	LJB 336F	RESL	1968	New
194	S337	LJB 337F	RESL	1968	New
195	S338	LJB 338F	RESL	1968	New
259	621	GJB 259	LWL	1952	New
263	625	GJB 263	LWL	1952	New
265	627	GJB 265	LWL	1952	New
267	629	GJB 267	LWL	1952	New
269	631	GJB 269	LWL	1952	New

<u>Notes:</u> UW – United Welsh   UAS – United Automobile Services
BOC – Bristol Omnibus   R&W – Red & White Services
* did not operate with new fleet number due to withdrawal.
+ former coach fleet number of vehicle under conversion.

Seen above is ex-United Auto Car 127 (SHN 728) at Henley with white fleet numerals, whilst below former United Welsh Car 148 (KWN 794) has a metal plate, Graham Low's view also showing its emergency door.

Bracknell Garage still had a varied allocation, with Bristol KSW, LD, LS, LH, MW, RE, FLF and VRT-types there. The garage is seen from the southern end of the yard on a very cold morning – note the icicles on the front of RESL6G Car S333 (LJB 333F)! To the left is Bristol KSW6B Car 659 (HBL 61) and Bristol LS6B Car 713 (HMO 869) without fleet number in the process of becoming Car 119. The capacity of this garage was soon outstripped as the town grew.

Newbury still offered a wide variety of buses, with a high number of secondhand types also present. 1953 former coach S315 (TWL 55) is seen in its final form when the lower front end was rebuilt after an accident, working the 106 to Upper Lambourn. Next to it is former United Auto Bristol KSW6B Car 690 (PHN 821) waiting a turn on Route 111 through to Bucklebury, or if was a Thursday onto Stanford Dingley, the latter bus outlasting the LS by 2 years.

With the last of the half-cab Bristol saloons now gone, the Newbury saloon duties fell to Bristol LS, MW, RE and LH-types, and again there were secondhand examples. On the left is 1969 LH6L Car 209 (VMO 226H) on the 114 to East Woodhay, and to its right is another ex-United Auto bus, an LS5G of 1953 Car 128 (SHN 729) on the 120 service to Frilsham via Hermitage, one of a number of rural routes still hanging on.

164

1970

The formation of the National Bus Company one year previously on 1st January 1969 had so far had no visible impact on the operations at *Thames Valley*, but it had at last brought together the bus interests of both the former Tilling Group and British Electric Traction operators. These companies had been neighbours since the pioneering days, and many had territorial agreements with each other, though now they also shared Directors following some cross-fertilisation as a result of the new common control.

As noted in the previous chapter, further Bristol SUS–type buses were being sought, though only 16 had been built for *Southern/Western National* and another 9 for *Bristol OC*. The latter responded with its No.306 (846 THY), new in 1963 with ECW B30F body, and this became Car 199 in January.

Western National followed this up with a pair of 1960 examples, also with ECW B30F bodies, previously Nos.612/3 (668/9 COD), which became Cars 196/7. All of these buses had an overall length of 24ft 4ins and weighed in at 4tons 3cwts unladen, so the limit of 15 passengers still applied when crossing the weight-restricted Marlow Bridge over the River Thames, and notices were once again displayed in these buses to that effect.

Bristol SUS4A Car 197 enters Maidenhead Bus Station from Marlow on Route 18.

This lightweight model had been put together to meet a need along the narrow lanes of the West Country etc., but they were not particularly reliable vehicles, at least by the time they reached the *'Valley'*, and their 4.1 litre 72bhp Albion engines found the climb up Bisham Hill a struggle with a load on board, whereas drivers were none too impressed with the brakes on the descent of that same road. Due to repeated issues, it was soon decided that a further bus would be a good idea, as it could also cover the lightly-loaded Route 14 operations to Bray, Holyport and Paley Street.

Prior to the acquisition of the fifth Bristol SUS4A the Route 14 duties usually fell to a Bristol LS-type, and former United Auto Car 127 (SHN 728) is seen above on the afternoon short-working to Foxley Corner. SU-type Car 199 (846 THY) is seen below at Maidenhead Bus Station ready for a Route 14 journey to Paley Street, waiting on the same stand once used by the 1937 Leyland 'Cubs' used for the Marlow route.

As *Western National* could spare no further buses, another came from *Bristol OC* as its No.305 of 1963, which had an ECW B30F body and arrived on 21st February to became Car 158 (845 THY).

We have already seen how the bus services were daily relied upon by workers, shoppers and school-children, but it should also be appreciated how much of a part they played in providing leisure travel. Many people still took the bus regularly to attend all manner of club or church activities, and the author would often finish an evening stroll with a pint in one of the Binfield or Warfield pubs, safe in the knowledge that the bus time table could be relied upon. Straying further afield for live music in Windsor, there was no hesitation in going for the last Route 53 at 10.30pm, or when coming home from his girlfriend Suzi at the other end of the route, catching the 11pm 53 at the Bull & Butcher in Owlsmoor, that bus having reached Camberley as the last through journey on Route 3.

165

The heating modifications on the Bristol VRT's also continued, with Cars 500/1 (SRX 944/5G) and 502-4 (UBL 243-5G) going to Lowestoft between January and September, mostly for about a fortnight at a time, though 501 was absent for some 3 months!

Within the Company workshops the seating on 1956 Bristol LD6G Car 751 was altered in February from its 56 coach seats to bus seating in a LD33/27RD layout, whilst a surprise out-turn from the paint-shop was 1952 Bristol LWL6B Car 263 (GJB 263), which would be withdrawn just 6 months later!

Former United Welsh Car 635 (OCY 961) rests under the canopy of Windsor Central Station on Route 92.

Former Western National Bristol SUS Car 196 (668 COD) was caught by Philip Wallis crossing Marlow Bridge to the Berkshire bank at Bisham.

Two of the Bristol LD6G buses on hire from *United Welsh* were sold to *Thames Valley* in January, when Nos.311/5 (OCY 958/62) became Cars 626/8, both remaining at Bracknell. The other pair on hire, Nos.313/4 (OCY 960/1) was duly acquired in May as Cars 634/5, and they too continued to operate mainly on the 3 and 90-group routes from Bracknell Garage.

Car 626 (OCY 958) is seen emerging from Reading Bus Station on Route 3 for Camberley, still wearing its United Welsh paintwork with two cream bands but now with added platform door.

From Sunday 4th January Aylesbury got a new bus station which backed onto the new shopping precinct and County Hall, so the *Thames Valley* Routes 21/21a (to High Wycombe via the main road) and 80 (also to High Wycombe but via Lacey Green) transferred from their old haunt at Kingsbury Square. In the meantime work on the Newlands Bus Station in High Wycombe was well underway, though the outline as seen from the road looked more like a prison block! With the anticipated move to this new site Jim Vockings and Freddie Ferguson were both made up to Inspectors during March.

Also concerning the Wycombe area, the 28th January saw a reduction in the timetable for Route 37 (High Wycombe – Lane End – Henley), which included the withdrawal of Sunday journeys through to Henley. Also from that date Route 27a (to Great Missenden via Little Kingshill) lost its Sunday service, though the direct Route 27 continued to link High Wycombe and Great Missenden on an hourly headway.

Platform doors continued to be fitted to 'Lodekkas' without them, and between January and July former *United Welsh* Cars 620/2 (OCY 955/7), 623/4 (NCY 637/8), 626/8 (OCY 958/62), 632/3 (OCY 954/6), 772-5 (LWN 48-51) and 776/7 (JCY 993/4) were all dealt with. Heaters continued to be fitted to other buses, *Smith's* doing 18 during January and February.

Over at Newbury Route 116 (Newbury – Stockcross – Hungerford) had several journeys diverted to serve Hungerford Newtown and these, along with the shorts on Wednesdays between Hungerford and Hungerford Newtown, were now designated as Route 136, a duty usually covered by a Bristol LS saloon.

In the meantime another notable retirement had taken place from the ranks of the old drivers originally at the Ascot Garage, when Alf Waterman finally stepped out of the cab after 43 years service. He had started in 1927, not long before that garage received its first batch of Leyland 'Titan' TD1's, living a few miles away at Woodside, from where he cycled until he could afford his first motorcycle. He covered all the Ascot duties transferring to the Bracknell Garage in June 1960 with the closure of Ascot.

As he was due to retire soon, 1969 had seen him hired to Bray Studios to drive Bristol RESL6G Car S332 (LJB 332F) during the filming of 'I Start Counting', the first feature role for 16-year old Jenny Agutter and her co-star Simon Ward, the latter playing the part of the serial-killer bus conductor and Miss Agutter as a 14-year old convent schoolgirl. Much of the filming was done around Bracknell and featured Point Royal flats, Rectory Row shops and included some scenes of old Bracknell buildings being demolished. There were also some rural scenes, and during those the author encountered S332 on Holyport Green, where he met Alf, who was proud to receive a letter from the Director praising his professionalism during the filming, whilst the bus displayed 'Tittle Row 22' on the blinds for the road scenes.

Bristol MW6G Car 166 (PRX 933) in its new role as a service saloon on Route 35 to Downley village hall.

A number of changes took place in the Service Vehicle fleet, with outgoing vehicles consisting of a 1964 Ford 'Zephyr' car (ARX 554B) out in February, the GM's 1967 Wolseley 6/110 car (LRX 457E) out in March, followed by 1965 Leyland 15cwt Van No.55 (GMO 831C) in July. The GM got a Triumph 2.5-litre car (WMO 953H), whilst the other incoming vehicles came as Bedford CAV Van Nos.71 and 73 (SRD 167/8H) in January, and a Vauxhall 'Ventura' car (XBL 396H) during February. Fuller details of the allocations of the Service Vehicles will be found in Appendix 2 on pages 219/20.

The days of the Bristol KSW6B buses on mainline duties were now largely a thing of the past, though they could still be seen quite widely at the start of the year. Car 739 (JRX 814) was one of those rebuilt from coach seating and is seen at Newbury Wharf on Route 2 to Reading, by then an unusual outing for the type.

As noted in the previous chapter, the bus terminus at Camberley had been relocated to Knoll Road, and Bristol FLF Car 838 (UJB 204) was photographed there by Philip Wallis on a short-working on the 4.

The last of the 1959 batch of Bristol MW6G coaches converted to B41F for service work was completed in February as Car 166 (PRX 933), originally delivered as *South Midland* coach 807. It was sent to Wycombe, spending some time allocated to Fingest Dormy Shed. It is interesting to note that the 1969 re-numbering of saloons had left the numbers 167 to 178 vacant, and it is reasonable to assume that conversion of the rest of the MW-types, and even the earlier Bristol RELH6G's was envisaged, had other factors not intervened.

A trio of photos all with a High Wycombe theme – Car 166 (PRX 933) is seen outside the Fingest Dormy Shed in this photo by Graham Low, as it prepares to return to High Wycombe via Lane End on Route 37. This shed had been home to a wide range of types over the years since opening in 1930, though out-stationing in the area pre-dated that. It was also used regularly to store de-licensed coaches during the Winter months, as well as buses for the 36 and 37 services.

The days of the Wycombe Marsh Garage were now numbered as the Newlands project took shape, and this March 1970 Philip Wallis photo shows the For Sale board above Bristol LWL6B Car 621 (GJB 259), as yet not re-numbered under the 1969 scheme. The original part of the garage, which opened in 1924, is shown, though over the years it was successively extended and the roadway to the right in Micklefield Road provided other entrances.

In another Philip Wallis view we see Bristol FLF-type Car D58 (PBL 58F) leaving Windsor Central Station on Route 20a up to High Wycombe. The buses used the stands on the right of the photo, mainly under the ornate arched canopy, with some room beyond for turning and lay overs for relief buses when Ascot Race traffic was on. This terminus was handy for train connections and the shopping areas, as well as being not far from the riverside and castle.

The coach-seated Bristol MW6G Cars 852/3 (VJB 943/4) had for many years been used on longer runs such as the 75 to Guildford and the A to London, but in their final guise they lost their dual-purpose livery. Now as Car 179 (VJB 943), and back in ordinary bus livery, this example is seen on the 11 to Bucklebury, passing the white-painted building that was Thames Valley's original office in St. Mary's Butts, Reading.

Since 1969 there had been a marked decline in the general appearance of the fleet, with minor damage to panels going un-repaired for weeks or even months at a time, torn adverts left hanging, blinds missing or damaged, along with a general down-at-heel look to paintwork. Shortages of serviceable buses, or breakdowns in service, had became a daily issue, and even *South Midland* was not immune to such problems, having to borrow a Strachans B53F-bodied Ford R226 (MBW 159E) from *Worth's* of Enstone during February.

Bristol LD6G Car 796 (NCY 635) was still running in the paintwork it came from United Welsh with in 1968, with no fleet number or destination blind, as seen in Newbury on Route 108 to who-knows-where!

This situation was not, of course, unique to *Thames Valley,* as most operators felt the competition from other fields of employment that offered better pay and more sociable working hours. As one former *'Valley* driver once told the author 'why drive around in traffic from the crack of dawn, when you can get more money sweeping floors at the Mars factory'. Even the mighty *Midland Red*, based in a wide area around the West Midlands, found itself having to send buses out to local motor garages and dealers for attention. Spare parts were also often an issue, in part due to frequent industrial disputes endemic to Britain at that time.

Bristol RESL6G Car 189 (LJB 332F) seen on more mundane duties after co-starring with Jenny Agutter the previous year, coming over Windsor Bridge, which as the sign states had a 12-ton limit at the time.

From 28th February a number of changes took place in the Wycombe area, with Local Service 42 (Wycombe Marsh – Booker Hill Estate) being reduced, particularly on Saturdays, whilst Routes 39 (High Wycombe – Stokenchurch – Watlington) and 40 (High Wycombe – Stokenchurch – Radnage) both had their mileage cut. However, Route 31 (Wycombe – Naphill – Lacey Green) went over to double-deck operation, though to a reduced frequency, whilst Local Service 33 (Town Centre – Desborough Castle Estate) finally went over to double-deckers, with the route being diverted via Whitelands Road – Chairborough Road – Rutland Avenue, though again the frequency was amended from every 7/8 minutes to 10. At the same time the separate workings as Route 33a onto Link Road on the Desborough Castle Estate were deleted, as the revised routed covered that area.

Buses on the rural services saw some pruning, with a general reduction on Route 34 (Wycombe – Speen), whilst Route 36 (Wycombe – Lane End – Cadmore End - Henley) lost a number of journeys including those on a Sunday onto Henley. However, a new service 30 catered for the Plomers Hill Estate, out via Hughenden Avenue to Tinkers Wood Road, and returning via Hithercroft School as well. It should of course be noted that the Local Service 33 had been the haunt of the Bristol LWL6B buses, and the surviving few were now used on the 26, 42 and 81a Local Services, with 265 on hand for towing duties.

From 2nd March the link from Wildridings School in Netherton at Bracknell was extended deeper into the developing Great Hollands Estate to reach Yardley and Viking, which added the destination line Bracknell (Great Hollands) to the blinds for Route 53. Also, north of Ascot, the Cranbourne School Special was withdrawn from that same date as no longer required. In the Maidenhead area, a 10.10pm journey was added at weekends to Route 18 between Maidenhead and RAF Danesfield, some 2.75 miles west of Marlow from 7th March, but these were discontinued from 12th December as only poorly used.

Quite a few changes were made to services operated by Bracknell Garage, with effect from 7th March:
Routes 51/51a/51b (Windsor Local Services) – Revised with reduced evening and Sunday journeys;
Routes 52/56 (Bracknell Local Services) – Journeys from Bullbrook no longer used the High Street, but via Church Road and Station Road instead;
Routes 53/53a (Windsor – Camberley) – Route south of Bracknell now via Bagshot Road and South Hill Road, due to closure of Crowthorne Road section over Mill Lane (now a footbridge and cycleway only);
Routes 54/94/98 (Bracknell Local Services) – Routes replaced by new circular services running as –
54 – Station Road – Northway – London Road – Long Hill Road – Lilyhill Road - Bay Road – Deepfield Road – Church Road – Bagshot Road – Downshire Way – Wildridings Road – Ringmead – Great Hollands Road – Crowthorne Road;
58 – Bagshot Road – Downshire Way – Crowthorne Road – Great Hollands Road – Ringmead – Wildridings Road – Crowthorne Road – Station Road – Northway – Deepfield Road – Bay Road – Lilyhill Road – Long Hill Road – London Road – Church Road; 'b' variants via Doncastle Road (Rowney).

The Sunningdale services were also altered, with some Route 59 journeys through to Windsor in response to complaints about changing buses at Fernbank Corner. Philip Wallis found Bristol KSW6B Car 744 (JRX 819) in Broomhall Lane, Sunningdale.

Routes 55/55a Bracknell – Warfield – Hawthorn Hill) – Extended through to Maidenhead and incorporating Route 14, but no longer served short section between Touchen End (Hinds Head) –Paley Street, and worked by both Bracknell and Maidenhead;
Routes 58/58a (Sunningdale – Ascot - Bracknell – Wildridings - Services withdrawn;
Routes 59/59a (Brookside – Ascot – Sunningdale) – Services revised with some through journeys between Sunningdale and Windsor at work times;
Routes 90/90a/91/91a/92/92a (Windsor – Bracknell – Reading corridor) – Journeys towards Reading now via Church Road and Station Road due to closure of High Street in Bracknell to traffic.

In order to achieve the changes on the services for Wildridings, Southern Industrrial Area and Great Hollands Estate a new bus-only lane was constructed at the northern end of Mill Pond, which allowed buses direct access from Wildridings Road onto the under-carriageway of Mill Lane flyover, and this had a gap in the central reservation, with bus-activated traffic lights, another TRRL local experiment in co-operation with Bracknell Development Corporation. A further link between Lovelace Road on the Southern Industrial Area and Ringmead was added at a later stage in local developments.

One of the memorable features of the Route 92/92a journey via Binfield was the old hump-backed bridge over Framptons Brook, just by the lake of Binfield Manor and east of the Stag & Hounds Y-road fork, and Bracknell-based Bristol FLF6G Car D26 (GJB 874C) is seen passing over it towards Windsor.

Whilst on the subject of the 90-group mainline routes, mention was made in the 1946 – 1960 volume of the alternative names Conductor Rance called out for some of the stops. Mike Waring has been able to add a few more, with 'Three Jumpers' (Three Frogs, Wokingham), 'Paradise Street' (Seaford Road, with something of a reputation at the time), 'Wokingham Without' (Station Road), 'Crimpy College' (Crimpy Crisps Factory, Winnersh Crossroads), 'Winnersh Post Office, Off-license and Harberdashery' (for the Winnersh Post Office, west of the crossroads).

A further trio of 1952 Bristol KSW6B's with ECW L27/28R bodies were ousted in March as Cars 650 (GJB 288) and 651/2 (HBL 53/4), whilst during April just one saloon left, in the shape of Car 126 (HMO 838), a Bristol LS6B best remembered for the pock-marked seating rails taken from a *Smith's Luxury Coaches* former *City of Oxford* AEC 'Regent' when it had been converted from a coach in 1965.

Former Lincolnshire RCC Bristol LD6B Car 605 (LFW 329) was caught above by Philip Wallis in West Street as it passed through Marlow on Route 28, the line of bunting indicating regatta week in that town. Below we see Car 607 (NBE 133) freshly repainted and ready for Route 8 from Reading and Henley.

Incoming Bristol 'Lodekka' buses acquired during March broke new ground, with some from *Crosville Motor Services* of Chester and *Lincolnshire Road Car*. Both of these operators provided buses of rather variable condition, which meant that some languished for many months before time could be found to prepare them for service, and at one point it looked likely that the degree of cannibalisation might prevent several of them ever entering active use!

Those from *Lincolnshire* were Bristol LD6B's new in 1955 as Nos.2321/6/30 (LFW 329 and NBE 129/33), the former with an ECW L33/25RD body and the other pair with LD33/27R bodywork. These became Cars 605-7, with the first allocated to High Wycombe and the latter two both to Reading.

Another of the Lincolnshire examples was Car 606 (NBE 129), which is seen after a platform door had been added, with blinds set for Route 4a to Arborfield, Barkham and Wokingham, a service warranting 60-seaters due to the presence of the Army Apprentices College at the REME Arborfield Garrison and the army families living on the military housing estate.

The *Crosville* contingent were also 1955 Bristol LD6B's, all with ECW L33/27RD bodies and with fleet numbers DLB776/81, which became Cars 601/3 (XFM 187/92) and were allocated to Reading and High Wycombe.

Former Crosville MS Car 601 (XFM 187) is seen in Lower Thorn Street yard after its repaint, its radiator grille surround already over-painted by Crosville.

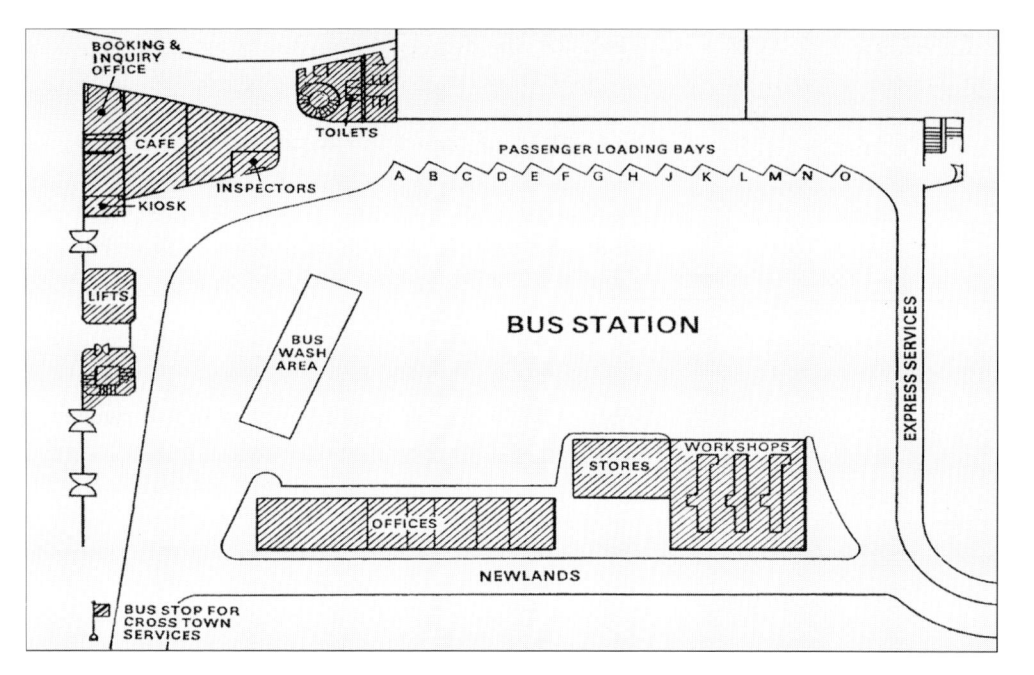

The layout plan for the Newlands Bus Station at High Wycombe is seen on the left. Incoming buses dropped passengers off at Stops 1 and 2 (not marked and left of the bus wash area), then proceeded to the central waiting area opposite the relevant stand until it was vacant. The stop shown for Cross Town Services was used by Routes 26/26a/326, those buses not entering the bus station, but using the road marked Newlands to exit the site.

Bus services were allocated to the bays as follows:
Bay A – Route 33 (to Desborough Castle Estate)
Bay B – Routes 20/20a (to Maidenhead and Windsor)
Bay C – Routes 20/20a (to Maidenhead and Windsor) and 21/21a (to Aylesbury)
Bay D – Routes 25/25a (to Flackwell H./Bourne End)
Bay E – Routes 25 (Flackwell Hth) and 28 (to Marlow or Reading) and *London Country Bus Services**
Bay F – Routes of *London Country Bus Services**
Bay G – Routes 28 (to Marlow or Reading) 38 (to Booker)
Bay H – Routes 28 and 30 (Tinkers Wood circular)
Bay J – Routes 27/27a (to Great Missenden)
Bay K – Route 31 (to Naphill and Lacey Green)
Bay L – Routes 32 (to Bledlow Ridge and Chinnor), 34 (to Speen) and 80 (to Lacey Green /Aylesbury)
Bay M – Route 35 (to Downley)
Bay N – Routes 36 (to Lane End and Cadmore End) and 37 (to Lane End/Fingest/Hambleden/Henley)
Bay O – Routes 39 (to Watlington), 40 (to Radnage), 41 (Ibstone) and *City of Oxford* 75 (to Oxford)
Stop 1 – Local Service Route 38
Stop 2 – Local Service Routes 42 and 81/81a
Western end – Express services
* 305 (to The Chalfonts/Uxbridge), 441 (to Slough/Staines) and 455 (to Beaconsfield/Uxbridge).

The new Bus Station was much better lit than the one at Reading and offered more waiting space with seats, café and toilets. The clear bay numbers and illuminated advert panels all added to a good facility when first opened.

The major event of March was the official opening of the new High Wycombe Bus Station at Newlands on Friday 20th March, when the Minister of Transport Fred Mulley cut the tape to allow Wycombe's senior driver Cyril ('Bob') Harding to drive Bristol FLF6G Car D56 (PBL 56F) in. Bob was then 70 years old and had for decades been based at the Fingest Dormy Shed, and he had originally come to *TV* with the purchase of the *Chiltern Bus Co. Ltd.* in 1936, having started out with *Charlie Holland* and marrying his daughter along the way, a busman throughout.

Bob Harding is seen on the left, with his long-term regular Conductor Tommy Wandlass, in front of one of the 1935 Leyland 'Tiger' TS7 buses that were the mainstay of Fingest Shed operations for some years.

The public opening of the new facility was due for Sunday 4th April, though this had to be subsequently delayed until 6th June due to disputes over staff car parking and a new productivity agreement which, in true Wycombe style was gone over line-by-line by the Union. Indeed, the new facility was not only a bus station, but replaced the split-site garages at Wycombe Marsh and Desborough Road, along with Frogmoor Bus Station and the Enquiry Office at 37 Frogmoor, which had come into the fold from the *Penn Bus Co.* in 1935, also serving as the local Traffic Office.

When new the facility looked quite bright, but with 650 *Thames Valley* departures daily, grime from the diesel engines soon attached itself to the bare concrete surfaces, whilst in due course lower standards of care added to the sometimes unpleasant state of the bus station. Indeed, the author cannot look at an interior photo without it evoking that heady mix of greasy-spoon cafe, smelly toilets and diesel, whilst the inclusion of the bus garage element inevitably led to much noise of revving engines and dropped tools etc.!

Jim Vockings recalls that at the time of the transfer to Newlands the Chief Inspector became Eddie Edwards (in place of Percy Hounslow, who retired), supported by Inspectors Freddie Burridge, Bill Dunford, 'Curly' Fay, Freddie Ferguson, and Jim himself, along with Mobile Inspectors Jimmy Green and George Grant. In all 289 *Thames Valley* employees were transferred to the new site and all the old premises were sold off. However, the 'Marsh Garage Foreman E. ('Mac') McCormack, who had some years earlier taken over from Frank Stacey, did not want to transfer so he left, and Graham Rackley came from Reading in his place. The arrangements for out-stationing by *Royal Blue* also transferred to that site and continued until 1973.

All in all, and despite the comments on its later grubbiness, the bus station offered the passenger easy and level access to the new Octagon Shopping Precinct and onwards to the older parts of the town, whilst car drivers had to use the multi-storey car park away from ground level. The County Architect who oversaw the project had already been involved in new thinking over the Milton Keynes City, and his consideration for bus passengers was indeed praised by the *Thames Valley* Chairman Mr. D.S. Deacon, who had recently written to various Local Authorities urging them to adopt schemes giving buses preference in town centres over the tide of private motorists.

Above we see Harry Kercher pacing out bus spaces at Frogmoor, and Traffic Superintendent Joe Morris with chalk and tape measure in hand during a discussion between Management and Union. Below is Harry's wife Mabel with shovel helping to dig Fingest Car S330 (JCY 996) out of a snowdrift on Route 37.

The Kerchers were another husband-and-wife team in the Wycombe area, Kathleen 'Mabel' Ryan having started at Wycombe Marsh in 1950, duly meeting Harry and marrying in 1955. At first they worked as a crew, but after daughter Judy came along in 1957 they arranged alternate shifts so one of them was at their home at Wisteria Cottage in Turville, and Mabel moved to the nearby Fingest Dormy Shed. Harry had started in 1947 and was a keen Union member and Ted Tapper's right-hand man, and it was not unknown for him to ring Joe Morris in the early hours with an ultimatum to resolve an issue, or there would be no buses in the morning! Harry later became the Driving Instructor and was responsible in 1973 for passing the first female driver at Wycombe, Mrs. Frances Monks.

A younger Mabel Kercher stands right centre in front of one of the Bristol LWL6B coaches new in 1951.

Mabel is remembered widely for helping old ladies and young mums with their shopping bags or pushchairs, taking them to the door if nearby a stop. She was a keen knitter, always with something on the go in quiet moments on the bus, and if she heard someone was expecting would knit baby items for them. Sometimes the bell rang in the middle of nowhere and Mabel jumped out and over a gate to pick mushrooms in the field! Another time her regular driver Alex Lambley and her helped a poor Turville family who could not afford a lorry move to Henley by loading all their furniture etc. onto the bus, such was the care given by the country bus crews then.

Another trio of Bristol LD6B buses of 1955/6 came from *Crosville* in April, with its DLB742 (VFM 607) carrying an ECW LD33/27R body becoming Car 600 and allocated to Reading, whilst the other pair were Nos.DLB779/84 with ECW LD33/27RD bodies, and these became Cars 602/4 (XFM 190/5) and both were sent to High Wycombe as replacements for withdrawn Bristol KSW6B's on Local Services.

Car 602 (XFM 190) is seen above passing the old market building in High Wycombe on Local Service Route 42. As with other Crosville examples this arrived with the radiator surround already over-painted. The XFM batch had short radiators from new, whereas the VFM examples originally had the full-length version. Below we see another similar bus on Route 42, Car 604 (XFM 195) as it leaves the new bus station at Newlands with platform door closed.

A routine inspection of the weight-restricted Windsor Bridge, which spanned the River Thames between the town and Eton, revealed serious structural defects with the framework, resulting in its closure to all traffic other than the emergency services from 10th April. Route 22 (Maidenhead – Dorney – Eton Wick – Eton – Windsor) was therefore truncated on the Eton side at the Burning Bush, any passengers for Windsor having to take the short walk over the bridge. In the meantime the Windsor Relief Road had taken most traffic away from using the old route along Eton High Street, and as residents in that area soon appreciated how much quieter the area was, no effort was ever made to resolve the problems, though *TV* evidently only regarded this as a temporary close at the time.

Former Crosville Bristol LD6B Car 600 (VFM 607) is seen in Weldale Street yard at Reading Garage, which had been extended even further westwards after the demolition of the last of the cottages on that side.

As already noted, failing buses were a frequent issue, and on one occasion in late April the Victoria-based Inspector was faced with a bus with electrical problems, so he commandeered a spare *South Midland* coach to cover the Route A journey to Reading!

There were also some new buses for the fleet, this time with one-man double-deck operation planned for expansion at Maidenhead. For this a pair of Bristol VRT/SL6G buses with ECW H39/31F bodies arrived in May as Cars 513/4 (XMO 541/2H).

During June Maidenhead Local Service Route 15 to Curls Lane Estate was converted to double-deck one-man working, and Car 513 (XMO 541H) is seen on the forecourt of Maidenhead Garage.

Also arriving in May was a further pair of Bristol LH6L saloons, carrying ECW B41F bodies and both were allocated to High Wycombe, as Cars 216/7 (XRX 819/20H).

With the virtual demise of rear-entrance Bristol LWL buses at High Wycombe, most single-deck workings were now one-man-operated, which incidentally is a correct description as it should be appreciated that there were no female drivers on the 'Valley at that time. Car 216 (XRX 819H) was caught by Graham Low on Route 35 to Downley soon after delivery.

Also received in May were the first pair of a quartet of new touring coaches for the *South Midland* fleet, these being 41-seater Duple 'Commander' MkIV-bodied Bristol LH6L's, which had Leyland 400/75 diesel engines similar to the previous batch. Cars 436/7 (YBL 925/6H) were licensed from May, whilst Car 438 (YBL 927H) was delayed until July, finally followed by Car 439 (YBL 928H) in September, just as the touring season was drawing to a close!

Car 436 (YBL 925H) is seen at Oxford's Gloucester Green Bus Station in very shiny brand new condition. The three huge side windows mirror the buildings across the road, but were rather expensive to replace in the case of breakage. Forced air ventilation was by now very common on coach bodywork.

Another interesting trio of shots from Philip Wallis and his travels around the 'Valley. Outside Reading General Station we see both the reserve coaches in use on the Rail-Air Link, with Bedford SB13 Car C408 (838 CRX) on the stand after transfer in June, whilst Bristol MW6G Car 866 (520 ABL) is waiting behind in reserve. Scenes such as this would soon lead to an increase in the frequency of the service.

Mention has already been made of the new terminus at Knoll Road in Camberley, which was actually nearer to the new shopping area, library civic offices and station, but suffered from a total lack of facilities – not even any shelters! The open nature of the site is apparent is this view of Bristol KSW6B Car 747 (JRX 822) coming in on Route 49 from Wokingham and Bristol VRT/SL6G Car 512 (VMO 231H) on Route 53 for Windsor.

Royal Ascot Races during June had for many years seen various measures to control traffic at that busy time, and Bristol LS6B Car 118 (HMO 858) is seen turning into Station Hill for Sunningdale on Route 59, its front end carrying various damage yet to be rectified. Note the temporary roundabout constructed by the Police, with the race track behind the Horse & Groom pub. To the right is Zaradi's tobacco shop, a long-time TV parcel agent on the corner of the High Street.

May also saw yet another source of secondhand buses being tapped, with the arrival from *Midland General* of 1956 ECW-bodied Bristol LS6G No.245 (959 ARA), which took the vacant fleet number 144 and was allocated to High Wycombe.

Car 144 stands in Weldale Street yard after being re-painted and awaiting dispatch to High Wycombe. The bodies on these buses were unlike TV's own examples and the destination screens also featured single-track numerals.

As a result of these various incoming buses, a number of older types were ousted in May, including a pair of the Bristol LWL6B's still in use, 1952 ECW B39R-bodied Cars 259/69 (GJB 259/69), now displaced from Route 33, along with a pair of Bristol KSW6B's of 1952/3 with ECW L27/28R bodywork, Cars 657/69 (HBL 59/71). The ranks of the native 1954 Bristol LS6B's were further thinned with the departure of Cars 117/9 (HMO 857/9).

Another former Midland General saloon was Car 145 (956 ARA), seen here turning from Tudor Road into Greyfriars Road, having arrived in Reading on Route 8 from Henley. The Tudor Arms pub stands behind the bus, then a Wethered's of Marlow house. This batch of buses featured semi-luxury seating when new and were used on longer routes.

Car 150 (961 ARA) emerges from the gloom of Reading Bus Station for its 9-mile journey to Twyford Station on Route 47. This batch of buses was in good condition, although this one has taken a few knocks.

During June further ex-*Midland General* Bristol LS6G saloons arrived as Cars 145/50 (956/61 ARA), formerly Nos.242/7, new in 1956 with ECW B45F bodies, but as with all acquired LS-type buses these were reduced to 41-seaters with the addition of a luggage pen. Both entered service at Reading, and it was something of a pity they had to lose the attractive blue and cream livery of their former owner.

The infamous low railway bridge on Finchampstead Road in Wokingham added yet another notch to its battered archway on Wednesday 13th May, when ex-*Thackray's Way* driver Lionel Godsell forgot to take the turn into Molly Millars Lane when working Route 3 towards the town centre! However, once again the Company was rather fortunate in that only one minor injury resulted, though the whole of the nearside upper-deck was badly crushed. A contemporary note indicated that this bus was a Bristol FLF this time, so the absence of 1963 Car D2 (840 CRX) at Lowestoft from 15th May until 23rd June would seem to fit the bill in respect of its identity. Other notable departures in that direction also saw 1960 Bristol MW6G coach 832 (UJB 198) away for 2 months from 6th March, whilst 1967 Bristol FLF6G Car D47 (LBL 847E) there from 25th April through to mid-June.

Disaster struck again on Tuesday 2nd June, though this time no bridge was involved! Rail-Air Bristol RELH coach C424 (RJB 424F) was travelling towards the airport near Littlewick Green on the M4, when a fire broke out. All 19 passengers were safely evacuated, but the coach had virtually burnt out by the time the fire was dealt with. The driver had radioed Western Tower, so Traffic Superintendent Arthur Waldron had dispatched another coach, though it took 45 minutes to reach the scene due to traffic congestion, and the press reports do not mention if the luggage was removed in time! As a result of this *South Midland* Bedford SB13 coach C408 (838 CRX) was transferred to Reading as an interim replacement vehicle.

Rail-Air Bristol RELH6G coach C424 (RJB 424F) is seen in the yard at Lower Thorn Street before the fire that reduced it to scrap.

A number of service changes took place in the High Wycombe area on 6th June, coinciding with finally the public use of Newlands Bus Station. With the closure of Wycombe Marsh Garage, buses on Local Services Routes 26, 42 and 81 now turned by way of Hatters Lane, Guinions Road and Micklefield Road to re-join the London Road, but this caused complaints from residents, so from 1st August this changed again to use the small triangular diversion of Abbey Barn Road and Ford Road south of the A40 instead. Buses on Routes 35 (from Downley), 36 (from Cadmore End), 37 (from Henley or Lane End), 39 (from Watlington), 40 (from Radnage) and 41 (from Ibstone) to High Wycombe Railway Station now terminted at the Castle Street stop instead, though the *City of Oxford* Route 75 from Oxford still reached the station.

Over at Maidenhead there were also changes from 6th June, when Routes 15 (to Curls Lane Estate) and 24a to 24a Cookham Rise) were both converted to one-man working, whilst Route 16 (to Warren Row and Henley) lost its Sunday service. The Maidenhead contribution to Windsor Local Service 51 was also put on o-m-o, though Bracknell continued with crew-operated double-deckers on its workings.

In general this was a quiet year for service changes, no doubt due to the re-scheduling work required with the opening of the Newlands Bus Station, along with the considerable time involved in yet another round of general fares increases.

June saw a further wave of older types being disposed of, with a another pair of 1952 Bristol LWL6B saloons with ECW B39R bodies as Cars 263/7 (GJB 263/7), which left only Car 265 (GJB 265) of that type still active. The ranks of Bristol KSW6B's also suffered further loses, with 1952 Cars 654/5 (HBL 56/7) and 1953 Car 700 (HMO 846), all with ECW L27/28R bodies. The secondhand Bristol LS-types also took a hit, with the weeding out of the poorest examples, ex-*United Welsh* Cars 150/1 (KWN 796/7) and 152 (MCY 39), all dating from 1955.

Reading Garage was also now suffering with a shortage of road crews, something it had not really experienced before, and this led to a number of cancellations of certain journeys on the Woodley Local Services from 27th June, whilst in the longer term these schedules had to be permanently reduced. At Bracknell there were public calls for the numerous buses on the expanding Local Services to bear proper destinations, one suggestion being that a list of points served should appear near the entrance to help identify the correct bus. However, in response Traffic Superintendent Arthur Waldron, who also had that garage under his care, stated that the bus workings were quite complex and 'would not make it possible'.

As mentioned earlier the 55/55a now ran through to Maidenhead incorporating the erstwhile former Blue Bus Route 14. Graham Low caught Bristol LH6L Car 210 (VMO 227H) leaving Bracknell Garage on the 55, whilst the author was surprised to find Bristol SU Car 196 (668 COD) inside that same garage one day! Both buses have sucker-boards reading Maidenhead (or Bracknell) via Holyport and Bray.

After having seen secondhand purchases from *Bristol, Crosville, Eastern National, Lincolnshire, Midland General, United Auto* and *United Welsh*, the appearance of *Royal Blue* Bristol LS6G coach 2203 (VDV 746) in the Lower Thorn Street yard on 11th July resulted in a number of rumours regarding its purpose. One rather unlikely theory was that this 1957 ECW C39F-bodied coach had been obtained to replace burnt-out Rail-Air coach C424 (RJB 424F)!

Royal Blue coach 2203 (VDV 746) as it was found wedged in between a green ex-Crosville LD and one of the native examples in Lower Thorn Street yard.

Another rumour, which had some truth in it, was that another dozen LS-types were 'on the way', which also no doubt inspired the third version that this was to be converted for bus duties, indeed the most likely of all those theories. The coach remained in situ until 19th August when, rather mundanely, it was collected by the dealer who had merely left it behind in July!

The general fares increase deposited with the Traffic Commissioner in May had caused a raft of complaints from both the public and all Local Authorities in the Company's operating area, several Councils calling for an enquiry into the matter. As it was, the numerous journey cancellations of recent times had also called into question the quality of a service for which the higher fares were now being sought. Although *Thames Valley* was not unique in its financial problems, the Traffic Commissioner dealt with a wide variety of operators, so the degree of his criticism of the Company can be said to be more objective than the generally knee-jerk reaction of the public and its elected representatives, particularly as many of the latter had already been invited by the Management to consider subsidising loss-making services. Indeed, Traffic Manager Spencer Gwinnell stated at the Public Hearing in Reading that 35.8% of the services were now regarded as unrenumerative.

Leaving aside the purely financial aspects of income and expenses, the Traffic Commissioner issued a press statement in which he gave *Thames Valley* a severe public dressing-down, highlighting its failures in both terms of reliability and policy-making, such a wide-ranging condemnation being a rarity. He noted that 180 out of the total 374 fleet were over 12 years old, compared with an average in his region of 10.5, whilst also that the Company had continued to purchase elderly buses unsuited to one-man-operation, despite the 25% grant subsidy provided by the Government for new vehicles suitable for more efficient working.

Although *TV* had 102 buses suitable for o-m-o, only 85 of those were in use as such. He added that the Company had the highest level of fares within his juristriction, whilst passenger loadings averaged only 2.98 per mile against a regional average of 4.07 from comparably-sized concerns, leading to a loss of income from 1969 of £63,538. He commented on the lack of progress in co-ordination with *Reading CT*, though to be fair the latter had hardly been working actively on that, possibly because it did not want to get too involved with a Company in apparent terminal decline? The Commissioner noted that some 3 million passenger journeys had been lost between 1966 and 1969, whilst between 1st January and 16th May 1970 alone 3,959 had been lost, attributable to staff shortages (2618), vehicle shortages (565), mechanical breakdowns (400) and traffic delays (376)!

The fares increase called for the minimum fare to rise from 3d to 5d, whilst most fares would rise by 8d, and in due course the Traffic Commissioner had little choice other than to grant the increases, whilst the effects on the elderly saw moves towards what is now termed Concessionary Travel, and a marked increase in the shift towards contracted school transport, very little of which benefited *Thames Valley*.

There had of course been some progress on one-man working recently, such as Maidenhead Local Service 15, and Bristol VRT/SL6G Car 514 (XMO 542H) is seen in this Graham Low view at the Bus Station.

Such was the Company's woes with shortages of vehicles that some rail replacement work was now being contracted out to other operators, and on 26th July *Smith's Luxury Coaches* of Reading provided 9 double-deckers and 2 coaches to cover journeys between that town and Bracknell or Blackwater, a situation not previously seen locally. However, there may have been some amusement at 83 Lower Thorn Street when word reached it that *Smith's* former *South Wales* AEC 'Regent' MkV double-decker (MCY 402) had been driven down the Finchampstead Road and under the low railway bridge with predictable results, raising the bridge's running total to *Thames Valley* 4, *Smith's* 1 and the bridge 5, not including any lorries!

Further service changes were introduced from 1st August, mainly in response to staffing shortages at Reading. The Woodley Local Services were reduced from 8 buses an hour to just 5, with most off-peak journeys on Route 45 withdrawn, and the Sunday headway now reduced to 2-hourly. Route 49 (Reading or Bracknell – Wokingham – Camberley) had some peak journeys onto Farley Hill in compensation for those taken off Route 4a (Reading – Arborfield – Wokingham), whilst the other Farley Hill projections were placed under Route 4 (Reading – Arborfield – Camberley). Route 6a (Reading – Odiham) no longer served Wellington Monument, but ran via the A32 instead, whilst Route 7 was mostly converted to one-manners on an hourly headway to Stoke Row and Borocourt Hospital, now with fewer journeys onto Nettlebed. Routes 8 (to Henley) and 8a (to Caversham Park) also went over to one-man, with Sunday runs reduced to 2 hourly, whilst Route 11 (to Bucklebury) officially went over to o-m-o, though odd crew-operated double-deckers might still turn up at times.

An unusual choice for Route 11 to Bucklebury was Bristol RELL6G Car 185 (CBL 355B), caught by Philip Wallis on the temporary stand on Station Hill during the snows of December 1970.

In the Newbury area 1st August saw a number of service revisions, including the first changes to those taken over from *Reliance MS* back in June 1966. Route 107 (Newbury – Brightwalton) now had the previous dead-running out to Brightwalton as a scheduled journey, whilst the Route 119 (Newbury – Cold Ash) 'Convent loop' journeys were now incorporated into the Cold Ash circular Route 109. On Route 103 (Newbury – Ecchinswell) buses now ran out of town via Racecourse Road rather than Queens Road, whilst on the Local Services most journeys on Route 126 were extended on from Almond Avenue to Brummell Road, and on the 128 onto Love Lane in place of the projections formerly worked under Route 127. Some services even saw their running times reduced for the first time since WW2, with Route 2 (Reading – Newbury) down by 5 minutes to 56, Route 4 (Reading – Camberley) also by 5 minutes to 57 and the 25-mile Route 5a (Reading – Wantage) by 10 minutes to 1 hour and 8 minutes.

During July more new saloons started to arrive, with a trio of Bristol RELL6G's with ECW B49F bodies, as Cars 224-6 (YBL 521-3H).

The new trio of Bristol RELL6G buses were based at Reading and took over on the Oxford Route 5. Car 224 (YBL 521H) is seen above at Gloucester Green Bus Station in Oxford, whilst similar Car 226 (YBL 523H) waits time at Wallingford Town Hall.

In an effort to increase seating capacity available and reduce relief workings, the former London express 1960/4 coach-seated Bristol FLF's were re-seated, though dealt with in a piecemeal fashion typical of that time, and also tied in with a trend towards stripping vehicles prior to disposal. 1960 Cars 835-8 (UJB 201-4) each got an additional pair of seats in the lower saloon in place of the extra luggage rack, making them now CH37/30F and dealt with during March (835), April (838) and June (836/7), whereas similar Car 834 (UJB 200) was fully re-seated as a bus to H38/32F layout in April. These were followed by the 1964 batch, Cars D4-7 (ABL 116-9B) and D8 (BRX 141B), also altered to CH37/30F layout during September (D6/8), October (D4), November (D7) and December (D5). Also noted in Weldale Street yard during September was coach-seated Bristol LS6B Car 113 (HMO 838) being stripped of seating etc.

A further ECW B41F-bodied Bristol LH6L saloon arrived in July as Car 218 (ABL 121J), and in August it was joined by similar Car 219 (ABL 122J), both of which went to Maidenhead for the increased use of one-manners from that garage in preparation for further route conversions to o-m-o later in the year.

New Bristol LH6L Car 219 (ABL 122J) is seen at the layover point in Eton for Route 22 resulting from the closure to traffic of Windsor Bridge, in this case on a short-working to Eton Wick (Colenorton Crescent).

However, and despite the recent comments by the Traffic Commissioner, the tide of secondhand double-deckers had not ceased, with July seeing further buses from the *Crosville* fleet added. These were 1955/6 Bristol LD6B's with ECW LD33/27RD bodies which had been Nos. DLB753/7/85, and they became Cars 609/10 (VFM 618/22) and 614 (XFM 196), the latter allocated to Reading and the other pair to Wycombe.

Former Crosville Car 609 (VFM 618) departs from Newlands Bus Station for Booker on Route 38.

Recent arrivals resulted in the demise of various Bristol KSW6B buses with ECW L27/28R bodies in July, as 1952/3 Cars 654/5/64 (HBL 56/7/66), along with ex-*United Welsh* 1953 Car 673 (JCY 990), the first of the secondhand examples to depart. Another Bristol LS6B of 1954 with ECW B41F body was also ousted in July as Car 120 (HMO 860). August saw just one disposal, of 1953 Bristol KSW6B Car 697 (HMO 843), carrying ECW L27/28R bodywork, whilst during that month similar 1952 example Car 658 (HBL 60) became a Driver Training Bus. As will be noted the ranks of the Bristol KSW's were being steadily depleted, replaced by slightly newer LD's!

A number of changes took place to the yards of the Reading Garage complex during this time. The entrance from Lower Thorn Street was lost with the building of the sunken carriageway of the Inner Distribution Road. The yard on that side was further reduced by a building to house the computer section, after which this yard was not used much by vehicles on active service, but tended to house new vehicles or those waiting re-painting. On the other hand, the yard on Weldale Street had expanded considerably through the demolition of all the Company-owned cottages, and was now the main throughfare for the many buses kept outside at night. A new canteen was also constructed towards the garage end of that yard.

Another ex-Crosville LD6B, Car 614 (XFM 196) is seen in the Weldale Street yard with blinds set for Route 90 and the new canteen block to its right.

August saw a further raft of 6 secondhand Bristol LD-types arriving from *Lincolnshire* and *Crosville*, the former being its Nos.2314/6 (LFW 322/4) and 2327 (NBE 130). The first became Car 615 and was an ECW LD33/25RD-bodied 1955 LD6B which went to Reading, whilst the second was also new in 1955 but now an LD6G with ECW LD33/25RD bodywork that still retained the long type of radiator grille, and this became Car 616 allocated to Newbury. The third bus was an LD6B new in 1955 but with an ECW LD33/27R body, which became Car 617. Although re-painted it was noted as unallocated at September and October 1970, and still so at June and September 1971, and was often noted in Weldale Street yard, so it was probably kept as an engineering float to cover buses in for overhaul.

From the *Crosville* stable came its 1955 Nos.DLB746/52 (VFM 611/7) and 1956 DLB782 (XFM 193), all with Bristol 6-cylinder engines and ECW 60-seater bodies, though the first one lacked the platform doors found on the other pair. These became Cars 608 (VFM 611) allocated to Reading, 611 (VFM 617) at Newbury and 613 (XFM 193) was sent to High Wycombe.

Former Lincolnshire Car 616 (LFW 324) was the first example in the Thames Valley fleet to carry the long-type radiator grille, and it is seen at Swindon Bus Station on Route 106 from Lambourn and Newbury.

With the start of the Autumn term in September, there were additional school-related short-workings from the south of Wokingham, with new housing built around California Crossroads, whilst additional housing in Sandhurst generated further secondary school pupils needing transport to Bracknell schools.

The already beleagured Company was hit by a work-to-rule from 13th September, which included the non-acceptance of standing passengers, whilst the local Reading newspaper noted that recently some buses had been sent to *Western National* in Plymouth for overhauls due to a shortage of maintenance staff!

Withdrawals for September saw the remaining 1964 Duple 'Super Vega' C37F-bodied Bedford SB13's departing, these being *South Midland* Cars C407-9 (837/8/42 CRX). Two Bristol LS-types were also ousted, one as Car 122 (HMO 864), a 1954 LS6B with ECW B41F body, and the other being Car 113 (TWL 58), this being the penultimate LS-type coach-to-bus conversion left and latterly with a 6-cylinder Gardner engine and ECW DP39F body, which was stripped before final disposal. On the double-deck front only one bus left that month, it being former *United Auto* Bristol KSW6B Car 689 (PHN 829) of 1952 with standard ECW L27/28R body, whilst the following month saw native 1954 example Car 739 (JRX 813) going, by then with an ECW L27/26RD layout.

September also saw one of the 1969 Bristol LH6L's out of action after running into a wall at Maidenhead, and Car 210 (VMO 227H) was with ECW from 22nd of that month until 27th November. Similar bus 212 (VMO 232H) also went there for 5th November until 11th December following another unplanned event to that Reading-based bus.

Other *Thames Valley* buses taking the sea air went there to be rebuilt with platform doors, with former *Crosville* Cars 600 (VFM 607) returning in October and 608 (VFM 611) in November, followed by ex-*Lincolnshire* Car 607 (NBE 133) in December.

Routes A and B (from Victoria) were amended from 24th October to leave via Ebury Street – Eccleston Street – Kings Road – Hobart Place – Grosvener Place – Hyde Park Corner. Also from 26th of that month, buses on Route A from the London direction were switched from using Bracknell High Street in favour of the loop via Church Road and Station Road, no bus services now using that road.

Two of the outgoing buses of the Autumn are seen in Weldale Street yard. Above is Bristol LS6G Car 113 (TWL 58), partially stripped and standing next to one of the ex-Crosville LD's yet to go through the Works, whilst below we see Bristol KSW6B Car 697 (HMO 843) in a slightly earlier view.

Also from 26th October, a large area of the Reading Bus Station floor had to be re-laid, due to poor work by the original contractor, so some services were transferred to temporary stands in the surrounding streets, an embarrassment the Company could have done without, and the routes affected were as below:

Garrard Street – Routes 3 (to Camberley); A/B (to London) and 90/90a/91/91a/92/92a (to Windsor), plus other express services;
Station Hill (Western Tower) – Routes 2 (to Newbury) and 11 (to Bucklebury);
Station Hill (Central Island) – Routes 6 (Basingstoke), 6a (to Odiham), 6b (to Basingstoke), 7 (to Nettlebed), 8 (to Henley) and 8a (to Caversham Park);
Station Hill (Phoenix House) – Routes 4 (Camberley), 4a (Arborfield and Wokingham) and 12 (Aldershot).

Such arrangements also saw *Thames Valley* buses using slightly different routes in and out of town in some cases, including its buses turning from Broad Street into St. Mary's Butts for the first time since the 1920's, when the Corporation banned that routing due to 'congestion'. Indeed, from 15th November all traffic other than buses and delivery vehicles was banned from the whole of Broad Street. This, along with the use of the bus-only contra-flow lane in Kings Road, attracted a fair amount of attention, with the T&RRL bringing parties of councillors etc. from other towns, and the *Reading CT* General Manager Royston Jenkins hosted a number of tours, but it would not be long before the town was swamped with traffic again!

Maidenhead got its first 36ft-long buses in the shape of a pair of Bristol RELL6G's with ECW B49F bodies in November for use on some Slough operations. These were Cars 227/8 (AMO 233/4J), the former of which is seen on Route 62 to Cippenham (The Green).

Also entering service in November were three further 30ft-long Bristol LH6L saloons with ECW B41F bodies as Cars 220-2 (AMO 235-7J), followed by similar Car 223 (AMO 238J) in December, and these were allocated to Bracknell (220), Newbury (223), Reading (221) and Wycombe (222).

Also completed for November was what had been intended as the first of the 1960 Bristol MW6G's from coach to bus work, as former *South Midland* 830 (UJB 196) re-emerged as B41F and as Car 167 at Newbury.

Philip Wallis caught converted Bristol MW Car 167 (UJB 196) on the steam ramp at Smith's of Reading, another example of work being subbed out to them.

Bristol LH6L Car 221 (AMO 236J) seen in Farnham Road at Guildford on Route 75 back to Reading.

Further secondhand saloons suitable for one-man were also forthcoming from *Midland General* in November as former Nos.244/8, Bristol LS6G's new in 1956 and with ECW bodies as B41F with *TV*. These became Cars 152/5 (958/62 ARA), and they were joined by similar buses from that source in December as Cars 151/6/7 (957/60/3 ARA), also new in 1956 as Nos.243/6/9, though Cars 156/7 still retained their original coach seating fitted to the batch for use on longer services, albeit now reduced to 41. These saloons were sent to the garages at Bracknell (151), Maidenhead (152) and Reading (155-7).

Even so, there were more 'Lodekkas' still arriving from other fleets, and a further 1955 ECW LD33/27RD-bodied LD6B arrived from *Crosville* in November as Car 612 (XFM 186), formerly No.DLB 775 and it was allocated to Reading Garage.

Ex-Crosville Car 612 (XFM 186) freshly re-painted.

However, further colour was added to Weldale Street yard that month with the arrival of the first double-decker from *Notts & Derby,* part of the group of former Balfour-Beatty operators now managed by *Midland General,* and also had the blue and cream livery. No.465 (14 DRB) was a Bristol LD6G new in 1958 with ECW LD33/25RD bodywork. Being of a non-Tilling external scheme, buses from this source featured red interior paintwork and blue moquette seating in the lower saloon, very much in keeping with pre-war *TV* standards, though the upper-deck seating was blue leatherette. The latter feature was in connection with their use in colliery areas, and platform signs required miners in overalls to occupy the top deck only. It also featured fluorescent lighting, whilst the destination blinds were of a non-standard format, with the ultimate box being narrower but deeper than the Tilling standard, and the intermediate box being shallower as a result, whilst the route number blinds were of a single-track type. This bus became Car 636 and was allocated to Reading.

Former Notts & Derby Car 636 (14 DRB) was the best of all the LD-types so far acquired, and is seen in Weldale Street yard with amended destination boxes.

The sole 1962 Bristol MW6G coach with the revised style of ECW body, Car 866 (520 ABL), had latterly been reserved for helping out on the Rail-Air service, but from 1st December it was transferred to Newbury to take over an AWRE Harwell contract run from the UJB-registered 1960 *SM* Bristol MW recently in use.

There was further trouble on the Britwell Estate with youths, so from 12th December the later journeys were once again run short until the Police regained control. Also from that date a number of changes were made to Maidenhead area services, and Routes 60/69, 65/65a and 66/66a were now de-linked to the previous projections to operate between Langley or Slough and Maidenhead only. The section of Routes 65/65a from Maidenhead – The Walthams – Wokingham was now revised as Route 76/77, whilst the Tittle Row journeys of Route 17 (Maidenhead – Hurley – Henley) were also transferred to those services. The Route 60/69 journeys onto Pinkneys Green were transferred back to Route 18, which also had additional links from Marlow to Marlow Bottom added. The revised routes were worked by o-m-o saloons and ran as follows:

Route 76 – Maidenhead (Bus Station) – Cox Green – Woodlands Park – The Walthams – Wokingham*
Route 77 – Maidenhead (BS) – Tittle Row – Woodlands Park – The Walthams – Wokingham*
Route 78 – Maidenhead (BS) – St.Marks Road – Halifax Road#
Route 79 – Maidenhead (BS) – Belmont Road – Halifax Road#
Notes - * Only 3 daily journeys reached Wokingham, and no longer at times suitable for workpeople.
Had some eastwards projections to Summerleaze Road to avoid need to change bus at Maidenhead.

1953 Bristol LS6G Car 105 (HBL 85) is seen on a short-working of Route 76 to Woodlands Park at the Bus Station in Maidenhead with unusual blind layout.

Despite the increase in one-man working, there were still further Bristol LD-types coming in to replace the Bristol KSW-type double-deckers mainly used on town services, with examples arriving in December from the *Bristol* and *Lincolnshire* fleets, introducing further variety into the range of the 'Lodekka' fleet.

Also seen on the stands at Maidenhead, and offering a comparison of body styles, is Bristol LS6G Car 152 (958 ARA) recently bought from Midland General, and covering Route 24 to Cookham Dean (Quarry Wood Road) – all set out on a single-line blind!

The incoming buses from the *Bristol* fleet were 1955 LD6B-types with ECW LD33/25RD bodies, formerly Nos.L8255/60, which became Cars 629/30 (THW 745/50) and were both allocated to Reading. It should be noted that incoming saloons were taking numbers previously used by buses of the same model, whilst the 'Lodekkas' were allocated those from KSW or LWL-types, often from batches not entirely extinct, making it all quite a lot to keep up with! Also, although the author does recall at least one LD-type with a fleet number marked in yellow crayon prior to going through the workshops, at the time it was difficult to tell if these were pre-planned to any extent.

Former Bristol OC Car 629 (THW 745) is seen leaving Reading Bus Station on service to Mortimer Station, though no route number is shown. This bus arrived with the longer style of grille, but later acquired a shorter polished version following a front-end collision. Note the BOC-style destination boxes.

The other pair of LD-types arrived on 18th December, and these were in the reversed cream and green livery used by *Lincolnshire* for the Skegness seafront route.

The pair were formerly Nos.2309/10 (LFW 317/8), both being 1954 LD6B-types with 58-seater ECW bodies still retaining open rear platforms in keeping with the nature of the service they had been employed on. However, the sea air had done these buses no favour and, apart from a possible tie with a couple of the *Crosville* examples, the author would award the prize for the 'Worst Lodekka Acquired' to this pair! Indeed, as Cars 618/9 they were both allocated to Reading for only some 7 months of use, taking on the appearance of 'spare' buses and never being fitted with platform doors - the 'Skeggy rust-buckets'.

Ex-Lincolnshire Car 618 (LFW 317) is seen in the Weldale Street yard at Reading, staff cars now parking in an elevated area reached by the slope to the left of the bus and back towards Chatham Road.

With all these arrivals there were further inroads into the ranks of the Bristol KSW6B-types with ECW L27/28R bodies. November saw the end for 1953 Cars 663 (HBL 65) and 694 (HMO 840), along with former *United Welsh* example Car 672 (JCY 989), also new in 1953. During December 1953 Cars 668/70 (HBL 70/2) departed, along with similar Cars 699 and 703 (HMO 845/9). The only saloon to go during December was another 1953 vehicle, also formerly *United Welsh,* as Bristol LS6B Car 116 (JCY 997) with ECW B41F bodywork.

For the first time in its history, the company ran no services on Boxing Day, not even the London express routes, the sole exception being the Rail-Air Link at the insistence of *British Rail*. However, the area suffered from heavy snowfalls overnight on 26th/27th December, causing some disruption when services resumed. Indeed, at Reading, the bus station slope once again proved problematical, causing all buses to have to use the temporary stands put in place a little earlier for the remedial work on the concrete flooring. At some times there were buses parked on both sides of Garrard Street, and others on Station Hill.

The other former Bristol OC LD6B acquired during December was Car 630 (THW 750), also with the longer style of grille on a 3-piece front cowling. It is seen departing from Reading Bus Station on Route 43a to Woodley (Tippings Lane), with no 'a' shown.

At a time when *Thames Valley* was beset with so many problems a number of rumours regarding its future were in circulation. The at times severe loss of services out to the large Woodley estates, dependent as many residents were on transport to Reading for work and shopping, led to calls for *Reading BC* to take the services over, though at that time those areas were outside of the Borough boundary. Indeed, during the earlier fares Public Hearing, the Commissioner had intimated that if the Company wished to withdraw from services it could no longer maintain, he would then look favourably on other operators wishing to offer replacement facilities, perhaps using smaller buses in respect of the very rural areas.

Another of the former Midland General Bristol LS6G saloons was Car 151 (957 ARA), which was allocated to Bracknell and is seen in Market Street ready for the 57 to Sunningdale.

So the news that *South Midland* was to be transferred under *City of Oxford* was taken by local enthusiasts as confirmation that some fractionalisation of *Thames Valley's* operations might well follow. Surrounded as it was by other bus companies now under the National Bus Company, it was not hard to visualise how those concerns might be used in order to dispense with the Reading-based concern. As it was the *'Valley* made connections with *Wilts & Dorset* at Basingstoke, and Newbury (not to mention a bus outstationed with them at Baughurst), *Bristol* at Hungerford and Swindon, *City of Oxford* at Reading, Wallingford, Oxford and Newbury, *Aldershot & District* at Aldershot, Reading, Camberley and Guildford and *United Counties* up at Aylesbury, whilst *London Country* had operations with the Company and other routes based at garages at Windsor, High Wycombe and Staines. From all these it is easy to consider how each operator could have increased its share of operations inwards towards the centre (i.e. Reading), leaving *Reading CT* to expand its coverage from that centre and *London Country* to take on everything else to the north and east of the established area. As it was, and as we shall see in the next chapter, the actual outcome of these rumblings would prove to be even more bizarre than expected!

The lack of any public explanation in respect of the transfer of the Oxford operations also gave the sense of a done deal. Indeed, *City of Oxford* had little recent experience of coach work and none of extended tours. All of the *South Midland* coaches, along with Botley Road Garage, and the Café and Enquiry Office at Gloucester Green, were transferred with effect from 1st January 1971, and these were:

Bedford SB13 – Cars 410-2 (EMO 551-3C)
Bedford VAM14 – Cars 413-6 (GRX 413-6D)
Bristol LS6G – Cars 440/1 (613/4 JPU)
Bristol MW6G – Cars 442 (618 JPU), 831-3 (UJB 197-9) and 858-60 (WRX 773-5)
Bristol REX6G – Car 403 (521 ABL)
Bristol RELH6G – Cars 404/5 (834/5 CRX) and 421-3 (LJB 421-3E)
Bristol LH6L – Cars 428-31 (RJB 428-31F), 432-5 (UMO 688-91G) and 436-9 (YBL 925-8H)

The Oxford-based Service Vehicles also passed to *City of Oxford*, these being the Austin 'Gypsy' Van No.59 (GBL 227C), the Inspector's Austin 1100 car (PJB 421F) and the Traffic Superintendent's Austin 1300 car (RJB 934F).

Typical of the outgoing Bristol KSW6B's was Car 670 (HBL 72), seen at Slough on Route 62 to Cippenham, a service now covered by one-man 36ft Bristol RE's.

1971

This year started off fairly quietly, but a lot of effort was going on behind the scenes to shed mileage and assist in reducing the operating deficit of the previous year. On Sunday 31st January the following service revisions took place throughout the Company's area:

Route 5 (Reading – Oxford) – Now incorporated the Moulsford (Fair Mile Hospital) service on Sundays;
Route 5a (Reading – Wantage) – Sunday service ends;
Route 5b (Reading – Yattendon – Newbury) – Sunday service withdrawn, some weekday journeys extended from Kiln Corner onto Compton (and also via Purley Village) as Route 5c, in compensation for withdrawal of Route 102. Tidmarsh journeys now transferred onto Route 11 as Route 11a;
Route 6a (Reading – Odiham) – Service completely withdrawn, but some provision between Reading and Spencers Wood by new Route 4b;

Bristol MW6G Car 163 (PRX 930) prepares for an afternoon journey on Route 4b to Spencers Wood.

Route 11 (Reading – Bucklebury Common) – Sunday service withdrawn. Certain journeys now transferred from Route 5b to serve Tidmarsh as Route 11a;
Route 16 (Maidenhead – Warren Row – Henley) – Service completely withdrawn, but action delayed due to protests (see later in this chapter);
Route 26 (Wycombe Marsh/Bowerdean Rd. – Sands) – Sunday service withdrawn;
Route 27 (High Wycombe – Great Missenden) – The Sunday service reduced to 2-hourly from hourly;
Route 28 (Reading – Marlow – High Wycombe) – On High Wycombe – Marlow shorts, all but 2 evening journeys on Sundays withdrawn;
Route 30 (High Wycombe – Plomer Hill Estate) – No service on Sundays;
Route 31 (High Wycombe – Lacey Green) – 4 trips on Tuesdays/Thursdays/Saturdays extended to Longwick (Red Lion) via Princes Risborough as compensation for withdrawn Route 80. Sunday service reduced to 2-hourly;

Route 32 (High Wycombe – Bledlow Ridge/Chinnor) – Sunday service withdrawn;
Route 34 (High Wycombe – Speen) – Sunday service withdrawn. Certain weekday journeys via Bryants Bottom and Great Hampden as Route 34a to cover for withdrawn Route 80;
Route 35 (High Wycombe – Downley) – Sunday service reduced to 2-hourly;
Route 36 (High Wycombe – Lane End – Cadmore End) – Sunday service reduced;
Route 37 (High Wycombe – Lane End – Henley) – Sunday journeys Wycombe – Lane End reduced;
Route 41 (High Wycombe – Ibstone) – Sunday service withdrawn;
Route 42 (Wycombe Marsh – Booker Hill Estate) – Sunday service withdrawn, but Route 38 re-timed to provide link;
Route 50 (Reading – Wallingford) – Now included the Fair Mile Hospital journeys on Thursdays;
Route 80 (High Wycombe – Lacey Green – Princes Risborough) - Service completely withdrawn. *United Counties* Route 365 now covered Aylesbury – Longwick – Princes Risborough, plus see Routes 31 and 34;
Route 81 (Wycombe Marsh – Booker) – Sunday service withdrawn;
Route 104 (Newbury – Ashford Hill) – Service completely withdrawn, but see Route 122;
Route 105 (Newbury – Curridge) – Service completely withdrawn, but see Route 129;
Route 107 (Newbury – Brightwalton) – Sunday service withdrawn;
Route 113 (Newbury - Inkpen – Hungerford) – Sunday service withdrawn, and now fully one-man;
Route 116 (Newbury – Stockcross – Hungerford) – Sunday service withdrawn;
Route 119 (Newbury – Cold Ash) – Sunday service withdrawn. 2 journeys on Thursdays extended to serve Frilsham in place of Route 120;
Route 120 (Newbury – Frilsham) - Service completely withdrawn, but see Route 119;

The complete withdrawal of services such as Route 120 was keenly felt by many villagers who relied on the buses. Bristol MW6G Car 182 (VJB 946) was caught by Philip Wallis the previous Summer as it rounded into a recently demolished Market Street.

Route 121 (Newbury – Penwood) Service withdrawn completely;
Route 122 (Newbury - Kingsclere – Basingstoke) – Some journeys added between Newbury and Ashford Hill on Thursdays in compensation for withdrawn Route 104 and known as Route 122a;
Route 129 (Newbury – Hampstead Norris – Compton) – Now included Thursday-only journeys Newbury – Curridge formerly covered by Route 105.

On the same date the Bracknell – Holyport – Bray – Maidenhead operations were revised, with Routes 55 and 55a now replaced by the revival of Route 14. The route now only operated direct from Bracknell along Warfield Road, without journeys via Jigs Lane and Warfield Street, which was more highly populated, with the Warfield Caravan Site and other housing. 4 or 5 journeys ran through between Maidenhead and Bracknell an both garages were involved, but many other trips ran as shorts from Maidenhead to Foxley Corner or (once again) Paley Street (Sheepcote Lane), the latter largely being in the interest of safely turning the bus, whilst through journeys dropped Paley Street passengers on the road at nearby Touchen End (Hinds Head). Some additional passengers were generated by having suitable timings passing Wick Hill for Wick Hill and The Garth Schools. It is worth noting that the Jealotts Hill stop was incorrectly given as the Old Leathern Bottle, whereas it was actually the New one!

When working towards Reading on Route 5b, Bristol LS5G Car 124 (HMO 836), was in collision with an articulated lorry at Hermitage on Monday 11th January. The Driver's Defect Card read 'slight damage to near-side, draughty at high speeds'! Needless to say, this bus did not return to service.

Incidentally, the Thames Valley Social Club still arranged its annual children's outing to the pantomime, and on Saturday 2nd January a pair of Bristol FLF's took 120 children and minders to the London Palladium to see Cilla Black in Aladdin.

Ex-Bristol Car 625 (THW 743) leaves from Reading's Station Hill on Route 44 for Woodley and Twyford.

Despite some new Bristol RELL and VRT vehicles being on order, further secondhand 'Lodekkas' arrived during January. Three came from *Bristol OC*, as ECW LD33/25RD-bodied LD6B Nos. L8252-4 (THW 742-4) of 1955, which became Cars 621/5/7, with the first pair allocated to Reading and the latter to High Wycombe. The Reading examples both retained their original long radiator grilles, where Car 627 had already received the shorter type before arrival. These buses were of course 16 years old and rather average.

The other incoming buses were once again from *Notts & Derby*, and were in much better condition at only 13 years old. These Bristol LD6G types also carried ECW LD33/25RD bodies, fitted out as noted under Car 636 (14 DRB) in the previous chapter. These were Nos.467-70 (16-9 DRB), which became Cars 637-40, and were shared between Newbury (638/40) and Reading (637/9).

Car 640 (19 DRB) seen in its Notts & Derby livery.

188

Former Notts & Derby Car 639 (18 DRB) is also seen above in Weldale Street yard as it arrived and showing the style of destination screens fitted as new. Behind it is Car D6 (ABL 118B), which was one of a number of bad accidents in early 1971, evidently when working Route B towards Reading. Below we see Car 637 (16 DRB) after overhaul and repainting.

The arrival of further newer types heralded the demise of 1953 ECW L27/28R-bodied Bristol KSW6B Cars 702/4 (HMO 848/50), a pair allocated to Newbury since new, along with similar and former *United Auto* Cars 690/1 (PHN 821 and 819), built in 1952 and also from the Newbury stable during their 3-year stay. Only one saloon was disposed of in January, as 1954 ECW B41F-bodied Bristol LS6B Car 123 (HMO 865). During that month another Bristol FLF was lost temporarily, when Car 842 (WJB 226) was found to have a cracked chassis and was stored at Maidenhead.

It should also be noted that, unlike all native Bristol LD's or acquired buses of that type fitted with platform doors, either as new or subsequently, those from the *Midland General* group fleets featured power operated 4-leaf folding doors. Also noteworthy is the fact that, although many buses were fitted with rear doors of the 2-leaf manually operated variety, they were not popular with conductors on busier services!

The recent service reductions led to a great number of complaints, often aired through the local press and from all over the Company's area. Residents in the areas affected varied from those inconvenienced, such as the changes in the Warfield area, to those whose lifeline had, quite literally, been cut off at very short notice. The decline of village shops is nothing new, and many had already lost them by this time. Parish Councils had quite limited resources with which to consider subsidies, whilst the County Councils were unwilling to accept responsibility. Oxfordshire did decide to appoint a Transport Co-ordinator, though the initial concern was undertaking its responsibilities for home-to-school travel for eligible school children, most of whom had until then managed with free passes on service routes, plus some appropriately timed relief workings. The introduction of adult fares for children travelling before 9.15am on Mondays to Fridays was really the final straw.

The Newbury area came off worst generally, and in some cases the Parishes did negotiate some limited return of service, though only effective for shopping, leaving scholars and workers without a link that had existed for around 50 years. As a result of this the Ashford Hill journeys via Route 122 and Frilsham links via Route 119 were arranged during the notice period, also being subsidised by Newbury Town Council. Neither the LA's or the Company showed much expertise when negotiating such subsidies, the former feeling they were held over a barrel, and the latter lacking experience in dealing with such bodies.

An increasing trend was the stripping of withdrawn Bristol LS-types for parts, and Car 106 (HBL 86) is seen In Weldale Street yard around March 1971.

Ex-Midland General Bristol LS6G Car 126 (966 ARA) is seen after repainting and awaiting collection from Reading by a High Wycombe driver.

The other time-consuming matter during early 1971 was the introduction of decimal currency, which came into use from 15th February, with all fares charts being revised and staff trained. Some coins were new, such as the 1penny, half-penny and 50pence, whereas others were old types now with new values, e.g. the 1shilling (now 5p), Florin (old 2shilling now 10p) and even the old three-penny bit, with a phased change-over period of 18 months. This led to a varied mix of coins for the conductors bag, whilst due to there not always being a direct conversion to costs, the trend was to round upwards, causing many to feel that life got more expensive as a result, which did not sit well with the difficulties already being experienced.

At the same time revised Parcel Rates were also put in place, with those up to 7lbs at 10p (old 2shillings), up to 14lbs for 13p (old 2shillings 6pence) and 18p for up to 28lbs (old 3s 6d). However, the reductions in the bus map had severely reduced the use of this facility.

There were a couple of notable retirements from High Wycombe at this time, and no doubt Cashier Charlie Fox was relieved to be going with the above in mind, after 21 years of service at Wycombe Marsh mainly. The other was Fitter George Bishop, who retired after 34 years, though his job title belies the much wider involvement both he and his family had with pioneer bus operations in the Lane End area. Indeed, he had in due course become part of the *Chiltern Bus Company* and came to *Thames Valley* when that was acquired in May 1936. Fuller details of the background to that can be found in the *Thames Valley 1931-1945* volume.

Another trio of former *Midland General* 1956 Bristol LS6G's with ECW bodies arrived during February, and these were re-seated to 41 by *TV* before service. Originally Nos.250/2/3 (964/6/7 ARA), they became Cars 125, 126 and 132 and were sent to Bracknell (125/32) and High Wycombe (126). A further Bristol LS6G was also forthcoming from the same group, but latterly running as *Mansfield District* No.200 (PNN 769), a 1954 example which had started out as a coach and saw conversion for bus work in July 1967, when it carried dual *Midland General-Mansfield District* fleetnames. 41 coach seats had been retained, and had a cream and black livery. This became Car 119 and was allocated to Newbury.

Just as the last of the native coach-to-bus Bristol LS conversions was leaving the fleet, this example came from the east Midlands. Car 119 (PNN 769) arrived with 41 coach seats, as shown here at The Wharf in Newbury on Route 5b for Reading, but in July the front nearside pair was removed for a luggage pen.

The *Mansfield District* fleet featured a non-standard green and cream livery for service buses, similar in its application to the parent *Midland General,* whilst the interiors also had a green scheme in place of the blue found on the *Midland General* and *Notts & Derby* buses. A pair of Bristol LD6G's arrived from that fleet in February, Nos.513 (WAL 440) and 516 (213 ANN), both new in 1958 and with ECW LD33/25RD bodies. These became Cars 642/3 and both were sent to Maidenhead Garage.

Former Mansfield District Bristol LD6G Car 642 (WAL 440) is seen at Maidenhead Bus Station ready for busy Route 66a to Slough via the Trading Estate. In this case the ultimate screen has been used, whilst other examples saw single-line blinds fitted to the intermediate screen instead, painted over in this case.

190

Also on a Slough service, Route 65a via the Trading Estate, is ex-Mansfield District Car 643 (213 ANN). Also note that because of the livery style of these buses they were built without the upper-deck beading.

With the recent service reductions and the secondhand acquisitions, February saw the Bristol KSW6B buses taking a big reduction. 1953 ECW L27/28R-bodied Cars 665/6 (HBL 67/8) and similar 1954 Cars 727/8/31/2/5-7/44 (JRX 802/3/6/7/10-2/9) all went, along with the last of the secondhand examples, 1952 ex-*United Autos* Car 688 (PHN 828).

Car 666 (HBL 68) was one of the outgoing KSW6B's, and is seen here a little earlier when on Route 20 from Maidenhead to Windsor.

A pair of 1954 Bristol LS5G's with ECW B41F bodies also went in February, these being long-time Bracknell Cars 110/1 (HMO 854/5), whilst that garage received Bristol KSW6B Cars 729/30 (JRX 804/5), a pair originally allocated for Stokenchurch duties during February, along with the final bus of that type purchased new, Car 749 (JRX 824) from Reading. Despite these changes there was still a shortage of serviceable buses, so *City of Oxford* loaned its AEC 'Reliances' Nos.751 (751 HFC) and 753 (753 KFC) for use on Route 12 (Reading – Aldershot) from 2nd to 5th February, and were garaged at Reading overnight.

February also saw the end of an era, when the final example of the 85 rear-entrance Bristol L-series buses bought new by the '*Valley*' between 1947 and 1952 was taken out of service.

Last of the line, 1952 Bristol LWL6B Car 265 (GJB 265) is seen in Newlands Bus Station on Route 38 in from Booker. This also doubled up as Wycombe's tow bus, and as can be seen was still in good condition.

There was another long-term loss to the fleet from Thursday 18th February, when 1964 Bristol RELL6G Car 185 (CBL 355B) received extensive front end damage. As noted in the last chapter, this bus saw use on Route 11 to Bucklebury Common, hardly a suitable use for a 36-footer, and that service inter-worked with Route 8 (to Henley). The latter featured several blind bends, and it was out at Shiplake that the bus collided with a van. Being an unusual body style, and with extensive mechanical damage, this bus languished in Weldale Street yard for many months before eventually returning to service.

Also written off in March was Route Servicing Vehicle ED53 (FPU 510), former Bristol K5G Car 460, which came off worse after a collision with a concrete-mixer lorry out Mortimer way.

Wilts & Dorset Bristol FLF No.681 (EMR 297D) is seen with Thames Valley Car 616 (LFW 324) on the rail replacement workings on 21st March, in this photo at Reading General Station by Philip Wallis. Wilts & Dorset had been placed under the control of Hants & Dorset in 1964, hence the advert for the latter's services on this bus. As the W&D livery was similar, most passengers would not have noticed the loan of these buses on this occasion.

A shortage of buses also saw *Thames Valley* borrowing buses several buses from *Wilts & Dorset* in order to cover rail replacement duties over the evening of Saturday 20th and all day on Sunday 21st March to cover the Reading – Wokingham section.

Secondhand buses were still being fitted with platform doors, and the final examples travelling to Lowestoft returned as ex-*United Welsh* Car 624 (OCY 960) in January, former *Lincolnshire* Car 606 (NBE 129) in February, and another ex-*United Welsh* example, Car 635 (OCY 961) during March. Others were altered within the Company's workshops, but full details are lacking. By the Summer of 1971 it was stated that only former *Lincolnshire* Cars 618/9 (LFW 317/8) did not have platform doors, though no evidence relating to that feature on Car 617 (NBE 130) from that same source has so far come to light.

Other alterations also took place in order to increase seating capacity, when the coach-seated pair of Bristol LD6G's for some years associated with the longer services from Newbury, Cars 763/4 (MBL 844/5) were re-seated with bus seating as LD33/27RD during April (764) and May (763).

The remaining Bristol LS-types were also reviewed, leading to a number receiving Gardner 6HLW units in place of their original Bristol engines, with ex-*United Welsh* Car 148 (KWN 794) in January, Car 147 (HMO 870) in April, another ex-*United Welsh* Car 149 (KWN 795) in June, Car 118 (HMO 858) in July, ex-*United Welsh* Car 153 (OCY 947) in August, then finally Car 121 (HMO 863) in October. During this time LS-type Car 106 (HBL 86) was noted being stripped in May, and Cars 100/1 (HBL 79/80) and ex-*United Autos* Car 128 (SHN 729) were so in September, whilst earlier accident victim Car 124 (HMO 836) finally went for scrap in July. In all cases every usable part was removed, especially those hard-to-find items for these ageing types.

The fleet also found itself under fire once again during early March, though this time it was literally the case! A number of late-night buses in the Baughurst and Tadley area were found to have been damaged by stones or air-gun pellets, leading to a press report that the Police were patrolling in an effort to catch the culprit, and fortunately the practice then ceased before someone was injured.

Of the various secondhand 'Lodekka's acquired, three were noted in March as still not prepared for service, these being ex-*Crosville* Cars 612 (XFM 186), which did enter service in May, 611 (VFM 617), which was being cannibalised but did also get completed in May, along with former *Lincolnshire* Car 617 (NBE 130), which sat in Weldale Street yard until it was suddenly cleaned up for re-painting and taken to The Colonnade on 24th August!

Damaged Bristol RELL6G Car 185 (CBL 355B) and ex-Crosville Bristol LD Car 612 (XFM 186) give the Weldale Street yard the appearance of a scrapyard.

During March it was publicly announced that the National Bus Company was to merge *Thames Valley* with the neighbouring *Aldershot & District* company!

This news came as an equal shock to all local bus enthusiasts and, regardless of whether your allegiance was to the red or the green, all those on either side of the A30 knew one thing – it just wouldn't work. Despite many years of being under the same original ownership (BET) and even having the same Chairman (Sidney Garcke), these adjacent operators had had remarkably little to do with each other over the 50-plus years of existence. As it was, the management of *Thames Valley* had acknowledged from an early date that the widening area of operation could only be effectively controlled by locally based managers, with the No.1 Area covering Reading and all its associated Dormy Sheds, whilst the No.2 Area took in the High Wycombe area, its Dormy Sheds and Maidenhead. When the Newbury area came into the fold No.3 Area was based upon it, and the *South Midland* operations formed the fourth division, with a sound system of Traffic Superintendents, Assistants and Inspectors making the whole work well. Quite how the persons responsible for this decision saw things working on a daily basis from the following 1st January seems to have gone un-recorded, lost in the 1970's dogma of operating-units and other accountancy-based jargon.

1971 saw the ranks of Bristol KSW6B's disappearing rapidly, and Car 733 (JRX 808) is seen still at work at Maidenhead Garage where, a little later, it would become the Driver Training Bus. Indeed the final trio of that type would survive on such duties into 1972.

As part of the announcement it was stated that the new concern would become the *Thames Valley & Aldershot Omnibus Co. Ltd.*, and that the Head Office would remain at Reading, in Thorn Walk as the old Lower Thorn Street had become since being paved over as part of the opening of the Reading IDR. Tom Pruett was due for retirement in 1972, and would stay in a consultancy capacity as Peter Scully (from *A&D*) took over as the new General Manager. Despite this location, there was a definite feeling that *Thames Valley* had been taken over by the Aldershot concern, not helped when the latter duly applied to take over all the Road Service Licenses held by the '*Valley*.

The second bus to bear the fleet number 641 (20 DRB) at Bracknell Garage was this ex-Notts & Derby Bristol LD6G.

March saw a further pair of Bristol LD6G's acquired from fleets of the *Midland General* group, both new in 1958 with ECW LD33/25RD bodies. One was from *Mansfield District*, its No.517 (214 ANN), which went to Newbury as Car 644, whilst the other was former *Notts & Derby* No.471 (20 DRB), which as Car 641 was sent to Bracknell.

With the announcement of the planned merger, a local paper interviewed Tom Pruett, and he stated that there were already much closer links with not only the Aldershot company, but with *City of Oxford, Wilts & Dorset and Hants & Dorset,* which once again raised the possibility that some of the operations might still be re-assigned to those operators. Certainly it would have made sense if *City of Oxford* had resumed control at Stokenchurch, or *Wilts & Dorset* taken in the Baughurst or Newbury areas for example.

At Newbury there was already some co-operation with Wilts & Dorset, and Bristol FLF6G Car 872 (540 BBL) was photographed by Philip Wallis on the joint Route 122 from that town to Basingstoke.

Graham Low found this fine line up of 'Lodekkas' in the Weldale Street yard, all of them secondhand purchases. Left to right these are ex-United Welsh Car 776 (JCY 993), ex-Lincolnshire Car 615 (LFW 322), ex-Notts & Derby Car 637 (14 DRB), and ex-Lincolnshire Car 606 (NBE 129). This photo continues on the right.

The outgoing toll of vehicles for March was a familiar mix of Bristol KSW6B double-deckers and Bristol LS-type saloons, all native examples this time around. The 'deckers were all 1954 deliveries, as Cars 705 (HMO 851) and 734/42 (JRX 809/17), the last of which had originally had coach seating but had been rebuilt to L27/26RD, whereas the others had standard ECW L27/28R bodies. The saloons were both new in 1953 and had ECW B41F bodies, as LS6G Car 106 (HBL 86) and LS5G Car 108 (HMO 852).

From 18th April the Bracknell Local Services 52/56 were revised and the frequency much reduced to an hourly headway off-peak and none on Sundays, whilst the route through Priestwood was altered. Buses had previously used Horsneille Lane, but complaints from drivers over parked cars, along with bus-related damage due to the use of the fairly narrow estate road, resulted in town-bound buses now carrying straight on at the Prince of Wales pub in Shepherds Lane to run via Folders Lane – Warfield Road – By-pass – Northway instead. The other factor was the closure of the gap in the By-pass opposite Bull Lane, which had been used by all traffic, but was closed following a number of bad high speed collisions. As it was, the revised route also provided a convenient link to the Wick Hill area schools. Journeys via Western Road continued to be designated 'a', whilst projections to Doncastle Road (Rowney's) were shown with a 'b' suffix and operated as suitable times for workers.

From Monday 19th April many off-peak journeys on Route 6 (Reading – Riseley – Basingstoke) were cut, whilst of a more drastic nature was the complete withdrawal of services on Routes 6b (Reading – Grazeley – Basingstoke) and 9a (Reading – Grazeley – Tadley), which overnight left whole communities without any public transport links. Also affected from that date was Route 50 (Reading – Wallingford), which was reduced to one return working, along with the Thursdays-only Moulsford (Fair Mile Hospital) journeys, to which the Sunday operation to the same point was switched from Route 5 with effect from 10th October. With such a reduced operation, it is rather surprising that the route continued as a separate one when it could easily have been rolled into Route 5?

During April there was a further cull of the ranks of Bristol KSW6B double-deckers with ECW L27/28R bodies, as 1953 Cars 667 (HBL 69) and 698 and 701 (HMO 844/7), along with 1954 examples 729/30/47 (JRX 804/5/22) of 1955. The only saloon to go was ex-*United Auto* Car 129 (SHN 730), a Bristol LS5G of 1953 with ECW B41F bodywork.

In the meantime loadings on the Rail-Air link saw the regular need for relief coaches, so plans were made to increase the frequency to half-hourly from 3rd May on weekdays and Saturdays. A further pair of dedicated coaches were ordered to assist the surviving Bristol RELH6G's, Cars C425-7 (RJB 425-7F), and were of that same type, though this time with Plaxton 'Panorama Elite' C51F bodywork. These arrived during April as Cars 400/1 (BJB 883/4J), with another quartet of similar coaches on order in due course.

Plaxton-bodied Bristol RELH6G Rail-Air coach 401 (BJB 884J) is seen inside the Reading Garage.

During the early months of the year all of the earlier Bristol VRT's were brought up to MkII specification, as the chassis type had to undergo quite a few changes in the light of daily operation. Not that they were bad buses, in fact a credit to the Brislington factory, but the usual process of working prototypes had not been possible due to the need to produce a bus suitable for the grants available to operators of one-man-operated buses. This led to the rapid development of this chassis, the 'rear-engined Lodekka' as it was at first conceived before attaining a separate identity.

The other LD-types in the line up were, left to right, ex-Crosville Car 608 (VFM 611), former Notts & Derby Car 639 (18 DRB), and then Cars 627 (THW 744) and 621 (THW 742) both of which emanated from the Bristol fleet. There was a wide variety of body details in the destination screens, windows and radiators!

The first new service buses of the year arrived in May as a further trio of Bristol RELL6G's with 36ft-long ECW B49F bodies, as Cars 229-31 (CMO 647-9J). Car 229 became Wycombe's first bus of that length, whilst the other pair was allocated to Reading.

The pair of new RELL's at Reading were generally found on Route 5 to Oxford or Route 12 to Aldershot, and Car 230 (CMO 648J) was caught leaving the Bus Station at Reading on the latter by Graham Low.

From 16th May Sunday operations from the Fingest Dormy Shed ceased, with Routes 36 (High Wycombe – Lane End – Cadmore End) and 37 (High Wycombe – Lane End – Henley) revised for reduced working by High Wycombe alone. However, this was by no means the end for the shed, which continued to 1976.

May was a fairly quiet month for withdrawals, as indeed the Summer tended to be, with only 1953 ECW L27/28R-bodied Bristol KSW6B Car 696 (HMO 842) ousted, along with ex-*United Autos* ECW B41F-bodied Bristol LS5G Car 128 (SHN 729) of the same vintage, the latter still in evidence in September as a stripped hulk. The other change to the fleet saw Bristol KSW6B Car 745 (JRX 820) assigned to Driver Training, though still retaining its PSV license.

Indeed, by June the once ubiquitous native fleet of 45 KSW-types had been reduced to a mere 11, with most of these earmarked for early withdrawal. These were allocated to Bracknell – Car 749 (JRX 824), Reading – Cars 739/40/5/6/8 (JRX 814/5/20/1/3), Newbury – Cars 726/41/3 (JRX 801/16/8), High Wycombe – Car 695 (HMO 841) and Maidenhead Car 733 (JRX 808).

Cars 733/48 were also being used for Driver Training in due course, and these retained their PSV licenses. The overall fleet strength at the start of June was officially stated at 334, comprising of 220 double-deckers, 104 single-deckers and 10 coaches. As some of the recently acquired buses were turned out from re-painting at The Colonnade, June saw further reductions in the Bristol KSW6B's, with the demise of 1953 ECW L27/28R-bodied Car 695 (HMO 841), similar 1954 Car 726 (JRX 801) and 1955 Cars 746/9 (JRX 821/4), along with 1954 Cars 739/40 (JRX 814/5), former London service buses later converted from 53 coach seats to L27/26RD with bus seats.

From Sunday 6th June the outstationing of buses for the London Route B at Samuelson's Garage ceased, bringing the practice of keeping them in the capitol since 1941 to a close. Therefore the 7.30 and 8.30am departures from London now ceased, and all buses ran out-and-back from Reading, with the first departure from Victoria now set back to 9.30am. The late evening departures from London now featured one bus leaving at 10.30pm to arrive back in Reading at 40 minutes past midnight on Mondays to Saturdays, whilst on Sundays a later journey left at 11.30pm and got to Reading at 1.40am. The Bristol VRT buses in use on the A and B services were at last converted to one-man-operation, though crew-operated Bristol FLF's could still be seen as peak-time reliefs.

Bristol RE Car 229 (CMO 647J) at High Wycombe.

195

Following a number of bad press reports in the High Wycombe area, the Traffic Superintendent Joe Morris arranged for some 38,000 questionnaires to be handed out on the buses during June, though only some 2,500 completed responses were returned for analysis. It was found that 60% of passengers felt that the local buses met their needs, though a letter in the Bucks Free Press soon pointed out that this also meant that 40% were not satisfied! The same correspondent also stated that the response indicated that many felt the Company incapable of running a better service, whilst the great number who had in recent times deserted the buses already were not involved in the process. Quite by coincidence, the Palace Cinema was then showing the feature film version of 'On the Buses', which some say could have been based on High Wycombe!

Another bridge closure resulted in Routes 20/20a (High Wycombe – Maidenhead – Windsor) having to be split again, when Cores Bridge between Wooburn Green and Bourne End was being worked on for 6 weeks from 28th June. As the route was worked from both ends, passengers were transferred between buses, for which the Union extracted an extra payment for conductors to supervise the transfer! Also from that same date Route 62 (Slough – Cippenham) had its weekday frequency cut to hourly and was withdrawn completely on Sundays.

The unreliability of buses in the Bracknell area, with frequent breakdowns at remote or awkward spots, and no towing wagon handy, led to the Council writing to the Company urging it to 'only use serviceable buses', otherwise it intended to contact the Ministry.

During July the remaining quartet of Bristol RELH6G coaches for the Rail-Air Link arrived as Cars 402-5 (CJB 587-90J), and these also had Plaxton 'Panorama Elite' C51F bodies, and were all allocated to Reading. As the popularity of this service grew, the Company now had these 6 new coaches, along with the 3 from the 1968 batch, and even a couple of the original 1967 Bedford VAM's to call upon.

Bristol RELH6G Car 405 (CJB 590J) is seen on the reserved loading bay at Reading General Station on a journey to Heathrow. These coaches featured Thames Valley fleetnames below the windscreen at first, but these later disappeared.

The first new double-deckers for some 14 months also arrived in July as Cars 515-8 (DRX 101-4K), and they were Bristol VRT/SL2/6G chassis with ECW H39/31F bodies. The first three were all allocated to Bracknell, whilst the fourth went to Maidenhead.

Two of the new Bristol VRT double-deckers in use on one-man services, with Car 516 (DRX 102K) seen above later in the year on Bracknell Local Service 51to Great Hollands, whilst Maidenhead-based Car 518 (DRX 104K) is on the Local Service Route 15.

With some new double-deckers into the fold, it was possible to shed the last of the Bristol KSW6B's still retaining the CL27/26RD layout as originally used on the London services, these being Newbury-based Cars 741/3 (JRX 816/8), along with 1952 ECW B41F-bodied Bristol LS6G Car 100 (HBL 79). Also ousted in July after very little use during their 8-month stay were the poorest of the ex-*Lincolnshire* Bristol LD6B Cars 616/8/9 (LFW 324/17/8), whilst the ranks of the KSW6B stood at just the trio of Cars 733/45/8 (JRX 808/20/3), now in use as the Driver Training Buses at Maidenhead, Reading and High Wycombe.

Route 12 (Reading – Aldershot) was due to go over to one-man from 25th July, though the initial coverage by *TV* did include some crewed workings due to still awaiting further full-size saloons, though *Aldershot & District* did even manage conversion from 5th July. In the meantime changes were made to delivery plans within the NBC in order to speed up completion of further Bristol RELL's for the *Thames Valley* fleet.

Former Bristol OC Car 629 (THW 745) 'Lodekka' received this shorter radiator grille during the Summer of 1971 following an accident. It is seen on the contra-flow bus lane in Kings Road with Reading College of Art & Design to the left, the same place the author obtained his training in graphic design.

Despite the extensive revisions earlier in the year, it was found necessary to make further changes to services from Newbury with effect from 11th July:

Route 101 (to East Ilsley and Harwell) – Certain journeys on Thursdays and Saturdays diverted though Peasemore and Stanmore;
Route 106 (to Lambourn and Swindon) – Generally reduced;
Route 107 (to Brightwalton) – Service reduced again;
Route 113 (to Inkpen and Hungerford) – Off-peak service reduced;
Route 114 (to East Woodhay) – Generally reduced;
Route 115 (to Woolton Hill) – Generally reduced.

Buses had been outstationed at Lambourn for many years, but with these changes the allocation was altered to a pair of the Bristol MW6G coach-to-bus conversions, as Cars 159/161 (ORX 631/3).

During August a further two Bristol LD6G buses with ECW LD33/25RD bodies joined the fleet. One was from *Midland General*, No.477 and new in 1959, and it became Car 647 (515 JRA) and allocated to Reading. The other was also new in 1959 as No.520 (191 BRR) in the *Mansfield District* fleet, and as Car 648 it was sent to High Wycombe.

It will be recalled that some of the Bristol FLF buses delivered between 1961 and 1963 had been fitted with illuminated advert panels on the offside of the upper deck, though these were effective only if well looked after. During 1971 a number of these were removed as buses passed through for re-paints, as Cars 850 (WJB 234), 870 (538 BBL) and D2 (840 CRX) in July, Car 851 (WJB 235) in September, Car 845 (WJB 229) in December, along with Cars 848 (WJB 232) and 871 (539 BBL) at dates not recorded. Also in July, 1967-8 Bristol FLF6G Cars D50 (LBL 850E) and D54 (PBL 53F) had their seating reverted to the full H38/32F after some time as the designated spare buses for the London express services, though both Cars D57/60 (PBL 57/60F) remained with the additional luggage space for those duties. Other seating changes affected the 1960 former London duty FLF's with sliding door, with Car 836 (UJB 202) re-seated with bus seats in the upper deck only to give H38/30F, but retaining coach seating in the lower saloon in August, whilst similar Car 835 (UJB 201) was fully re-seated with bus seats as H38/32F in October.

Over at Bracknell there were complaints again about the extensive use of the destination 'Local Service' on so many routes serving the expanding town, and in reply Ken Rogerson (TS at Maidenhead, who now also covered Bracknell) said he would bear that in mind when planning changes from that Autumn.

The two additional buses from the east Midlands are seen here, with Car 647 (515 JRA) forming a School Special above, whilst Car 648 (191 BRR) is seen below fresh out of shops amongst building work in the Weldale Street yard.

197

Another selection of views by Philip Wallis showing TV buses in three different towns. This scene in the Market Place at Henley sees Bristol LD6B Car 766 (MBL 847) on Route 8 for Reading before one-man-operation took over, whilst the Bristol MW6G Car 162 (ORX 634) is on the threatened Route 16 from Maidenhead through the sparsely populated areas of Warren Row and Crazies Hill. The painted bus stop indicator on the right was provided by the Town Council.

In Reading town centre Broad Street was now restricted to buses and some deliveries, whilst the buses used Queen Victoria Street one way only. 1960 Bristol FLF6G Car 839 (WJB 223) is seen working towards Colemans Moor Road in Woodley on Route 44a. These road changes, along with the contra-flow bus lane in Kings Road did assist the buses with time-keeping, but general traffic congestion soon eroded such advantages, which also affected the reliability of services and led to a loss of passengers.

Towards the south of the Company's area, Route 122 ran to Basingstoke from Newbury and was a joint operation with Wilts & Dorset. The latter's bus station in the town is seen in this view of Bristol FLF6G Car D55 (PBL 55F) about to return to Newbury, with a similar Wilts & Dorset bus and one of the Aldershot & District Bristol RE's in the background. Note also the Christmas trees in this photo taken in December.

Mention was made back in January of the intention to withdraw Route 16 (Maidenhead – Warren Row – Henley), which had led to protests over the schoolchildren who would lose their transport link to school. The service was indeed finally withdrawn from 29th August, but certain journeys on Route 17 (Maidenhead – Hurley – Henley) were diverted in a loop via Crazies Hill and designated Route 17a.

From that same date the services to Cookham from Maidenhead, Routes 23 (Maidenhead – Spencers Estate/Cookham Dean) and 24/24a (Maidenhead – Cookham Rise/Cookham Dean) were re-organised as follows:

Route 71 – Maidenhead (Bus Station) – Marlow Road – Furze Platt (Golden Harp) – Spencers Estate – Whyteladyes Lane – Cookham Rise (Westwood Grn.) – Cookham (Station);
Route 71a – Maidenhead (BS) – Marlow Rd. – Furze Platt (Golden Harp) – Spencers Estate – Whyteladyes Lane – Cookham (Station);
Route 72 – Maidenhead (BS) – Spencers Bridge – Cookham Rise (Westwood Grn.) – Cookham (Station) – Cookham Dean (Quarry Wood Road);
Route 73 – Maidenhead (BS) – Spencers Bridge – Pinkneys Grn. (Brick Kiln) – Cookham Dn. (Church).

Also altered at the same date was Route 18 (M'head – Marlow), which lost the projections onwards from Marlow Bottom to Chisbridge Cross, whilst in the Slough area Routes 62 (Slough – Cippenham), 63 (Slough – Britwell) and 68 (Maidenhead – Cliveden – Hatcham Park – Burnham – Slough) all went fully over to one-man-operation at that point.

Another photo by Philip Wallis shows Bristol FLF6B Car 869 (537 BBL) on Route 12 from Aldershot and passing the Wellington Monument at Heckfield Heath.

There were some revisions to Route 14 (Maidenhead – Holyport – Paley Street or Bracknell) from August 29th, though Jigs Lane and Warfield Street were still not served, and the campaign by residents continued.

Although no new vehicles entered service in August, those already acquired were prepared for service, and that led to the release of some of the less good of the LD-types, former *Lincolnshire* Cars 606/7 (NBE 129/33), along with ex-*Crosville* Car 601 (XFM 187). Also ousted was another of the first batch of Bristol LS6G buses of 1952/3, as Car 102 (HBL 81) with ECW B41F body. This meant that out of the 43 native LS-types, including those converted from coaches to buses, only Cars 101/3/4/5/7 (HBL 80/3/4/5/7) and 118/21/46/7 (HMO 858/63/8/70) were still in service, whereas there were still 32 secondhand examples in the fleet at August 1971.

Timetable changes had not occurred across the *TV* area on a common date, so between July and September separate area booklets based on Bracknell, High Wycombe, Maidenhead, Newbury and Reading were issued instead, with a charge of 5p per issue.

Bristol RELL6G Car 233 (DRX 626K) passes through Wallingford on Route 5 to Reading.

As noted earlier there was a need for more full-length saloons, and during September 6 Bristol RELL-types were received. The first three numerically were the remainder of the order part-delivered in May, as Cars 232-4 (DRX 625-7K), fitted with ECW B49F bodies and Gardner 6HLX engines. These were allocated to Reading (232/3) and Wycombe (234), and another 6 similar buses were on order, though they would not arrive until after the change of ownership, as Cars 480/1 (DRX 628/9K) and 491-4 (DRX 630-3K), these originally being intended as Cars 235-40.

The other trio received in September were Leyland-engined Bristol RELL's, fitted with ECW B50F bodies, incorporating differences in specification due to having originally been intended for *Southdown*. They became Cars 241 (EBL 390K) and 242/3 (EBL 437/8K), and once again they were only part of a larger batch diverted to *TV* but arriving in 1972 as Cars 482-5 (EBL 439/40/1/61K) under the new scheme. Whereas new saloons had for some time had no rear destination screens, these had the numeral box, with red background to their blinds, though it is unlikely that the rear feature was actually used by *TV*.

The last saloons delivered new to Thames Valley were the trio of Bristol RELL6L's, and Cars 241 (EBL 390K) and 243 (EBL 438K) are seen in Thorn Walk yard having just arrived from Lowestoft.

From 5th September a number of changes took place in the High Wycombe area, with a view to saving bus miles on Routes 36 (High Wycombe – Land End – Cadmore End) and 37 (High Wycombe – Lane End – Henley). The 37 now ran onto Henley on Thursdays and Saturdays only, and in general off-peak journeys were reduced on both routes. At Stokenchurch Dormy Shed most journeys on Routes 39 (High Wycombe – Watlington), 40 (High Wycombe – Radnage) and 41 (High Wycombe – Ibstone) went over to one-man, as did Newlands-based Routes 81/81a to Booker Estate. On Route 30 (to Plomer Hill Estate) timings were altered to provide suitable journeys between Wycombe and the new Downley Secondary School. Also, from 29th September, there were further cuts to frequency on Route 32 (High Wycombe – Bledlow Ridge – Chinnor), one of the services taken over from *Fred Crook* and his *Booker Bus Service* in June 1937.

Yet another pair of former *Midland General* Bristol LS6G saloons were acquired in September, though these came south after service with *East Midland!* These 1955 buses had originally been Nos.234/5 (XNU 415/6), before becoming *East Midland* Nos.R315/6, then finally *TV* Cars 123/4 and allocated to Bracknell, now down-seated to B41F.

Car 123 (XNU 415) is seen outside the Market Street garage in Bracknell just in from Sunningdale on Route 57. Note the larger fleetname split into two.

A further Bristol LD6G also came from *Mansfield District* in September, a 1958 ECW LD33/25RD-bodied bus new as No.518 (215 ANN), which became Car 645 and was allocated to Reading.

Disposals for September followed the pattern of August, with a clearout of secondhand 'Lodekkas', as former *Crosville* Cars 600/9 (VFM 607/18), 602 (XFM 190) and 612 (XFM 186), along with ex-*Lincolnshire* Car 617 (NBE 130). Another native 1953 Bristol LS6G also went as Car 101 (HBL 80), along with the last Bristol LS5G in the fleet, former *Bristol OC* Car 131 (PHW 931).

During September a pair of *Aldershot & District* AEC 'Reliance' coaches, Nos.101/2 (YCG 101/2J) were seen with *Alder Valley* fleetnames, and about the same time *Thames Valley* Bedford VAM coaches C417/8 (LJB 417/8E) were similarly noted at Reading garage, and it was confirmed that this would be the working title of the new concern, contrived to avoid any sense of dominance by one partner over the other. However, the application by the Aldershot company to take over the Road Service Licenses of *TV* hardly did much to cheer the generally demoralised staff of the latter.

Whilst many of the Bracknell-based routes were around the growing housing estates of the New Town, others took buses out to some leafy spots, and Bristol LH6L Car 220 (AMO 235J) is seen on Route 59 as it turns at Brookside, on the edge of Windsor Forest.

The issue of a new livery for the combined fleet also saw the Directors endeavouring not to favour one existing scheme over the other. *A&D's* 1958 AEC 'Reliance' No.316 (SOU 474) was painted in a mix of green and red, in different proportions on either side, whilst *TV's* ex-*United Welsh* Bristol LD Car 794 (JCY 992) was given a blue scheme, and an edict was issued that none of these should be photographed. In the end a dark red scheme, similar to *Ribble Motor Services* was selected, though it did not wear well.

A further phase in the evolution of Bracknell Local Services took place from 10th October, in order to keep up with further housing developments, whilst other services operating from that garage were also reviewed for more economic working.

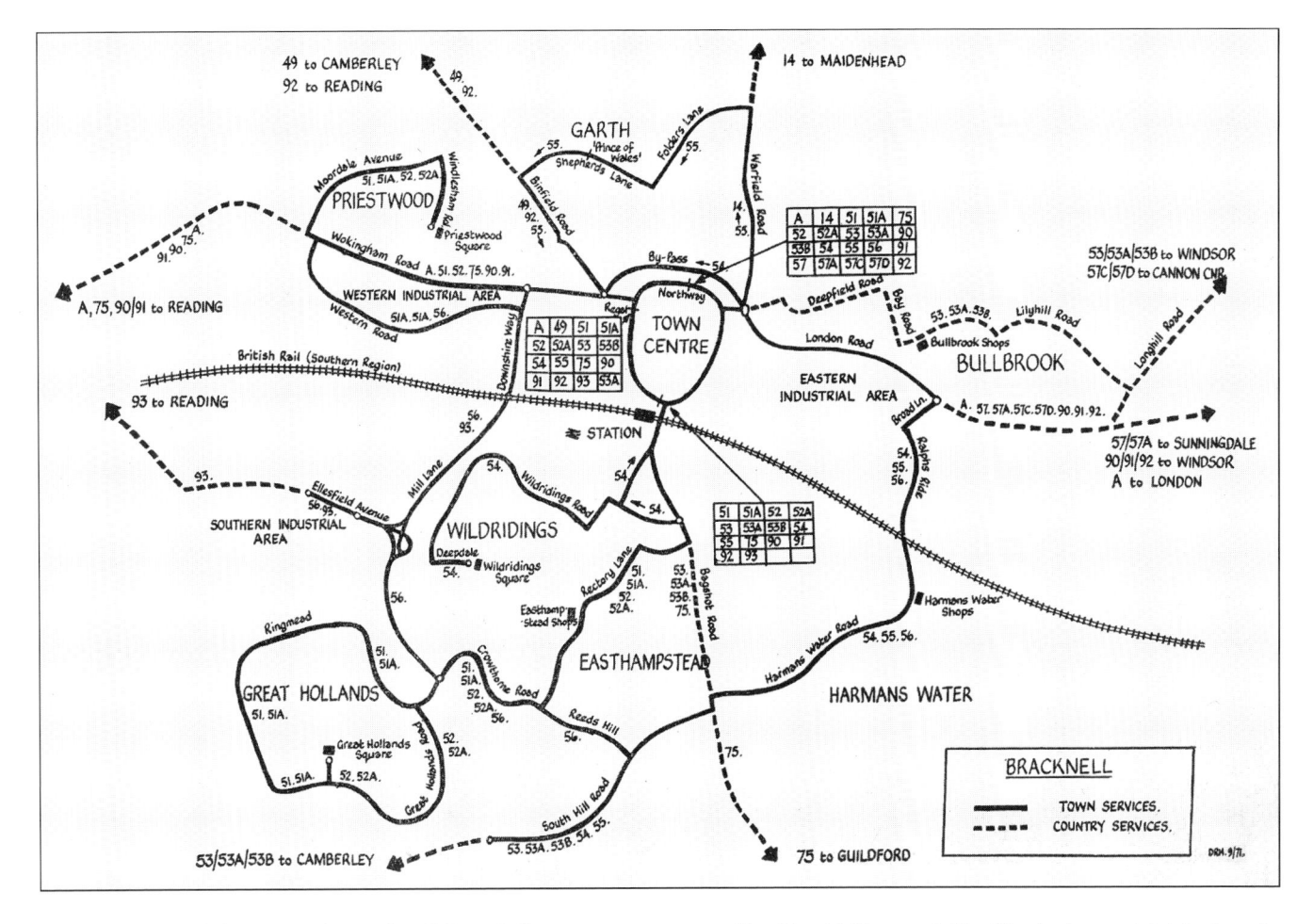

Official map of the revised Bracknell Local Services as prepared by David Howard, Traffic Assistant Maidenhead.

In respect of the Windsor Local Services, the existing circular Routes 51 (Central Station – Peascod Street – St. Leonards Road – Hatch Lane – St. Leonards Road – Victoria Street – Central Station), 51a (Central Station – Peascod Street – St. Leonards Road – Hatch Lane – Clewer Hill Road – Foster Avenue – Wolf Lane – Dedworth Road – Clarence Road – Victoria St. – Central Station) and 51b (Central Station – Victoria Street – Clarence Road – Dedworth Road – Wolf Ln. – Foster Avenue – Clewer Hill Road – Hatch Lane – St. Leonards Road – Victoria St. – Central Station) were replaced by new out-and-back services.

These were Routes 48 (Central Station – St. Leonards Road – Hatch Lane – Dedworth (The Wolf) – Tinkers Lane) and 48a (Central Station – Clewer (Three Elms) – Dedworth (The Wolf) – Tinkers Lane). However, the two saloons now employed on these one-man workings, ran out on one route and returned on the other, making it effectively still a circular operation, resulting in a basic half-hourly headway, with Route 48 taking 19 minutes and the 48a taking 14. Sundays were now much less frequent than before, with a 2-hourly headway, and there was now no involvement by the Maidenhead Garage.

In Bracknell the existing Routes 52 (Town Centre – Priestwood – Town Centre – Southern Industrial Area – Easthampstead – Harmanswater – Bullbrook – Town Centre) and 56 (in reverse order) were revised with a Great Hollands element to form new Route 51 (Great Hollands Square – Ringmead – Crowthorne Road – Rectory Lane – Town Centre – Wokingham Road – Moordale Avenue – Priestwood Square), with new Route 52 operating the reverse direction, and both having 'a' journeys via Western Road at times.

Former Midland General Bristol LS6G Car 125 (964 ARA) at Windsor Central Station on Route 48a, with damaged front end, in a photo by Philip Wallis.

The other areas around the town were now catered for by revised services as follows, each out-and-back:

Route 54 – Wildridings Shops – Station – Regal Cinema – Northway – Bullbrook – Harmanswater

Shops – South Hill Road – Easthampstead (Mill Lane);
Route 55 – Priestwood (Prince of Wales) – Northway – Bullbrook – Harmanswater Shops – South Hill Road – Easthampstead (Mill Lane);
Route 56 – Northway – Bullbrook – Harmanswater Shops – South Hill Road – Easthampstead (Church Hill House Hospital) – Ellesfield Avenue (Clark Eaton) – Western Road (Ferranti), with returning journeys terminating at Bracknell Station.

Ex-Midland General Bristol LS6G Car 151 (957 ARA) was based at Bracknell and is seen on Route 49 duty. Note the unusual side beading beyond the entrance door, a reminder its earlier employment on express services with a fleetname mounted in that position.

The other service changes in the Bracknell area affected the following:

Route 49 – Service revised with reduced frequency;
Route 53b – Additional variant of Route 53 running via new housing estate in Yeovil Road area of Owlsmoor, as loop from Branksome Hill Road – Yeovil Road – College Road;

Philip Wallis caught Bristol VRT Car 508 (VMO 223H) leaving Windsor Central Station on the 53b.

Routes 57c/57d – Diverted via Chavey Down between Long Hill Road and The Royal Foresters crossroads;
Routes 59/59a – Lost journeys starting at Brookside as part of a general reduction in service. These were further amended from 1st November to take in Perry Oaks (Lily Hill Drive) and Lily Hill Road;
Routes 90/91/92 – No longer with 'a' variants running the loop to Ascot (Horse & Groom), but turned on the roundabout at Heatherwood Hospital, with an additional stop fixed west of the junction. This was a rather windswept place and originally lacked a shelter, whilst buses travelling to or from Windsor used the same stop, after which only the Sunningdale services from Bracknell and the 59 from Windsor served the Horse & Groom stop, plus the London A service;
Route 93 – A new limited-stop peak-time service between Bracknell and Reading, calling only at Regal – Wokingham Road (Sperry's) – Southern Ind. Area (Ellesfield Avenue) – Binfield (Shoulder of Mutton) – Wokingham (Three Frogs) – Wokingham (Broad St.) – Emmbrook (Rifle Volunteer) - Winnersh crossroads – Loddon Bridge – Earley (Three Tuns) – Cemetery Junction – Reading (Broad St.) – Reading Bus Station. The timings morning and afternoon were obviously aimed at office workers, whilst during the daytime some short-workings ran as only Bracknell (Station or Regal) – Southern Industrial Area (Ellesfield Ave.).

At the same time the Reading-based Route 4 took in new housing at Rosemary Lane between Darby Green and Blackwater, and after that journeys continuing along the main road were designated as Route 4c, and that was also used for the Camberley – Yateley shorts.

LD6G Car 646 (216 ANN) at Reading on Route 9b.

October saw only one new entrant to the fleet, as Car 646 (216 ANN), another Bristol LD6G from the *Mansfield District* fleet, new in 1958 with ECW LD33/25RD body as No.519, allocated to Reading. This would actually be the final Bristol LD-type to be acquired by *Thames Valley*, though not the last secondhand purchase, as we shall soon see.

The Thames-side towns were an integral part of the Thames Valley routes, with buses passing from Berkshire in neighbouring Counties, and these three photos from Philip Wallis show buses in those towns. Former United Welsh Car 776 (JCY 993) turns from Henley's Market Place into Duke Street on Route 8 bound for Reading. For many years the buses from Reading, High Wycombe and Maidenhead Garages used the cluster of stops near the Town Hall.

The bridge carrying the A-roads from Twyford and Hurley into Henley over the River Thames was an impressive affair, but there were notices fixed at either end warning the drivers of traction engines not to exceed the loading restrictions! At a mere 8.5 tons Bristol FLF6G Car 878 (546 BBL) is within the limit as it passes from Oxfordshire to Berkshire on Route 28 bound for Reading. This service had its origins in the Marlow & District company.

Windsor is a riverside town known to many, dominated by its complex castle grounds, attracting tourists by the coach-load, then more recently from across the globe. It also provided another hub for Thames Valley services to Maidenhead, Reading, Aylesbury, High Wycombe and Camberley, along with Local Services, but was a 'border' town shared with the London Transport area. Bristol FLF6G Car D21 (FBL 485C) is seen by the Harte & Garter Hotel on Route 20 to High Wycombe.

Continuing the theme of the Thames bridges, the view above by Philip Wallis shows Bristol FLF6B Car 870 (538 BBL) crossing Staines bridge from the Surrey bank into Middlesex as it helps out at Whitsun on Route A towards London's Victoria Coach Station. In contrast below, we see the tree-lined Ray Mead Road by Boulters Lock, on the Maidenhead bank of the river with Bristol FLF6G Car D3 (841 CRX) working Route 20 towards Windsor. The railings lining the riverbank were used as a guide by bus drivers during floods in earlier days when buses were much higher built!

Further secondhand 'Lodekkas' departed from the fleet during October, as former *Crosville* Car 608 (VFM 611) and ex-*Bristol OC* Cars 621/5 (THW 742/3), along with the original batch of such purchases, the former *United Welsh* Cars 770-5 (LWN 52/3 and 48-51).

October also saw another odd re-allocation, when 36ft-long Bristol RELL6G Car 186 (CBL 356B) was sent out to Newbury, hardly the best area for a bus of such a length! Indeed, one West Berkshire Parish Council commenting at that time about the service cuts in the area made reference to the 'monstrously large buses' currently being used on rural routes!

It has already been noted that the patronage of bus services had declined since its zenith around the start of this volume, the causes being a mixture of private car ownership, traffic congestion, increasing fares and unreliability of services, along with more recent cuts to routes. During the decade under review this can be demonstrated by the following figures, which do highlight the peak use as occurring in the year 1961-

Year Ended	Miles Operated	Passengers
31.12 1960	1,775,488	15,340,217
30.12.1961	1,890,603	15,455,909
29.12.1962	1,980,205	15,137,052
28.12.1963	2,072,994	15,058,462
26.12.1964	2,105,771	14,979,779
31.12.1965	2,077,310	14,171,474
31.12.1966	2,183,525	14,004,423
30.12.1967	2,306,595	14,437,333
28.12.1968	2,360,862	14,264,152
27.12.1969	2,469,142	14,128,969
26.12.1970	2,552,392	13,558,683
25.12.1971	2,806,067	12,840,869

Notes: The increase in mileage from 1967 onwards is largely attributable to the Reading – Heathrow Rail – Air Link service, along with higher route mileages due to one-way traffic schemes.

The effects of fare rises can also be gauged by the following adult single fare comparisons from either end of the decade -

Journey	1961	1971	= to
Reading – Newbury	3s 1d	23p	4s 6d
Newbury – Harwell AERE	2s 8d	21p	4s 2d
Newbury – Lambourn	2s 5d	20p	4s 0d
Newbury – Oxford	4s 5d	27p	5s 4d
Newbury – Basingstoke	2s 11d	22p	4s 4d
Bracknell – Camberley	1s 10d	15p	3s 0d
Bracknell – Windsor	2s 1d	15p	3s 0d
Bracknell – Reading	2s 0d	15p	3s 0d
Reading – Windsor	4s 0d	25p	5s 0d
Camberley – Windsor	3s 7d	24p	4s 8d
Bracknell – Guildford	2s 7d	16p	3s 2d
Reading – London (VCS)	5s 0d	43p	8s 6d
Reading – Ascot	2s 8d	19p	3s 8d
Reading – Twyford	1s 3d	11p	2s 2d
Maidenhead – Windsor	1s 7d	14p	2s 8d
M'head – High Wycombe	2s 1d	16p	3s 2d
Maidenhead – Slough	1s 3d	11p	2s 2d
M'head – London (VCS)	4s 0d	36p	7s 2d
Maidenhead – Reading	2s 4d	18p	3s 6d
High Wycombe – Reading	4s 0d	28p	5s 6d
High Wycombe – Henley	2s 11d	19p	3s 8d
High Wycombe – Lane End	1s 2d	11p	2s 2d
Wycombe - Stokenchurch	1s 5d	12p	2s 5d
Wycombe – Watlington	2s 5d	18p	3s 7d
High Wycombe – Marlow	1s 1d	10p	2s 0d

On this page we see some of the buses leaving the fleet during the final year of Thames Valley. Bristol KSW's and LS's bore the brunt of the disposals, but all the same there was variety within their ranks.

This Bristol LS coach-to-bus conversion left the fleet after an accident as Car 124 (HMO 836), but is seen here in earlier days as S310 and when Route 120 ran through to the village of Aldworth.

The native Bristol LS-types were mostly updated with the thin MW-style strip in place of the heavy front bumper originally fitted. However, accidents to their front end led to greater variety of badges, vents and dumb-iron flaps over the years. Above we see Car 101 (HBL 80) at High Wycombe on Route 30 to Plomer Hill Estate, whilst below is Car 111 (HMO 855) of the Bracknell allocation with blinds set for a short on the 53a to Little Sandhurst.

The native contingent of Bristol KSW6B double-decks had been joined by others acquired secondhand. One of the latter is seen above as Car 690 (PHN 821), new in 1952 to United Automobile Services of Darlington, which spent all its days with the 'Valley at Newbury. Below there is Car 732 (JRX 807), new in 1954 and seen in the old Southern yard between turns on Route 9b to Mortimer or Baughurst and based at Reading.

A start was also made on disposing of secondhand 'Lodekkas', and former United Welsh Car 774 (LWN 50) is seen in Weldale Street yard, apparently going to Whitley Wood, though not applicable to the 43 seen in the route number box. This bus was one of the original batch purchased in 1966, and it came as a surprise to see these go, as others from the same source were certainly in less good condition.

205

It should be noted that buses repainted during 1971 often appeared with the older and larger size of fleetname, and when used on saloons these were split into two lines, and obviously the intention was to use up some rediscovered stocks of the transfers.

The final secondhand purchase of the 120 vehicles obtained between March 1966 and November 1971 arrived to become Car 588 (566 ERR). This broke new ground for the *Valley*, being the first (and only) FS6G variant of the Bristol 'Lodekka' to be acquired. New in 1960 to *Mansfield District* as No.530 and with an ECW H33/27RD on its flat-floor chassis, it was allocated to Reading Garage. It will be noted that the fleet number was the first to be re-issued in the 500 series, though this was actually the number it would become under the scheme now worked out for combining the two fleets for use from January 1972.

Bristol FS6G Car 588 (566 ERR) after it emerged from the paint-shop. As with other later examples from the Midland General group it was the practice to adapt the intermediate destination box for a single-line display and to over-paint the ultimate box.

During November some of the recently delivered Bristol RELL6L saloons, Cars 241-3 (EBL 390 and 437/8K) were noted in use on the London A and B routes, but with two-man crews, having taken the place of Bristol FLF double-deckers used at times.

December saw the last service change under the old firm, when the residents of Warfield were successful in their campaign to have journeys via Jigs Lane and Warfield Street reinstated. From 16th December some journeys on Thursdays, the market day in Bracknell, were operated via those points and tabled as Route 14a. These journeys ran through between Maidenhead and Bracknell, and were based on existing timings diverted away from the direct route via Wick Hill and covered by the Bracknell-based bus, which at that point was Bristol SUS4A Car 158 (845 THY). Also based at the garage at that time was one of the former Rail-Air Bedford VAM-type coaches C419 (LJB 419E) for relief duties, which continued a tradition stemming back to Ascot Garage during the 1950's.

The final bus delivered to the old firm was Bristol VRT Car 922 (FBL 114K), seen here on the journey from Lowestoft painted in the new dark red livery.

No buses were withdrawn in December, but that month saw the final new vehicles delivered to the *Thames Valley* fleet, though already bearing numbers in the new scheme, as Cars 920-2 (FBL 112-4K). All were Bristol VRT/SL2/6G chassis carrying ECW H39/31F bodywork for one-man working from the Reading Garage.

All in all 332 buses and coaches passed from *TV* into the combined fleet, including the surviving trio of Bristol KSW6B's which, although on Driver Training, still retained PSV licenses. The new fleet numbers will be found in the last column on the fleet list which starts on the next page. Only three *TV* buses are recorded as re-painted into the dark red scheme prior to January 1972, these being Bristol FLF6G Car D21 (FBL 485C), Bristol LS6G Car 145 (956 ARA) and Bristol LH6L Car 210 (VMO 227H), though none entered service in that form prior to the merger date, by which time they bore their new fleet numbers.

And so it was, that at the stroke of midnight on 31st December 1971, the old *Thames Valley* company ceased to exist. It should, however, be rightly recalled for its many achievements over the years, and the high standards once the expected norm for the fleet and the efficient operation of its widespread bus services.

Appendix 1

THE THAMES VALLEY FLEET

Vehicles operated or acquired between January 1961 and December 1971

Vehicles rebuilt and re-numbered are shown when they re-entered service in their new guise.
Details of re-numbering in later years are shown in the appropriate places, whilst vehicles passing to Alder Valley
are shown with new fleet number in the right hand column in lieu of a disposal date.

Standard body codes:	B - single-deck saloon bus	DP - dual-purpose bus with coach seating	C - coach
L - lowbridge double-decker	H - highbridge double-decker or flat-floor Lodekka		LD - Lodekka low height double-decker
F- full-front on half-cab chassis	CH - flat-floor Lodekka with coach seats		CLD - Lodekka with coach seats
Entrance position:	F - front entrance R - rear entrance C - centre entrance D - dual entrance RD- rear platform door fitted		
Other codes:	8 (as suffix) indicates an 8ft wide body on a 7ft 6ins chassis (51) - indicates year of newer body fitted		
Example:	CLD31/25RD = coach-seated Lodekka with 31 seats on upper deck, 25 seats on lower deck and rear platform door		

Fleet No.	Reg. No.	Chassis Make	Chassis Type	Bodybuilder	Body Type	Date New	Date Acq.	Date Out
439	CRX 548	Bristol	K6A	Eastern Coach Works	L27/28R	May-46	New	Mar-64
440	CRX 549	Bristol	K6A	Eastern Coach Works	L27/28R	May-46	New	Dec-63
441	CRX 550	Bristol	K6A	Eastern Coach Works	L27/28R	Jun-46	New	Jan-66
442	CRX 551	Bristol	K6A	Eastern Coach Works	L27/28R	Jun-46	New	Apr-62
443	DBL 151	Bristol	K6A	Eastern Coach Works	L27/28R	Sep-46	New	Apr-63
444	DBL 152	Bristol	K6A	Eastern Coach Works	L27/28R	Sep-46	New	Oct-62
445	DBL 153	Bristol	K6A	Eastern Coach Works	L27/28R	Sep-46	New	Apr-63
446	DBL 154	Bristol	K6A	Eastern Coach Works	L27/28R	Oct-46	New	Feb-65
447	DBL 155	Bristol	K6A	Eastern Coach Works	L27/28R	Oct-46	New	Jul-65
448	DBL 156	Bristol	K6A	Eastern Coach Works	L27/28R	Nov-46	New	May-65
449	DBL 157	Bristol	K6A	Eastern Coach Works	L27/28R	Dec-46	New	Oct-62
450	DBL 158	Bristol	K6A	Eastern Coach Works	L27/28R	Dec-46	New	Oct-65
451	DBL 159	Bristol	K6A	Eastern Coach Works	L27/28R	Dec-46	New	Oct-62
452	DBL 160	Bristol	K6A	Eastern Coach Works	L27/28R	Dec-46	New	Feb-66
453	DBL 161	Bristol	K6B	Eastern Coach Works	L27/28R	Jan-47	New	Feb-63
454	DBL 162	Bristol	K6B	Eastern Coach Works	L27/28R	Apr-47	New	Oct-65
466	DMO 670	Bristol	K6A	Eastern Coach Works	L27/28R	Nov-47	New	Oct-62
467	DMO 671	Bristol	K6A	Eastern Coach Works	L27/28R	Dec-47	New	Oct-62
468	DMO 672	Bristol	K6B	Eastern Coach Works	L27/28R	Mar-48	New	Mar-65
469	DMO 673	Bristol	K6B	Eastern Coach Works	L27/28R	Mar-48	New	Oct-66
470	DMO 674	Bristol	K6B	Eastern Coach Works	L27/28R	Apr-48	New	Apr-63
471	DMO 675	Bristol	K6B	Eastern Coach Works	L27/28R	Apr-48	New	May-66
492	EJB 214	Bristol	K6B	Eastern Coach Works	L27/28R	Nov-48	New	Dec-63
493	EJB 215	Bristol	K6B	Eastern Coach Works	L27/28R	Dec-48	New	Aug-65
494	EJB 216	Bristol	K6B	Eastern Coach Works	L27/28R	Dec-48	New	Aug-65
495	EJB 217	Bristol	K6B	Eastern Coach Works	L27/28R	Dec-48	New	Aug-65
496	EJB 218	Bristol	K6B	Eastern Coach Works	L27/28R	Dec-48	New	Jul-65
497	EJB 219	Bristol	K6B	Eastern Coach Works	L27/28R	Jan-49	New	Jul-66
498	EJB 220	Bristol	K6B	Eastern Coach Works	L27/28R	Jan-49	New	Jul-65
499	EJB 221	Bristol	K6B	Eastern Coach Works	L27/28R	Dec-48	New	Dec-65
500	EJB 222	Bristol	K6B	Eastern Coach Works	L27/28R	Jan-49	New	Dec-65
501	EJB 223	Bristol	K6B	Eastern Coach Works	L27/28R	Jan-49	New	Dec-63
502	EJB 224	Bristol	K6B	Eastern Coach Works	L27/28R	Jan-49	New	Dec-65
503	EJB 225	Bristol	K6B	Eastern Coach Works	L27/28R	Jan-49	New	Aug-65
504	EJB 226	Bristol	K6B	Eastern Coach Works	L27/28R	Jan-49	New	Jul-66
505	EJB 227	Bristol	K6B	Eastern Coach Works	L27/28R	Jan-49	New	Dec-65
506	EJB 228	Bristol	K6B	Eastern Coach Works	L27/28R	Jan-49	New	Aug-66
507	EJB 229	Bristol	K6B	Eastern Coach Works	L27/28R	Jul-49	New	Nov-66
508	EJB 230	Bristol	K6B	Eastern Coach Works	L27/28R	Jul-49	New	Aug-66
509	EJB 231	Bristol	K6B	Eastern Coach Works	L27/28R	Jul-49	New	Mar-66
513	EJB 235	Bristol	K6B	Eastern Coach Works	L27/28R	Jul-49	New	Jan-67
514	EJB 236	Bristol	K6B	Eastern Coach Works	L27/28R	Aug-49	New	Jan-67
515	EJB 237	Bristol	K6B	Eastern Coach Works	L27/28R	Aug-49	New	Feb-66
516	EJB 238	Bristol	K6B	Eastern Coach Works	L27/28R	Aug-49	New	Aug-66
517	EJB 239	Bristol	K6B	Eastern Coach Works	L27/28R	Aug-49	New	Jul-66
518	EJB 240	Bristol	K6B	Eastern Coach Works	L27/28R	Aug-49	New	Jul-66
519	EJB 241	Bristol	K6B	Eastern Coach Works	L27/28R	Aug-49	New	Jul-66
524	FBL 26	Bristol	K6B	Eastern Coach Works	L27/28R	Nov-49	New	Oct-66
525	FBL 27	Bristol	K6B	Eastern Coach Works	L27/28R	Dec-49	New	Jul-66
526	FBL 28	Bristol	K6B	Eastern Coach Works	L27/28R	Jan-50	New	Jan-67
527	FBL 29	Bristol	K6B	Eastern Coach Works	L27/28R	Feb-50	New	Jan-67
528	FBL 30	Bristol	K6B	Eastern Coach Works	L27/28R	Feb-50	New	Jan-67
529	FBL 31	Bristol	K6B	Eastern Coach Works	L27/28R	Mar-50	New	Mar-67
530	FBL 32	Bristol	K6B	Eastern Coach Works	L27/28R	Apr-50	New	Nov-66
531	FBL 33	Bristol	K6B	Eastern Coach Works	L27/28R	Apr-50	New	Mar-67
532	FMO 7	Bristol	K6B	Eastern Coach Works	L27/28R	Apr-50	New	May-67

Fleet No.	Reg. No.	Chassis Make	Chassis Type	Bodybuilder	Body Type	Date New	Date Acq.	Date Out
533	FMO 8	Bristol	K6B	Eastern Coach Works	L27/28R	Apr-50	New	May-67
555	FMO 937	Bristol	L6B	Windover	C33F	Jul-50	New	Oct-61
170	FMO 515	Guy	Arab 111 6LW	Duple	L27/26RD	Feb-50	New	Apr-68
171	FMO 516	Guy	Arab 111 6LW	Duple	L27/26RD	Feb-50	New	Apr-68

These Guy buses were new to Newbury & District Motor Services Ltd.

Fleet No.	Reg. No.	Chassis Make	Chassis Type	Bodybuilder	Body Type	Date New	Date Acq.	Date Out
172/H10	FMO 517	Guy	Arab 111 6LW	Duple	H31/26R	May-50	New	Mar-68

This Guy bus was ordered for Venture, Basingstoke, but diverted to Newbury, for the rest of the batch see 175-8 below

Fleet No.	Reg. No.	Chassis Make	Chassis Type	Bodybuilder	Body Type	Date New	Date Acq.	Date Out
175/H13	HOT 391	Guy	Arab 111 6LW	Duple	H31/26R	Apr-50	Jan-51	Mar-68
176/H14	HOT 392	Guy	Arab 111 6LW	Duple	H31/26R	Apr-50	Jan-51	Apr-68
177/H15	HOT 393	Guy	Arab 111 6LW	Duple	H31/26R	Apr-50	Jan-51	Mar-68
178/H16	HOT 394	Guy	Arab 111 6LW	Duple	H31/26R	Apr-50	Jan-51	Mar-68

These Guys were acquired with N&D, but were originally Venture of Basingstoke, transferred for standardistion

Fleet No.	Reg. No.	Chassis Make	Chassis Type	Bodybuilder	Body Type	Date New	Date Acq.	Date Out
559	FMO 941	Bristol	LL6B	Eastern Coach Works	B39R	Aug-50	New	Mar-67
560	FMO 942	Bristol	LL6B	Eastern Coach Works	B39R	Nov-50	New	Apr-68
564	FMO 946	Bristol	LL6B	Eastern Coach Works	B39F	Nov-50	New	May-67
565	FMO 947	Bristol	LL6B	Eastern Coach Works	B39F	Dec-50	New	Aug-68
566	FMO 948	Bristol	LL6B	Eastern Coach Works	B39F	Dec-50	New	Jun-68
567	FMO 949	Bristol	LL6B	Eastern Coach Works	B39F	Dec-50	New	Aug-68
568	FMO 950	Bristol	LL6B	Eastern Coach Works	B39F	Dec-50	New	Aug-68
569	FMO 951	Bristol	LL6B	Eastern Coach Works	B39R	Dec-50	New	May-68
570	FMO 952	Bristol	LL6B	Eastern Coach Works	B39R	Jan-51	New	Oct-61
571	FMO 953	Bristol	LL6B	Eastern Coach Works	B39R	Jan-51	New	Dec-67
572	FMO 954	Bristol	LL6B	Eastern Coach Works	B39R	Feb-51	New	Jan-61
573	FMO 955	Bristol	LL6B	Eastern Coach Works	B39R	Jan-51	New	Oct-61
574	FMO 956	Bristol	LL6B	Eastern Coach Works	B39R	Jan-51	New	Aug-68
575	FMO 957	Bristol	LL6B	Eastern Coach Works	B39R	Jan-51	New	Oct-61
576	FMO 958	Bristol	LL6B	Eastern Coach Works	B39R	Feb-51	New	Oct-61
577	FMO 959	Bristol	LWL6B	Eastern Coach Works	B39R	Mar-51	New	Apr-62
578	FMO 960	Bristol	LWL6B	Eastern Coach Works	B39R	Mar-51	New	Apr-62
579	FMO 961	Bristol	LWL6B	Eastern Coach Works	B39R	Mar-51	New	Apr-62
580	FMO 962	Bristol	LWL6B	Eastern Coach Works	B39R	Mar-51	New	Apr-62
581	FMO 963	Bristol	LWL6B	Eastern Coach Works	B39R	Mar-51	New	Feb-62
582	FMO 964	Bristol	LWL6B	Eastern Coach Works	B39R	Mar-51	New	Mar-66
583	FMO 965	Bristol	LWL6B	Eastern Coach Works	B39R	Mar-51	New	Apr-62
584	FMO 966	Bristol	LWL6B	Eastern Coach Works	B39R	Mar-51	New	Sep-62
585	FMO 967	Bristol	LWL6B	Eastern Coach Works	B39R	Mar-51	New	Feb-62
586	FMO 968	Bristol	KS6B	Eastern Coach Works	L27/28R	Aug-50	New	Mar-68
587	FMO 969	Bristol	KS6B	Eastern Coach Works	L27/28R	Sep-50	New	Sep-68
588	FMO 970	Bristol	KS6B	Eastern Coach Works	L27/28R	Sep-50	New	Jul-68
589	FMO 971	Bristol	KS6B	Eastern Coach Works	L27/28R	Nov-50	New	May-68
590	FMO 972	Bristol	KS6B	Eastern Coach Works	L27/28R	Nov-50	New	Aug-68
591	FMO 973	Bristol	KS6B	Eastern Coach Works	L27/28R	Nov-50	New	Dec-67
592	FMO 974	Bristol	KS6B	Eastern Coach Works	L27/28R	Nov-50	New	Aug-68
593	FMO 975	Bristol	KS6B	Eastern Coach Works	L27/28R	Nov-50	New	Aug-68
594	FMO 976	Bristol	KS6B	Eastern Coach Works	L27/28R	Nov-50	New	Oct-68
595	FMO 977	Bristol	KS6B	Eastern Coach Works	CL27/26RD	Jan-51	New	Dec-68
596	FMO 978	Bristol	KS6B	Eastern Coach Works	CL27/26RD	Jan-51	New	Apr-69
597	FMO 979	Bristol	KS6B	Eastern Coach Works	CL27/26RD	Jan-51	New	Oct-68
598	FMO 980	Bristol	KS6B	Eastern Coach Works	CL27/26RD	Jan-51	New	Apr-69
599	FMO 981	Bristol	KS6B	Eastern Coach Works	CL27/26RD	Jan-51	New	Feb-69
600	FMO 982	Bristol	KS6B	Eastern Coach Works	CL27/26RD	Jan-51	New	Oct-68
601	FMO 983	Bristol	KSW6B	Eastern Coach Works	L27/28R	Dec-50	New	Apr-69
602	FMO 984	Bristol	KSW6B	Eastern Coach Works	L27/28R	Dec-50	New	Sep-69
603	FMO 985	Bristol	KSW6B	Eastern Coach Works	L27/28R	Dec-50	New	Oct-68
607	GBL 871	Bristol	LWL6B	Eastern Coach Works	FC37F	Jul-51	New	Dec-63
608	GBL 872	Bristol	LWL6B	Eastern Coach Works	FC37F	Jul-51	New	Apr-64
609	GBL 873	Bristol	LWL6B	Eastern Coach Works	FC37F	Aug-51	New	May-64
610	GBL 874	Bristol	LWL6B	Eastern Coach Works	FC37F	Aug-51	New	Apr-64
611	GBL 875	Bristol	LWL6B	Eastern Coach Works	FC37F	Aug-51	New	Dec-63
612	GBL 876	Bristol	LWL6B	Eastern Coach Works	FC37F	Aug-51	New	May-62
613	GJB 251	Bristol	LWL6B	Eastern Coach Works	B39R	Oct-51	New	Mar-68
614	GJB 252	Bristol	LWL6B	Eastern Coach Works	B39R	Oct-51	New	Aug-64
615	GJB 253	Bristol	LWL6B	Eastern Coach Works	B39R	Jan-52	New	Aug-68
616	GJB 254	Bristol	LWL6B	Eastern Coach Works	B39R	Jan-52	New	Apr-69

Car 616 ceased PSV duties July 1965, serving as an Enquiry Office at Maidenhead, then as a driver training vehicle

Fleet No.	Reg. No.	Chassis Make	Chassis Type	Bodybuilder	Body Type	Date New	Date Acq.	Date Out
617	GJB 255	Bristol	LWL6B	Eastern Coach Works	B39R	Jan-52	New	Feb-65
618	GJB 256	Bristol	LWL6B	Eastern Coach Works	B39R	Jan-52	New	Feb-65
619	GJB 257	Bristol	LWL6B	Eastern Coach Works	B39R	Jan-52	New	Jul-66
620	GJB 258	Bristol	LWL6B	Eastern Coach Works	B39R	Jan-52	New	Dec-68

Fleet No.	Reg. No.	Chassis Make	Chassis Type	Bodybuilder	Body Type	Date New	Date Acq.	Date Out
621/259	GJB 259	Bristol	LWL6B	Eastern Coach Works	B39R	Jan-52	New	May-70
622	GJB 260	Bristol	LWL6B	Eastern Coach Works	B39R	Feb-52	New	Mar-65
623	GJB 261	Bristol	LWL6B	Eastern Coach Works	B39R	Feb-52	New	May-64
624	GJB 262	Bristol	LWL6B	Eastern Coach Works	B39R	Feb-52	New	Apr-68
625/263	GJB 263	Bristol	LWL6B	Eastern Coach Works	B39R	Feb-52	New	Jun-70
626	GJB 264	Bristol	LWL6B	Eastern Coach Works	B39R	Feb-52	New	Mar-68
627/265	GJB 265	Bristol	LWL6B	Eastern Coach Works	B39R	Feb-52	New	Feb-71
628	GJB 266	Bristol	LWL6B	Eastern Coach Works	B39R	Mar-52	New	Nov-68
629/267	GJB 267	Bristol	LWL6B	Eastern Coach Works	B39R	Apr-52	New	Jun-70
630	GJB 268	Bristol	LWL6B	Eastern Coach Works	B39R	Mar-52	New	Dec-68
631/269	GJB 269	Bristol	LWL6B	Eastern Coach Works	B39R	Mar-52	New	May-70
632	GJB 270	Bristol	LWL6B	Eastern Coach Works	B39R	Apr-52	New	Oct-68
633	GJB 271	Bristol	LWL6B	Eastern Coach Works	B39R	Apr-52	New	Nov-68
634	GJB 272	Bristol	KSW6B	Eastern Coach Works	L27/28R	Jun-51	New	Dec-68
635	GJB 273	Bristol	KSW6B	Eastern Coach Works	L27/28R	Jul-51	New	Mar-69
636	GJB 274	Bristol	KSW6B	Eastern Coach Works	L27/28R	Jul-51	New	Mar-69
637	GJB 275	Bristol	KSW6B	Eastern Coach Works	CL27/26RD	Oct-51	New	Sep-69
638	GJB 276	Bristol	KSW6B	Eastern Coach Works	CL27/26RD	Oct-51	New	Apr-69
639	GJB 277	Bristol	KSW6B	Eastern Coach Works	CL27/26RD	Oct-51	New	Apr-69
640	GJB 278	Bristol	KSW6B	Eastern Coach Works	L27/28R	Oct-51	New	Apr-69
641	GJB 279	Bristol	KSW6B	Eastern Coach Works	L27/28R	Oct-51	New	May-69
642	GJB 280	Bristol	KSW6B	Eastern Coach Works	L27/28R	Oct-51	New	May-69
643	GJB 281	Bristol	KSW6B	Eastern Coach Works	L27/28R	Nov-51	New	May-69
644	GJB 282	Bristol	KSW6B	Eastern Coach Works	L27/28R	Nov-51	New	May-69
645	GJB 283	Bristol	KSW6B	Eastern Coach Works	L27/28R	Nov-51	New	Apr-69
646	GJB 284	Bristol	KSW6B	Eastern Coach Works	L27/28R	Nov-51	New	Apr-69
647	GJB 285	Bristol	KSW6B	Eastern Coach Works	L27/28R	Nov-51	New	May-69
648	GJB 286	Bristol	KSW6B	Eastern Coach Works	L27/28R	Jan-52	New	Nov-69
649	GJB 287	Bristol	KSW6B	Eastern Coach Works	L27/28R	Jan-52	New	May-69
650	GJB 288	Bristol	KSW6B	Eastern Coach Works	L27/28R	Jan-52	New	Mar-70
79	SFC 565	Bristol	LS6G	Eastern Coach Works	C39F	Jun-52	New	Sep-65
80	SFC 566	Bristol	LS6G	Eastern Coach Works	C39F	Jun-52	New	Sep-65
81	SFC 567	Bristol	LS6G	Eastern Coach Works	C39F	Jun-52	New	Sep-65
82	SFC 568	Bristol	LS6G	Eastern Coach Works	C39F	Oct-52	New	Sep-65
83	SFC 569	Bristol	LS6G	Eastern Coach Works	C39F	Oct-52	New	Sep-65
84	SFC 570	Bristol	LS6G	Eastern Coach Works	C39F	Oct-52	New	Oct-61
85	SFC 571	AEC	Regal IV	Eastern Coach Works	C37F	Aug-52	New	Oct-67

Coaches 79-85 were for South Midland, the AEC having been ordered by the Red & White Group

Fleet No.	Reg. No.	Chassis Make	Chassis Type	Bodybuilder	Body Type	Date New	Date Acq.	Date Out
73	EBD 236	Bristol	L6B	Eastern Coach Works	FC31F	May-50	May-52	Oct-61
75	FRP 832	Bristol	LL6B	Eastern Coach Works	FC37F8	Feb-51	May-52	Dec-62
76	FRP 833	Bristol	LL6B	Eastern Coach Works	FC37F8	Feb-51	May-52	May-63
77	FRP 834	Bristol	LL6B	Eastern Coach Works	FC37F8	Feb-51	May-52	Aug-63
78	FRP 836	Bristol	LL6B	Eastern Coach Works	FC37F8	Feb-51	May-52	Mar-63

These vehicles were acquired by South Midland from United Counties Omnibus Co. Ltd.

Fleet No.	Reg. No.	Chassis Make	Chassis Type	Bodybuilder	Body Type	Date New	Date Acq.	Date Out
651	HBL 53	Bristol	KSW6B	Eastern Coach Works	L27/28R	Jul-52	New	Mar-70
652	HBL 54	Bristol	KSW6B	Eastern Coach Works	L27/28R	Jul-52	New	Mar-70
653	HBL 55	Bristol	KSW6B	Eastern Coach Works	L27/28R	Aug-52	New	Nov-69
654	HBL 56	Bristol	KSW6B	Eastern Coach Works	L27/28R	Sep-52	New	Jul-70
655	HBL 57	Bristol	KSW6B	Eastern Coach Works	L27/28R	Sep-52	New	Jul-70
656	HBL 58	Bristol	KSW6B	Eastern Coach Works	L27/28R	Sep-52	New	Nov-69
657	HBL 59	Bristol	KSW6B	Eastern Coach Works	L27/28R	Sep-52	New	May-70
658	HBL 60	Bristol	KSW6B	Eastern Coach Works	L27/28R	Sep-52	New	Jun-70
659	HBL 61	Bristol	KSW6B	Eastern Coach Works	L27/28R	Nov-52	New	Sep-69
660	HBL 62	Bristol	KSW6B	Eastern Coach Works	L27/28R	Nov-52	New	Sep-69
661	HBL 63	Bristol	KSW6B	Eastern Coach Works	L27/28R	Nov-52	New	Sep-69
662	HBL 64	Bristol	KSW6B	Eastern Coach Works	CL27/28R	Nov-52	New	Jun-70
663	HBL 65	Bristol	KSW6B	Eastern Coach Works	L27/28R	Jan-53	New	Nov-70
664	HBL 66	Bristol	KSW6B	Eastern Coach Works	L27/28R	May-53	New	Jul-70
665	HBL 67	Bristol	KSW6B	Eastern Coach Works	L27/28R	May-53	New	Feb-71
666	HBL 68	Bristol	KSW6B	Eastern Coach Works	L27/28R	May-53	New	Feb-71
667	HBL 69	Bristol	KSW6B	Eastern Coach Works	L27/28R	Jun-53	New	Apr-71
668	HBL 70	Bristol	KSW6B	Eastern Coach Works	L27/28R	Jun-53	New	Dec-70
669	HBL 71	Bristol	KSW6B	Eastern Coach Works	L27/28R	Jun-53	New	May-70
670	HBL 72	Bristol	KSW6B	Eastern Coach Works	L27/28R	Jun-53	New	Dec-70
671	HBL 73	Bristol	LS6G	Eastern Coach Works	C39F	Jun-52	New	Oct-67
672	HBL 74	Bristol	LS6G	Eastern Coach Works	C39F	Jul-52	New	Aug-66
673	HBL 75	Bristol	LS6G	Eastern Coach Works	C39F	Jul-52	New	Oct-65
674	HBL 76	Bristol	LS6G	Eastern Coach Works	C39F	Sep-52	New	Nov-66
675	HBL 77	Bristol	LS6G	Eastern Coach Works	C39F	Sep-52	New	Oct-67

Fleet No.	Reg. No.	Chassis Make	Chassis Type	Bodybuilder	Body Type	Date New	Date Acq.	Date Out
676	HBL 78	Bristol	LS6G	Eastern Coach Works	C39F	Sep-52	New	Jul-68
677/100	HBL 79	Bristol	LS6G	Eastern Coach Works	B45F	Nov-52	New	Jul-71
678/101	HBL 80	Bristol	LS6G	Eastern Coach Works	B45F	Nov-52	New	Sep-71
679/102	HBL 81	Bristol	LS6G	Eastern Coach Works	B45F	Jan-53	New	Aug-71
680	HBL 82	Bristol	LS6G	Eastern Coach Works	B45F	Mar-53	New	Mar-69
681/103	HBL 83	Bristol	LS6G	Eastern Coach Works	B45F	Feb-53	New	To AV 201
682/104	HBL 84	Bristol	LS6G	Eastern Coach Works	B45F	Mar-53	New	To AV 202
683/105	HBL 85	Bristol	LS6G	Eastern Coach Works	B45F	Apr-53	New	To AV 203
684/106	HBL 86	Bristol	LS6G	Eastern Coach Works	B45F	May-53	New	Mar-71
685/107	HBL 87	Bristol	LS6G	Eastern Coach Works	B45F	May-53	New	To AV 204
686	HBL 88	Bristol	LS5G	Eastern Coach Works	B41F	Jun-53	New	Oct-68
687	HBL 89	Bristol	LS5G	Eastern Coach Works	B41F	Aug-53	New	Nov-68
90	TWL 55	Bristol	LS6B	Eastern Coach Works	C37F	Jun-53	New	See S315
91	TWL 56	Bristol	LS6B	Eastern Coach Works	C37F	Jun-53	New	See S316
92	TWL 57	Bristol	LS6B	Eastern Coach Works	C37F	Jun-53	New	See S317
93	TWL 58	Bristol	LS6B	Eastern Coach Works	C37F	Jul-53	New	See S318
94	TWL 59	Bristol	LS6B	Eastern Coach Works	C37F	Aug-53	New	See S319
95	TWL 60	Bristol	LS6B	Eastern Coach Works	C37F	Oct-53	New	See S320

Coaches 90-5 were for the South Midland fleet

Fleet No.	Reg. No.	Chassis Make	Chassis Type	Bodybuilder	Body Type	Date New	Date Acq.	Date Out
688	HMO 834	Bristol	LS6B	Eastern Coach Works	C39F	Oct-53	New	See S309
689	HMO 835	Bristol	LS6B	Eastern Coach Works	C39F	Oct-53	New	See S310
690	HMO 836	Bristol	LS6B	Eastern Coach Works	C39F	Oct-53	New	See S311
691	HMO 837	Bristol	LS6B	Eastern Coach Works	C39F	Feb-54	New	See S312
692	HMO 838	Bristol	LS6B	Eastern Coach Works	C39F	Feb-54	New	See S313
693	HMO 839	Bristol	LS6B	Eastern Coach Works	C39F	Feb-54	New	See S314
694	HMO 840	Bristol	KSW6B	Eastern Coach Works	L27/28R	Jul-53	New	Nov-70
695	HMO 841	Bristol	KSW6B	Eastern Coach Works	L27/28R	Jul-53	New	Jun-71
696	HMO 842	Bristol	KSW6B	Eastern Coach Works	L27/28R	Sep-53	New	May-71
697	HMO 843	Bristol	KSW6B	Eastern Coach Works	L27/28R	Sep-53	New	Aug-70
698	HMO 844	Bristol	KSW6B	Eastern Coach Works	L27/28R	Sep-53	New	Apr-71
699	HMO 845	Bristol	KSW6B	Eastern Coach Works	L27/28R	Oct-53	New	Dec-70
700	HMO 846	Bristol	KSW6B	Eastern Coach Works	L27/28R	Oct-53	New	Jun-70
701	HMO 847	Bristol	KSW6B	Eastern Coach Works	L27/28R	Oct-53	New	Apr-71
702	HMO 848	Bristol	KSW6B	Eastern Coach Works	L27/28R	Oct-53	New	Jan-71
703	HMO 849	Bristol	KSW6B	Eastern Coach Works	L27/28R	Dec-53	New	Dec-70
704	HMO 850	Bristol	KSW6B	Eastern Coach Works	L27/28R	Dec-53	New	Jan-71
705	HMO 851	Bristol	KSW6B	Eastern Coach Works	L27/28R	Jan-54	New	Mar-71
706/108	HMO 852	Bristol	LS5G	Eastern Coach Works	B41F	Oct-53	New	Mar-71
707/109	HMO 853	Bristol	LS5G (later 6B)	Eastern Coach Works	B41F	Oct-53	New	Nov-69
708/110	HMO 854	Bristol	LS5G	Eastern Coach Works	B41F	Nov-53	New	Feb-71
709/111	HMO 855	Bristol	LS5G	Eastern Coach Works	B45F	Dec-53	New	Feb-71
710	HMO 856	Bristol	LS6B	Eastern Coach Works	B45F	Nov-53	New	Nov-68
711/117	HMO 857	Bristol	LS6B	Eastern Coach Works	B41F	Jan-54	New	May-70
712/118	HMO 858	Bristol	LS6B (later 6G)	Eastern Coach Works	B41F	Jan-54	New	To AV 208
713/119	HMO 859	Bristol	LS6B	Eastern Coach Works	B41F	Jan-54	New	May-70
714/120	HMO 860	Bristol	LS6B	Eastern Coach Works	B41F	Jan-54	New	Jul-70
715	HMO 861	Bristol	LS6B	Eastern Coach Works	B45F	May-54	New	Oct-65
716	HMO 862	Bristol	LS6B	Eastern Coach Works	B45F	May-54	New	Mar-69
717/121	HMO 863	Bristol	LS6B (later 6G)	Eastern Coach Works	B45F	Jun-54	New	To AV 211
718/122	HMO 864	Bristol	LS6B	Eastern Coach Works	B45F	Jun-54	New	Sep-70
719/123	HMO 865	Bristol	LS6B	Eastern Coach Works	B45F	Nov-54	New	Jan-71
720/144	HMO 866	Bristol	LS6B	Eastern Coach Works	B45F	Nov-54	New	Nov-69
721/145	HMO 867	Bristol	LS6B	Eastern Coach Works	B41F	Nov-54	New	Nov-69
722/146	HMO 868	Bristol	LS6B (later 6G)	Eastern Coach Works	B41F	Dec-54	New	To AV 227
723	HMO 869	Bristol	LS6B	Eastern Coach Works	DP41F	Jun-55	New	Nov-68
724/147	HMO 870	Bristol	LS6B (later 6G)	Eastern Coach Works	B41F	Jun-55	New	To AV 228
725	HMO 871	Bristol	LS6B	Eastern Coach Works	DP41F	Jun-55	New	Nov-68
726	JRX 801	Bristol	KSW6B	Eastern Coach Works	L27/28R	Aug-54	New	Jun-71
727	JRX 802	Bristol	KSW6B	Eastern Coach Works	L27/28R	Aug-54	New	Feb-71
728	JRX 803	Bristol	KSW6B	Eastern Coach Works	L27/28R	Sep-54	New	Feb-71
729	JRX 804	Bristol	KSW6B	Eastern Coach Works	L27/28R	Aug-54	New	Apr-71
730	JRX 805	Bristol	KSW6B	Eastern Coach Works	L27/28R	Sep-54	New	Apr-71
731	JRX 806	Bristol	KSW6B	Eastern Coach Works	L27/28R	Sep-54	New	Feb-71
732	JRX 807	Bristol	KSW6B	Eastern Coach Works	L27/28R	Sep-54	New	Feb-71
733	JRX 808	Bristol	KSW6B	Eastern Coach Works	L27/28R	Sep-54	New	To AV 27
734	JRX 809	Bristol	KSW6B	Eastern Coach Works	L27/28R	Sep-54	New	Mar-71
735	JRX 810	Bristol	KSW6B	Eastern Coach Works	L27/28R	Sep-54	New	Feb-71
736	JRX 811	Bristol	KSW6B	Eastern Coach Works	L27/28R	Sep-54	New	Feb-71
737	JRX 812	Bristol	KSW6B	Eastern Coach Works	L27/28R	Sep-54	New	Feb-71

Fleet No.	Reg. No.	Chassis Make	Chassis Type	Bodybuilder	Body Type	Date New	Date Acq.	Date Out
738	JRX 813	Bristol	KSW6B	Eastern Coach Works	CL27/26RD	Sep-54	New	Oct-70
739	JRX 814	Bristol	KSW6B	Eastern Coach Works	CL27/26RD	Sep-54	New	Jun-71
740	JRX 815	Bristol	KSW6B	Eastern Coach Works	CL27/26RD	Sep-54	New	Jun-71
741	JRX 816	Bristol	KSW6B	Eastern Coach Works	CL27/26RD	Sep-54	New	Jul-71
742	JRX 817	Bristol	KSW6B	Eastern Coach Works	CL27/26RD	Sep-54	New	Mar-71
743	JRX 818	Bristol	KSW6B	Eastern Coach Works	CL27/26RD	Sep-54	New	Jul-71
744	JRX 819	Bristol	KSW6B	Eastern Coach Works	L27/28R	Oct-54	New	Feb-71
745	JRX 820	Bristol	KSW6B	Eastern Coach Works	L27/28R	Sep-55	New	To AV 28
746	JRX 821	Bristol	KSW6B	Eastern Coach Works	L27/28R	Sep-55	New	Jun-71
747	JRX 822	Bristol	KSW6B	Eastern Coach Works	L27/28R	Sep-55	New	Apr-71
748	JRX 823	Bristol	KSW6B	Eastern Coach Works	L27/28R	Sep-55	New	To AV 29
749	JRX 824	Bristol	KSW6B	Eastern Coach Works	L27/28R	Sep-55	New	Jun-71

When the Bristol KSW6B's were transferred to Alder Valley it was for use as Driver Training Buses

Fleet No.	Reg. No.	Chassis Make	Chassis Type	Bodybuilder	Body Type	Date New	Date Acq.	Date Out
750	MBL 831	Bristol	LD6G	Eastern Coach Works	CLD31/25RD	May-56	New	To AV 523
751	MBL 832	Bristol	LD6G	Eastern Coach Works	CLD31/25RD	Mar-56	New	To AV 524
752	MBL 833	Bristol	LD6G	Eastern Coach Works	CLD31/25RD	Mar-56	New	To AV 525
753	MBL 834	Bristol	LD6G	Eastern Coach Works	CLD31/25RD	Mar-56	New	To AV 526
754	MBL 835	Bristol	LD6G	Eastern Coach Works	CLD31/25RD	Mar-56	New	To AV 527
755	MBL 836	Bristol	LD6B	Eastern Coach Works	LD33/27R	Mar-56	New	To AV 528
756	MBL 837	Bristol	LD6B	Eastern Coach Works	LD33/27R	Mar-56	New	To AV 529
757	MBL 838	Bristol	LD6B	Eastern Coach Works	LD33/27R	Mar-56	New	To AV 530
758	MBL 839	Bristol	LD6G	Eastern Coach Works	LD33/27R	May-56	New	To AV 531
759	MBL 840	Bristol	LD6G	Eastern Coach Works	LD33/27R	Jun-56	New	To AV 532
760	MBL 841	Bristol	LD6G	Eastern Coach Works	CLD31/25RD	Jun-56	New	To AV 533
761	MBL 842	Bristol	LD6G	Eastern Coach Works	LD33/27RD	May-56	New	To AV 534
762	MBL 843	Bristol	LD6G	Eastern Coach Works	LD33/27RD	Jun-56	New	To AV 535
763	MBL 844	Bristol	LD6G	Eastern Coach Works	CLD31/24RD	May-56	New	To AV 536
764	MBL 845	Bristol	LD6G	Eastern Coach Works	CLD31/25RD	Jun-56	New	To AV 537
765	MBL 846	Bristol	LD5G (later 6G)	Eastern Coach Works	LD33/27R	Jul-56	New	To AV 538
766	MBL 847	Bristol	LD5G (later 6B)	Eastern Coach Works	LD33/27R	Jul-56	New	To AV 539
767	MBL 848	Bristol	LD5G (later 6B)	Eastern Coach Works	LD33/27R	Jul-56	New	To AV 540
768	MBL 849	Bristol	LD5G (later 6B)	Eastern Coach Works	LD33/27R	Jul-56	New	To AV 541
769	MBL 850	Bristol	LD5G (later 6B)	Eastern Coach Works	LD33/27R	Jul-56	New	To AV 542
774/S301	NBL 731	Bristol	SC4LK	Eastern Coach Works	B35F	Dec-56	New	Dec-69
775/S302	NBL 732	Bristol	SC4LK	Eastern Coach Works	B35F	Dec-56	New	Dec-69
776/S303	NBL 733	Bristol	SC4LK	Eastern Coach Works	B35F	Dec-56	New	Dec-69
777/S304	NBL 734	Bristol	SC4LK	Eastern Coach Works	B35F	Jan-57	New	Nov-69

774-7 were re-numbered S301-4 in July 1966 and again in the 1969 scheme as 155-158

Fleet No.	Reg. No.	Chassis Make	Chassis Type	Bodybuilder	Body Type	Date New	Date Acq.	Date Out
778	NBL 735	Bristol	SC4LK	Eastern Coach Works	B35F	Jan-57	New	Jul-63
779	NBL 736	Bristol	LDL6G	Eastern Coach Works	LD37/33R	Nov-57	New	To AV 548
780	NBL 737	Bristol	LD5G (later 6B)	Eastern Coach Works	LD33/27R	Jun-57	New	To AV 549
781	NBL 738	Bristol	LD5G (later 6B)	Eastern Coach Works	LD33/27R	Jun-57	New	To AV 550
782	NBL 739	Bristol	LD5G (later 6B)	Eastern Coach Works	LD33/27R	Aug-57	New	To AV 551
783	NBL 740	Bristol	LD5G (later 6B)	Eastern Coach Works	LD33/27R	Oct-57	New	To AV 552
784	NBL 741	Bristol	LD5G (later 6B)	Eastern Coach Works	LD33/27R	Nov-57	New	To AV 553
785	NBL 742	Bristol	LD5G (later 6B)	Eastern Coach Works	LD33/27R	Nov-57	New	To AV 554
786	NBL 743	Bristol	LD6G	Eastern Coach Works	LD33/27R	Dec-57	New	To AV 555
787	NBL 744	Bristol	LD6G	Eastern Coach Works	LD33/27R	Jan-58	New	To AV 556
788	NBL 745	Bristol	LD6G	Eastern Coach Works	LD33/27R	Jan-58	New	To AV 557
789	NBL 746	Bristol	LD5G (later 6B)	Eastern Coach Works	LD33/27R	Feb-58	New	To AV 558
790	NBL 747	Bristol	LD6G	Eastern Coach Works	LD33/27R	Feb-58	New	To AV 559
791	NBL 748	Bristol	LD5G (later 6B)	Eastern Coach Works	LD33/27R	Mar-58	New	To AV 560
792	NBL 749	Bristol	LD6G	Eastern Coach Works	LD33/27R	Sep-58	New	To AV 561
793	NBL 750	Bristol	LD6G	Eastern Coach Works	LD33/27R	Sep-58	New	To AV 562
794	DMO 664	Bristol	LL5G	Eastern Coach Works	FB39F	Sep-47	Aug-58	Mar-67
795	DMO 665	Bristol	LL5G	Eastern Coach Works	FB39F	Feb-48	Jun-58	Jan-67
796	DMO 666	Bristol	LL5G	Eastern Coach Works	FB39F	Sep-47	Jun-58	Aug-67
797	DMO 667	Bristol	LL5G	Eastern Coach Works	FB39F	Oct-47	Aug-58	Mar-67
798	DMO 668	Bristol	LL5G	Eastern Coach Works	FB39F	Feb-48	Aug-58	Nov-66
799	DMO 669	Bristol	LL5G	Eastern Coach Works	FB39F	Oct-47	Aug-58	Nov-66
800	ORX 631	Bristol	MW6G	Eastern Coach Works	C34F	Mar-58	New	See 159
801	ORX 632	Bristol	MW6G	Eastern Coach Works	C34F	Mar-58	New	See 160
802	ORX 633	Bristol	MW6G	Eastern Coach Works	C34F	Apr-58	New	See 161
803	ORX 634	Bristol	MW6G	Eastern Coach Works	C32F	Apr-58	New	See 162
804	PRX 930	Bristol	MW6G	Eastern Coach Works	C34F	Mar-59	New	See 163
805	PRX 931	Bristol	MW6G	Eastern Coach Works	C34F	Apr-59	New	See 164
806	PRX 932	Bristol	MW6G	Eastern Coach Works	C34F	Apr-59	New	See 166
807	PRX 933	Bristol	MW6G	Eastern Coach Works	C34F	Mar-59	New	See 165

These MW6G coaches were for the South Midland fleet and were painted in the new maroon and cream livery

Fleet No.	Reg. No.	Chassis Make	Chassis Type	Bodybuilder	Body Type	Date New	Date Acq.	Date Out
808	PRX 926	Bristol	LD6G	Eastern Coach Works	LD33/27RD	Oct-58	New	To AV 563
809	PRX 927	Bristol	LD6G	Eastern Coach Works	LD33/27RD	Oct-58	New	To AV 564
810	PRX 928	Bristol	LD6B	Eastern Coach Works	LD33/27RD	Jan-59	New	To AV 565
811	PRX 929	Bristol	LD6B	Eastern Coach Works	LD33/27RD	Jan-59	New	To AV 566
812	SMO 78	Bristol	LD6G	Eastern Coach Works	LD33/27RD	Jun-59	New	To AV 567
813	SMO 79	Bristol	LD6G	Eastern Coach Works	LD33/27RD	Jun-59	New	To AV 568
814	SMO 80	Bristol	LD6G	Eastern Coach Works	LD33/27RD	Jun-59	New	To AV 569
815	SMO 81	Bristol	LD6B	Eastern Coach Works	LD33/27RD	Jul-59	New	To AV 570
816	SMO 82	Bristol	LD6B	Eastern Coach Works	LD33/27RD	Jul-59	New	To AV 571
817	FMO 21	Bristol	LL5G	Eastern Coach Works	FB39F	Mar-50	Feb-59	Jul-68
818	FMO 22	Bristol	LL5G	Eastern Coach Works	FB39F	Mar-50	Feb-59	Jun-68
819	FMO 23	Bristol	LL5G	Eastern Coach Works	FB39F	Mar-50	Feb-59	May-68
820	FMO 24	Bristol	LL5G	Eastern Coach Works	FB39F	Mar-50	Feb-59	Mar-68
821	FRP 835	Bristol	LL6B	Eastern Coach Works	FC37F8	Feb-51	Jan-59	Oct-61
822	FRP 837	Bristol	LL6B	Eastern Coach Works	FC37F8	Feb-51	Jan-59	Mar-62
823	FRP 838	Bristol	LL6B	Eastern Coach Works	FC37F8	Mar-51	Jan-59	Jul-63
824	FRP 839	Bristol	LL6B	Eastern Coach Works	FC37F8	Feb-51	Jan-59	Mar-62
825	FRP 840	Bristol	LL6B	Eastern Coach Works	FC37F8	Mar-51	Jan-59	Jan-62
826	FRP 841	Bristol	LL6B	Eastern Coach Works	FC37F8	Feb-51	Jan-59	Oct-61
827	FRP 842	Bristol	LL6B	Eastern Coach Works	FC37F8	Feb-51	Jan-59	Mar-62
828	FRP 843	Bristol	LL6B	Eastern Coach Works	FC37F8	Feb-51	Jan-59	Oct-61
829	FRP 844	Bristol	LL6B	Eastern Coach Works	FC37F8	Feb-51	Jan-59	Oct-61

Bristol LL6B coaches 821-9 were purchased from the United Counties Omnibus Co. Ltd

Fleet No.	Reg. No.	Chassis Make	Chassis Type	Bodybuilder	Body Type	Date New	Date Acq.	Date Out
436	KHU 624	Bristol	K6B	Eastern Coach Works	L27/28R	Sep-47	Jun-59	Jul-66
437	KHU 601	Bristol	K6B	Eastern Coach Works	L27/28R	Sep-47	Jun-59	Dec-63
438	HTT 980	Bristol	K5G	Eastern Coach Works	L27/28R	Oct-46	Jun-59	May-62
455	KHU 604	Bristol	K6B	Eastern Coach Works	L27/28R	Sep-47	Nov-59	Dec-63
456	KHW 633	Bristol	K6A	Eastern Coach Works	L27/28R	Nov-47	Nov-59	Mar-63
457	KHU 605	Bristol	K6A	Eastern Coach Works	L27/28R	Sep-47	Nov-59	Feb-65
458	KHU 606	Bristol	K6A	Eastern Coach Works	L27/28R	Sep-47	Nov-59	Apr-63
459	KHU 622	Bristol	K6A	Eastern Coach Works	L27/28R	Sep-47	Nov-59	Feb-65

These 8 Bristol K's were purchased from the Bristol Omnibus Co. Ltd.

Fleet No.	Reg. No.	Chassis Make	Chassis Type	Bodybuilder	Body Type	Date New	Date Acq.	Date Out
460	FPU 510	Bristol	K5G	Eastern Coach Works	L27/28R8 (51)	Nov-37	Nov-59	Oct-64

Car 460 was withdrawn from PSV use in October 1964 and became the Tree Lopper/Route Servicing Vehicle ED53

Fleet No.	Reg. No.	Chassis Make	Chassis Type	Bodybuilder	Body Type	Date New	Date Acq.	Date Out
461	FPU 509	Bristol	K5G	Eastern Coach Works	L27/28R8 (52)	Nov-37	Nov-59	Jul-65
462	FPU 515	Bristol	K5G	Eastern Coach Works	L27/28R8 (52)	Nov-37	Nov-59	Jan-65
463	FPU 517	Bristol	K5G	Eastern Coach Works	L27/28R8 (51)	Nov-37	Nov-59	Feb-66
464	FPU 511	Bristol	K5G	Eastern Coach Works	L27/28R8 (51)	Nov-37	Jan-60	May-65
465	FPU 513	Bristol	K5G	Eastern Coach Works	L27/28R (47)	Nov-37	Jan-60	Oct-62

These buses were purchased from United Counties O.C.Ltd., rebodied in the years shown in brackets, some with 8ft wide bodies

Fleet No.	Reg. No.	Chassis Make	Chassis Type	Bodybuilder	Body Type	Date New	Date Acq.	Date Out
472	JT 9354	Bristol	K5G	Eastern Coach Works	L27/28R (49)	May-38	Mar-60	Mar-64
473	JT 9355	Bristol	K5G	Eastern Coach Works	L27/28R (49)	Jul-38	Mar-60	Mar-64
474	JT 9360	Bristol	K5G	Eastern Coach Works	L27/28R (49)	Jul-38	Mar-60	Sep-64
475	FLJ 978	Bristol	K5G	Brush (bebuilt H&D)	L28/26R	Apr-42	Mar-60	Nov-64

These buses were purchased from Hants & Dorset M.S. Ltd., some rebodied as shown in brackets

Fleet No.	Reg. No.	Chassis Make	Chassis Type	Bodybuilder	Body Type	Date New	Date Acq.	Date Out
476	GNO 688	Bristol	K5G	Eastern Coach Works	L27/28R (48)	Jul-38	Apr-60	Apr-63
477	GNO 698	Bristol	K5G	Eastern Coach Works	L27/28R (48)	Jul-38	Apr-60	Oct-62

These buses were purchased from United Counties O.C.Ltd., carrying bodies built as shown in brackets

Fleet No.	Reg. No.	Chassis Make	Chassis Type	Bodybuilder	Body Type	Date New	Date Acq.	Date Out
830	UJB 196	Bristol	MW6G	Eastern Coach Works	C34F	Mar-60	New	See 167
831	UJB 197	Bristol	MW6G	Eastern Coach Works	C34F	Mar-60	New	Jan-71
832	UJB 198	Bristol	MW6G	Eastern Coach Works	C34F	Mar-60	New	Jan-71
833	UJB 199	Bristol	MW6G	Eastern Coach Works	C34F	Apr-60	New	Jan-71

These MW6G coaches were for the South Midland fleet and were painted in the maroon and cream livery

Fleet No.	Reg. No.	Chassis Make	Chassis Type	Bodybuilder	Body Type	Date New	Date Acq.	Date Out
834	UJB 200	Bristol	FLF6B(later 6G)	Eastern Coach Works	CH37/28F	Jul-60	New	To AV 601
852/179	VJB 943	Bristol	MW6G	Eastern Coach Works	DP41F	Jul-60	New	To AV 251
853/180	VJB 944	Bristol	MW6G	Eastern Coach Works	DP41F	Aug-60	New	To AV 252
854/181	VJB 945	Bristol	MW6G	Eastern Coach Works	B41F	Nov-60	New	To AV 253
855/182	VJB 946	Bristol	MW6G	Eastern Coach Works	B41F	Nov-60	New	To AV 254
835	UJB 201	Bristol	FLF6G	Eastern Coach Works	CH37/28F	Nov-60	New	To AV 602
836	UJB 202	Bristol	FLF6G	Eastern Coach Works	CH37/28F	Nov-60	New	To AV 603
837	UJB 203	Bristol	FLF6G	Eastern Coach Works	CH37/28F	Nov-60	New	To AV 604
838	UJB 204	Bristol	FLF6G	Eastern Coach Works	CH37/28F	Nov-60	New	To AV 605
856/183	VJB 947	Bristol	MW6G	Eastern Coach Works	B41F	Dec-60	New	To AV 255
857/184	VJB 948	Bristol	MW6G	Eastern Coach Works	B41F	Dec-60	New	To AV 256
839	WJB 223	Bristol	FLF6G	Eastern Coach Works	H38/32F	Dec-60	New	To AV 606
840	WJB 224	Bristol	FLF6G	Eastern Coach Works	H38/32F	Dec-60	New	To AV 607
841	WJB 225	Bristol	FLF6G	Eastern Coach Works	H38/32F	Jan-61	New	To AV 608
842	WJB 226	Bristol	FLF6G	Eastern Coach Works	H38/32F	Jan-61	New	To AV 609
843	WJB 227	Bristol	FLF6G	Eastern Coach Works	H38/32F	Jan-61	New	To AV 610

Fleet No.	Reg. No.	Chassis Make	Chassis Type	Bodybuilder	Body Type	Date New	Date Acq.	Date Out
844	WJB 228	Bristol	FLF6G	Eastern Coach Works	H38/32F	Jul-61	New	To AV 611
845	WJB 229	Bristol	FLF6G	Eastern Coach Works	H38/32F	Jul-61	New	To AV 612
846	WJB 230	Bristol	FLF6G	Eastern Coach Works	H38/32F	Jul-61	New	To AV 613
847	WJB 231	Bristol	FLF6G	Eastern Coach Works	H38/32F	Jul-61	New	To AV 614
848	WJB 232	Bristol	FLF6G	Eastern Coach Works	H38/32F	Jul-61	New	To AV 615
849	WJB 233	Bristol	FLF6G	Eastern Coach Works	H38/32F	Nov-61	New	To AV 616
850	WJB 234	Bristol	FLF6G	Eastern Coach Works	H38/32F	Nov-61	New	To AV 617
851	WJB 235	Bristol	FLF6G	Eastern Coach Works	H38/32F	Nov-61	New	To AV 618
858	WRX 773	Bristol	MW6G	Eastern Coach Works	C34F	May-61	New	Jan-71
859	WRX 774	Bristol	MW6G	Eastern Coach Works	C34F	May-61	New	Jan-71
860	WRX 775	Bristol	MW6G	Eastern Coach Works	C34F	Jun-61	New	Jan-71
861	WRX 776	Bedford	SB8 7ft. 6ins.	Duple Super Vega	C37F	May-61	New	Feb-68
862	516 ABL	Bedford	SB8 7ft. 6ins.	Duple Super Vega	C37F	May-62	New	Apr-68
863	517 ABL	Bedford	SB8 8ft.	Duple Super Vega	C37F	May-62	New	Jun-68
864	518 ABL	Bedford	SB8 8ft.	Duple Super Vega	C37F	May-62	New	May-68
865	519 ABL	Bedford	SB8 8ft.	Duple Super Vega	C37F	May-62	New	Jun-68

Coaches 858-865 were for the South Midland fleet in the maroon and cream livery

| 866 | 520 ABL | Bristol | MW6G | Eastern Coach Works | C39F | May-62 | New | To AV 31 |

Car 866 was for the Thames Valley fleet and was in the maroon and cream livery

| 867/403 | 521 ABL | Bristol | REX6G | Eastern Coach Works | C47F | Apr-63 | New | Jan-71 |

Car 867 was the high-floor RE prototype for the South Midland fleet in maroon and cream livery. Re-numbered in July 1969

868	536 BBL	Bristol	FLF6B	Eastern Coach Works	H38/32F	Sep-62	New	To AV 619
869	537 BBL	Bristol	FLF6B	Eastern Coach Works	H38/32F	Sep-62	New	To AV 620
870	538 BBL	Bristol	FLF6B	Eastern Coach Works	H38/32F	Sep-62	New	To AV 621
871	539 BBL	Bristol	FLF6B	Eastern Coach Works	H38/32F	Sep-62	New	To AV 622
872	540 BBL	Bristol	FLF6B	Eastern Coach Works	H38/32F	Sep-62	New	To AV 623
873	541 BBL	Bristol	FLF6B	Eastern Coach Works	H38/32F	Sep-62	New	To AV 624
874	542 BBL	Bristol	FLF6B	Eastern Coach Works	H38/32F	Sep-62	New	To AV 625
875	543 BBL	Bristol	FLF6G	Eastern Coach Works	H38/32F	Jan-63	New	To AV 626
876	544 BBL	Bristol	FLF6G	Eastern Coach Works	H38/32F	Jan-63	New	To AV 627
877	545 BBL	Bristol	FLF6G	Eastern Coach Works	H38/32F	Feb-63	New	To AV 628
878	546 BBL	Bristol	FLF6G	Eastern Coach Works	H38/32F	Feb-63	New	To AV 629
879	547 BBL	Bristol	FLF6G	Eastern Coach Works	H38/32F	Mar-63	New	To AV 630
880	548 BBL	Bristol	FLF6G	Eastern Coach Works	H38/32F	Mar-63	New	To AV 631
881	549 BBL	Bristol	FLF6G	Eastern Coach Works	H38/32F	Apr-63	New	To AV 632
C401	831 CRX	Bedford	SB8	Duple Bella Vega	C37F	Feb-63	New	Oct-68
C402	832 CRX	Bedford	SB8	Duple Bella Vega	C37F	Apr-63	New	Oct-68
C403	833 CRX	Bedford	SB8	Duple Bella Vega	C37F	Apr-63	New	Oct-68

Coaches C401-3 were for the South Midland fleet in the maroon and cream livery

D1	839 CRX	Bristol	FLF6G	Eastern Coach Works	H38/32F	Oct-63	New	To AV 633
D2	840 CRX	Bristol	FLF6G	Eastern Coach Works	H38/32F	Oct-63	New	To AV 634
D3	841 CRX	Bristol	FLF6G	Eastern Coach Works	H38/32F	Oct-63	New	To AV 635
S301	GFM 881	Bristol	L6A	Eastern Coach Works	B35F OMO	Mar-48	May-63	Nov-64
S302	GFM 882	Bristol	L6A	Eastern Coach Works	B35F OMO	Mar-48	May-63	Mar-65
S303	GFM 884	Bristol	L6A	Eastern Coach Works	B35F OMO	Apr-48	May-63	Nov-64
S304	GFM 887	Bristol	L6A	Eastern Coach Works	B35F OMO	May-48	May-63	Feb-65
S305	GFM 888	Bristol	L6A	Eastern Coach Works	B35F OMO	Mar-48	May-63	Dec-66
S309	HMO 835	Bristol	LS6B	Eastern Coach Works	B41F	See 689	Apr-64	Nov-68
S310/124	HMO 836	Bristol	LS6B (later 5G)	Eastern Coach Works	B41F	See 690	Apr-64	Apr-71
S311/125	HMO 837	Bristol	LS6B	Eastern Coach Works	B41F	See 691	Apr-64	Oct-69
C404	834 CRX	Bristol	RELH6G	Eastern Coach Works	C47F	Jan-64	New	Jan-71
C405	835 CRX	Bristol	RELH6G	Eastern Coach Works	C47F	Jan-64	New	Jan-71
C406	836 CRX	Bedford	SB13	Duple Super Vega	C37F	Jan-64	New	Nov-69
C407	837 CRX	Bedford	SB13	Duple Super Vega	C37F	Jan-64	New	Sep-70
C408	838 CRX	Bedford	SB13	Duple Super Vega	C37F	Jan-64	New	Sep-70
C409	842 CRX	Bedford	SB13	Duple Super Vega	C37F	Jan-64	New	Sep-70

Coaches C404/5/7-9 were for the South Midland fleet, and all including C406 were in the maroon and cream livery

D4	ABL 116B	Bristol	FLF6B	Eastern Coach Works	CH37/28F	Feb-64	New	To AV 636
D5	ABL 117B	Bristol	FLF6B	Eastern Coach Works	CH37/28F	Feb-64	New	To AV 637
D6	ABL 118B	Bristol	FLF6B	Eastern Coach Works	CH37/28F	Feb-64	New	To AV 638
D7	ABL 119B	Bristol	FLF6B	Eastern Coach Works	CH37/28F	Feb-64	New	To AV 639
D8	BRX 141B	Bristol	FLF6G	Eastern Coach Works	CH37/28F	Aug-64	New	To AV 640
D9	BRX 142B	Bristol	FLF6G	Eastern Coach Works	LD38/32F	Aug-64	New	To AV 641
S306/185	CBL 355B	Bristol	RELL6G	Eastern Coach Works	B54F	Oct-64	New	To AV 401
S307/186	CBL 356B	Bristol	RELL6G	Eastern Coach Works	B54F	Oct-64	New	To AV 402
S308/187	CBL 357B	Bristol	RELL6G	Eastern Coach Works	B54F	Oct-64	New	To AV 403
D10	CMO 833B	Bristol	FLF6G	Eastern Coach Works	H38/32F	Nov-64	New	To AV 642
D11	CMO 834B	Bristol	FLF6G	Eastern Coach Works	H38/32F	Nov-64	New	To AV 643
D12	CMO 835B	Bristol	FLF6G	Eastern Coach Works	H38/32F	Nov-64	New	To AV 644

Fleet No.	Reg. No.	Chassis Make	Chassis Type	Bodybuilder	Body Type	Date New	Date Acq.	Date Out
D13	CMO 836B	Bristol	FLF6G	Eastern Coach Works	H38/32F	Nov-64	New	To AV 645
D14	DJB 529C	Bristol	FLF6G	Eastern Coach Works	H38/32F	Jan-65	New	To AV 646
D15	DJB 530C	Bristol	FLF6G	Eastern Coach Works	H38/32F	Jan-65	New	To AV 647
D16	DRX 120C	Bristol	FLF6G	Eastern Coach Works	H38/32F	Feb-65	New	To AV 648
D17	DRX 121C	Bristol	FLF6G	Eastern Coach Works	H38/32F	Feb-65	New	To AV 649
D18	DRX 122C	Bristol	FLF6G	Eastern Coach Works	H38/32F	Mar-65	New	To AV 650
S312/126	HMO 838	Bristol	LS6B	Eastern Coach Works	B41F	See 692	Mar-65	Apr-70
S313	HMO 839	Bristol	LS6B	Eastern Coach Works	DP39F	See 693	Feb-65	Oct-68
C410	EMO 551C	Bedford	SB13	Harrington Crusader IV	C37F	Apr-65	New	Jan-71
C411	EMO 552C	Bedford	SB13	Harrington Crusader IV	C37F	Apr-65	New	Jan-71
C412	EMO 553C	Bedford	SB13	Harrington Crusader IV	C37F	Apr-65	New	Jan-71
D19	FBL 483C	Bristol	FLF6G	Eastern Coach Works	H38/32F	Jun-65	New	To AV 651
D20	FBL 484C	Bristol	FLF6G	Eastern Coach Works	H38/32F	Jun-65	New	To AV 652
D21	FBL 485C	Bristol	FLF6G	Eastern Coach Works	H38/32F	Jun-65	New	To AV 653
S314	HMO 834	Bristol	LS6B	Eastern Coach Works	DP39F	See 688	Jul-65	Nov-68
D22	FJB 738C	Bristol	FLF6G	Eastern Coach Works	H38/32F	Aug-65	New	To AV 654
D23	FJB 739C	Bristol	FLF6G	Eastern Coach Works	H38/32F	Aug-65	New	To AV 655
D24	FJB 740C	Bristol	FLF6G	Eastern Coach Works	H38/32F	Sep-65	New	To AV 656
D25	GBL 907C	Bristol	FLF6G	Eastern Coach Works	H38/32F	Oct-65	New	To AV 657
D26	GJB 874C	Bristol	FLF6G	Eastern Coach Works	H38/32F	Nov-65	New	To AV 658
D27	GMO 827C	Bristol	FLF6G	Eastern Coach Works	H38/32F	Dec-65	New	To AV 659
D28	GMO 828C	Bristol	FLF6G	Eastern Coach Works	H38/32F	Dec-65	New	To AV 660
D29	GRX 129D	Bristol	FLF6G	Eastern Coach Works	H38/32F	Jan-66	New	To AV 661
D30	GRX 130D	Bristol	FLF6G	Eastern Coach Works	H38/32F	Jan-66	New	To AV 662
D31	GRX 131D	Bristol	FLF6G	Eastern Coach Works	H38/32F	Jan-66	New	To AV 663
D32	GRX 132D	Bristol	FLF6G	Eastern Coach Works	H38/32F	Feb-66	New	To AV 664
D33	GRX 133D	Bristol	FLF6G	Eastern Coach Works	H38/32F	Feb-66	New	To AV 665
S315	TWL 55	Bristol	LS6B	Eastern Coach Works	DP39F	See 90	Feb-66	Sep-69
C413	GRX 413D	Bedford	VAM14	Duple Bella Venture	C41F	Mar-66	New	Jan-71
C414	GRX 414D	Bedford	VAM14	Duple Bella Venture	C41F	Mar-66	New	Jan-71
C415	GRX 415D	Bedford	VAM14	Duple Bella Venture	C41F	Mar-66	New	Jan-71
C416	GRX 416D	Bedford	VAM14	Duple Bella Venture	C41F	Mar-66	New	Jan-71

Coaches C413-6 were for the South Midland fleet in the maroon and cream livery

Fleet No.	Reg. No.	Chassis Make	Chassis Type	Bodybuilder	Body Type	Date New	Date Acq.	Date Out
S316	TWL 56	Bristol	LS6B	Eastern Coach Works	DP39F	See 91	May-66	Mar-69
D34	GRX 134D	Bristol	FLF6G	Eastern Coach Works	H38/32F	Jun-66	New	To AV 666
D35	GRX 135D	Bristol	FLF6G	Eastern Coach Works	H38/32F	Jun-66	New	To AV 667
D36	GRX 136D	Bristol	FLF6G	Eastern Coach Works	H38/32F	Jun-66	New	To AV 668
S317	TWL 57	Bristol	LS6B	Eastern Coach Works	DP39F	See 92	Jul-66	Mar-69
S318/113	TWL 58	Bristol	LS6B (later 6G)	Eastern Coach Works	DP39F	See 93	Jul-66	Sep-70
D37	GRX 137D	Bristol	FLF6G	Eastern Coach Works	H38/32F	Aug-66	New	To AV 669
D38	GRX 138D	Bristol	FLF6G	Eastern Coach Works	H38/32F	Aug-66	New	To AV 670
D39	GRX 139D	Bristol	FLF6G	Eastern Coach Works	H38/32F	Sep-66	New	To AV 671
D40	GRX 140D	Bristol	FLF6G	Eastern Coach Works	H38/32F	Sep-66	New	To AV 672
D41	GRX 141D	Bristol	FLF6G	Eastern Coach Works	H38/32F	Sep-66	New	To AV 673
D42	GRX 142D	Bristol	FLF6G	Eastern Coach Works	H38/32F	Oct-66	New	To AV 674
D43	GRX 143D	Bristol	FLF6G	Eastern Coach Works	H38/32F	Oct-66	New	To AV 675
D44	GRX 144D	Bristol	FLF6G	Eastern Coach Works	H38/32F	Oct-66	New	To AV 676
D45	GRX 145D	Bristol	FLF6G	Eastern Coach Works	H38/32F	Nov-66	New	To AV 677
D46	GRX 146D	Bristol	FLF6G	Eastern Coach Works	H38/32F	Dec-66	New	To AV 678
S320	TWL 60	Bristol	LS6B	Eastern Coach Works	DP39F	See 95	Dec-66	Mar-69

Special Note: *Between March 1966 and November 1971 the Company purchased 120 secondhand vehicles from other operators. For convenience of notation these are arranged after the end of new deliveries for each of these years. They are also segregated into their original owners.*
Also note that Bristol SC's 774-7 were re-numbered S301-4 during 1966 to vacate numbers for acquired LD's.

Fleet No.	Reg. No.	Chassis Make	Chassis Type	Bodybuilder	Body Type	Date New	Date Acq.	Date Out
S321/148	KWN 794	Bristol	LS6B (later 6G)	Eastern Coach Works	B40F	Jan-55	May-66	To AV 223
S322/149	KWN 795	Bristol	LS6B (later 6G)	Eastern Coach Works	B41F	Feb-55	May-66	To AV 224
S323/150	KWN 796	Bristol	LS6B	Eastern Coach Works	B41F	Jul-55	Jul-66	Jun-70
S324/151	KWN 797	Bristol	LS6B	Eastern Coach Works	B41F	Jul-55	Jul-66	Jun-70
S325/152	MCY 39	Bristol	LS6B	Eastern Coach Works	B41F	Jul-55	Jul-66	Jun-70
S326/116	JCY 997	Bristol	LS6B	Eastern Coach Works	B41F	Dec-53	Nov-66	Dec-70
S327/153	OCY 947	Bristol	LS5G (later 6G)	Eastern Coach Works	B41F	Jul-57	Nov-66	To AV 240
S328/154	OCY 948	Bristol	LS5G (later 6G)	Eastern Coach Works	B41F	Aug-57	Nov-66	To AV 241
672	JCY 989	Bristol	KSW6B	Eastern Coach Works	L27/28R	Jul-53	Nov-66	Sep-70
673	JCY 990	Bristol	KSW6B	Eastern Coach Works	L27/28R	Jul-53	Nov-66	Jul-70
770	LWN 52	Bristol	LD6B	Eastern Coach Works	LD33/27RD	Jun-55	Jun-66	Oct-71
771	LWN 53	Bristol	LD6B	Eastern Coach Works	LD33/27RD	Jul-55	Jun-66	Oct-71
772	LWN 48	Bristol	LD6B	Eastern Coach Works	LD33/25R	Apr-55	Jul-66	Oct-71
773	LWN 49	Bristol	LD6B	Eastern Coach Works	LD33/27R	May-55	Jul-66	To AV 512
774	LWN 50	Bristol	LD6B	Eastern Coach Works	LD33/27R	Jun-55	Jul-66	Oct-71

Fleet No.	Reg. No.	Chassis Make	Chassis Type	Bodybuilder	Body Type	Date New	Date Acq.	Date Out
775	LWN 51	Bristol	LD6B	Eastern Coach Works	LD33/27R	Jun-55	Jul-66	Oct-71
The above 16 vehicles were purchased from United Welsh Services Ltd.									
C417	LJB 417E	Bedford	VAM14	Duple Viceroy	C41F	Jan-67	New	To AV 32
C418	LJB 418E	Bedford	VAM14	Duple Viceroy	C41F	Jan-67	New	To AV 33
C419	LJB 419E	Bedford	VAM14	Duple Viceroy	C41F	Jan-67	New	To AV 34
C420	LJB 420E	Bedford	VAM14	Duple Viceroy	C41F	Jan-67	New	To AV 35
Bedford coaches C417-20 were in the Thames Valley fleet for the Reading - Heathrow Rail Air Link service									
D47	LBL 847E	Bristol	FLF6G	Eastern Coach Works	H38/32F	Jan-67	New	To AV 679
D48	LBL 848E	Bristol	FLF6G	Eastern Coach Works	H38/32F	Jan-67	New	To AV 680
D49	LBL 849E	Bristol	FLF6G	Eastern Coach Works	H38/32F	Feb-67	New	To AV 681
D50	LBL 850E	Bristol	FLF6G	Eastern Coach Works	H38/32F	Feb-67	New	To AV 682
D51	LBL 851E	Bristol	FLF6G	Eastern Coach Works	H38/32F	Mar-67	New	To AV 683
D52	LBL 852E	Bristol	FLF6G	Eastern Coach Works	H38/32F	Mar-67	New	To AV 684
D53	LBL 853E	Bristol	FLF6G	Eastern Coach Works	H38/32F	Jun-67	New	To AV 685
S319	TWL 59	Bristol	LS6B	Eastern Coach Works	DP39F	See 94	Jun-67	Dec-68
C421	LJB 421E	Bristol	RELH6G	Eastern Coach Works	DP47F	Apr-67	New	Jan-71
C422	LJB 422E	Bristol	RELH6G	Eastern Coach Works	DP47F	May-67	New	Jan-71
C423	LJB 423E	Bristol	RELH6G	Eastern Coach Works	DP47F	May-67	New	Jan-71
Bristol coaches C421-3 were in the South Midland fleet in maroon and cream livery									
776	JCY 993	Bristol	LD6G	Eastern Coach Works	LD33/25R	Mar-54	Jun-67	To AV 504
777	JCY 994	Bristol	LD6G	Eastern Coach Works	LD33/25R	Nov-54	Jun-67	Oct-71
778	JCY 991	Bristol	LD6G	Eastern Coach Works	LD33/25R	Feb-54	Dec-67	Aug-71
794	JCY 992	Bristol	LD6G	Eastern Coach Works	LD33/25RD	May-54	Dec-67	To AV 505
S329/114	JCY 995	Bristol	LS6B	Eastern Coach Works	B41F	Nov-53	Jan-67	Sep-71
S330/115	JCY 996	Bristol	LS6G	Eastern Coach Works	B41F	Nov-53	Jan-67	To AV 206
The above 6 vehicles were purchased from United Welsh Services Ltd.									
D54	PBL 53F	Bristol	FLF6G	Eastern Coach Works	H38/32F	Feb-68	New	To AV 686
D55	PBL 55F	Bristol	FLF6G	Eastern Coach Works	H38/32F	Feb-68	New	To AV 687
D56	PBL 56F	Bristol	FLF6G	Eastern Coach Works	H38/32F	Feb-68	New	To AV 688
D57	PBL 57F	Bristol	FLF6G	Eastern Coach Works	H38/32F	Feb-68	New	To AV 689
D58	PBL 58F	Bristol	FLF6G	Eastern Coach Works	H38/32F	Feb-68	New	To AV 690
D59	PBL 59F	Bristol	FLF6G	Eastern Coach Works	H38/32F	Feb-68	New	To AV 691
D60	PBL 60F	Bristol	FLF6G	Eastern Coach Works	H38/32F	Feb-68	New	To AV 692
S331/188	LJB 331F	Bristol	RESL6G	Eastern Coach Works	B40D	Mar-68	New	To AV 404
S332/189	LJB 332F	Bristol	RESL6G	Eastern Coach Works	B40D	Mar-68	New	To AV 405
S333/190	LJB 333F	Bristol	RESL6G	Eastern Coach Works	B40D	Mar-68	New	To AV 406
S334/191	LJB 334F	Bristol	RESL6G	Eastern Coach Works	B40D	Mar-68	New	To AV 407
S335/192	LJB 335F	Bristol	RESL6G	Eastern Coach Works	B40D	Mar-68	New	To AV 408
S336/193	LJB 336F	Bristol	RESL6G	Eastern Coach Works	B40D	Mar-68	New	To AV 409
S337/194	LJB 337F	Bristol	RESL6G	Eastern Coach Works	B40D	Mar-68	New	To AV 410
S338/195	LJB 338F	Bristol	RESL6G	Eastern Coach Works	B40D	Mar-68	New	To AV 411
C424	RJB 424F	Bristol	RELH6G	Duple Commander III	C49F	Apr-68	New	Jun-70
C425	RJB 425F	Bristol	RELH6G	Duple Commander III	C49F	Apr-68	New	To AV 56
C426	RJB 426F	Bristol	RELH6G	Duple Commander III	C49F	Apr-68	New	To AV 57
C427	RJB 427F	Bristol	RELH6G	Duple Commander III	C49F	Apr-68	New	To AV 58
Bristol coaches C424-7 were in the Thames Valley fleet for the Reading - Heathrow Rail Air Link service									
C428	RJB 428F	Bristol	LHL6L	Duple Commander III	C41F	May-68	New	Jan-71
C429	RJB 429F	Bristol	LHL6L	Duple Commander III	C41F	May-68	New	Jan-71
C430	RJB 430F	Bristol	LHL6L	Duple Commander III	C41F	May-68	New	Jan-71
C431	RJB 431F	Bristol	LHL6L	Duple Commander III	C41F	May-68	New	Jan-71
Bristol coaches C428-31 were in the South Midland fleet in maroon and cream livery									

Note: *From October 1968 new saloons were numbered in a new series commencing at 200, whilst new double-decks were in a series commencing at 500. Coaches continued the existing 400 series but without the C prefix. Acquired saloons continued in the 300 series, again with the S prefix discontinued, whilst acquired double-decks continued to use vacated numbers in the 700, 600 or finally 500 series. No existing vehicles were re-numbered at this point.*

Fleet No.	Reg. No.	Chassis Make	Chassis Type	Bodybuilder	Body Type	Date New	Date Acq.	Date Out
200	RRX 991G	Bristol	LH6L	Eastern Coach Works	B41F	Oct-68	New	To AV 257
201	RRX 992G	Bristol	LH6L	Eastern Coach Works	B41F	Oct-68	New	To AV 258
202	RRX 993G	Bristol	LH6L	Eastern Coach Works	B41F	Oct-68	New	To AV 259
203	RRX 994G	Bristol	LH6L	Eastern Coach Works	B41F	Oct-68	New	To AV 260
204	RRX 995G	Bristol	LH6L	Eastern Coach Works	B41F	Oct-68	New	To AV 261
205	RRX 996G	Bristol	LH6L	Eastern Coach Works	B41F	Oct-68	New	To AV 262
206	RRX 997G	Bristol	LH6L	Eastern Coach Works	B41F	Oct-68	New	To AV 263
207	RRX 998G	Bristol	LH6L	Eastern Coach Works	B41F	Oct-68	New	To AV 264
501	SRX 945G	Bristol	VRT/SL6G	Eastern Coach Works	H41/29F	Dec-68	New	To AV 902
688	PHN 828	Bristol	KSW6B	Eastern Coach Works	L27/28R	May-52	Jan-68	Feb-71
689	PHN 829	Bristol	KSW6B	Eastern Coach Works	L27/28R	Jun-52	Jan-68	Sep-70
690	PHN 821	Bristol	KSW6B	Eastern Coach Works	L27/28R	Jun-52	Jan-68	Jan-71
691	PHN 819	Bristol	KSW6B	Eastern Coach Works	L27/28R	May-52	Jan-68	Jan-71

Fleet No.	Reg. No.	Chassis Make	Chassis Type	Bodybuilder	Body Type	Date New	Date Acq.	Date Out
S339/127	SHN 728	Bristol	LS5G	Eastern Coach Works	B41F	Dec-53	Feb-68	To AV 207
S340/128	SHN 729	Bristol	LS5G	Eastern Coach Works	B41F	Dec-53	Feb-68	Apr-71
S341/129	SHN 730	Bristol	LS5G	Eastern Coach Works	B41F	Dec-53	Feb-68	Mar-71
	The above 7 buses were purchased from United Automobile Services Ltd.							
C432/440	613 JPU	Bristol	LS6G	Eastern Coach Works	C34F	Mar-57	Mar-68	Jan-71
C433/441	614 JPU	Bristol	LS6G	Eastern Coach Works	C34F	Mar-57	Mar-68	Jan-71
C434/442	618 JPU	Bristol	MW6G	Eastern Coach Works	C34F	Jan-58	Mar-68	Jan-71
	These coaches were purchased from the Eastern National Omnibus Co. Ltd., re-numbered 440-2 without C prefix in May 1969.							
S342	PHW 929	Bristol	LS5G	Eastern Coach Works	B41F	Jun-54	Mar-68	Mar-69
S343/130	PHW 930	Bristol	LS5G	Eastern Coach Works	B41F	Jun-54	Mar-68	To AV 210
S344/131	PHW 931	Bristol	LS5G	Eastern Coach Works	B41F	Jun-54	Mar-68	Sep-71
S345/132	PHW 932	Bristol	LS5G	Eastern Coach Works	B41F	Jun-54	Mar-68	Nov-69
	These buses were purchased from the Bristol Omnibus Co. Ltd.							
623	NCY 637	Bristol	LD6G	Eastern Coach Works	LD33/27R	Nov-56	Oct-68	To AV 517
624	NCY 638	Bristol	LD6G	Eastern Coach Works	LD33/27R	Nov-56	Oct-68	To AV 518
795	NCY 634	Bristol	LD6G	Eastern Coach Works	LD33/27R	Jul-56	Apr-68	To AV 519
796	NCY 635	Bristol	LD6G	Eastern Coach Works	LD33/27R	Jul-56	Apr-68	To AV 520
797	NCY 636	Bristol	LD6G	Eastern Coach Works	LD33/27R	Nov-56	Apr-68	To AV 521
798	OCY 953	Bristol	LD6G	Eastern Coach Works	LD33/27R	Feb-57	Apr-68	To AV 522
	These buses were purchased from United Welsh Services Ltd.							
346/133	MAX 116	Bristol	LS6G	Eastern Coach Works	B41F	Aug-54	Oct-68	To AV 212
347/134	MAX 117	Bristol	LS6G	Eastern Coach Works	B41F	Aug-54	Oct-68	To AV 213
348/135	MAX 118	Bristol	LS6G	Eastern Coach Works	B41F	Aug-54	Oct-68	To AV 214
349/136	MAX 119	Bristol	LS6G	Eastern Coach Works	B41F	Aug-54	Oct-68	To AV 215
350/137	MAX 122	Bristol	LS6G	Eastern Coach Works	B41F	Aug-54	Oct-68	To AV 217
351/138	MAX 123	Bristol	LS6G	Eastern Coach Works	B41F	Sep-54	Oct-68	To AV 218
352/139	MAX 126	Bristol	LS6G	Eastern Coach Works	B41F	Sep-54	Nov-68	To AV 220
353/140	MAX 127	Bristol	LS6G	Eastern Coach Works	B41F	Oct-54	Nov-68	To AV 221
354/141	MAX 121	Bristol	LS6G	Eastern Coach Works	B41F	Sep-54	Nov-68	To AV 216
355/142	MAX 125	Bristol	LS6G	Eastern Coach Works	B41F	Nov-54	Nov-68	To AV 219
356/143	MAX 128	Bristol	LS6G	Eastern Coach Works	B41F	Nov-54	Nov-68	To AV 222
	These buses were purchased from Red & White Services Ltd. Note that the S prefix was discontinued from this point.							
500	SRX 944G	Bristol	VRT/SL6G	Eastern Coach Works	H41/29F	Jan-69	New	To AV 901
502	UBL 243G	Bristol	VRT/SL6G	Eastern Coach Works	H39/31F	Apr-69	New	To AV 903
503	UBL 244G	Bristol	VRT/SL6G	Eastern Coach Works	H39/31F	Apr-69	New	To AV 904
504	UBL 245G	Bristol	VRT/SL6G	Eastern Coach Works	H39/31F	Apr-69	New	To AV 905
505	UBL 246G	Bristol	VRT/SL6G	Eastern Coach Works	H39/31F	Apr-69	New	To AV 906
506	UBL 247G	Bristol	VRT/SL6G	Eastern Coach Works	H39/31F	May-69	New	To AV 907
507	UBL 248G	Bristol	VRT/SL6G	Eastern Coach Works	H39/31F	May-69	New	To AV 908
432	UMO 688G	Bristol	LH6L	Duple Commander IV	C41F	May-69	New	Jan-71
433	UMO 689G	Bristol	LH6L	Duple Commander IV	C41F	May-69	New	Jan-71
434	UMO 690G	Bristol	LH6L	Duple Commander IV	C41F	May-69	New	Jan-71
435	UMO 691G	Bristol	LH6L	Duple Commander IV	C41F	May-69	New	Jan-71
	These coaches were for the South Midland fleet and were in the maroon and cream livery							
159	ORX 631	Bristol	MW6G	Eastern Coach Works	B41F	See 800	Mar-69	To AV 243
160	ORX 632	Bristol	MW6G	Eastern Coach Works	B41F	See 801	Jul-69	To AV 245
161	ORX 633	Bristol	MW6G	Eastern Coach Works	B41F	See 802	Jun-69	To AV 244
162	ORX 634	Bristol	MW6G	Eastern Coach Works	B41F	See 803	Apr-69	To AV 242
508	VMO 223H	Bristol	VRT/SL6G	Eastern Coach Works	H39/31F	Jul-69	New	To AV 909
509	VMO 224H	Bristol	VRT/SL6G	Eastern Coach Works	H39/31F	Aug-69	New	To AV 910
208	VMO 225H	Bristol	LH6L	Eastern Coach Works	B41F	Aug-69	New	To AV 265
209	VMO 226H	Bristol	LH6L	Eastern Coach Works	B41F	Aug-69	New	To AV 266
210	VMO 227H	Bristol	LH6L	Eastern Coach Works	B41F	Aug-69	New	To AV 267
211	VMO 228H	Bristol	LH6L	Eastern Coach Works	B41F	Aug-69	New	To AV 268
510	VMO 229H	Bristol	VRT/SL6G	Eastern Coach Works	H39/31F	Sep-69	New	To AV 911
511	VMO 230H	Bristol	VRT/SL6G	Eastern Coach Works	H39/31F	Oct-69	New	To AV 912
512	VMO 231H	Bristol	VRT/SL6G	Eastern Coach Works	H39/31F	Nov-69	New	To AV 913
212	VMO 232H	Bristol	LH6L	Eastern Coach Works	B41F	Nov-69	New	To AV 269
213	VMO 233H	Bristol	LH6L	Eastern Coach Works	B41F	Nov-69	New	To AV 270
214	VMO 234H	Bristol	LH6L	Eastern Coach Works	B41F	Nov-69	New	To AV 271
215	VMO 235H	Bristol	LH6L	Eastern Coach Works	B41F	Nov-69	New	To AV 272
163	PRX 930	Bristol	MW6G	Eastern Coach Works	B41F	See 804	Nov-69	To AV 246
164	PRX 931	Bristol	MW6G	Eastern Coach Works	B41F	See 805	Dec-69	To AV 247
165	PRX 932	Bristol	MW6G	Eastern Coach Works	B41F	See 806	Oct-69	To AV 248
632	OCY 954	Bristol	LD6G	Eastern Coach Works	LD33/27R	Feb-57	May-69	To AV 546
620	OCY 955	Bristol	LD6G	Eastern Coach Works	LD33/27R	Feb-57	Aug-69	To AV 543
633	OCY 956	Bristol	LD6G	Eastern Coach Works	LD33/27R	Feb-57	May-69	To AV 547
622	OCY 957	Bristol	LD6G	Eastern Coach Works	LD33/27R	May-57	Jun-69	To AV 544
	These 4 Lodekkas were purchased from United Welsh Services							

Fleet No.	Reg. No.	Chassis Make	Chassis Type	Bodybuilder	Body Type	Date New	Date Acq.	Date Out
308	AHW 227B	Bristol	SUS4A	Eastern Coach Works	B30F	Nov-64	On loan	Nov-69
198	844 THY	Bristol	SUS4A	Eastern Coach Works	B30F	Sep-63	Dec-69	To AV 497

The first of these SU's was loaned by Bristol Omnibus Co. Ltd. for evaluation only and was returned

Note: *From April 1969 most older saloons were re-numbered in a series commencing at 100 but took some time to complete.*
Surviving LWL6B's were, however, given numbers in the 200 series to correspond with their registrations.
New saloons received numbers in the 200 series, whilst secondhand saloons were accommodated in the 100 range.
No re-numbering of the double-deck fleet took place, but secondhand stock continued to take older vacated numbers.
The revised numbers for the LWL's are shown by a second number in the first column from 621 onwards.

Fleet No.	Reg. No.	Chassis Make	Chassis Type	Bodybuilder	Body Type	Date New	Date Acq.	Date Out
166	PRX 933	Bristol	MW6G	Eastern Coach Works	B41F	See 807	Feb-70	To AV 249
513	XMO 541H	Bristol	VRT/SL2/6G	Eastern Coach Works	H39/31F	May-70	New	To AV 914
514	XMO 542H	Bristol	VRT/SL2/6G	Eastern Coach Works	H39/31F	May-70	New	To AV 915
216	XRX 819H	Bristol	LH6L	Eastern Coach Works	B41F	May-70	New	To AV 273
217	XRX 820H	Bristol	LH6L	Eastern Coach Works	B41F	May-70	New	To AV 274
436	YBL 925H	Bristol	LH6L	Duple Commander IV	C41F	May-70	New	Jan-71
437	YBL 926H	Bristol	LH6L	Duple Commander IV	C41F	May-70	New	Jan-71
438	YBL 927H	Bristol	LH6L	Duple Commander IV	C41F	Jul-70	New	Jan-71
439	YBL 928H	Bristol	LH6L	Duple Commander IV	C41F	Sep-70	New	Jan-71

These coaches were for the South Midland fleet and were in the maroon and cream livery

Fleet No.	Reg. No.	Chassis Make	Chassis Type	Bodybuilder	Body Type	Date New	Date Acq.	Date Out
224	YJB 521H	Bristol	RELL6G	Eastern Coach Works	B49F	Jul-70	New	To AV 412
225	YJB 522H	Bristol	RELL6G	Eastern Coach Works	B49F	Jul-70	New	To AV 413
226	YJB 523H	Bristol	RELL6G	Eastern Coach Works	B49F	Jul-70	New	To AV 414
218	ABL 121J	Bristol	LH6L	Eastern Coach Works	B41F	Jul-70	New	To AV 275
219	ABL 122J	Bristol	LH6L	Eastern Coach Works	B41F	Aug-70	New	To AV 276
167	UJB 196	Bristol	MW6G	Eastern Coach Works	B41F	See 830	Nov-70	To AV 250
227	AMO 233J	Bristol	RELL6G	Eastern Coach Works	B49F	Nov-70	New	To AV 415
228	AMO 234J	Bristol	RELL6G	Eastern Coach Works	B49F	Nov-70	New	To AV 416
220	AMO 235J	Bristol	LH6L	Eastern Coach Works	B41F	Nov-70	New	To AV 277
221	AMO 236J	Bristol	LH6L	Eastern Coach Works	B41F	Nov-70	New	To AV 278
222	AMO 237J	Bristol	LH6L	Eastern Coach Works	B41F	Nov-70	New	To AV 279
223	AMO 238J	Bristol	LH6L	Eastern Coach Works	B41F	Dec-70	New	To AV 280
196	668 COD	Bristol	SUS4A	Eastern Coach Works	B30F	Mar-60	Jan-70	To AV 495
197	669 COD	Bristol	SUS4A	Eastern Coach Works	B30F	Mar-60	Jan-70	To AV 496

These Bristol SU's were purchased from the Western National Omnibus Co. Ltd.

Fleet No.	Reg. No.	Chassis Make	Chassis Type	Bodybuilder	Body Type	Date New	Date Acq.	Date Out
158	845 THY	Bristol	SUS4A	Eastern Coach Works	B30F	Sep-63	Feb-70	To AV 499
199	846 THY	Bristol	SUS4A	Eastern Coach Works	B30F	Sep-63	Jan-70	To AV 498
629	THW 745	Bristol	LD6B	Eastern Coach Works	LD33/25RD	Mar-55	Dec-70	To AV 510
630	THW 750	Bristol	LD6B	Eastern Coach Works	LD33/25RD	Jun-55	Dec-70	To AV 511

These 4 Bristols were purchased from the Bristol Omnibus Co. Ltd.

Fleet No.	Reg. No.	Chassis Make	Chassis Type	Bodybuilder	Body Type	Date New	Date Acq.	Date Out
626	OCY 958	Bristol	LD6G	Eastern Coach Works	LD33/27R	May-57	Jan-70	To AV 545
634	OCY 960	Bristol	LD6G	Eastern Coach Works	LD33/27R	Jan-58	May-70	To AV 573
635	OCY 961	Bristol	LD6G	Eastern Coach Works	LD33/27R	Mar-58	May-70	To AV 574
628	OCY 962	Bristol	LD6G	Eastern Coach Works	LD33/27R	Feb-58	Jan-70	To AV 572

These Bristol LD's were purchased from United Welsh Services Ltd.

Fleet No.	Reg. No.	Chassis Make	Chassis Type	Bodybuilder	Body Type	Date New	Date Acq.	Date Out
618	LFW 317	Bristol	LD6B	Eastern Coach Works	LD33/27R	Nov-54	Dec-70	Jul-71
619	LFW 318	Bristol	LD6B	Eastern Coach Works	LD33/27R	Nov-54	Dec-70	Jul-71
615	LFW 322	Bristol	LD6B	Eastern Coach Works	LD33/25RD	Feb-55	Aug-70	Oct-71
616	LFW 324	Bristol	LD6G	Eastern Coach Works	LD33/25RD	Apr-55	Aug-70	Jul-71
605	LFW 329	Bristol	LD6B	Eastern Coach Works	LD33/25RD	May-55	Mar-70	Nov-71
606	NBE 129	Bristol	LD6B	Eastern Coach Works	LD33/27R	Sep-55	Mar-70	Aug-71
617	NBE 130	Bristol	LD6B	Eastern Coach Works	LD33/27R	Sep-55	Aug-70	Sep-71
607	NBE 133	Bristol	LD6B	Eastern Coach Works	LD33/27R	Sep-55	Mar-70	Aug-71

These Bristol LD's were purchased from the Lincolnshire Road Car Co. Ltd.

Fleet No.	Reg. No.	Chassis Make	Chassis Type	Bodybuilder	Body Type	Date New	Date Acq.	Date Out
600	VFM 607	Bristol	LD6B	Eastern Coach Works	LD33/27R	Jul-55	Apr-70	Sep-71
608	VFM 611	Bristol	LD6B	Eastern Coach Works	LD33/27R	Jul-55	Aug-70	Oct-71
611	VFM 617	Bristol	LD6B	Eastern Coach Works	LD33/27RD	Jul-55	Aug-70	To AV 508
609	VFM 618	Bristol	LD6B	Eastern Coach Works	LD33/27RD	Jul-55	Jul-70	Sep-71
610	VFM 622	Bristol	LD6B	Eastern Coach Works	LD33/27RD	Jul-55	Jul-70	To AV 507
612	XFM 186	Bristol	LD6B	Eastern Coach Works	LD33/27RD	Sep-55	Nov-70	Sep-71
601	XFM 187	Bristol	LD6B	Eastern Coach Works	LD33/27RD	Sep-55	Mar-70	Aug-71
602	XFM 190	Bristol	LD6B	Eastern Coach Works	LD33/27RD	Oct-55	Apr-70	Sep-71
603	XFM 192	Bristol	LD6B	Eastern Coach Works	LD33/27RD	Mar-56	Mar-70	To AV 513
613	XFM 193	Bristol	LD6B	Eastern Coach Works	LD33/27RD	Mar-56	Aug-70	To AV 515
604	XFM 195	Bristol	LD6B	Eastern Coach Works	LD33/27RD	Mar-56	Apr-70	To AV 514
614	XFM 196	Bristol	LD6B	Eastern Coach Works	LD33/27RD	May-56	Jul-70	To AV 516

These Bristol LD's were purchased from Crosville Motor Services Ltd.

Fleet No.	Reg. No.	Chassis Make	Chassis Type	Bodybuilder	Body Type	Date New	Date Acq.	Date Out
145	956 ARA	Bristol	LS6G	Eastern Coach Works	B41F	May-56	Jun-70	To AV 230
151	957 ARA	Bristol	LS6G	Eastern Coach Works	B41F	May-56	Dec-70	To AV 231
152	958 ARA	Bristol	LS6G	Eastern Coach Works	B41F	May-56	Nov-70	To AV 232

Fleet No.	Reg. No.	Chassis Make	Chassis Type	Bodybuilder	Body Type	Date New	Date Acq.	Date Out
144	959 ARA	Bristol	LS6G	Eastern Coach Works	B41F	May-56	May-70	To AV 229
156	960 ARA	Bristol	LS6G	Eastern Coach Works	DP41F	May-56	Dec-70	To AV 233
150	961 ARA	Bristol	LS6G	Eastern Coach Works	B41F	Jul-56	Jun-70	To AV 237
155	962 ARA	Bristol	LS6G	Eastern Coach Works	B41F	Jul-56	Nov-70	To AV 238
157	963 ARA	Bristol	LS6G	Eastern Coach Works	DP41F	Jul-56	Dec-70	To AV 239

The above 8 Bristol LS's were purchased from the Midland General Omnibus Co. Ltd.

Fleet No.	Reg. No.	Chassis Make	Chassis Type	Bodybuilder	Body Type	Date New	Date Acq.	Date Out
636	14 DRB	Bristol	LD6G	Eastern Coach Works	LD33/25RD	Jan-58	Nov-70	To AV 575

This Bristol LD was purchased from the Nottinghamshire & Derbyshire Traction Co. Ltd.

Fleet No.	Reg. No.	Chassis Make	Chassis Type	Bodybuilder	Body Type	Date New	Date Acq.	Date Out
400	BJB 883J	Bristol	RELH6G	Plaxton Panorama Elite	C51F	Apr-71	New	To AV 59
401	BJB 884J	Bristol	RELH6G	Plaxton Panorama Elite	C51F	Apr-71	New	To AV 60
402	CJB 587J	Bristol	RELH6G	Plaxton Panorama Elite	C51F	Jul-71	New	To AV 61
403	CJB 588J	Bristol	RELH6G	Plaxton Panorama Elite	C51F	Jul-71	New	To AV 62
404	CJB 589J	Bristol	RELH6G	Plaxton Panorama Elite	C51F	Jul-71	New	To AV 63
405	CJB 590J	Bristol	RELH6G	Plaxton Panorama Elite	C51F	Jul-71	New	To AV 64

These coaches were for the Rail Air Link service from Reading - Heathrow Airport.

Fleet No.	Reg. No.	Chassis Make	Chassis Type	Bodybuilder	Body Type	Date New	Date Acq.	Date Out
229	CMO 647J	Bristol	RELL6G	Eastern Coach Works	B49F	May-71	New	To AV 471
230	CMO 648J	Bristol	RELL6G	Eastern Coach Works	B49F	May-71	New	To AV 472
231	CMO 649J	Bristol	RELL6G	Eastern Coach Works	B49F	May-71	New	To AV 473
515	DRX 101K	Bristol	VRT/SL2/6G	Eastern Coach Works	H39/31F	Jul-71	New	To AV 916
516	DRX 102K	Bristol	VRT/SL2/6G	Eastern Coach Works	H39/31F	Jul-71	New	To AV 917
517	DRX 103K	Bristol	VRT/SL2/6G	Eastern Coach Works	H39/31F	Jul-71	New	To AV 918
518	DRX 104K	Bristol	VRT/SL2/6G	Eastern Coach Works	H39/31F	Jul-71	New	To AV 919
232	DRX 625K	Bristol	RELL6G	Eastern Coach Works	B49F	Sep-71	New	To AV 474
233	DRX 626K	Bristol	RELL6G	Eastern Coach Works	B49F	Sep-71	New	To AV 475
234	DRX 627K	Bristol	RELL6G	Eastern Coach Works	B49F	Sep-71	New	To AV 476
241	EBL 390K	Bristol	RELL6L	Eastern Coach Works	B50F	Sep-71	New	To AV 477
242	EBL 437K	Bristol	RELL6L	Eastern Coach Works	B50F	Sep-71	New	To AV 478
243	EBL 438K	Bristol	RELL6L	Eastern Coach Works	B50F	Sep-71	New	To AV 479
920	FBL 112K	Bristol	VRT/SL2/6G	Eastern Coach Works	H39/31F	Dec-71	New	To AV 920
921	FBL 113K	Bristol	VRT/SL2/6G	Eastern Coach Works	H39/31F	Dec-71	New	To AV 921
922	FBL 114K	Bristol	VRT/SL2/6G	Eastern Coach Works	H39/31F	Dec-71	New	To AV 922
621	THW 742	Bristol	LD6B	Eastern Coach Works	LD33/25RD	Mar-55	Jan-71	Oct-71
625	THW 743	Bristol	LD6B	Eastern Coach Works	LD33/25RD	Mar-55	Jan-71	Oct-71
627	THW 744	Bristol	LD6B	Eastern Coach Works	LD33/25RD	Mar-55	Jan-71	To AV 509

These Bristol LD's were purchased from the Bristol Omnibus Co. Ltd.

Fleet No.	Reg. No.	Chassis Make	Chassis Type	Bodybuilder	Body Type	Date New	Date Acq.	Date Out
637	16 DRB	Bristol	LD6G	Eastern Coach Works	LD33/25RD	Feb-58	Jan-71	To AV 576
638	17 DRB	Bristol	LD6G	Eastern Coach Works	LD33/25RD	Mar-58	Jan-71	To AV 577
639	18 DRB	Bristol	LD6G	Eastern Coach Works	LD33/25RD	Mar-58	Jan-71	To AV 578
640	19 DRB	Bristol	LD6G	Eastern Coach Works	LD33/25RD	Mar-58	Jan-71	To AV 579
641	20 DRB	Bristol	LD6G	Eastern Coach Works	LD33/25RD	Sep-58	Mar-71	To AV 580

These Bristol LD's were purchased from the Nottinghamshire & Derbyshire Traction Co. Ltd.

Fleet No.	Reg. No.	Chassis Make	Chassis Type	Bodybuilder	Body Type	Date New	Date Acq.	Date Out
125	964 ARA	Bristol	LS6G	Eastern Coach Works	B41F	Jul-56	Feb-71	To AV 234
126	966 ARA	Bristol	LS6G	Eastern Coach Works	B41F	Jul-56	Feb-71	To AV 235
132	967 ARA	Bristol	LS6G	Eastern Coach Works	B41F	Jul-56	Feb-71	To AV 236
647	515 JRA	Bristol	LD6G	Eastern Coach Works	LD33/25RD	Aug-59	Aug-71	To AV 586

These 4 Bristols were purchased from the Midland General Omnibus Co. Ltd.

Fleet No.	Reg. No.	Chassis Make	Chassis Type	Bodybuilder	Body Type	Date New	Date Acq.	Date Out
123	XNU 415	Bristol	LS6G	Eastern Coach Works	B41F	Apr-55	Sep-71	To AV 225
124	XNU 416	Bristol	LS6G	Eastern Coach Works	B41F	Apr-55	Sep-71	To AV 226

These Bristol LS's were purchased from East Midland Motor Services Ltd., but were new to Midland General.

Fleet No.	Reg. No.	Chassis Make	Chassis Type	Bodybuilder	Body Type	Date New	Date Acq.	Date Out
119	PNN 769	Bristol	LS6G	Eastern Coach Works	DP41F	Apr-54	Feb-71	To AV 209
642	WAL 440	Bristol	LD6G	Eastern Coach Works	LD33/25RD	Jan-58	Feb-71	To AV 581
643	213 ANN	Bristol	LD6G	Eastern Coach Works	LD33/25RD	Oct-58	Feb-71	To AV 582
644	214 ANN	Bristol	LD6G	Eastern Coach Works	LD33/25RD	Oct-58	Mar-71	To AV 583
645	215 ANN	Bristol	LD6G	Eastern Coach Works	LD33/25RD	Dec-58	Sep-71	To AV 584
646	216 ANN	Bristol	LD6G	Eastern Coach Works	LD33/25RD	Dec-58	Oct-71	To AV 585
648	191 BRR	Bristol	LD6G	Eastern Coach Works	LD33/25RD	Jul-59	Aug-71	To AV 587
588	566 ERR	Bristol	FS6G	Eastern Coach Works	H33/27RD	Jun-60	Nov-71	To AV 588

These Bristols were purchased from the Mansfield District Traction Co. Ltd.

Notes: Vehicles are shown as they were at the start of January 1961, or in the form they subsequently entered service.
Engine changes after entry into service are shown in brackets after the original model designation, e.g. LS6B (later 6G) indicates that the vehicle was new (or entered service) with a 6-cylinder Bristol engine subsequently replaced by a 6-cylinder Gardner unit. Dates of engine changes are included in the main text.

Body alterations are not shown due to limitations of space. However, coaches were quite often re-seated for changing duties, whilst some buses were re-seated in due course, either for o-m-o working or during rebuilds, as detailed in the text.
Most of the LD-types were later fitted with platform doors, and full details of these alterations will be found in the text.
The bodies of Cars 170/1 were incorrectly listed in the Newbury & District Story, but were L27/26RD.
The engines of 170/1, 438 and 815/6 were shown incorrectly in the previous volume and are therefore corrected here.

Appendix 2 SERVICE VEHICLE FLEET 1961 - 1971

F. No.	Reg. No.	Chassis Make/Model	Type	Date New	Date In	Date Sold	Original Purpose	Allocation
19	*111 RD*	Ford (Canada) V8	4WD lorry	Ex-WD	Nov-46	To AV	Breakdown	Reading
	FRX 9	Morris Oxford	Car	Mar-50	New	Feb-61	Traffic Supt. Car	Reading
	FRX 647	Morris Oxford	Car	Jun-50	New	Feb-61	Traffic Supt. Car	Wycombe
31	GJB 552	Bedford 10/12cwt	Van	Mar-51	New	Oct-65	Depot van	Bracknell
	GJB 786	Vauxhall Velox	Car	Apr-51	New	Jul-61	Traffic Manager	Reading
35/27	RWL 71	Bedford 10/12cwt	Van	Jun-51	New	Oct-65	Depot van	Oxford
	RWL 72	Vauxhall Wyvern	Car	Jun-51	New	Jun-61	Staff car	Oxford
33	GMO 943	Austin A40	Van	Oct-51	New	Nov-66	Publicity Dept.	Reading
35	KBL 963	Fordson Thames 4D	Lorry	Sep-54	New	Nov-66	Stores lorry	Reading
	JRD 479	Ford Popular 10hp	Car	Dec-54	New	Jul-62	Inspectors	Newbury
	JRD 982	Ford Popular 10hp	Car	Nov-54	New	Jul-62	Asst. Traffic Man.	Reading
	LBL 331	Vauxhall Velox	Car	Apr-55	New	Jul-62	Traffic Manager	Reading
	XFC 888	Morris Oxford II	Car	May-55	New	Jul-62	Traffic Supt. Car	Oxford
37	MRX 113	Commer Cob	Van	Jun-56	New	May-68	Depot van	Newbury
39	MRX 114	Commer Cob	Van	Jun-56	New	Apr-67	Clerk of Works	Reading
41	MRX 115	Bedford CA5	Van	Jun-56	New	Oct-65	Depot van	Reading
	MRX 116	Ford Popular 10hp	Car	Jul-56	New	Jul-62	Inspectors	Reading
	MMO 731	Wolseley 6/90	Car	Jul-56	New	Jun-62	GM's car	Reading
43	BRX 921	Bristol K5G	Tree-lopper	Ex-bus	Oct-56	Nov-64	Route servicing	Reading
	RBL 109	Morris Minor 1000cc	Car	Oct-58	New	Feb-64	Company Sec.	Reading
RV.1	*323 RD*	AEC Matador	Crane Lorry	Ex-WD	Jan-60	To AV	Recovery Vehicle	Reading
45	UJB 298	Bedford CAV	Van (grey livery)	Feb-60	New	Nov-68	Clerk of Works	Reading
47	UJB 299	Bedford CAV	Van	Feb-60	New	Mar-69	Depot van	Wycombe
	UMO 568	Morris Minor 1000cc	Car	Mar-60	New	Apr-68	Company Sec.	Reading
	WMO 52	Austin A40	Car	Nov-60	New	Nov-67	Traffic Supt. Car	Wycombe
	WMO 279	Morris Oxford	Car	Nov-60	New	Apr-68	Chief Engineer	Reading
	YBL 283	Vauxhall Victor	Car	Jul-61	New	Jun-68	Traffic Manager	Reading
	YBL 284	Vauxhall Victor	Car	Jul-61	New	Mar-69	Asst. Chief Eng.	Reading
	764 BJB	Ford Anglia	Car	Jul-62	New	Jun-68	Inspectors	Newbury
	457 BMO	Wolseley 6/110	Car	Jul-62	New	Feb-67	GM's car	Reading
	460 BMO	Vauxhall Velox	Car	Jul-62	New	Feb-68	Traffic Supt. Car	Oxford
49	765 BJB	Ford Thames 307E	Van	Jul-62	New	May-68	Inspectors	Reading
	592 BMO	Austin A40	Car	Aug-62	New	Aug-68	Asst. Traffic Man.	Reading
51	32 GBL	Ford Thames 307E	Van	Feb-64	New	Jul-69	Inspectors	Newbury
	ARX 554B	Ford Zephyr	Car	Apr-64	New	Feb-70	Chief Engineer	Reading
ED53	FPU 510	Bristol K5G	Tree-lopper	Ex-bus	Dec-64	Mar-71	Route servicing	Reading
55	FMO 831C	Leyland 15cwt	Van	Jul-65	New	Jul-70	Depot van	Reading
57	GMO 760C	Leyland 15cwt	Van	Oct-65	New	To AV	Depot van	Wycombe
59	GJB 227C	Austin Gypsy	Van	Oct-65	New	Jan-71	Recovery Vehicle	Oxford
	HBL 297D	Austin 1100	Car	Jan-66	New	To AV	Company Sec.	Reading
61	KRX 261D	Bedford CALV30	Van	Oct-66	New	To AV	Depot van	Maidenhead
63	KRX 563D	Bedford KDLC1	Dropside Lorry	Oct-66	New	To AV	Stores lorry	Reading
	LJB 229E	Austin 1100	Car	Jan-67	New	To AV	Traffic Supt. Car	Wycombe
	LJB 230E	Austin 1100	Car	Jan-67	New	To AV	Traffic Supt. Car	Maidenhead
	LRX 475E	Wolseley 6/110	Car	Feb-67	New	Mar-70	GM's car	Reading
65	LRX 865E	Bedford CALV30	Van	Mar-67	New	To AV	Publicity Dept.	Reading
67	MMO 367E	Bedford CALV30	Van	May-67	New	To AV	Depot van	Bracknell
	PJB 98F	Wolseley 18/85	Car	Jan-68	New	To AV	Traffic Manager	Reading
49	PJB 349F	Ford 7cwt	Van	Feb-68	New	To AV	Inspectors	Reading
	PJB 421F	Austin 1100	Car	Feb-68	New	To AV	Inspectors	Oxford
	PJB 422F	Austin 1100	Car	Feb-68	New	To AV	Inspectors	Wycombe
	PJB 423F	Austin 1100	Car	Feb-68	New	To AV	Traffic Supt. Car	Reading
37	RJB 37F	Bedford CAV	Van 10/12cwt	May-68	New	To AV	Depot van	Newbury
45	RJB 45F	Bedford CAV	Van 15/17cwt	May-68	New	To AV	Clerk of Works	Reading
	RJB 934F	Austin 1300	Car	May-68	New	Jan-71	Traffic Supt. Car	Oxford
	TJB 348G	Austin 1300 Estate	Car	Nov-68	New	To AV	Asst. Traffic Man.	Reading
69	VBL 838H	Ford Escort	Van	Aug-69	New	To AV	Inspectors	Wycombe
71	SRD 167H	Bedford CAV	Van	Jan-70	New	To AV	Depot van	Reading
73	SRD 168H	Bedford CAV	Van	Jan-70	New	To AV	Depot van	Wycombe
	XBL 396H	Vauxhall Ventura	Car	Feb-70	New	To AV	Chief Engineer	Reading

	WMO 953H	Triumph 2.5 litre	Car	Mar-70	New	To AV	GM's car	Reading
Notes:	19 and 21 operated on the Trade Plates as shown in italics, 19 also ran on Trade Plate 533 MO. 19 was originally at Maidenhead.								
	Lorries 19 and 21 were purchased from Government Surplus sales. 33 (GMO 943) transferred to Maidenhead in early 1960.								
	31 (GJB 552) was originally at Reading, allocated to Ascot garage by August 1957, transferring to Bracknell in June 1960.								
	39 (MRX 114) became the Publicity van in 1960, then replaced 31 at Bracknell in October 1965.								
	47 (UJB 299) was repainted as the Publicity Van in October 1965 and transferred to Reading.								
	RWL 71 and RWL 72 were owned by South Midland M.S. Ltd.								
	Van RWL 71 was apparently also numbered 35 in error, being re-numbered as 27 c.1957.								
	RV.1 used Trade Plate 323 RD and had a new body constructed by Thames Valley on an ex-WD chassis.								
	ED53 was former bus 460 and was painted in an all-over green livery with gold lettering.								
	The cars did not have fleet numbers allocated, but were recorded by their registration numbers.								

Appendix 3   Garages, Dormy Sheds & Outstations 1961 - 1971

BRACKNELL - Pre-cast concrete and brick-built garage in Market Street, opened June 1960 to replace Ascot Garage and Crowthorne Dormy Shed. Site leased from Bracknell Development Corporation.

DESBOROUGH ROAD - Brick and steel-built garage in Desborough Road, High Wycome, purchased in June 1946 as a running shed to supplement capacity and reduce dead mileage. Closed June 1970 when Newlands Bus Station opened.

FINGEST - Pre-fabricated wooden-framed steel-clad dormy shed in Turville Road, erected in 1930. In this period it was home to two single-deckers for Routes 36 and 37, Bristol LWL's mostly, replaced by o-m-o Bristol LS's in 1969.

HIGH WYCOMBE (NEWLANDS) - Concrete-built bus station and open garage complex opened June 1970. When open it replaced the bus station at Frogmoor and the garages at Desborough Road and Wycombe Marsh.

HUNGERFORD - Outstation with open parking by part-time drivers for two contract coaches used on Great Bedwyn to Harwell (AERE) and Chilton Foliat to Harwell (AERE). Ceased with termination of contracts 30th April 1962.

KINGSCLERE - Oustation with open parking in yard of The Crown in Newbury Road, later relocated to the yard of the Kingsclere & Whitchurch RDC in Swan Street, for 1 double-decker on Route 122 (Newbury - Kingsclere - Basingstoke).

LAMBOURN - Outstation with open parking in Newbury Street. At 1961 the allocation was one double-decker for Route 106 (Newbury - Lambourn - Swindon), along with two contract coaches for Lambourn to Didcot (ROF) and Ramsbury to Harwell (AERE), the Didcot run ceasing 24th February 1962 and the Harwell contract on 30the April 1962. One of the two coaches also covered journeys on the Wednesdays-only Lambourn - Shefford - Hungerford Route 106a. After closure of the Lambourn Valley Railway the allocation rose, and by August 1965 there was a pair of double-decks and two saloons.

LONDON - Thames Valley kept a pair of double-deckers for Route B (Reading - Maidenhead - London Victoria) at the nearby garage of Samuelson's New Transport in Eccleston Road overnight, worked by London-based crews. This ceased on 6th June 1971, ending many years of outstationing at various London locations for the route to Reading. South Midland oustationed two coaches in London to cover early departures on the London - High Wycombe - Oxford and London - Henley-on-Thames - Oxford routes. By 1961 these were kept at the London Transport Gillingham Street garage in Victoria, but this arrangement ceased on 16th May 1963, when they transferred to Samuelson's garage. On 14th March 1965 they relocated again to the London Transport Walworth Garage in Camberwell New Road.

MAIDENHEAD - Brick and steel-built garage, originally opened 1916 by British Automobile Traction, and extended several times during 1920's and 1930's and situated in Bridge Street.

NEWBURY - Brick and steel-built garage, originally built for Newbury & District and rebuilt and extended under Red & White in 1944. Situated in Mill Lane, with the nearby former Thames Valley dormy shed still in use as a paintshop/store.

OXFORD - Brick and steel-built garage in Botley Road, originally built for Varsity Express in 1929, acquired by United Counties, passing to Thames Valley in May 1952 with Oxford - High Wycombe - London service, and then extended.

PRINCES RISBOROUGH - Pre-fabricated wooden-framed steel-clad dormy shed erected in Longwick Road in 1933. Two double-deckers outstationed for Route 20/20a (Aylesbury - High Wycombe - Maidenhead - Windsor), one rotated weekly with Wycombe Marsh garage. Later covered Route 21/21a (Aylesbury - High Wycombe) after being split.

READING - Brick and steel-built complex of garage and works, as well as Head Office and other subsidary buildings on site in Lower Thorn Street and Weldale Road. Yard area continued to expand along Weldale Street, with new staff canteen in due course. Also controlled activities at The Colonnade, Cemetery Junction, as additional works and paintshop. Original garage had opened in 1922 as Somerset Place, duly incorporated into first phase of rebuilding and known as Lower Thorn Street.

STOKENCHURCH - Brick and steel-built dormy shed in London Road, originally built for City of Oxford Motor Services in 1924, passing to Thames Valley in July 1937 with Routes 39 (High Wycombe - Watlington), 40 (High Wycombe - Radnage) and 41 (High Wycombe - Ibstone). Two double-deckers kept there for those workings, one rotated with Wycombe Marsh on a weekly basis. COMS continued to base buses there for other services, at times allocating more than TV.

WORCESTER - At 1961 a South Midland coach was outstationed for the service to London and was kept outside at the Croft Road coach park, having moved there from Newport Street bus station during 1959. In August 1964 it was relocated to the Padmore Street garage of Midland Red. A second coach was added in the Summer months for the Southsea service.

WYCOMBE MARSH - Brick and steel-built garage complex opened in 1924, much extended rearwards in phases during late 1920's and 1930's. On London Road, Wycombe Marsh, with additional entrances in Micklefield Road. Closed in June 1970, being replaced by facilities at the Newlands bus station and garage complex. Controlled dormy sheds at Stockenchurch, Fingest and Princes Risborough.

OTHER COMPANY VEHICLES - Wilts & Dorset kept one single-deck bus for Route 135 (Newbury - Whitchurch) at the Newbury garage, whilst Royal Blue outstationed a coach at Desborough Road (later Newlands) for expess service to the West Country.

Appendix 4
Working Arrangements
At 1st November 1961

Scheduled Allocations to Garages -
Includes outstationed vehicles

Garage	D/D	S/D	Coaches	Totals
Bracknell	21	7	0	28
High Wycombe*	40	29	0	69
Maidenhead	67	15	0	82
Newbury*	36	12	6	54
Oxford*	0	0	26	26
Reading*	66	29	2	97
Total Licensed	230	92	34	356
Delicensed	4	0	22	26
For Sale	0	0	6	6
Total Owned	234	92	62	388

Scheduled Workings By Garage –

BRACKNELL

Route No.	D/D	S/D	Coaches	Totals
2 and 3	9	0	0	9
2a, 2b and 2c	2	0	0	2
3a	0	1	0	1
51a and 51b	2	0	0	2
52	0	1	0	1
53, 53a, 55 and 55a	0	4	0	4
54	0	1	0	1
Relief Workings	7	0	7	7

HIGH WYCOMBE
(D = Desborough Road or D/W shared with Wycombe Marsh, all others by Wycombe Marsh or as indicated)

Route No.	D/D	S/D	Coaches	Totals
20 and 20a	10	0	0	10
(2 at Princes Risborough)				
25	0	3	0	3
26 and 26a (D)	2	0	0	2
27 (D/W)	4	0	0	4
28	7	0	0	7
31 (D/W)	0	3	0	3
32	0	1	0	1
33 (D)	0	4	0	4
34	0	1	0	1
35	0	2	0	2
36 and 37	0	5	0	5
(2 at Fingest)				
38 (D)	2	0	0	2
39, 40 and 41	4	0	0	4
(2 at Stokenchurch)				
42 (D)	4	0	0	4
80	0	2	0	2
81 (D)	1	0	0	1
Relief Workings	3	6	0	9

MAIDENHEAD

Route No.	D/D	S/D	Coaches	Totals
1	2	0	0	2
15	1	0	0	1
16, 17, 18 and 18b	0	7	0	7
18a	3	0	0	3
19	1	0	0	1
20 and 20a	8	0	0	8
21	5	0	0	5
23	2	0	0	2
24	0	2	0	2
51	1	0	0	1
60, 60a, 61, 61a, 62, 63, 64, 65, 65a, 66, 66a, 67, 67a, 70	32	0	0	32
Relief Workings	9	4	0	13

NEWBURY

Route No.	D/D	S/D	Coaches	Totals
1	3	0	0	3
5b	1	0	0	1
101 and 102	1	0	0	1
106 and 106a	5	0	1	6
(2 at Lambourn)	(106a covered by coach)			
109 and 111	1	1	0	2
110	2	0	0	2
112	2	0	0	2
113	2	0	0	2
121	1	0	0	1
122 (at Kingsclere)	1	0	0	1
127 and 128a	2	0	2	0
128	1	0	0	1
101a, 103, 104, 105, 106 shorts, 108, 114, 114a, 115, 116, 120, 120a, 126, 129	0	9	0	9
Relief Workings	6	0	0	6
Contracts	7	0	4	11

OXFORD (South Midland) incl. London and Worcester
26 coaches active for express services, contracts and private hire work.

READING

Route No.	D/D	S/D	Coaches	Totals
A	2	0	0	2
B (2 at Victoria)	6	0	0	6
1	6	0	0	6
1a	5	0	0	5
1b	0	1	0	1
1c	1	0	0	1
2 and 3	4	0	0	4
4	3	0	0	3
4a	2	0	0	2
5	0	3	0	3
5a	0	1	0	1
5b	1	0	0	1
6	3	0	0	3
6a	0	1	0	1
6b (ex other duties)	0	1	0	1
7	3	0	0	3
8 and 11	4	0	0	4
9 (1 at Baughurst)	4	0	0	4
9a	0	1	0	1
12	1	0	0	1
28 and 37	1	0	0	1
50	0	1	0	1
75	0	1	0	1
102	0	3	0	3
Relief Workings	19	11	0	30
Contracts	0	1	0	1

Note - The numbers shown under routes may not exactly agree with garage summaries due to inter-worked duties.

Appendix 5
Official Fleet Allocations at 1st July 1963

The oldest vehicle delivered new to Thames Valley in service at this date was Bristol K6A-type Car 439 (CRX 548). New in 1946 it carries the earlier style of Eastern Coach Work's lowbridge body, though it was still in fair shape when seen in the Southern yard at Reading Stations in 1962 as part of the relief pool, as indicated by the duty plate 65. Note also the rather limited blind display, as keeping the old 49-inch blinds up to date was no longer economical for buses with limited duties. Some of those had blinds in the lower box showing only the route number placed.

BRACKNELL –
Double-deckers: Bristol K5G 462, 463, 464, Bristol KSW6B 640, 641, 642, 643, 644, 710, 703, 705, 744, 745, 746, 747, Bristol LD5G 766, 767, Bristol LDL6G 779, Bristol FLF6G 843, 847
Single-deckers: Bristol LWL6B 624, Bristol LS5G 706, 709, Bristol LS6B 711, 712, 713, 718, 719, 721, 724

HIGH WYCOMBE - Combined allocation for both Desborough Road and Wycombe Marsh garages and dormy sheds at Fingest, Princes Risborough and Stokenchurch –
Double-deckers: Bristol K6B 468, 469, 495, 496, 505, 506, 508, 513, 518, 519, 533, Bristol KS6B 591, Bristol KSW6B 636, 647, 652, 658, 695, 730, 731, Bristol LD6B 810, 811, Bristol LD6G 761, 786, 787, 788, 808, 809, 812, 813, Bristol FLF6B 870, 873, 874, Bristol FLF6G 840, 841, 848, 880
Single-deckers: Bristol LL5G 797, 798, 799, Bristol LL6B 559, 560, 567, 568, 569, 571, 574, Bristol LWL6B 614, 615, 618, 619, 620, 621, 622, 623, 628, 630, Bristol LS5G 678, 679, 680, 681
Coaches: Bristol LS6G 672

MAIDENHEAD –
Double-deckers: Bristol K5G 460, 461, Bristol K6A 447, 448, 457, Bristol K6B 492, 498, 499, 500, 501, 502, 503, 504, 514, 515, 516, 527, 528, 530, 531, 532, Bristol KS6B 592, 593, 598, 599, 600, Bristol KSW6B 603, 635, 649, 650, 651, 655, 657, 661, 662, 666, 667, 670, 698, 699, 732, 733, 734, Bristol LD5G 765, 783, 784, 789, 791, 792, 793, Bristol LD6B 755, 756, 757, 815, 816, Bristol FLF6B 871, Bristol FLF6G 842, 850, 851, 875, 876, 877, 879
Single-deckers: Bristol LL5G 819, Bristol LS6B 715, Bristol LS6G 677, Bristol SC4LK 774, 775, 776, 777

NEWBURY – including outstations at Lambourn and Kingsclere:
Double-deckers: Guy 'Arab' MkIII 6LW 170, 171 (lowbridge), H10, H13, H14, H15, H16 (highbridge), Bristol K5G 472, Bristol K6A 446, Bristol K6B 509, 524, 525, Bristol KS6B 596, 597, Bristol KSW6B 602, 669, 702, 704, 726, 727, 728, 741, 743, Bristol LD5G 780, 781, 782, Bristol LD6G 754, 763, 764, 790, Bristol FLF6B 872
Single-deckers: Bristol L6A S303, Bristol LL5G 794, 795, Bristol LL6B 564, 565, 566, Bristol LS5G 687, 707, 710, Bristol LS6B 717, 725, Bristol MW6G 854, 855, 856, 857
Coaches: Bristol LS6G 674, 676

OXFORD – including outstations at Worcester and London –
Coaches: AEC 'Regal' MkIV 85, Bedford SB8 861, 862, 863, 864, 865, C401, C402, C403, Bristol LWL6B 608, 609, 610, Bristol LS6B 90, 91, 92, 93, 94, 688, 689, 690, 691, 692, Bristol LS6G 79, 80, 81, 82, 83, 671, 673, Bristol MW6G 800, 801, 802, 803, 804, 805, 806, 807, 830, 831, 832, 833, 858, 859, 860, Bristol REX6G 867

READING – including bus outstationed at Wilts & Dorset Baughurst dormy shed and in London–
Double-deckers: Bristol K5G 473, 474, 475, Bristol K6A 439, 441, 450, 452, 459, Bristol K6B 436, 437, 454, 455, 471, 493, 494, 497, 517, 526, 529, Bristol KS6B 586, 587, 588, 589, 590, 594, 595, Bristol KSW6B 601, 634, 638, 639, 646, 648, 654, 656, 659, 660, 663, 664, 665, 668, 694, 697, 700, 729, 735, 736, 737, 738, 739, 740, 742, 748, 749, Bristol LD5G 768, 769, 785, Bristol LD6G 750, 751, 752, 753, 760, 762, Bristol FLF6B 834, 868, 869, Bristol FLF6G 835, 836, 837, 838, 844, 845, 846, 849, 878, 881
Single-deckers: Bristol L6A S302, Bristol LL5G 796, 817, 818, 820, Bristol LWL6B 582, 613, 616, 617, 629, 631, 633, Bristol LS5G 682, 683, 684, 685, 686, 706, Bristol LS6B 714, 716, 720, 722, 723, Bristol MW6G 852, 853
Coaches: Bristol LWL6B 607, 611, Bristol LS6B 693, Bristol LS6G 675, Bristol MW6G 866

UNLICENSED VEHICLES –
Double-deckers: Bristol KSW6B 637, 645
Single-deckers: Bristol L6A S301, S304, S305, Bristol SC4LK 778
Coaches: None

Appendix 6
Official Fleet Allocations at 1st June 1968

BRACKNELL:
Double-deckers: Bristol KS6B 599, Bristol KSW6B 640, 641, 642, 643, 644, 653, 659, 703, 744, 747, Bristol LD6B 770, 771, 772, 775, Bristol FLF6G 843, 847, D9, D19, D26, D45, D46, D47, D59
Single-deckers: Bristol LS5G 706, 708, 709, Bristol LS6B 711, 712, 713, 716, 718, 721, S312, S317, S320, Bristol RESL6G S333, S334, S338

HIGH WYCOMBE – Combined allocation for both Desborough Road and Wycombe Marsh garages and dormy sheds at Fingest, Princes Risborough and Stokenchurch –
Double-deckers: Bristol KSW6B 602, 634, 636, 647, 652, 662, 695, 730, 731, Bristol LD6B 810, 811, Bristol LD6G 758, 759, 761, 778, 786, 787, 788, 794, 797, 808, 809, 812, 813, 814, Bristol FLF6B 874, Bristol FLF6G 840, 841, 848, 874, 880, 881, D3, D12, D14, D15, D25, D27, D32, D34, D36, D37, D42, D51, D52, D56
Single-deckers: Bristol LL5G 817, Bristol LL6B 567, 568, 569, 574, Bristol LWL6B 615, 620, 621, 625, 627, 628, 629, 630, 631, 632, 633, Bristol LS6B 719, 722, Bristol LS6G 678, 679, 680, 681, 682, S330

MAIDENHEAD –
Double-deckers: Bristol KS6B 598, 600, Bristol KSW6B 649, 650, 651, 655, 657, 660, 661, 666, 667, 698, 699, 733, 734, Bristol LD6B 755, 756, 757, 783, 784, 789, 791, 815, 816, Bristol LD6G 765, 792, 793, 798, Bristol FLF6B 871, Bristol FLF6G 842, 850, 851, 871, 875, 876, 877, 879, D1, D10, D11, D16, D20, D21, D22, D23, D28, D29, D33, D35, D38, D39, D40, D53, D58
Single-deckers: Bristol LS5G S339, S340, S341, Bristol LS6B 714, S316, S318, S321, Bristol LS6G 677, 685, Bristol SC4LK S301, S302, S303, S304, Bristol RESL6G S331, S332

NEWBURY – including outstations at Lambourn and Kingsclere –
Double-deckers: Bristol KS6B 595, 596, Bristol KSW6B 601, 672, 673, 688, 689, 690, 691, 702, 704, 726, 727, 728, 741, 743, Bristol LD6B 780, 781, 782, Bristol LD6G 754, 763, 764, 790, 795, 796, Bristol FLF6B 872, Bristol FLF6G D18, D41, D55
Single-deckers: Bristol LS5G 687, 707, S342, S343, S344, S345, Bristol LS6B 710, 717, 725, S315, S319, S322, S323, S324, S329, Bristol LS6G 683, Bristol MW6G 854, 855, 856, 857, Bristol RESL6G S337
Coaches: Bristol MW6G 802, 803

OXFORD – including outstations at Worcester and London –
Coaches: Bedford SB8 865, C401, C402, C403, Bedford SB13 C411, Bedford VAM14 C417, C418, Bristol MW6G 800, 801, 804, 805, 806, 807, 830, 831, 832, 833, 858, 859, 860, Bristol REX6G 867, Bristol RELH6G C404, C405, C421, C422, C423, Bristol LHL6L C428, C429, C430, C431

Vehicles of only 7ft 6ins width were now getting in short supply at Thames Valley. Bristol KS6B Car 589 (FMO 971) was one of those with bus seats from new, whilst those originally fitted with coach seats for the London Route B were duly rebuilt with cut-down seats. It is seen in the yard at Lower Thorn Street and awaits the afternoon peak workings, with similar bus 594 (FMO 976) on a short-working on Route 1 to Theale. On the single-deck front only the SC's, one LL5G, and four LL6B's were now of that width, the latter at High Wycombe on Local Service Route 33.

READING – including bus outstationed at Wilts & Dorset Baughurst dormy shed and in London–
Double-deckers: Bristol KS6B 589, 590, 593, 594, 597, Bristol KSW6B 637, 639, 646, 648, 654, 656, 658, 664, 665, 668, 694, 696, 697, 700, 701, 705, 729, 732, 735, 736, 737, 738, 739, 740, 742, 745, 746, 748, 749, Bristol LD6B 766, 767, 768, 769, 773, 774, 785, Bristol LD6G 750, 751, 752, 753, 760, 762, 776, 777, Bristol LDL6G 779, Bristol FLF6B 868, 869, 870, 873, 874, D4, D5, D6, D7, Bristol FLF6G 834, 835, 836, 837, 838, 845, 846, 849, D2, D8, D13, D17, D24, D30, D31, D43, D44, D48, D49, D50, D54, D57, D60
Single-deckers: Bristol LS5G 686, S310, S327, S328, Bristol LS6B 720, 723, 724, S309, S311, S313, S314, S325, S326, Bristol LS6G 684, Bristol MW6G 852, 853, Bristol RELL6G S306, S307, S308, Bristol RESL6G S335, S336
Coaches: Bedford SB8 863, Bedford VAM14 C419, C420, Bristol LS6G 676, Bristol MW6G 866, Bristol RELH6G C424, C425, C426, C427

UNLICENSED VEHICLES:
Double-deckers: Bristol KS6B 587, 592, 598, Bristol KSW6B 603, 635, Bristol FLF6G 844
Single-deckers: Bristol LL5G 818
Coaches: Bedford SB13 C406, C407, C408, C409, C410, C412, Bedford VAM14 C413, C414, C415, C416

Index to Other Operators In The Main Text

A-B

Aldershot & District Traction Co. Ltd. *7 8 14 31 67 114 186 192 193 196 198 200*
Alpha Coaches (Carter) *10 17 31 57*
Austin, Albert *93*
Bath Tramways *160*
Blue Bus Service (Ron Cole) *157*
Blue Bus Services (Albert Cole) *91 93 94 95*
Blue Bus (West Bros.) *157*
Blue Star Service (Spratley) *31*
Bray Transport *93*
Brighton, Hove & District Omnibus Co. Ltd. *15 140*
Brimblecombe Bros. *17*
Bristol Greyhound *59 81 91 94 112*
Bristol Omnibus Co. Ltd. *10 23 32 40 43 55 73 74 87 97 103 119 126 127 133 140 147 150 160 161 163 165 184 185 186 195 197 200 204*
British Automobile Traction Co. Ltd. *26*

C

Central SMT *87*
Chiltern Bus Co. Ltd. *173 190*
Cole (Albert and Ron) –see Blue Bus Services
Cooper's Car Hire *35 76 97*
City of Oxford Motor Services Ltd. *7 8 9 10 40 43 44 50 55 56 63 66 68 72 76 88 96 98 106 148 149 154 155 171 178 186 191 193*
Crook, Fred (Booker Bus Service) *16 47 94 157 200*
Crosville Motor Services Ltd. *48 56 62 63 67 75 76 90 102 171 172 174 175 178 179 181 183 184 192 195 199 200 204*
Cumberland Motor Services Ltd. *9*

D-E-F-G

Denham Bros. *11 30*
Direct Bus Service (Lintott's) *5*
Dring's Coaches *10*
Durnford Bros. *63*
Eastern Counties Omnibus Co.Ltd. *47*
Eastern National Omnibus Co. Ltd. *8 12 66 136 152 178*
Eastern Scottish M.T. *200*
East Kent Road Car Co. Ltd. *16*
East Midland Motor Services Ltd. *200*
Ford, A. & Son *12*
Gough's Coaches *17 29*
Green Line Coaches Ltd. *11*
Greenslade's Tours *52*

H-I-J-K

Hants & Dorset Motor Services Ltd. *10 39 63 64 66 71 93 114 192 193*
Harris, J.H. – see Pixey B.S.
Hedges, George – see Reliance M.S.
Holland, Charlie *173*
Holman, Tom *88*
House Bros. *47*
Imperial Bus Service (Moore) *102 103*
Kent's Coaches *12*
King Alfred Motor Services Ltd. *8*

L-M

Ledbury Transport Co. Ltd. *90 146 177*
Lincolnshire Road Car Co. Ltd. *127 171 178 181 182 184 185 192 194 196 199 200*
Lintott's – see Direct Bus Service
London Transport/London Country *8 12 15 20 27 34 40 49 50 58 61 71 73 74 76 89 91 96 133 140 172 186*
Lovegrove Bros. *12*
Mansfield District Traction Co. Ltd. *190 191 193 197 202 206*
Marlow & District Motor Services Ltd. *75*
Midland General Omnibus Co. Ltd. *104 126 177 178 183 184 185 186 189 190 193 197 200 201 202 206*
Midland Red *66, 169*
Moore, A. & Son –see Imperial B.S.

N-O

Newbury & District Motor Services Ltd. *5 8 10 25 29 30 56 77 88 93 113 136*
Notts & Derby (Nottinghamshire & Derbyshire Traction Co. Ltd.) *184 188 189 190 193 194 195*

P-Q-R

Pangbourne Coaches *15 76*
Penn Bus Company *36 77 142 173*
Pixey Bus Service (J.H. Harris) *45*
Reading & District Motor Services *56*
Reading Corporation Transport *3 42 54 61 63 64 68 82 87 91 93 101 103 112 114 125 133 140 147 183 186*
Red & White United Transport Ltd./Red & White Services Ltd. *5 58 63 78 88 113 116 129 142 143 144 147 148 163*
Reliance Motor Services Ltd. *10 12 17 32 63 93 95 96 109 111 154 180*
Ribble Motor Services Ltd. *200*
Rickards, Charles & Son *104*
Royal Blue Coaches *51 173 178 179*

S-T

Samuelson's Garage *49 58 59 91 195*
Scottish Motor Traction Co. Ltd. *12*
Smith's Luxury Coaches (Reading) Ltd. *10 11 12 17 59 76 114 158 162 166 171 179 183*
Southampton Corporation Transport *103*
Southdown Motor Services Ltd. *199*
Southern National Omnibus Co. Ltd. *10 104 160 165*
Southern Vectis Omnibus Co. Ltd. *40*
Spratley, J. & Son – see Blue Star Service
Sugg, Fred – see Penn Bus Company
Swindon Corporation Transport *51*
South Midland Motor Services Ltd. *2 5 6 7 11 13 14 15 16 20 23 24 27 31 32 39 41 42 43 44 45 49 50 53 54 55 57 58 63 66 68 74 76 77 78 81 82 84 91 93 94 96 97 107 108 109 113 123 124 129 131 136 138 139 143 148 150 152 155 158 169 175 177 182 183 184 186 193*
Thackray's Way – see Ledbury Transport
Tillings Transport Ltd. *12*
Timson, A. & Sons Ltd. *97*

U-V

Ulster Transport Authority *58*
United Automobile Services Ltd. *9 68 131 132 133 137 163 164 165 178 182 189 191 192 194 195 205*
United Counties Omnibus Co. Ltd. *8 11 15 23 27 29 37 39 40 43 49 50 66 70 74 78 81 91 186*
United Welsh Services Ltd. *77 94 96 97 100 102 105 107 109 111 126 127 130 131 138 143 144 150 153 155 156 160 161 163 166 178 185 192 194 200 202 204 205*

W-X-Y-Z

Venture Ltd. *8 51 93*
Walwyn's Coaches *57*
Western National Omnibus Co. Ltd. *10 12 32 104 160 165 166 182*
West Yorkshire Road Car. Co. Ltd. *87*
White, W.J. & Son *10*
Wilts & Dorset Motor Services Ltd. *8 10 12 25 30 35 51 65 82 85 93 98 186 192 193 198*
Worth's of Enstone *169*

Operators whose services were acquired by Thames Valley 1961 to 1971

Albert Cole (Blue Bus Services), Slough – 4th June 1966
Maidenhead – Dorney – Eton Wick – Eton – Windsor (Castle) as Route 22

Reliance Motor Services Ltd., Brightwalton – 25th June 1966
Brightwalton – Newbury – as Route 107
Cold Ash – Newbury - as Route 119
Newbury – Wantage - not operated

Ron Cole (Blue Bus Service), Bray – 4th October 1969
Maidenhead – Bray – Holyport – Paley Street – as Route 14